THE ORAL TRADITION OF CLASSICAL ARABIC POETRY

THE ORAL TRADITION OF CLASSICAL ARABIC POETRY

Its Character and Implications

BY MICHAEL ZWETTLER

Ohio State University Press : Columbus

Library of Congress Cataloguing in Publication Data

Zwettler, Michael.
The oral tradition of classical Arabic poetry.

Bibliography: p.
Includes index.
1. Arabic poetry—To 622—History and criticism. 2. Arabic poetry—622–750—History and criticism. 3. Oral tradition—Arabia. I. Title.
PJ7541.Z9 1978 892'.7'1009 77-25386
ISBN 0-8142-0273-X

*

To my family: Janett, Robert, and Rebecca Zwettler

*

Contents

Preface ix

Notes on Transliteration, Abbreviations, and Dates xi

CHAPTER ONE

Oral Tradition and Traditional Texts: Questions of Application 3

CHAPTER TWO

The Oral Tradition of Classical Arabic Poetry 41

CHAPTER THREE

The Classical ᶜ*Arabīya* as the Language of an Oral Poetry 98

CHAPTER FOUR

Variation and Attribution in the Tradition of Classical Arabic Poetry 189

Appendixes 235

Bibliography 275

Index 299

*

Preface

Throughout centuries of Arabic literary scholarship, there has been little serious doubt that pre- and early Islamic Arabic poetry had been produced and transmitted through the operation of some kind of "oral tradition." What that fact really meant, however, and what the character and implications of such a tradition might have been, were questions that were seldom, if ever, asked. But some have been asking them in recent years. They are asked here, as well, and a considered attempt has been made to answer them, in terms of the "oral-formulaic" theory of poetic composition worked out by Milman Parry, Albert Lord, and others.

The subject of this study—the *oral* tradition of classical Arabic poetry—grew out of another one, an investigation of the *textual* tradition of the poetry, to which it is the natural and necessary antecedent. My thanks go to Professor Marsden Jones, of the American University in Cairo, who lured me into the earlier topic and who inspired in me a true interest in, and appreciation for, classical Arabic poetry.

I am very grateful to Professors Mounah Khouri, Joseph Duggan, William Brinner, Michael Nagler, and Ariel Bloch—all of the University of California, Berkeley—who helped and guided me in seeing this work through its preliminary phase as my doctoral dissertation. Their forthright, friendly assistance and criticism made the labor enlightening and worthwhile, though not necessarily always easier. In addition, I have subsequently benefited from coming to know and converse with Professor James Monroe, also of Berkeley, whose own concern and original work in the field of oral-formulaic theory had developed parallel to mine. I particularly appreciate the support and advice that have been extended to me, so graciously and from so far away, by Professor Anton Spitaler of the University of Munich.

A special vote of thanks is due the inter-library loan departments of the University of California, Berkeley, and the Ohio State University, both of which provided me promptly and considerately with many sources that otherwise would have remained inaccessible.

And, finally, to the many friends and colleagues who bore me up, bore with me, and were bored by me throughout this long and arduous gestation period—*alf šukr*!

*

Notes on Transliteration, Abbreviations, and Dates

1. The system of transcribing Arabic words employed in this study is as follows, in the order of the Arabic alphabet:

' b t ṯ j ḥ x d ḏ r z s š ṣ

ḍ ṭ ẓ ᶜ ġ f q k l m n h w y

Vowels and diphthongs are indicated as follows:

a i u

ā ī ū

aw ay

Long vowels immediately preceding the prosthetic hamza (*hamzat al-waṣl*) are transcribed as short vowels (e.g., *ayyuha l-laylu, Abu l-Faḍl, iḏa s-tadbarta-hu, ᶜala l-wana*). Word-initial hamza is not indicated, but it is indicated elsewhere in a word (e.g., *iskān, al-Aṣmaᶜī*; but *Qur'ān, Abu l-ᶜAlā'*).

2. Sources referred to throughout this study will generally be noted in the body of the text. Abbreviations of references used will be clarified in full in the Bibliography, which is divided into four sections:

I. Abbreviations of Journals, Encyclopedias, etc.
II. Poetry and Poetical Collections
III. Recensions of the *Mu*^{c}*allaqa* of Imra'alqays and Related Material
IV. General Bibliography

3. Where two dates are indicated with a slash (/) separating them, the first number denotes the date of the Muslim era (after the Hijra) and the second the date of the Christian era (A.D.).

4. All translations are mine unless otherwise indicated.

THE
ORAL TRADITION
OF CLASSICAL ARABIC
POETRY

*

Chapter One

Oral Tradition and Traditional Texts
Questions of Application

A. The intention of this study initially was to trace the "tradition" of classical[1] Arabic poetry in the sense of its *textual* tradition—that is, the self-conscious and deliberate process, undertaken by a society (or properly, by a class of specialists more or less authorized by the society), of setting down, dealing with, and passing on verbal works of recognized importance in its cultural, intellectual, and spiritual life. These works, it seemed, could enjoy the status of "sacred scriptures" in the society, in which case the society tends to be "convinced that God himself wrote, dictated, or inspired them" (Leipoldt/Morenz *HS* 53). "Tradition" then becomes inextricably entangled with religion, and the process follows a course largely determined by pious or hieratic interests. Alternatively, these works could have in the society's eyes a value that is predominantly secular or profane (although it might be asked to what extent verbal art could ever have been viewed by *homo religiosus* of the pre-modern world without some reference to religion or some sense of the sacral overtones in poetic language).[2] In that case "tradition," as process, has ordinarily evolved along quite different lines. And this evolution, as it took place for classical Arabic poetry during the second/eighth–fourth/tenth centuries, was to have been the subject of this work.

The process does begin, however, with "setting down" these verbal works in some written form—with *textualization*. And here it was that the focus of the entire study began to shift. For whether sacred or secular, the works—particularly the poetical works—that have given rise to a textual tradition seem invariably to have existed in some sort of oral form prior to being set down. This oral form of the work was, to a certain extent, preserved by memory and passed on by word of mouth. Such a process (or one might better say, state of affairs) has long been accepted by scholars who spoke of a period of "oral transmission" or "oral tradition"—whether of biblical books or of the Homeric epics. As they did in the latter case, "scholars could call in to their help the 'fantastic memories' so 'well attested' of illiterate people. They felt that a text could remain from one generation to another unaltered, or altered only by inconsequential lapses of memory" (Lord *ST* 9). The same, in general, has been true of Arabic literary studies.[3]

Yet, another possibility exists. Although "fantastic memories" *have been* "well attested," among literate as well as illiterate peoples, accounting, for instance, for the accepted belief "that if all the written and printed copies of the Rigveda were lost, the text could be restored at once with complete accuracy,"[4] nevertheless there is good reason for thinking that the works we are considering may have originated through modes of *composition* that are distinctly oral, rather than literary, as we know them. The pioneer studies of Milman Parry and Albert B. Lord on the genesis of the orally composed epic and the nature of the "oral-formulaic technique" of verse composition[5] have fundamentally affected our understanding of, and approach to, pre-literate and non-literary verbal art. Their observations and conclusions, as well as subsequent qualifications and extensions made by other scholars,[6] have demonstrated that the earliest text of such a work—epic, ballad, or even prose narrative[7]—may well have been, in reality, a written record of the words uttered during a single performance by a singer, poet, or narrator who was, at the same time, not reciting from memory, but rather composing the work so taken down. In other words, the "oral transmitter" of the textual critics must be seen, first, in his primary office as performer. But the very nature and exigencies of oral performance resulted in a technique of presentation that was simultaneously a technique of oral composition along lines that will be discussed later. Thus, however similar two performances might have been, the intention of the singer-poet was never to reproduce a set version of his work (much less a non-existent "text"), but rather to entertain and enthrall his audience anew. It is to be expected, then, that this fact, if it is true, often underlies the poetical texts that are both the subject and the raison d'être of a textual tradition as it subsequently evolves.

Lord admits—a point that should not be forgotten—that these "records" possibly do not represent fully the oral poet's techniques of composition during an ordinary performance: he was now performing at the behest of a scribe, who undoubtedly wrote more slowly than he could compose, and without the benefit of music, tempo, or audience rapport to advance the process. Yet, despite these unaccustomed deviations from his normal mode of performance, the oral composer finally became used to the process of dictation and the work was set down (*ST* 124).

Lord's depiction of the textualization of an oral epic-song bears quoting at length, as it is not without relevance to the earliest setting-down of any orally composed work.

> A written text was thus made of the words of song. It was a record of a special performance, a command performance under unusual circumstances. Such has been the experience of many singers in many lands, from the first recorded text, I believe, to present times. And what has been said of other performances can be said of it; for though it is written, it is oral. The singer who dictated it was its "author," and it reflected a single moment in the tradition. It was unique.
>
> Yet, unwittingly perhaps, a fixed text was established. Proteus was photographed, and no matter under what other forms he might appear in the future, this would become the shape that was changed; this would be the "original". Of course, the singer was not affected at all. He continued, as did his confrères, to compose and sing as he always had and as they always had. The tradition went on. Nor was his audience affected. They thought in his terms, in the terms of multiformity. But there was another world, of those who could read and write, of those who came to think of the written text not as the recording of a moment of the tradition but as *the* song. This was to become the difference between the oral way of thought and the written way. (*ST* 124–25)

The student and critic of pre- and early Islamic poetry can no longer afford to ignore the implications of these observations, and of the theory of oral-traditional[8] composition in general. The same "superficial observer" (*oberflächlicher Beobachter*) who is struck by "the uniformity of content which, again and again, in various poems, can give expression to the same ideas in more or less modified form" (Bräunlich *VLB* 212)[9] cannot help but notice the pertinence of Parry's and Lord's discoveries to a reevaluation precisely of this aspect of Arabic poetry, not to mention many others. Although their findings were made chiefly in the area of Homeric and Yugoslavian epic poetry, they themselves saw their wider applications.[10] Indeed, "orality" has been demonstrated, not only in other Greek poetry such as Hesiod, the Homeric Hymns, Delphic oracular utterances, and the fragments of Panyassis, but also in areas as diverse as Old and Middle English poetry, medieval French and German epics, Old Testament verse, Babylonian and Hittite epic, Toda ritual songs, Coorg dance songs, Spanish and English ballads, and more.[11]

A.1 Milman Parry completely revised Homeric scholarship's view of the "repetitions" in the *Odyssey* and the *Iliad,* of the "stock epithets," "epic clichés," and "stereotyped phrases," by introducing his notion of the oral "formula": "a group of words which is regularly employed under the same metrical conditions to express a given essential idea" (*SET* I 80 = *MHV* 270). The technique of oral verse-making is determined by the presence of a system of such formulas—"a group of phrases which have the same metrical value and which are enough alike in thought and word to leave no doubt that the poet who used them knew them not only as a single formula, but also as formulas of a certain type" (*SET* I 85 = *MHV* 275).

In an important contribution to our understanding of this technique of composition, Joseph A. Russo proposes "broader criteria than those now being used [i.e., those established by Parry and accepted and promulgated by Lord] to judge what may be called a 'formula' or 'formulaic' in early Greek hexameter poetry" (Russo *CLHF* 235). He observes the recurrent correspondence in the Homeric poems of "three identical usages: the same parts of speech, the same metrical word types, the same position in the line," and suggests that, rather than basing formulaic analysis on verbatim repetition of a phrase or at least a word, one ought to seek "localized phrases whose resemblance goes no further than the use of identical metrical word-types of the same grammatical and syntactic pattern, as truly representing certain more general types of formulaic systems" (*CLHF* 237).[12] The aim, as Russo defines it, is

> to demonstrate the need for a new approach to Homeric [and, by implication (I would add), other metrically determined poetic] formulas based on subtle repetitions of word patterns rather than on verbatim repetition of words. . . . Word-types are highly localized because the thoroughly formulaic texture of Homeric verse requires that any given word be used only in a very limited number of ways. Formulaic verse not only repeats identical phrases; it also demands certain established rhythmical patterns. (*CLHF* 246)

More recently, Michael Nagler has reviewed later developments in the study of oral-formulaic poetry. These have resulted, he finds, in a wide recognition that much of earlier recorded "literature" has features of oral-formulaic poetry. But "formulaicness" involves more than verbatim repetition of phrases or lines in a given body of poetry, as Russo has shown (Nagler *TGV* 269–74).[13] He maintains that "formula" is too limiting and inexact a term for designating the phonetic, syntactic, verbal, rhythmic, and ideational resemblances or "corresponsions"—"the irrefutable statistical facts that distinguish the texts of Homer from those of poets known to have composed by writing" (*TGV* 274).[14] Nagler's interest is less in the occurrence of repetitions or corresponsions in the lines of the poem than in what he refers to as "a mental template in the mind of the oral poet" which is responsible for that occurrence. Borrowing from the approaches and terminology of linguistic philosophers, structural anthropologists, and folklorists, he suggests that a group of corresponsional phrases within a poem would better be considered "not a closed 'system' [like a 'formula' or 'formula-system'] but an open-ended 'family', and each phrase in the group would be considered an allomorph, not of any other existing phrase, but of some central Gestalt—for want of a better term—which is the real mental template underlying the production of all such phrases" (*TGV* 281). Similarly the structure of *langue* lies behind the statistical occurrences of *parole* and the structural model of a myth is realized in each of its versions (*TGV* 283–84).[15] Other analogous cases are considered as well:

> All of these precedents from other areas of inquiry do not prove that a preverbal Gestalt generating a family of allomorphs must be the best conceptual framework for the Homeric formula, but they do show that it is at least a possibility that the prevailing concept of the fixed and determinable structure, be it superficial (the completed phrase) or relatively deep (e.g., the localization of a metrical sequence), is not *a priori* the only working model for the production of phrases in oral epic composition. (*TGV* 284)

Whether, however, one accepts Nagler's "generative view" of oral composition, or the formulaic view as advanced by Russo or by Parry and Lord, it is unquestionable that in a poem so composed we are in the presence of a form of verbal art learned, produced, and transmitted in a manner quite different from that of a literary work.[16] The training of a Yugoslav bard-poet is described by Lord (*ST* 20–26), who holds it as representative of the formation of most oral singer-poets. He traces three stages. During the first, the would-be singer listens to older singers, absorbing their themes, images, rhythms, and language. Then he imitates the techniques of composition of his master—not at all, it is insisted, by memorizing his songs, but rather by accumulating, through repeated practice, the formulas and formulaic expressions[17] that will facilitate composition. Throughout this stage, "he is like a child learning words, or anyone learning a language without a school method; except that the language here being learned is the special language of poetry" (*ST* 22). Finally, the third stage begins when the poet-singer sings his first entire song before a critical audience and continues until "he has enough command of the formula technique to sing any song he hears, and enough thematic material at hand to lengthen or shorten a song according to his own desires and to create a new song if he sees fit" (*ST* 26).[18]

Nagler agrees essentially with Lord in regard to the three stages in the making of an oral poet. The second stage, though, involves not the aspiring poet's assimilation of formulaic "prototypes" (phrases for use under the pressure of composition and performance) but rather his unconscious absorption of hundreds of lines containing units—verbal, metrical, and syntactic—that are not necessarily identical, but that exhibit strong "family" resemblences.[19] Thence

> he develops an intuitive "feel" for a fluid Gestalt which he retains in his unconscious mind, probably in the same unknown way that the phrasal impulses of any language are retained in the mind when not in use. He then tries to realize that Gestalt at appropriate times *and in appropriate ways*—i.e., into the appropriate forms of its various parameters—in his fledgling attempts at verse-making (Lord's second stage), further securing the patterns in his mind by actually practising them. . . . What he learns is a method rather than its products. (*TGV* 285)

One can emphasize again that, for Parry, Lord, Russo, Nagler, and all who in any serious way subscribe to their views, the training process outlined above results in the formation of a poet-singer whose productions are to be distinguished from those of a literary (i.e., literate) artist, above all, in the nature of their composition. A poet who is formed in an oral tradition is not to be thought of as a reciter of memorized poems. The oral poet is not "*merely* a transmitter" (*ST* 5, 279 n. 7). Neither is he to be seen, both Lord and Nagler insist, as drawing from an accumulated store of memorized phrases and motifs to piece together the poem he presents (e.g., *ST* 42–43; *TGV* 284–86). "He does not 'memorize' formulas any more than we as children 'memorize' language. He learns them by hearing them in other singers' songs, and by habitual usage they becoming part of his singing as well" (*ST* 36). Nor, finally, can oral composition be equated with improvisation in a broad sense; the whole process is far too complex and subtle to be adequately designated by so imprecise a term (*ST* 5; cf. chap. 4, § D, below).

The essence of oral art lies in the *identity* of the act of poetizing with the act of performance. Herein resides the primary difference between oral and written verbal art—a difference that accounts not only for the peculiar training undergone by the oral poet and his resultant mode of formulaic mental operation but also for the unique form of his poetical productions. "An oral poem is not composed *for* but *in* performance. . . . Singing, performing, composing are facets of the same act" (*ST* 13). And it is the fact of his being a performer that has dictated the poet's method of composition. His state of "interaction with a highly critical and highly appreciative audience" (*TGV* 285) is, beyond doubt, the dominant and determining factor of his performance and, hence, of his poem. No matter where and before whom the performance takes place, "the essential element of the occasion of singing that influences the form of the poetry is the variability and instability of the audience" (*ST* 16). Here, then, in his need to capture and hold the attention of his hearers by the strength of his verses and his voice—to produce line after line continuously as long as his audience remains—is to be found the reason-for-being of the oral poet's mode of composition and of the characteristic elements in his poetry. Whether we call them "formulaic" or speak of them as having a Gestalt in common (*TGV* 380), the groups of repeated, parallel, or corresponsional phrases—so readily observable in the texts of oral poems—"were useful not, as some have supposed, merely to the audience if at all, but also and even more to the singer in the rapid composition" of his song (*ST* 30). In other words, these verbal configurations of sounds, rhythm, syntax, diction, meaning, and, I would add, context—all of these recurrent verbal phenomena would perhaps much better be interpreted as *implements* utilized in an ongoing process of composition, rather than as *elements* or *components* of a finished product.[20]

There are few characterizations of the nature of oral composition, as set forth in the Parry-Lord formulaic theory, more apt and concise than that of F. P. Magoun:

> It will be well to stress the fact that orally composed poetry by unlettered singers—or occasionally by lettered singers composing according to the techniques of their unlettered fellows[21]—as opposed to the work of lettered poets with ready access to writing materials, is put together not word by word with deliberation and at leisure but rapidly in the presence of a live audience by means of ready-made phrases filling just measures of isochronous verse capable of expressing every idea that the singer may wish to express in various metrical situations. These phrases may be called formulas and their use distinguishes the verse of the orally composed poems of unlettered singers whether Anglo-Saxon, Faroese, Finnish, Homeric, or Serbo-Croatian, to mention no others. (*BSC* 52)

Although Magoun's statement may appear somewhat of an oversimplification in the light of Lord's, Russo's, or Nagler's later elaborations of Parry's formulaic principle, it does nevertheless effectively describe the conditions under which the oral poet labors and the end that he strives to achieve.

Furthermore, the end Magoun suggests—"filling just measures of isochronous verse"—lies behind another feature that both Parry and Lord consider "a characteristic of oral composition and . . . one of the easiest touchstones to apply in testing the orality of a poem" (*ST* 54; cf. 131)—namely, the absence of necessary enjambement (see chap. 2, §B, below). The end-stopped line, equally with formulaic diction, is determined by a poem's origin in a situation of "interaction" between the poet and his audience. For, Lord asserts, the true art of the oral poet lies in his ability to create, and not simply recall, phrases that, when uttered in combination, will produce an effective line and succession of lines. "It is this facility rather than his memory of relatively fixed formulas that marks him as a skillful singer in performance" (*ST* 42–43).

A.2 For the reader and critic of poems that originated in an oral tradition, probably the most important implication of these findings is, as intimated earlier, the consideration that every performance of a poem entails a new and separate creation of the poem.[23] A singer may sing—or a poet perform—many times in his life a work that both he and his audience will recognize each time as one and the same. Or he may hear the song of another bard and perform it afterward, confident that he is repeating it as he heard it and that his audience will recognize its identity. But, in both cases, Parry and Lord have shown, there are more or less substantial variations from one performance or performer to the next. Emphasizing the "fluidity" of the oral tradition, as opposed to the "stability" of the written tradition, Lord declares that an understanding of the nature and genesis of an oral poem forces one to give up all ideas of finding or establishing its "original" version, for "in oral tradition the idea of an original is illogical" (*ST* 101).

> It follows, then, that we cannot correctly speak of a "variant", since there is no "original" to be varied! Yet songs are related to one another in varying degrees; not, however, in the relationship of variant to original, in spite of the recourse so often made to an erroneous concept of "oral transmission"; for "oral transmission", "oral composition", "oral creation", and "oral performance" are all one and the same thing. Our greatest error is to attempt to make "scientifically" rigid a phenomenon that is fluid. (Ibid.)[24]

Oral traditionists would have us recognize, therefore, that texts of works identifiable as products of an oral tradition are neither more nor, indeed, less than written records of the words uttered by the singer or poet during a single performance. Those texts that purport to record the same poem as rendered by a single performer on different occasions or by two or more performers will be bound to contain differences from one to another. For the oral epic, with which he is primarily concerned, Lord notes that, in the cases he has examined, the basic story was transmitted intact. The discernible changes, besides, generally involved addition, omission, and transposal of lines or material as a result of variations in style, training, or background from one poet to another or from one period in a poet's career to another (*ST*, esp. chap. 5).[25]

As noted at the beginning of the discussion, neither the poet nor his audience nor the tradition itself was affected by the simple writing-down of the performed poem. But that other world—"of those who could read and write, of those who came to think of the written text not as the recording of a moment of the tradition but as *the* song" (see above)—sometimes succeeded in imposing its notion of the fixed text, the "original" version, of *the* song, upon the literate members of the poet's public, as well as upon the poets themselves. The recorded texts acquired an unwarranted authority. They were read and even altered by individual readers in solitude. They were memorized by singers and reciters, who now became "transmitters" in truth. A gradual development took place in the poet's technique and his intention: he no longer strived to recreate *the* song as traditional configuration; rather he sought to reproduce *a* song as transmitted text. In this way, an isolated performance was adopted as the script for all subsequent performances.

> But this process is not a transition from an oral to a literary technique of composition. It is a transition from oral composition to simple performance of a fixed text, from composition to reproduction. This is one of the most common ways in which an oral tradition may die; not when writing is introduced, but when published song texts are spread among singers. (*ST* 130; cf. 109)[26]

In describing the post–World War II literarization of the poetic art in Yugoslavia, Lord states that, with the arrival of the set, "correct" text of the epic song, which was to be memorized and reproduced word for word, "the death knell of the oral process had been sounded" (*ST* 137).

A.3 After the foregoing discussion, it should be apparent that I hold the findings of scholars like Parry, Lord, Russo, and Nagler, with regard to poetry composed in an oral tradition, to be extremely relevant to the study of the recorded body of pre- and early Islamic Arabic poetry. Not only would "orality," were it to be shown in the case of this poetry, explain many of its "stereotyped," "repetitious," or "traditional" features and enable them to be better appreciated as intrinsic to the act of composition; it would also go far toward accounting for the often-noted instability of the textual tradition—particularly the presence of so many variant readings for almost every important line and the fragmentary or unfinished state of so many selections.[27] Moreover, and perhaps more importantly, if available texts of early Arabic poetry manifest characteristics that make plausible or probable its composition by means of techniques similar to those described above, then it may prove necessary or desirable to revise substantially our opinions on such perennial questions as literary plagiarisms among the early poets (*sariqāt*)[28] or the authenticity of the poetry itself.

I do not yet wish to pursue in any great detail the thorny issue of "authentic" and "forged" poetry—of transmitters with or without "integrity."

Nevertheless, the question cannot be entirely ignored in a study of the tradition of classical Arabic poetry. For, though critics from Abū ᶜAmr b. al-ᶜ Alā' and Ibn Sallām al-Jumaḥī to Ahlwardt, Margoliouth, and Ṭāhā Ḥusayn have cast doubt both on the reliability of many transmitters of the ancient poetry and on the authenticity of much of the transmitted poetry, their criticisms have generally failed to consider certain important facts that have since been brought out in a decisive fashion. One may, I think, grant that these doubts, at least in their extreme form as expressed by Margoliouth and Ṭāhā Ḥusayn,[29] have largely been laid to rest through the efforts of later scholars.[30]

There remains, however, at the root of even the most balanced and reflective defenses of the poetry and transmitters, the same presupposition—the same fundamental premise—of an "original version" of the poem to which all other versions are related as "variants." This seems to have been the view of the early Arab philologists and textual critics who sought to establish the works of the classical poets in *ne varietur* texts and who deplored the multiplicity of variants, alterations, misattributions, and the general "corruption" of the tradition. It has certainly been the view of more recent scholars. The very methodology to textual scholarship, as it has evolved to our time and as it has been usually applied in editing texts of early Arabic poetry, presumes the existence of an original manuscript (or, occasionally, "family" of manuscripts) from which later copies derived.[31] There is no doubt that this methodology has proven invaluable in establishing the original, or near-original, version of a written composition. Textual criticism has also brought us much closer to the texts of the Homeric epics and other oral poems as they were read and accepted by readers at the beginning of a textual tradition. But in this second case the "established text" must needs have been, by virtue of its origin in an oral tradition, either the record of a single special rendition or else an editorial synthesis or collation of several such records. Of course, the latter circumstance would be especially true of texts prepared by men who had a particular interest in such work and who were, to some extent, specially trained in techniques for "determining" the "correct" reading from several alternatives—i.e., the men who were operating in, and carrying on, a textual tradition.

Unfortunately, there seem as yet to have been few efforts to approach the problems of editing a poetical work that exhibits features of "orality" or of studying the textual history of such a work while giving consideration to the fluidity of the oral tradition.[32] Such an undertaking has been suggested and, to some extent, outlined by Lord with particular reference to the texts of the Homeric, South-Slavic, and certain medieval epics;[33] but the observations and indications he has made do not go far enough, nor do they seem to have impressed contemporary textual scholars too greatly. Of such a work as a history of the textual tradition of ancient and medieval literature, published in 1961, one reviewer has remarked, "the problem of the oral tradition is scarcely raised."[34] Another work, A. Dain's *Les Manuscrits*, offers invaluable information on the nature and course of the textual tradition of classical literature, but it does not at all envision any difficulty involved in the transference to writing of an oral-traditional poem.[35] Most recently R. Pfeiffer, in his *History of Classical Scholarship*, has admitted that the first period in the transmission of Greek literature was "probably . . . a time of *merely* oral composition and oral tradition of poetry" (*HCS* 25; my italics). But the implications of Parry's and Lord's view of "oral-composition" (as opposed to "oral-tradition")[36] for the study of the textual tradition of Homer and other early poets are dismissed in a (rather caustic) footnote, yet without their cogency being in the least diminished. Pfeiffer continues:

> The second stage, *we assume without further proof*, began with the introduction of alphabetic writing. Epic poets, heirs of an ancient oral tradition, began to put down their great compositions in this new script:[37] we still possess as the product of that creative epic age the two "Homeric" poems. The transmission remained oral: the poets themselves and the rhapsodes that followed them recited their works to an audience; and this oral tradition was secured by the script which *must* have been to a certain degree under proper control. . . . The power of memory was unchallenged, and the tradition of poetry and early philosophy remained oral. (Ibid.; my italics)

However, it was just this view of "oral tradition" as simply "oral transmission" that Lord described as a compromise to account for the fate of the Homeric poems during the years between Homer's death and the development of a viable writing system. Understood in this sense, "oral tradition was a fickle mistress with whom to flirt" (*ST* 9). Lord discounts, as we have seen, the "myth" of the "fantastic memories" so "well attested" of illiterate people and holds that "the main points of confusion in the theory . . . arose from the belief that in oral tradition there is a fixed text which is transmitted unchanged from one generation to another" (*ST* 9–10).

At this point, one might recognize a close similarity between opinions about the composition of the Homeric epics generally held by scholars prior to Parry and Lord (and still supported by several)[38] and the practically universal belief regarding the genesis of early Arabic poetry.[39] There has been, from the time of the medieval Muslim philologists to our own, an unwillingness to consider any possibility other than that of an original version of a poem—whether memorized or written—or rather, perhaps, simply an unawareness that such a possibility might exist. The nineteenth-century scholar and editor

John Kosegarten admirably sums up this traditional view for both his predecessors and his successors:

> The poetry of the Arabs, in the ages which preceded the rise of Islamism, was perpetuated by oral tradition; for in ancient times, when writing was not used or scarcely used, memory was exercised and strengthened to a degree now almost unknown. In those countries of Arabia where Arabian poetry may be justly considered to have had its origin or to have attained its earliest growth, there lived reciters, or Rāwis, as the Arabs called them, who got by heart numerous songs of their poets, and recited them, occasionally, in public assemblies and private parties. (*PH* i)

This impression, in essence, has been shared by a great majority of medieval and modern scholars who have dealt to any degree with early Arabic poetry. Students of Homer as well had felt the need to bridge the gap between their poet's death and the institution of an adequate script, and hence, besides taking recourse in a somewhat romanticized idea of "oral tradition," they also adopted two other alternatives: either advancing Homer's date to a period when writing was possible (or rather, feasible), or seeking to prove that writing did exist as early as the traditional date of Homer (*ST* 8–9). The first approach is not far removed from that of Margoliouth and Ṭāhā Ḥusayn, who proposed as more credible the idea that the origins of pre-Islamic poetry were to be found at a later post-Islamic date. As already mentioned, their hypotheses have been in large part discredited. Other scholars have chosen the second approach.[40] But, although the existence of writing may now be presumed to have been far more widespread among the pre-Islamic Arabs than has been thought previously, its mere existence and even its use for recording some poems by no means imply that it was utilized by the poet himself in the composition of his work (Blachère *HLA* 86). We have to overcome a tendency to naïveté concerning literacy. As Sterling Dow has cautioned in regard to the discovery of pre-Homeric literacy:

> Literacy is usually spoken of, for instance, as a simple indivisible essence (so that we say "the Mykenians were literate"), whereas in reality literacy is a complex skill applicable to a wide variety of purposes, in fact, to practically all the purposes of human communication. It would obviously be hazardous to assume that as soon as a person—child, barbarian, or Minoan—learns to write, he will use writing for the full range of purposes familiar to us. (Quoted in *ST* 150)

Yet even were the presence of an extensive written literature among the pre-Islamic Arabs to be proved, it would not follow that an oral poetry could not also be produced at the same time. Following Lord's findings, "we have . . . seen that oral literature can and does exist side by side with written literature" (*ST* 150).

A.4 Before considering the "orality" of early Arabic poetry, however, it may be well to note in reservation the following statement by Professor Lord: "It may not be possible in the case of many of our medieval texts to know with certainty whether we are dealing with an oral or a written product, but we may reach a high degree of *probability* in our research . . ." (*ST* 220). As it stands, and in view of the detailed and conclusive arguments he presents, the statement is quite acceptable. But, he continues, ". . . especially if we realize the certainty that it is either one or the other" (ibid.). Herein lies the sticking point for many who tend otherwise to accept Lord's and Parry's general thesis of oral-traditional composition. For Lord maintains, with almost dogmatic insistence, the impossibility of a text that is transitional between an oral tradition of verbal art and a written literary tradition—not the recording of a special, yet still purely oral, performance; nor the written work of a man who might earlier in his life have been an oral poet and subsequently came to compose in writing; nor, finally, "a *period* of transition between oral and written style, or between illiteracy and literacy; but a *text*, product of the creative brain of a single individual" (*ST* 129). The two techniques—of oral and written composition—are, according to Lord,

> contradictory and mutually exclusive. Once the oral technique is lost, it is never regained. The written technique on the other hand, is not compatible with the oral technique, and the two could not possibly combine, to form another, a third, a "transitional" technique. It is conceived that a man might be an oral poet in his younger years and written poet later in life, but it is not possible that he be *both* an oral and a written poet at any given time in his career. The two by their very nature are mutually exclusive. We may in actuality discover what might be called special categories of texts, but it is doubtful that they should be labelled "transitional," that is, part way between oral and written techniques. (Ibid.)[41]

However, Lord's view subsequently has met with serious, considered opposition from at least two quarters. In a study of "The Literary Character of Anglo-Saxon Formulaic Poetry," Larry D. Benson has made the highly significant point "that poems which we can be sure were not orally composed use formulas as frequently and sometimes more frequently than supposedly oral compositions" (*LC* 335 cf. 336–37, 339–40). Working with poems that he holds to have originated in a "lettered tradition," Benson reaches the following conclusions:

> Only our assumptions about formulaic poetry lead us to believe that such a style is necessarily connected with oral composition, and those assumptions, drawn from other literatures and other times, do not fit the facts of the Old English period; in that age literate poets could and did write heavily formulaic verse and . . . they could do so pen in hand . . . not because the demands of the meter or

> the pressures of oral composition prevent the poet from pausing to select some more suitable phrase but because this phrase *is* suitable, is part of a poetic diction that is clearly oral in origin but that is now just as clearly a literary convention. (*LC* 339; cf. 337)

According to Benson's findings, then (and contrary to Lord's position), "difficult theoretically as they may be, we must admit the possibility of 'transitional texts'" (*LC* 337). However, though I am not in a position to dispute his arguments concerning the "literary character" of the poems he discusses, I must object to a premise upon which he founds his study. "We know," Benson contends, "that there was a lettered as well as an oral tradition in Old English times, and we know too that the difficulties of collecting even modern oral poetry would argue for the fact that our surviving texts come from this lettered tradition" (*LC* 334). In a note, he adds, "By 'lettered tradition' I mean a tradition consisting of poems written by scribes for an audience of readers, poems which *thereby* have a fixed text that is transmitted to an audience by reading (probably aloud). . . . I also mean poems composed in writing" (*LC* 334 n. 4, my italics). Now, in my opinion, this postulate cannot be accepted as it stands. The very concept of an "audience of readers" goes against almost everything we know of the publication and circulation of poetical works during the era before printing and large-scale book production, particularly in the early (Western) Middle Ages.[42] Benson himself, as we have seen, admits that the formulaic diction of his "lettered" poet "is clearly oral in origin but . . . is now just as clearly a literary convention." But a literary convention, especially one so all-pervasive as this one,[43] is not employed merely out of authorial whim: it meets some requirement of the poet, it satisfies some taste of his audience, it somehow *functions*. And, on whatever other levels formulaic diction might have functioned—whether used by an unlettered oral poet or by a lettered poet composing according to the techniques of his unlettered predecessor (Magoun *BSC* 52; see above)—there can be no doubt that for the medieval poet in general, it functioned because it seemed to meet best his requirement of satisfying the taste of an audience that would be, first and foremost, precisely that—an *audientia*. For, during the Middle Ages, as H. J. Chaytor has shown most convincingly,[44] and throughout all antiquity,[45] poetry was meant to be heard, not read, *even by those who could read*; and *reading* of poetry—to the extent that it took place at all—was also, with but rare exceptions, a vocal operation (and in the Middle Ages, at least, according to Chaytor, a laborious, painful, and slow one; see below). The Anglo-Saxon poems discussed by Benson, regardless of their mode of composition, abound in formulaic and thematic usages, just as do the *chansons de geste, romans d'aventure,* and lyric poems of which Chaytor speaks at length,[46] just as do the Homeric and South-Slavic epics, just as do the Eddic and skaldic poems of the North, just as do—I hope to show—the pre-and early Islamic Arabic *qaṣīdas* and other poems. They abound in such usages because, to borrow Chaytor's words, "the whole technique of [such poems] . . . presupposed . . . a hearing, not a reading public. When culture had reached that stage at which the individual read to himself for his own enjoyment, a different kind of literature was in demand" (*FSP* 13).

Hence, in presuming an "audience of readers," Benson stands on very shaky ground. Albert Baugh's remarks on this subject are very much to the point and can be applied far more widely than just to the Middle English romanciers of whom he speaks:

> The ability to read is not the same thing as the habit of reading. With books as expensive as they were anything like a reading public did not exist. Since poets and versifiers were aware of this, they wrote with oral presentation in mind, adopting a style, so far as they were capable of it, natural to live presentation. They could hardly have failed to put themselves in the place of the minstrel or to imagine themselves as addressing a body of listeners. (*MER* 9–10)[47]

The "lettered tradition" visualized by Benson involves a further oversimplification of a most complex problem—namely, the nature of the delivery and transmission of the poems. One cannot, as he does, simply imply that "reading (probably aloud)" from a "fixed text," as the means of transmitting poetical works to an audience, was the only natural, clear-cut alternative to oral performance-*cum*-composition.[48] Chaytor (*FSP* chap. 1) offers a detailed discussion of the subject of reading and writing and their relation to oral delivery of medieval Western European poetry. He describes minutely the act of reading as it must have taken place in the medieval and classical world (*FSP* 5–10) and concludes thus: "The medieval reader, with few exceptions, did not read as we do; he was in the stage of our muttering childhood learner; each word was for him a separate entity and at times a problem, which he whispered to himself when he found the solution" (*FSP* 10). Later he adds:

> Whenever we encounter anyone poring over a newspaper, and whispering the words to himself as he laboriously spells his way through the sheet, we set him down as uneducated. It is not commonly realized that this was the manner of reading generally practised in the ancient world and during the early days of Christianity. . . . This ancient practice was continued in medieval times, until it was killed by the dissemination of printed matter, and the habit of mind which it implies deserves the notice of those who take in hand the editing of medieval texts. (*FSP* 13)

Indeed, it should be added, this habit of mind, coupled with the fact that the reader would in most cases be "confronted . . . by a manuscript often crabbed in script and full of contractions" (*FSP* 14),[49] deserves the notice of those who would contend that reading aloud was a common mode of presenting poems to a pre-Renaissance audience. We can recognize, as Baugh does for Middle English romances, that poems in general could be "sometimes sung, sometimes recited, and sometimes read from a book" (*MER* 23). Yet, the weight of the whole history of orally rendered poetry is preponderantly on the side of the first two. Even were we to question Chaytor's thesis regarding medieval reading habits and presume that readers existed in sufficient numbers who so far surpassed the "average" stumbling decipherer of texts whom he describes that they could read aloud,[50] not merely at a pace and volume adequate to the demands of an often discriminating audience, but also with the proper range of expression and vocal interpretation stipulated by the rhetorical aesthetic in which medieval poetry was composed (see *FSP* 48–67)—even then we could not dispute what has been affirmed by centuries of observers and preservers of the custom of orally rendered poetry, affirmed concerning the biblical psalmists and Homeric rhapsodes, the Arabic *rāwīs* and the Gallic jongleurs, the Slavic guslars and the Icelandic skalds, and many more. Whether before kings or commoners; whether speaking or singing; whether playing upon a harp, a gusle, a lute, or upon nothing at all; whether composing a poem or song as he presents it or presenting it as composed beforehand: the oral performer is almost never represented as one who reads aloud. In fact, in many traditions, such as those where the performer accompanied himself upon an instrument or enlivened his delivery by means of gestures, the notion that he held a book is out of the question.[51] Notable also is the tendency among all traditions where oral delivery of poetry was customary to recognize—even to insist upon—the preeminent role played by memory in carrying on the tradition.[52] Mythical or not, accounts of the phenomenal memories and prodigious mnemonic feats of performers and poets have been abundantly related for all these traditions—not only for those like the Vedic, the Greek rhapsodic or the later jongleur traditions where actual memorization from a text seems to have been the rule, but also for those that are "oral traditions" in the sense outlined above, where composition and performance are the same act. For even here, the oral poet *and* his public, as Lord has indicated, ordinarily conceive of his act of performance-*cum*-composition—of rendition—as a re-creation of a preexistent song from memory; and the poet himself would emphatically claim that his presentation of a poem is a verbatim "recitation" of it as he heard or performed it before (*ST* 26–29). Finally, it seems to have been true that in most literate, even highly literate, societies before the invention of printing—when books were the possession of the rich and the concern of the scholarly, and when poetry was, as we have seen, often written according to conventions probably inherited from a pre-literary oral tradition—poems continued to be rendered orally and usually by singing or recitation from a memorized text.[53] The very educational systems that brought about relatively high rates of literacy among certain segments, at least, of some pre-modern societies and fostered a proliferation of the written word—ancient India, for instance, the Greco-Roman world, and Arab-Islamic civilization—relied heavily upon memorization and recitation as a chief means of ensuring the acquisition and retention of knowledge; and conspicuous among the works so studied, learned, and recited were poetical texts.[54]

In Islam, particularly, the precedence of memorization and oral *transmission* in the service of the philological and religious sciences was maintained, as a fact or a fiction, throughout the Middle Ages, side by side with a prolific written tradition.[55] Even so staunch an advocate of the book and the written word as al-Jāḥiẓ does not hesitate to affirm the priority of oral transmission and the need for a retentive memory in the process of learning.[56]

One cannot, therefore, as Benson does, so lightly eliminate the problems of the origin and transmission of poetical texts whose content and style presuppose *some* form of oral delivery.[57] If they were, in fact, initially composed in writing rather than in performance, they would have been susceptible of at least three modes of delivery and publication employed in antiquity and the Middle Ages—singing, reciting, *and* reading aloud (apart, of course, from scribal copying, which is not in question at the moment). Now, authorities seem agreed that of the three, the sung and recited performance *from memory* were by far the most common during most of the Middle Ages.[58] The process of reading, on the other hand, involved such concentration and labor, even for practiced readers, that one cannot believe a representative audience of any taste would have suffered being read to, when two such satisfactory and proven techniques of rendition as singing and recitation were available. And if we admit the relative infrequency of oral delivery of poetical works from a text and, correspondingly, the prevalence of the sung or recited performance, we must also, it seems to me, accept the textual difficulties inherent in any oral-*transmission* process—difficulties described by Chaytor in considerable detail. Moreover, that these textual difficulties are not unrelated to—or at least not dissimilar from—those associated with the textual tradition of oral poetry is suggested by Lord (*ST* 202–20) and made clearer in a study by Michael Curschmann.

A.5 Curschmann's article, "Oral Poetry in Medieval English, French, and German Literature: Some Notes on Recent Research," makes the case for the existence of "transitional" texts, only to propose finally, "Perhaps we should not speak of transitional texts at all'' (*OPML* 49).[59] Although he questions Lord's doctrine of the mutual exclusiveness of the techniques of oral and written composition, he does not resort to Benson's view of poems ''written by scribes'' who employ formulaic techniques and who compose ''for an audience of readers.'' Rather, he raises the fundamental textual question of the recording of orally composed poetry. Lord (*ST* 128) holds that such recordings ''are *not* 'transitional', but are in a class by themselves.'' But, Curschmann says,

> of all of Parry's and Lord's observations this is the one most difficult to generalize: that the Yugoslavian singers find it difficult either to recite slowly enough for someone to follow in long-hand or (if they are literate) to write their songs down themselves. Consequently it is in this purely technical matter [of the recording process] that the theory of oral-formulaic composition has its most patent defects. (*OPML* 45)

Referring to Magoun's theory that the Anglo-Saxon poems we have are recordings, made by monastic scribes, of oral performances (*BSC* 60), Curschmann says,

> But to produce such a text the singer would have had to recite very slowly, much slower in fact than he would have to in our days of better transcribing techniques (not to mention the tape-recorder). Can we expect him to have tried carefully to preserve in the process the oral nature of his composition? The same reservations apply if we assume that he dictated to himself—''an uncommon if not awkward procedure.'' . . . In either case, for the finished product to be strictly oral, the singer would have had to possess the modern scholar's awareness of an absolute difference between written and oral. And if the singer had simply sung, without paying attention to the scribe's capacity, these texts would be even more garbled than we think they are. They would have to be considered even less reliable witnesses of the manner in which they were put together. (*OPML* 45)

Curschmann's reservations about self-dictated texts are not, however, entirely justified. As Dain has shown, self-dictation was the usual procedure followed by ancient and medieval copyists and accounts for many of the ''aural'' textual errors usually ascribed to copying from oral dictation (see n. 35). Moreover, the copyist progressed by means of small word-groups capable of being taken in at a single glance, immediately memorized, recited over, and written down; and there seems to be no reason why one who was writing without a textual exemplar—i.e., composing with pen in hand—should have proceeded in a way significantly different as regards the mechanics of the operation. And if that were true, the operation itself can be seen as not radically removed from that which Lord describes as resulting in *oral dictated* and *oral autograph* texts (*ST* 149–50). Hence, it would not be surprising to discover in these "written" compositions a large-scale conformity to products of an oral tradition, not because of conscious imitation, but rather because similar—or at least not contradictory—factors determined the mode of composition.

Furthermore, Curschmann's analysis is weakened by his accepting too readily certain conclusions about the "transitional"—even "written"—character of the *chansons de geste* and the *Chanson de Roland*, in particular (*OLMP* 46–47)—conclusions that current research shows to be highly dubious[60] and that already seem to have ignored the important findings of Ramón Menéndez Pidal, to whose work Curschmann makes no allusion.[61]

Nevertheless, Curschmann's study raises important considerations not only for textual criticism, where they are fundamental, but also for any accurate understanding and sensitive reading of a poem that bears evidence of "formulaic" composition. For such a poem, regardless of how it might have originated, exists for us only as a *text or collection of texts*. Most importantly, Curschmann warns against "indiscriminate application of Parry's methods" (*OPLM* 47–48). On the basis of differences in form and length between the long epic and various shorter genres, objections to such application have been raised or considered for the biblical psalms,[62] the English and Scottish ballad,[63] non-narrative Old English poems,[64] and the old Spanish ballad.[65] They may with equal justice be considered in the case of the Arabic *qaṣīda* (see below). Curschmann writes:

> But the problems involved here are certainly more basic. To come to grips with them we have to consider the phenomen of formulaic usage in all its facets and ramifications. . . . At present we cannot yet properly assess the usefulness of Parry's findings for our analysis of the various literary genres which are distinguised by abundant use of formulas or other prefabricated units. What we have seen so far suggests caution, however. (*OPML* 48)

What Curschmann can lead us to conclude, therefore, is the following: from the point of view of the literary critic who would satisfactorily interpret a work exhibiting formulaic usages or from that of the textual critic who would effectively come to grips with the problematical "fluidity" of the manuscript transmission of such a work, the question of a "transitional text" is not really to the point. The exigencies of oral rendition, which originally conditioned the phenomena we have come to associate with oral composition, were not relaxed simply because the poet or his listening audience happened to be literate. Lord tends to minimize the "usefulness" of formulaic elements to the audience and to stress instead their value to the singer in "rapid composition" (see above). But this is, in a sense, to beg the question: for, as Chaytor has said of medieval methods of oral delivery, "It is at least certain that the methods in vogue would not have persisted, had they not been to the taste of the audiences'' (*FSP* 67); and Lord himself continually attaches great importance to the audience as the determining factor in oral delivery (see above). Thus, in composing with the verbal techniques of the singer-poet, the scribe-poet and writer-poet (to use Curschmann's terms [*OPML* 49]) could hardly, in many—even most—cases, have been making a conscious choice of style. We must ask ourselves to what extent the very idea of ''poetry'' and ''poem'' as such, during those eras when it was regarded preeminently as an *aural* experience (regardless of how composed), would not have been of necessity conceived in terms of its pre-literate manifestations—i.e., in terms of a poetic of oral composition as we have come to know it. Would it not be true, under those conditions, that to prove that a poem produced during such an era is formulaic would be only to prove that it is a poem produced during such an era?[66]

Much more useful, in Curschmann's opinion, would be not to exercise oneself in trying to decide the oral or written origin of a given piece. ''Orally composed'' poems cannot really be identified as such beyond doubt, unless one (or one's recorder) is present at the performance taking down every word the poet utters. Historical evidences of oral composition, such as Bede's story of Caedmon or the sketches of extemporaneous performances in Arabic anecdotal literature, though they may demonstrate the existence of a living oral tradition, cannot be adduced to account for the state of specific texts. Rather, what we can seek to do is to determine whether the oral devices in a given poem, such as formulaic diction, lack of enjambement, recurrent motifs, and so on, are themselves primarily responsible for the structure of a poem, thus indicating the probable nature of its composition—in or for public oral performance; or whether other features are present, which are not—and perhaps cannot be—set forth exactly, but which somehow indicate that the author's formal approach to his composition was significantly determined by concerns outside those of public performance. It is when the ''writer-poet'' has recourse to, and aims for effects in, the realm ''beyond the scope of oral poetry'' (*OPML* 49); when, moreover, ''the use of oral devices . . . has a clearly subservient function'' to some overriding tectonic principle which itself is clearly non-oral (*OPML* 50): that we may be able to speak of ''a type [of poem] somewhere between oral and written'' (*OPML* 51). One of Curschmann's most telling examples is that of the Old Saxon *Heliand*, a highly formulaic poem assumed by some scholars to have been orally composed, but more recently shown to have been structured with ''careful and elaborate advance planning,'' the plan being ''based on the theological significance of formal proportions and the medieval symbolism of numbers''

(*OPML* 50). Curschmann also examines two twelfth century German *Spielmannsepen*, the *Orendel* and *Salman und Morolf*, both constructed in the manner of demonstrably oral poems with a high ratio of traditional themes and formulaic passages. Yet they also show evidence of "an overall plan": in both cases, Curschmann claims, "the author . . . is pursuing a modern theme through the forms of an ancient technique of composition" (*OPML* 52). Thus, again, it is the deliberate subordination, or rather, perhaps, exploitation of oral-traditional devices by an author "for compositional purposes beyond the scope of oral poetry" that, in Curschmann's view, would constitute a point of departure from oral-traditional composition that is capable of being ascertained (although with a certain amount of subjective judgment) and that reveals an *essential* change both in the poet's approach to his art and in the public he seeks to affect.

Curschmann's study adds something to our understanding of the formulaic poetry that makes up so much of our premodern "literature," and his distinction between poems in which oral-formulaic elements form the primary structuring principle and those in which such elements are subordinated to another, usually literary or learned, principle provides a more useful critical tool than Lord's oral-written dichotomy. But, as Curschmann notes (*OPML* 51 n. 53), Lord himself hinted that his distinction was not so rigid in practice as in theory: "Yet after all that has been said about *oral* composition as a technique of line and song construction, it seems that the term of greater significance is *traditional*. Oral tells us 'how,' but traditional tells us 'what,' and even more, 'of what kind' and 'of what force'" (*ST* 220). I would agree fully that the key word is *traditional,* but *oral* could also tell us much if our question were "why." One matter that should be apparent after the foregoing discussion is the large measure to which poetical composition, in many societies at many times, was absolutely conditioned by the occasion or prospect of oral rendition. This is self-evident in the case of orally composed poems. It seems also to have been the case for a great many poems that, although perhaps initially set down in writing, are so structured with a view to oral rendition—i.e., so formulaic and additive in style[67]—as to be, *for all practical purposes*, indistinguishable from "orally composed" poetry.

A.6 One could even wonder whether all early formulaic texts, insofar as the possibility—even probability—of scribal redaction of "oral texts" can never be excluded, ought not to be classified in a single category of "traditional" texts. This would be consistent with Curschmann's position and would have the advantage of benefiting from the insights and terminology developed by Parry, Lord, Nagler, and others. One would then have to recognize that oral performance of poetical works was a very complex operation, even when the performer did not simultaneously compose the poem he presented. We have had occasion earlier to refer to H. J. Chaytor's penetrating study of the world of poets and public, writers and readers, before the common existence of printed books. His discussion of the poet's and the performer's art, or "craft" (*FSP* 48–53, 114–29), though not couched in the terms of later theorists of oral poetry, is directly relevant to both the compositional and the textual problems of "traditional" poetry in the sense described above. When we consider the techniques and attitudes of the jongleur during performance and compare them, say, with those of the rhapsode,[68] the Arabic *rāwī* (see chap. 2 below), or other representatives of the custom of oral delivery, we cannot but see as misleading Lord's distinction not only between an "oral" and a "written" text but also between oral performance-*cum*-composition and oral performance from a "memorized" text.

Lord has, as was seen, cautioned against a tendency to naïveté with regard to literacy. But in his concern to uphold the excellence of the pristine oral-tradition carried on by illiterate or semiliterate singer-poets, as against the "meretricious virtues of [literary] art" (*ST* 221), he himself has been guilty of a kind of naïveté. Basing his judgment mainly on his experiences with Slavic singers who have since 1918 taken to memorizing the set text of published songs and performing them so that "one can follow the text in the book" (*ST* 137), he deplores what he regards as the generally pernicious effects of conscious memorization upon an oral tradition (see above). It perhaps need not be mentioned that literacy and becoming literate in a world where one is surrounded by printed books and the written word in all its forms is hardly to be compared with what the situation must have involved in the medieval and ancient pre-printing world; nor that a performer's awareness of the existence of hundreds, perhaps thousands, of reduplicated printed copies of the poem he performed could well inhibit his faculty for improvisation, whereas no such consideration would have inhibited a pre-printing performer, who probably would have owned, or had access to, one of but very few "copies" of the poem.[69]

Lord is insistent, with regard to variations in the oral tradition of a song from one performance to another, that however "chaotic and arbitrary" they may appear to the "superficial observer," in reality they are not.

> It cannot be said that "anything goes." Nor are these changes due in the ordinary sense to failure of memory of a fixed text, first, of course, because there is no fixed text, second, because there is no concept among singers of memorization as we know it, and third, because at a number of points in any song there are forces leading in several directions, any one of which the singer may take. (*ST* 120; cf. 22, 109)

Now, this is an extremely valuable insight into the operations of a mode of poetical composition and performance, but the principle here articulated is by no means so limited in application to orally composed poetry as Lord would have it. That rhapsodes, jongleurs, *rāwīs*, minstrels, and the like had among the tools of their trade, besides a capacious memory, a notable capacity for improvisation has been observed and documented.[70] Scholars have sometimes discerned in different manuscript copies of a work, all of which unquestionably derived from a single original, variants that cannot be accounted for by scribal error, but must have been the result of the performer's oral "interpretation" of the work. The fact that a definite and substantial *textual*, as opposed to *thematic* or *structural*, correspondence among the copies can be observed is certainly evidence that memorization must have been an operative factor in producing the texts, but hardly "memorization as we know it." No one would, I imagine, claim that each of these texts represents a separate and unique act of composition. Nor can one, on the other hand, treat such variants simply as "corruptions" of the text, for the concept would have had no more meaning for a virtuoso oral performer, "more concerned with the effectiveness of his 'interpretation' than with strict fidelity to his author's intentions" (Davison in *CH* 218), than it did for an unlettered oral poet whose "every performance is a separate song" (*ST* 4). There may be a greater measure of "stability" in recorded copies of text-based performances, but neither poem nor performer should on that account be deemed any the less "traditional"—particularly in the event that texts of the work exhibit throughout the oral-formulaic qualities associated with "traditional" poetry.

It cannot be assumed that "memorization" by reading or hearing a "fixed text" would have been for a professional performer, trained and immersed in a tradition of orally rendered poetry, the same as "memorization as we know it." At a time when sharp distinctions between the written and the spoken word did not always exist (particularly in the case of poetry, which anyway presupposed a listening audience), it would be difficult to maintain that such a performer's thorough exposure to both oral poems and poems composed for oral performance would not have furnished him with a sense of composition by means of "oral" formulas, themes, and such, analagous to, if not identical with, that of the oral poet himself. Peter Wolf, alluding to the fact that grammarians in late antiquity often composed poetry, notes that "this is only natural. From the Homeric rhapsodes down through the Hellenistic age to our own present day, those who preserved poetry have themselves composed it and the poets have concerned themselves with transmitted poetry" (*VSS* 39). And evident as this has been in the "lettered tradition" of the grammarians, it has been even more so in the "oral tradition" of formulaic poetry, whether lettered or unlettered.

The parallel that has been drawn between the approach and techniques of the jazz musician and those of the oral poet has equal—maybe more—validity with reference to those of the oral performer or renderant.[71] Robert Stevick, for example, makes these pertinent observations:

> In a traditional oral (or musical art form—as opposed to a tradition perpetuated in writing or notation—memory of past performances will have a very large effect on any further performance; any familiarity at all with successive jazz performances suggests strongly that performers (and particularly professional ones) repeat earlier performances as entities, subject only to such changes as faulty memory, momentary experiments, or effects of audience reaction may produce. They do not build each performance merely a phrase at a time. Composition, in this respect, represents relatively slight modifications within an entire "piece" or a substantial stretch of the selection being presented. But composition in improvisational art, for traditional themes handled repeatedly by professional performers, can hardly be conceived of entirely as fresh creation measure-by-measure, phrase-by-phrase. (*OFA* 385–86)

But improvisation upon a set text, just as upon a set score, would certainly have presented no inordinate problems to a professional performer. Indeed, as we have seen, textual evidence indicates that it did not. And if the poem itself was written with oral delivery in mind, fully reflecting the mnemotechnic, generative usages characteristic of oral poetry (not necessarily in conscious imitation of oral poetry but simply because that was the form a poem was expected to have), it would have been especially conducive to improvisational "interpretation" by a traditional performer. Thus, it can be said of the oral performer at certain periods that, no less than the oral bard, his technique too "is a technique of remembering rather than of memorization" (Lord, in Wace/Stubbings *CH* 185).

Literacy then, as the ability to write (even to write poems), cannot of itself have constituted "the vast cultural change [it takes] to develop a new kind of poetic" (Lord *ST* 128), as long as that poetic continued to be dictated by the fact that poems were, above all, things to be performed aloud and heard. Literacy, too, as the ability to read, "is not the same thing as the habit of reading" (see above): poems were rendered orally before lettered, as well as unlettered, audiences, and whether those poems were "composed" during rendition or were rendered on the basis of a written "original" seems to have made little essential difference either in their formulaic and thematic structuring, in accordance with the poetic of oral performance or in the "fluid" and "multiform" state of their textual tradition. Returning, however, to Benson's premised "lettered tradition," "consisting of poems written by scribes for an audience of readers" (p. 16 above), we have seen that to accept such a concept as appropriate to the circumstances of early medieval poetry is not justified by what we know of the tradition of oral rendition. Nor, as later considerations have shown, are we justified in assuming that "poems written by scribes" would, in any case, have been intended "for an audience of readers." Merely to adduce evidence of the poet's "learnedness" or of the verbal and thematic complexity of his poem does not "prove" (1) that he was writing, nor (2) that he was writing to be read. Given the orientation of ancient and medieval education toward oral dictation, lecture, and recitation, exposure to knowledge so promulgated—especially in certain more cultured milieux—could not have been too hard to come by, even for an illiterate, though undoubtedly sensitive, poet. An obvious case in point would be that of Caedman, to whom "quite learned men . . . expounded . . . a certain topic of Sacred Story or Teaching, bidding him, if he could, to turn this into poetical rhythm. Whereupon he, undertaking the task, departed and, coming back next morning, recited what he had been ordered to recite, composed in excellent verse" (Bede, quoted in Magoun *BSC* 50). But it is not even necessary to presume that a "traditional" poet need be illiterate. Furthermore, as Parry, Lord, Nagler, Duggan, and several other scholars have consistently pointed out, verbal and thematic complexity is precisely the hallmark of the finest "traditional" poems preserved to us. For sheer complexity, for instance, one could hardly rival the Old Norse Skaldic poems, whose origins in a tradition that banked heavily upon extemporaneous composition had been recognized long before Parry's studies first appeared.[72]

Behind the idea of such a "lettered tradition" as Benson supposes, there lies, nevertheless, a profound poetic truth that both Chaytor and Lord, to mention only two, were at pains to bring out, though each approached it from a different angle. For Lord, as noted above, poems that were composed in writing would differ essentially, *by virtue of that very fact*, from those composed during oral rendition. Although this distinction is finally reduced to one between the poems of a *traditional* oral singer and those of a *nontraditional* literary artist, the difference between their poems is still just as essential, and it results from different *modes* of composition. Chaytor is equally convinced that two intrinsically different kinds of poems can be observed in the evolution of medieval verse: one "composed to be heard, not read, . . . intended to give pleasure to the ear" (*FSP* 52); the other directed to "a public which would read for itself, for information, reflection and pleasure" (*FSP* 80). In his view, then, the difference has come about because of different *motives* for composition. "Oral," Lord has said, "tells us 'how'" (*ST* 220). As I suggested and as the works of Chaytor and Curschmann, at least, have made likely, "oral" does not always tell us "how;" but rather, and much more to the point, "oral" tells us "why"—why, that is, the work has such a form and style. The crucial distinction, then (if one must have crucial distinctions), is not to be made between "oral" composition and "written" composition. It ought, instead, to be made between "heard" poetry and "read" poetry. "Traditional," in Lord's sense, still "tells us 'what', and even more, 'of what kind' and 'of what force'." But now the realm of the "traditional" can be extended—not unreasonably, I believe, nor unrealistically—to include poems whose style and structure, comprising all the characteristics usually identified with oral poetry, leave little or no doubt that the *primary* purpose of their composition was *to be heard*—that they were composed in, and/or for, public oral presentation.

B. Naturally, as was intimated above, the theory of oral-formulaic composition and rendition cannot be applied to classical Arabic poetry without reservation. The distinctive nature and evolution of this poetry preclude our simply taking over conclusions reached about epic verse for service in analyzing the *qaṣīda* and other forms of Arabic verse. Important differences between the two genres must be taken into account; although, as Curschmann noted, such differences, where formulaic usage is concerned, are not necessarily critical (*OPML* 48; see § A.5, above).

B.1 First, Parry and particularly Lord often stress the narrative character of Homeric and South Slavic verse. "The ideal [of the oral tradition] is a true story well and truly retold" (*ST* 29; cf. 6–7). Although narrative or dramatic elements frequently do occur in early Arabic poetry, such occurrences are limited to episodes or passages within the larger context of the poem (cf. Bräunlich *VLB* 244). The Arabic *qaṣīda* has itself been typified as an "odic" composition or as a "descriptive lyric" (Ahlwardt *PP* 30; Bräunlich *VLB* 244; Arberry *SO* 15). Sir William Jones attributed to the *qaṣīda* of Imra'alqays, at least, the form of a "dramatick pastoral" (in Arberry *SO* 15). R. Jacobi, however, has discussed several attempts to classify the *qaṣīda* in terms of Western genres and indicates the futility of doing so, "if the concepts 'epic', 'lyric', 'dramatic', were today still to be understood, as they have been throughout the centuries, as poetic schemata or moulds (*Schablonen*) that only give to a material its external form" (*SPAQ* 208). There is, nevertheless, she finds, a striking appropriateness in the expression "epic" as a term applied to the *style* of the classical *qaṣīda*. Following E. Staiger's fundamental analysis (in his *Grundbegriffe der Poetik*) of the essential features of "epic" style, rather than of the epic as such, Jacobi observes that the characteristics of that style, which Staiger had deduced primarily on the basis of the Homeric epics, conformed to those of the *qaṣīda* style "astonishingly exactly" (*SPAQ* 209–12).

Thus, the generic differences between the *qaṣīda* and the epic poems considered by Parry, Lord, Duggan, and others should not, of themselves, prevent application of the oral-traditional theory to early Arabic poetry. We should also realize that the qualities of "epic" style, identified by Jacobi as present in the pre- and early Islamic *qaṣīda*, correspond "astonishingly exactly" to those that have been determined by the Chadwicks and M. Bowra to characterize "heroic" poetry (Chadwicks *GL*; Bowra *HP* passim), a poetry one of whose chief properties is its orality. Unquestionably, the persons, exploits, circumstances, and communities made manifest in the lines of classical Arabic poetry share, to a remarkable degree, the features set forth by the Chadwicks as essential to oral heroic literature (*GL* III 727–41). And although they do not treat or refer to Arabic poetry specifically, one can easily see that early Arab poets have composed in all the genres that "are found to be cultivated where writing is unknown or not used for literary purposes" (*GL* III 700)—all, that is, but epic or extensive narrative verse (see *GL* III 697–726, 802–53, and passim). In this regard, their poems are no more exceptional—and are considerably more "heroic"[73]—than many other non-epic forms of oral poetry. Even M. Bowra, who would seem to insist that "heroic poetry is essentially narrative" (*HP* 4), could hardly deny that Arabic poetry has a "heroic outlook, which admires man for doing his utmost with his actual, human gifts" (*HP* 5); and we, who read Bowra's brilliant comparative study of oral epic traditions among many different peoples, will come upon innumerable parallels with the Arabic tradition, non-narrative though it be.

Granting, then, the real "heroicness" of classical Arabic poetry, we should beware—as Benedetto Croce would have us beware—of attaching too much importance in aesthetic and literary analysis to differences in *genre* or *kind*. The differences between epic and *qaṣīda*, narrative and lyric or ode, are actual and observable. But while they may be useful for purposes of discussion or categorization, they must never blind us to the reality of the "individual expressive fact," without which all such artistic or literary kinds—being after all merely schemata logically deduced from existing "facts"—are empty names. The effects of this "greatest triumph of the intellectualist error" in aesthetic theory, the idea of artistic and literary kinds, are evident even within the Arabic tradition itself, with the enthronement of the *qaṣīda* upon the high altar of verbal art and the denial of artistic merit to other forms of expression and, conspicuously, to *rajaz* poetry.[74] The Bedouin who rendered his *qaṣīda* or *urjūza* before a sixth-century Arab audience may not have been telling a story or making an epic; but he was an oral poet poetizing in a heroic tradition, and I maintain that we have to approach his poems with this in mind.

B.2 Other objections that might be raised to including classical Arabic verse under the Parry-Lord definition of oral poetry are somewhat more serious and must be dealt with. The oral-formulaic theory evolved out of consideration of the two Homeric epics—together some 27,000 lines. It was expanded and further elaborated through analysis of texts—Yugoslavian epic-songs, Anglo-Saxon epics, *chansons de geste*, and so on—that, although generally shorter than the *Iliad* or the *Odyssey*, usually well exceed 200 lines. The verses of the Arabic ode (as we have it recorded), on the other hand, may vary in number, "but are seldom less than twenty-five or more than a hundred" (Nicholson *LHA* 77). Yet R. Culley has published an important study exploring in depth the question of *Oral Formulaic Language in the Biblical Psalms*—a genre often mentioned as similar in many essential features (including length) to the Arabic *qaṣīda*. And Ruth House Weber, who has had to meet the same objection in adapting Parry's oral-formulaic theory to the exigencies of the Spanish ballad, makes the point that

> it is not to be expected that Parry's studies on Homer should provide the answer to stylistic problems of the popular ballad, for the epic and the ballad require individual treatment. The length of the epic has been instrumental in its being being restricted to the hands of professional minstrels. Contrariwise, the greater brevity of the ballad has allowed it to be subjected to the more precarious vicissitudes of amateur handling. (*FDSB* 176)[75]

Ramón Menéndez Pidal expresses in the following terms the effect likely to be exerted upon the textual state of an oral poem, particularly a shorter one, by any appreciable amateur handling.

> There is a difference between *geste* and ballad as concerns the audience. A ballad is widely diffused, for numerous hearers can recall and repeat it. It is harder to learn a *geste* by reason of the poem's greater length. But undoubtedly there was among the hearers such an individual sufficiently endowed with memory to recall the whole *geste*, though more imperfectly than the *jongleur* by profession. Besides, we should view as rather frequent the collaboration of hearers who would learn and circulate the fragments, the most famous bits of a *geste*, thus contributing to the development of variants. (*CR* 59)

In many cases, specifically that of the early Arabic tradition, it would be inappropriate to make a sharp distinction between professional poets and amateurs.[76] Nevertheless, the observations of Weber and Menéndez Pidal with regard to the part played by amateurs in transmitting a "traditional" poem can still be applied to the classical *qaṣīda*. Referring to the Arab partisan or tribal poet, for instance, Blachère indicates that "in principle, all the members of the group or tribe made themselves gratuitous transmitters [of his poems]" (*HLA* 91). The anecdotal literary histories and other such cultural-historical sources are replete with accounts of the enthusiasm of rulers, notables, religious and military leaders, and others, for both hearing *and reciting* poetry.[77] But this "amateur" interest must be—as it usually was during the earliest periods about which we have information—seen as set apart from the more specialized activity of poet and *rāwī*. What influence such "amateur" reciters of poetry might have exercised on the textual tradition of the *qaṣīda* would be impossible to ascertain at this point.[78] It is essential to ask, however, whether someone who undertook to write down a poem from dictation (in an era when the act of writing itself was at best laborious and was performed, it seems, only for relatively limited purposes and by trained scribes) would have contented himself with anything less than the rendition of a properly qualified renderant whose poetic skill and faithfulness to the tradition had been demonstrated.

The fact that the *qaṣīda* is much shorter than the epic admits of a second consideration, viz., the extent to which memory and memorization might in fact have played a role in transmitting and preserving early Arabic poems before they were written down.[79] In a study of oral poetry in the Old English *Seafarer*, J. J. Campbell has raised this important question with particular reference to shorter Old English poems. (His remarks are also suggestive of the amateur's capacity for reproducing a poem he has heard performed.) Campbell says:

> Each poem need not necessarily have been composed spontaneously as an entirely new poem every time a poet told a given story. It is completely reasonable to expect that every member of the Old English poetic audience would remember a certain number of the poetic formulas, although his knowledge would be far inferior to that of the professional scop. . . . Further, members of the audience must often have had favorite poems which were so striking and memorable in the form in which they heard them from an expert scop that they could remember and repeat some sections in their original state. This memorizing probably would be more likely for laymen with little experience in fresh improvisation, but even professional singers might try to keep especially effective passages intact. (*OPS* 88)[80]

And J. B. Hainsworth has expressed a similar opinion:

> Of course a poem that is improvised as a whole may contain recited components (or indeed vice versa). This may well be the case with Homer: it is a common assumption in discussions of the Catalogue [of Ships]: we may also reasonably call recitation the repeated lines that arise when messages are delivered or commands executed. But the "typical scenes" (e.g., of arming and sacrificing) are a marginal and instructive case: . . . these are not ready-made packages. (*FHF* 2 n. 1)

Now, two factors are present in Arabic poetry that would be of great value both to the oral-formulaic poet and to the mnemonically oriented transmitter or reciter. One of these is the prosodic form of the poetry—certainly among the most invariable and demanding meter- and rhyme-conventions in world literature.[81] The other is the Arabic language itself, whose highly patterned morphology affords, as Professor H. A. R. Gibb has observed,

> an enormous number of words whose vowel schemes are exactly alike. Every noun of agent from the simple verb, for example, is formed exactly like *qātil* [(a killer)]: *rākib* (a rider), *kātib* (a writer), *ḥāmil* (carrier), &c. Inevitably, therefore, rhyme and assonance play a very large part in Arabic literary style from the first, not only in poetry but in prose as well, and alliteration and *jeux de mots*, so far from being avoided, are regarded as special ornaments in belles-lettres. (*ALI* 8)

These factors of meter, rhyme, assonance, alliteration, and wordplay naturally offer a vast store of the stuff that, as we have seen, formulas are made of. But they can serve equally as convenient mnemonic aids in memorized transmission of a poem. Thus, even if we grant the oral-traditional origins of most pre- and early Islamic poems, we must still inquire whether our extant poetical texts are records of given performances of odes composed *during* performance or *while* dictating, as Parry and Lord maintain of Homeric, Yugoslavian, and other epics; or whether they are indeed simply the setting down in writing of poems that have been memorized at the time of their composition and *transmitted* orally, largely intact, as exponents of the conventional theory of "oral tradition" (i.e., oral transmission of a memorized "text") have ordinarily presumed (cf. Monroe *OCPP* 40).

C. Confronted by the problematical features that generally differentiate "traditional" texts from texts obviously composed and transmitted in writing, scholars have sometimes turned to the research of folklorists, since poetry of the "folk" shares with "traditional" or "early" poetry a number of these same features. Chief among them are (1) a very wide repertoire of phrases, phrase-patterns, images, themes, even whole passages, that recur from poem to poem within a given corpus of poetry (and even within a single poem) and (2) a large measure of substantive variation from one version—or rendition—of a poem to another (cf. Zwettler *BFOT* 199). Scholars of "traditional" poetry have given lip service to the idea of an "oral tradition" through which the poems would have been preserved and transmitted down to the time of their textualization. But they have proceeded to blame the preliterate oral tradents—their "lapses of memory," "insensitivity," "incompetence," "irresponsibility," "over-inventiveness," even "unscrupulosity"—for the "conventionalizations," "confusions," "inconsistencies," "interpolations," "fabrications," "misattributions," "plagiarisms," and so on that are alleged to have "corrupted" the texts of those poems. Yet analogous phenomena have been noted as standard, even typical, attendants to "folk-poetry" as it is normally produced and rendered, without any such accusations being leveled against *its* representatives. And in the past some Arabists—most prominently, Karl Petráček (*DSSV*, *QAAL*, *VAL*) and Alfred Bloch (esp. *KWAV*)—have tentatively advanced the notion of applying folklore studies to the study of early Arabic poetry.

Elsewhere I have given considerable attention to this aspect of Arabic literary scholarship and to the questions raised by viewing classical Arabic poetry through folklorists' eyes (Zwettler *BFOT*). There it was observed that the one essential characteristic of "folk-poetry," in regard to which folklorists of all persuasions seem to be in accord, is that of "orality." F. Utley, after analyzing a wide range of definitions of "folk literature," offered the following "operational definition": "Folk literature is *orally transmitted literature* wherever found, among primitive isolates or civilized marginal cultures, urban or rural societies, dominant or subordinate groups" (in Dundes *SF* 13; my italics; cf. Zwettler *BFOT* 210).

> The folkloristic emphasis on oral *transmission* was carried an important step further with the work of the Homerists (and Slavicists), Milman Parry and Albert Lord, and other subscribers to the oral-traditional theory of poetry. Applying to the Homeric epics principles derived from observing and recording the processes of a living oral ["folk"] tradition (mainly South Slavic), they have been able to show that poetry of this kind—formulaic in diction, uniform in sensibility, multiform in aspect—is not just *orally transmitted*. It is also, and at the same time, *orally composed*—albeit with the aim of rendering a previously heard poem as excellently and as accurately as possible. Thus, the very features of fluidity and formularity—as well as those of avoidance of self-conscious originality, uncertain attribution, linguistic archaism, and others—, all of which folklore scholarship has usually accepted as unavoidable *consequences* of oral transmission by and among the folk, would be far better and more realistically understood as natural *concomitants* of a living and continuous tradition of oral rendition by and among an unlettered people. (Zwettler *BFOT* 211; cf. Lord *ST* 6–7; Parry in Lord *HPH* 37–40 = Parry *MHV* 469–73)

Both Bloch and Petráček, in applying the findings of folklore scholarship to their study of classical Arabic poetry, readily granted the fact of its oral *transmission*—though only in passing (Bloch *VSA* 3, 18, and passim; Petráček *DSSV* 6 n. 2, 11, 14; *QAAL* 404). But regrettably this passing acknowledgment went no further than the "lip service" alluded to above. Nevertheless, by calling attention to the folkloric affinities of the poetry, these two scholars have done serious students of early Arabic literature a valuable, though largely unrecognized, service: "For the findings of the folklorists with respect to folk 'literature' can bring the Arabist to a revaluation and a new understanding of precisely some of the most deprecated and least appreciated aspects of the classical poetry" (Zwettler *BFOT* 211).

It is, however, the circumstance of "orality" that has become accepted as the decisive factor that determines and identifies "folk-poetry," as distinct from "literary" or "art-poetry." So, too, scholars of various early literatures are coming to understand that "orality" must have been a most important—if not *the* most important—determinant of the anomalous, "corrupted," and otherwise inexplicable condition wherein they find the "traditional texts" with which their scholarship deals. The present study contends and hopes to demonstrate that "in the light of the Parry-Lord theory of oral-formulaic poetic composition and rendition, *judiciously adapted and applied to the particular circumstances of pre- and early Islamic Arab culture and Arabic poetry*, . . . these 'corrupted' texts [of classical Arabic poems] will appear in their true significance" (Zwettler *BFOT* 212; cf. Monroe *OCPP*, esp. 42–44).

1. There has been a certain amount of ambiguity among Arabists in their usage of the term *classical* to designate a particular period or body of Arabic literature. The word is sometimes employed to refer loosely to the entire output of poetic and belle-lettristic compositions produced in Arabic throughout most of the Middle Ages (e.g., Gibb *ALI* chap. 1 and passim; Wickens *AL* 22–45 passim). Sometimes, too, the early ᶜAbbāsid era (ca. second/ninth—fourth/eleventh centuries) is styled the "classical" age of Islamic civilization, with the adjective being applied to its literary productions as well (e.g., Brockelmann *GAL* and *Suppl* I, 2. Buch, 1. Abschnitt: "Die klassische Periode von ca 750 bis ca 1000"; Gabrieli *LT* 89, 92; Sourdel *CIC* 16–17 [including the later Umayyad period] and passim). Most often, however, and most properly "classical" Arabic poetry is considered to be that whose "tradition" is the subject of this study—viz., the poetry said to have been composed during the years extending from the later fifth century A.D. to (at the latest) the early second/eighth century (e.g., Ahlwardt *UPPA* 19; Nöldeke *BSS* 1–2; von Grunebaum *GSAP* 125–29 = *KD* 20–24; Fück *Ar* chaps. 1–2 passim; Fleisch *AC* 6). Blachère (*HLA* 84), debating what to call the poetry of this same period, chooses "archaïque" over "classique" because the latter adjective, he contends, "ne semble pas . . . convenir car il suppose un jugement de valeur qui interviendra seulement plus tard." But it is always the case that, when the term *classic* is applied to a work, a later judgment of value is implied. And when an extant body of poetry owes its preservation largely to a "classicistic" impulse, as did pre- and early Islamic poetry, and when that poetic corpus has itself undergone a more or less deliberate process of "classicization," the term *classical*—used advisedly—can fulfill an important twofold function: (1) it quite successfully designates a particular period or body of poetry that, certainly in the case of Arabic literature, is clearly distinguishable from later productions, and (2) it provides a key to our understanding of the role played by that poetry in the culture of subsequent generations and of the fate it underwent at their hands.

2. See, e.g., M. Picard, *Man and Language*, pp. 137–42; M. Eliade, *The Sacred and the Profane*, pp. 8–18; G. van der Leeuw, *Sacred and Profane Beauty*, pp. 115–31; cf. R. Christiansen, "Myth, Metaphor, and Simile," in Sebeok *MS* 64–80.

3. Cf., e.g., Nöldeke *BKPA* vii.

4. Chadwicks *GL* II 463; quoted in Chaytor *FSP* 116.

5. Parry *MHV* and Lord *ST*.

6. See, especially, Curschmann *OPML* and references cited; Nagler *TGV*, esp. 269 n. 1, 272 n. 7; Culley *OFL*, esp. "Appendix."

7. On the oral prose narrative, see Vansina *OT;* R. Dorson, "Oral Styles of American Folk Narrators," in Sebeok *SL* 27–51 (with additional comments, 52–53); and others.

8. At this point I must admit that, despite the careful distinctions in usage of the word *tradition* made at the beginning of this study, I have been forced to lapse into the ambiguity inherent in the English word itself. Usually, therefore, when speaking of "tradition" in the sense defined on p. 3, I shall refer to it as the "textual tradition."

9. For other expressions of what von Grunebaum (*GSAP* 127 = *KS* 21) calls "the long prevailing conviction of the stagnating uniformity of classical poetry," see references in Bräunlich *VLB* 213 n. 1. F. Krenkow ("Ḳaṣīda," *EI*[1] II 799) complains, rather immoderately, that after a point "the monotony becomes nauseous." Gibb's (*ALI* 21–22) is perhaps one of the least disparaging expressions of this theme.

10. See, e.g., Lord *ST* chap. 10.

11. See n. 6, above.

12. Russo takes pains, it should be mentioned, to point out that Parry himself cautioned against too strict an application of the verbatim requirement for formulaic analysis and that his own study resulted from following up "one of Parry's most important suggestions of the wide ranging possibilities for formulaic expression without literal repetition [which had] . . . been left unexplored by later critics" (*CLHF* 237; cf. 235–37 and n. 14).

13. See n. 6, above.

14. See Nagler *TGV* 274–81. For "corresponsion" and other terms, see esp. 275. In his dissertation (Nagler *FMHE* 52), however, Nagler does propose as a definition of oral "formula" the following: "an utterance in oral poetry, usually a phrase or more in length, which strongly corresponds with some other utterance in rhyme, meter, lexicography, syntax, semantics, phonemics, content, or any combination of these criteria."

15. Lord (*ST* 279 n. 7) relates Saussure's distinction between *langue* and *parole* to oral poetry, suggesting further "that we have in the case of oral epic performance something that is neither *langue* nor *parole,* but some third form; as Lévi-Strauss has intimated in the case of myths"; see "The Structural Study of Myth," *JAF* 68 (1955): 430 (also in Sebeok *MS* 84–85; cf. 92–94). Lord adds: "Or again with Levi-Strauss we might question whether we have something that is both *langue* and *parole* at the same time under different aspects, thus making a third form of communciation, or of relationship, peculiar to oral verbal art." Cf. also *ST* 285 n. 15.

16. Cf. Lord *ST* 20–22, 130–32, and passim.

17. By "formulaic expressions," Lord denotes "a line or half line constructed on the pattern of the formulas" (for which, see Parry's definition quoted above, p. 6)—*ST* 4.

18. Cf., esp., *ST* chap. 3 for a more detailed account of the genesis and assimilation of formulas in the young poet's mind. See also, e.g., Magoun *BSC;* cf. reservations of J. Campbell *OPS*, esp. 87–88.

19. See Nagler *TGV* 274–80, 285, for examples. He willingly admits that "a measure of subjectivity would seem inevitable once one goes beyond statistical description" (*TGV* 280 n. 20).

20. Cf. n. 14, above. Nagler, citing from Lord and from his own experience, indicates the extent to which our record of a "finished" song may mislead us as to the real nature of the performance as experienced both by the poet and by his audience. "According to Professor Lord, a South Slavic singer will occasionally omit a structurally significant portion from one of his songs. When confronted with such an omission, his first reaction will be to deny it outright, 'Of course I sang that part.' Could this not mean that to the singer and his regular audience, for whom the total effect of his performance is real and the fact (or printed record) of his actual words unimaginably abstract, the 'missing' part was there, implicitly sensed because part of the total Gestalt?" (*TGV* 308). He adds, "My own recordings in the field . . . have corroborated the well known fact that Cretan singers often break off a performance of a song, not only long before the

end of the piece, but even in the middle of a sentence, with resulting loss of intelligibility. Of course, their concentration on the music partially explains this catalexis of the words, but it is also to be explained by the presence of the omitted portion in the memory of the hearers'' (ibid. n. 70). Thus, the word-complexes we have been considering—whether on the level of verbatim repetitions, recurrence of word patterns, realizations of a pre-verbal Gestalt, or larger thematic structures—so far from being ''elements'' or ''components'' in a poem, do actually and concretely *implement* the composition and performance of the poem, *even though they might never be verbalized by the poet and, hence, might never appear in a recorded text.* It need hardly be pointed out how important this fact is for understanding many problems inherent in the textualization of an oral poetry and the early stages of its textual tradition.

21. On the question of ''lettered singers'' writing oral poetry, see §§ A.5--6, below.

22. See n. 18, above.

23. But see discussion, pp. 23–28, below.

24. Cf. the cogent remarks of A. E. Houseman, quoted in Chaytor *FSP* 152: ''Textual criticism is not a branch of mathematics, nor indeed an exact science at all. It deals with a matter not rigid and constant like lines and numbers, but fluid and variable; namely, the frailties and aberrations of the human mind, and of its insubordinate servants, the human fingers. It is, therefore, not susceptible of hard and fast rules. It would be much easier, if it were; and that is why people try to pretend that it is so, or at least behave as if they thought so. Of course you can have hard and fast rules if you like, but then you will have false rules and they will lead you wrong; because their simplicity will render them inapplicable to problems which are not simple, but complicated by the play of personality. A textual critic engaged upon his business is not at all like Newton investigating the motions of the planets; he is much more like a dog hunting for fleas. If a dog hunted for fleas on mathematical principles, basing his researches on statistics of area and density of population, he would never catch a flea, except by accident. They require to be treated as individuals, and every problem which presents itself to the textual critic must be regarded as possibly unique.''

25. As an immediately familiar example of the extent to which oral rendition can occasion extensive variation in the form and phrasing of a verbal work without noticeable effect upon its identity, I have often called my students' attention to joke-telling. They, in turn, have cited as a known instance of oral formularity politicians' impromptu press conferences.

26. Cf. Jones *CMOT:* ''In a dying [oral] tradition, memorization must play a role far different from that which it plays in a thriving tradition'' (102).

27. See, e.g., Nöldeke *BKPA* xi–xvi; Ahlwardt *Divans* viii–ix; Bräunlich *FEAP*, esp. 825; F. Krenkow, ''Ḳaṣīda,'' EI^1 ii 796; idem, ''Shā^{c}ir,'' EI^1 iv 286; Blachère *HLA* 88–90, 179–84.

28. The comprehensive treatment of this subject by G. E. von Gruenbaum (*CPAT* = KD 101–29) deals chiefly with the phenomenon as it occurred or was viewed during the post-classical (^{c}Abbāsid) period, rather than as it existed during the classical pre-and early Islamic period with which this study is concerned.

29. Margoliouth *OAP*; Ṭāhā Ḥusayn *Fi š-ši^{c}r al-jāhilī* (Cairo: 1926); followed by a slightly modified restatement, *FAJ*.

30. See esp. references cited in Brockelmann *GAL Suppl* I 32 n. 2; Blachère *HLA* 179. More recently Arberry *SO* 228–45; Asad *MSJ* 321–478. Cf. also, however, J. Stetkevych, ''Some Observations on Arabic Poetry,'' p. 2.

31. For a concise discussion of the shortcomings of this methodology as applied to works affected by oral tradition, such as the medieval *chansons de geste*, romances, etc., see Chaytor *FSP* 148–52 (Appendix D).

32. See, for Old English poetry, in particular references in W. A. O'Neil, ''Another Look . . . ,'' p. 596 n. 2.

33. See Lord *ST* 63, 105, 113, 119–20, 123, and chaps. 6–10 passim.

34. Herbert Hunger et al. *GTAML* i. The reviewer is J. Irigoin in *BZ* 55 (1962): 317.

35. Dain does, however, make important observations on the relation of dictation and self-dictation to the copying of manuscripts: see *MSS* 20–22, 44–46; cf. Hall *CCT* 183–84.

36. Or "oral-transmission," for Pfeiffer uses the two terms synonymously.

37. Here Pfeiffer notes (*HCS* 25 n. 1) that the "opposite view," based on Parry's collection of formulaic material, "only proves that Greek epic poems were the result of a long oral tradition and were destined for further oral transmission; there is no decisive argument against the composition of *Iliad* and *Odyssey* in writing." Yet the demonstrations of Parry and, following him, Lord and many other scholars constitute a far more decisive argument then Pfeiffer's not wholly warranted assumption of a literary composition of the epics. Cf. chap. 2, nn. 40, 117.

38. E.g., Pfeiffer, above; Lesky *HGL* 37–39; others mentioned in Nagler *FMHE* 4–7.

39. See Lord *ST* 5–12 for a summary of developments in Homeric scholarship relevant to this question.

40. E.g., I. Goldziher, "Der Dīwān des Garwal b. Aus Al-Huṭej'a," A. *Einleitung*, pp. 18–19; augmented and elaborated by Amīn *FI* 166–69; Abbott *RNAS* 51–54; and, above all, Asad *MSJ* 23–184, who conclusively demonstrates that the second- and third-century editors of *jāhili* poetry employed as sources both the oral recitations of the *ruwāt and* written documents of varying authority, many of which had been set down before or during the early years of Islam. Cf. Sezgin *GAS* II 14–33, 36.

41. Cf. Lord *ST* 129–38, 198–221 (esp. 220–21), 289 n. 9.

42. See, e.g., Chaytor *FSP* chap. 6 and passim.

43. See, e.g., Benson *LC* 336: "To prove that an Old English poem is formulaic is only to prove that it is an old English poem." Cf. n. 47, below; but Curschmann notes that "to use the term 'conventions' in this context, as J. J. Campbell has done in "Oral Poetry in *The Seafarer*" [(n. 18, above), and as Benson also has done (n. 47, below)] . . . is to lose again some of the insight which we have gained into the problems involved" (*OPML* 48 n. 46).

44. *FSP* 10–13, chaps. 4 and 6.

45. Recently B. M. W. Knox, "Silent Reading in Antiquity," has exposed many weaknesses in the long-accepted thesis of J. Balogh ("Voces Paginarum," *Philologus* 82 (1927): 84–109, 202–40; repr. Leipzig: 1927) that silent reading in the Greco-Roman world was not simply unusual but just about unheard of. Knox is, however, in complete accord with Balogh's assertion that the normal way to read a *literary* work was aloud, whether in the presence of others or alone (see Knox, pp. 421–28, where he critically reexamines much of Balogh's evidence and reaffirms [p. 427] "that ancient reading of literary texts was usually vocal").

46. Although Chaytor does not use the terminology of the formulists nor allude to the work of Parry (who was writing well before 1945, when Chaytor's book first appeared), many of his observations are of the greatest value and relevance to any student of formulaic poetry. In fact, his final chapter (*FSP* 115–37, with Appendix D, 148–52), read against the background of oral-formulaic studies, remains still the most important and suggestive essay toward developing a viable text-critical approach to works affected by an oral-traditional poetic. The poetry with which Chaytor is concerned has been discussed in terms of oral-formulaic theory; see, for references, Curschmann *OPML* passim; add also J. Duggan, "Formulas in the *Couronnement de Louis*" and, esp., idem *CR*.

47. Benson *LC* 340 seems to dismiss such "references to the oral tradition" in Anglo-Saxon verse as "conventional." Cf. n. 43, above.

48. Cf., among others, Crosby *OD;* Baugh *MER,* esp. 18–23.

49. Cf. W. Rutherford, *A Chapter of the History of Annotation, being Scholia Aristophanica III,* p. 47 (on the Hellenistic manuscript tradition): "Everybody who read hand-written books for knowledge and profit had to be something of a textual critic."

50. "Read aloud" as opposed to whisper, mutter, or mumble; Chaytor *FSP* 14–16, 147.

51. See, e.g., Chaytor *FSP* 117–18; Baugh *MER* 21.

52. See esp. J. A. Notopoulos, "Mnemosyne in Oral Literature"; R. Harriott, *Poetry and Criticism before Plato,* on the role of Mnemosyne in the mythology of ancient Greek poets (index, *s. v.*).

53. See esp. Chaytor *FSP* chap. 6; Baugh *Mer* 18–19. On techniques of the rhapsodes see, in *CH*, M. Bowra (pp. 22–23), J. A. Davison (pp. 218--19), and L. H. Jeffery (pp. 557–58); also R. C. Jebb, *Homer: An Introduction to the Iliad and the Odyssey,* pp. 78–80. P. Collart (in Mazon *Intro* 61 n. 2) remarks, apropos of certain annotations found in some papyrus exemplars of the *Iliad:* "Les plus intéressantes sont les indications scéniques, qui donnent à penser que ces livres sont des exemplaires de rhapsodes. Xenophon, *Banquet* III 6, nous apprend qu-on entendait presque journellement à Athènes des rhapsodes qui savaient par coeur tous les poèmes homériques, et les papyrus . . . nous montrent qu'au moins jusqu'au IIIe s. ap. J.-C. on engageait des "homéristes," pour déclamer des tirades aux fétes des villages égyptiens."

54. See, e.g., A. S. Altekar, *Education in Ancient India,* pp. 145–50, 160--64; Marrou *HEA* 215, 231, 375; Wolf *VSS* 33–34; Goldziher *EM* 201a.

55. See Goldziher *MS* 194–202; Rosenthal *TAMS* 6–7; Asad *MSJ* 255–83; esp. Abbott *SALP* I 9, 13, 22–23, 52–56; Sezgin *GAS* II 28–33.

56. See, e.g., Jāḥiẓ *KH* I 49–102; *Risāla fāla fī madḥ al-kutub,* ed. A. Rufai; *Risāla fī l-mu*^{c}*allim*, trans. in Rescher *EU* 102–3. Cf. also Zarnūjī *TMTT*passim, esp. chaps. 6 and 12.

57. Note Duggan's critique of Benson, *SR* 30–33.

58. Again, Chaytor *FSP* chap. 6; Baugh *MER* 18–21; Crosby *OD* 94. Cf., however, the study of M. Tyssens ("Le Jongleur et l'ècrit," *Mélanges offerts à René Crozet*, 1:685–95), who holds that recitation from memory of the *chansons de geste* "n'était pas la une pratique obligée, ni même la pratique la plus courante" (p. 695).

. 59. The works cited by Curschmann are the following: J. Rychner, *La Chanson de geste. Essai sur l'art épique des jongleurs* (Geneva and Lille: 1955); S. G. Nichols, Jr., *Formulaic Diction and Thematic Composition in the Chanson de Roland* (Chapel Hill, N.C.: 1961); A. Bonjour, "Poésie heroique du moyen âge et critique littéraire," *Romania* 78 (1957): 243–55; M. de Riquer, *Les Chansons de geste françaises,* 2d ed. (Paris: 1957).

60. Consultation with Professor J. Duggan on this point has been my most valuable source of information. Cf. his article cited in n. 46 above; also his longer study *SR*.

61. Menéndez Pidal *CR,* esp. chap. 2; cf. § B.2 of this study below.

62. Culley *OFL,* esp. chap. 4.

63. Friedman *FIT*.

64. Stevick *OFA*, esp. 387.

65. Webber *FDSB*, esp. 176–77.

66. Paraphrasing Benson *LC* 336; see n. 43, above.

67. On the "adding style" of oral-formulaic poetry, see Parry *EHV* = *MHV* 251–65; Lord *ST* 54–55.

68. See n. 53, above.

69. On the relevance of texts to the Arabic oral tradition, see chap. 2, n. 117.

70. See, e.g., Davison in *CH* 118; Chaytor *FSP* chap. 6 and App. D; Baugh *MER* 28–30; idem, "Improvisation in the Middle English Romance" (for the Arabic *rāwī*, see below).

71. Stevick *OFA* 385–86; Havelock *Preface to Plato,* p. 147. Both references are cited by Nagler *TGV* 284 n. 26, who adds: "Lest the analogy be discounted on the grounds of artistic quality, as that of the South-Slavic songs often is, we may suggest as well the classical music of India." See also n. 25 above; Chap. 4, § D.3 c, below. For "renderant," see Zwettler, *BFOT*, esp. p. 199, n. 5.

72. See, e.g., L. Hollander, *The Skalds*, Introduction, and references cited there.

73. See M. Bravmann, "Heroic Motives in Early Arabic Literature."

74. See B. Croce, *Aesthetic*, pp. 35–38; cf. F. Gabrieli, "Elementi epici nell'antica poesia araba."

75. With the exception of fifteen ballads of from 238 to 612 lines and one of 1,366 lines, the length of most of the remaining 182 ballads treated by Weber ranges only slightly more than that of the *qaṣīda*; see *FDSB* 259–64. More recently Edwards *LHTC* has made special mention of the differences in traditional style and diction, particularly in formula density, which might be met with in oral poems considerably shorter than the Homeric epics, such as the Hesiodic poems; see esp. *LHTC* 42–45, 191–92. Cf. also Duggan *SR* 219–20.

76. Cf., on this question, Bloch *KWAV* 237–38, quoted in Zwettler *BFOT* 208–9.

77. See, e.g., Asad *MSJ* 188–221; Maslūt *NI* 24–37; cf. Ibn ^{c}Abdrabbih *IF* V 283–302; Ibn Rašīq *Umda* I 27–40.

78. One could suggest that the inordinate disparities, both in sequence and in "interpolation" or "omission" of verses, which predominate in the *mu*^{c}*allaqa* of ^{c}Amr b. Kulṯūm, for instance (see Nöldeke *FM* I 13–20, 24–32; Arberry *SO* 200), might well be due to the fact (recorded in *Ag* IX 183) "that the Banū Taghlib, his tribe, admired the poem so greatly that 'young and old were for ever reciting it'" (Arberry *SO* 191), to the extent that they were often ridiculed (*hujū*) on account of it.

79. Cf. Monroe *OCPP* 40.

80. W. A. O'Neil's critique of Campbell's article ("Another Look . . .") does not take issue with these observations, but only with Campbell's conclusions regarding the *Seafarer*. Cf. above, § A.5; also Zwettler *BFOT* 211 and n. 43.

81. For an interesting, though superficial and rather dated, discussion of rhyme in which it is suggested, not improbably, that it is the Arabic contribution to world—or at least European—poetry, see Fabre-d'Olivet, *Le Vers dorés*, pp. 120–42. On the likelihood that greater complexity of form and diction in an oral poetical tradition would lead to greater stability among versions of a poem, see Chadwicks *GL* III 868. Vansina has discussed, with considerable perception, the problems posed by oral traditions of more or less free or fixed forms (*OT* passim, esp. 22–23, 56–57, 121–29); but unfortunately he does not explicitly discuss the mnemotechnical aspects of poetic form and diction in relation to their effect in stabilizing the transmission of so-called formal testimonies or fixed texts. See also Parry *MHV* 442–43.

*

Chapter Two

The Oral Tradition of Classical Arabic Poetry

Having followed the discussion thus far, one may well ask to what extent the principle of "orality" can be applied to classical Arabic poetry. That is to say, does pre- and early Islamic verse exhibit those particular features that have come to be acknowledged by many authorities as characteristics of oral-traditional poetry?

Parry and Lord, together with most scholars who wholly or in part have adopted their theory of "oral composition," recognize three sets of tests for determining the likelihood of a given poem's "orality" (see Lord *ST* 130–31, 144–47). On the verbal level, the presence of formulaic techniques is, without doubt, according to Lord, "the surest proof now known of oral composition" (*ST* 144). Another corroborating test is that of enjambement: the infrequent occurrence of necessary enjambement is "a characteristic of oral composition and is one of the easiest touchstones to apply in testing the orality of a poem" (*ST* 54; cf. 131, 145). Finally, thematic analysis offers a third indication of a poem's origin in an oral tradition, for the oral poet "needs well-established themes for rapid composition" (*ST* 131; cf. chap. 4 and 145–47).

A. Identical or similar word-groups, corresponsional phonetic or syntactic phrases, appearance of like syntactical or grammatical units in the same metrical position—these and other recurrent or anaphoric[1] verbal phenomena, which conform precisely to the descriptions of formulaic diction for other traditions, can be seen throughout our texts of classical Arabic poems. The evidence submitted in Appendix A of this study and discussed below, a formulaic analysis of Imra'alqays' *mu^{c}allaqa*, should support this contention. Although it might be objected that the results of such an analysis would only hold good for the single poem to which it was applied, I do not think that that objection requires serious consideration.

A.1 In the first place, adequate and comprehensive auxiliary materials (concordances, inventories of themes and grammatical forms, collections of parallel lines and passages, even computer studies) simply have not been prepared on a scale that would permit a more exhaustive survey of all the available early poetic texts (with their variants). One could glean an abundant supply of recurring phrases and constructions just by attentive reading of a fairly large corpus of poems. But this would give us nothing like the statistical accuracy needed to determine if such formulaic elements make up a "significant"[2] proportion of the corpus as a whole; and the approach itself would be quite inefficient and would suffer from the inevitable effects of human error and fatigue (cf. Monroe *OCPP* 32–33). Besides, from the point of view of its textual state and its range of variation, the ode of IQ can be taken as representative of a majority of classical Arabic poems; and in that respect, too, it indicates its affiliation with other traditions of oral poetry. Discovering a "significant" proportion of formulaic elements in this poem would establish a high degree of probability that other poems so constituted and so rendered could be expected to exhibit similar results.

At any rate, it is no longer possible to subscribe to conclusions about the nature of IQ's *mu^{c}allaqa* such as those advanced by S. Gandz in the introduction to his translation and commentary of the poem (*G* pp. 3–5). Gandz first holds, on the basis of arguments deriving from an essentially external apprehension of the poetic of the *qaṣīdas*, that "the poem must certainly be denied any homogeneous character. It presents itself to us as a compilation of a man whose concern was to select the best from the various *qaṣīdas* of IQ and combine it into one larger whole covered up by a single rhyme" (*G* p. 3).

Gandz's reasons for this view include the observations that (1) the poem has four verses with double-rhymes (i.e., *taṣrī^{c}*),[3] hence four different opening lines; (2) that it lacks a proper conclusion; and (3) that its four (?) sections are without adequate transitional and connecting elements either between or within themselves. Ibn Rašīq's discussion of *taṣrī^{c}* (*Umda* I 173–78), as well as any extensive reading of classical *qaṣīdas*, would serve to indicate that double-rhymed verses often occurred elsewhere than at the beginning of a poem, sometimes (but not necessarily) introducing a new section. The content of the verses cited in this ode, however (see note 3), does not at all suit them for traditional *qaṣīda* first lines. What *actually*—rather than *theoretically*—constituted a "proper" conclusion to a *qaṣīda* is, given the diversity of known examples (see, e.g., Gibb *ALI* 18; and esp. Jacobi *SPAQ* 65–100), debatable at best. And the question of unity and unifying elements in classical Arabic poetry must be completely reexamined in the light of studies like those of M. Bateson, R. Jacobi, and K. Abu-Deeb. In the case of IQ's *muᶜallaqa* the question must decidedly be answered in favor of the poet.

Gandz's clinching ground for arguing the compilatory character and doubtful authenticity of the *muᶜallaqa* is the fact that "more than half of the verses recur in IQ's *dīwān*, either according to their tenor, or else quite literally with only different rhyme-words" (*G* p. 4). We are provided with an appendix (*G* pp. 112–25) in which such recurrences have been carefully inventoried; and these, together with a great many others from the poems of IQ and a large number of his fellow classical poets, have been utilized in the formulaic analysis of the *muᶜallaqa* offered in Appendix A to this study. For, as I have already suggested (chap. 1, § A.3, above), by far the most reasonable assumption that one can make regarding these recurrences is that they bear witness to the existence and vitality of *a tradition of oral-formulaic poetic composition and rendition* among the early Arabs, which, despite particularities of genre, form, cultural background, and the like, conforms closely to those of other peoples whose poetry has been examined from this point of view.

A.2 About the time that this work was completed in its original form and submitted in the summer of 1972 as my doctoral dissertation, an article appeared by J. Monroe, entitled "Oral Composition in Pre-Islamic Poetry." Monroe's study deals with some of the same issues as the present work and reaches, by and large, some of the same conclusions. Naturally, the format of his study—a fifty-three-page article—precludes much of the lengthy, perhaps sometimes labored, argumentation and documentation presented here. Furthermore, my approach to, and method of, formulaic analysis differ to some extent from his.

In the first place, as already indicated, I have limited my analysis to a single poem in a single meter (*ṭawīl*), the *muᶜallaqa* of Imra'alqays, but have subjected to analysis the entire eighty-two verses of the poem in Ibn al-Anbārī's recension. Monroe, on the other hand, has analyzed the first ten verses of four classical odes (*OCPP* 32–35, 44–53): the same *muᶜallaqa* of IQ[4] (m. *ṭawīl*); the *muᶜallaqa* of Labīd (*DLab* 48; m. *kāmil*); an *m*-rhymed ode by Zuhayr (*DZuh* 18; m. *wāfir*); and a *d*-rhymed ode by an-Nābiġa (*DNab* 5; m. *basīṭ*).

This approach is similar to that employed by Parry in his analysis of the first twenty-five lines of the *Iliad* and the *Odyssey (SET* I 73–147, esp. 118–21 = *MHV* 266–324), by Lord in analyzing the first fifteen lines of a rendition of the Yugoslav *Song of Baghdad* (*ST* 46), and by several others.[5] Yet, as J. Duggan maintains, there can be a fundamental objection to such an approach, in particular to the size and choice of samples taken for analysis.

> The shorter the random sample, the less chance that it will reflect the characteristics of the entire text under consideration, and random samples taken from one place in the poem and counted in two digit amounts[6] are hopelessly inadequate. . . . Random samples—and the beginning of a poem, chosen because it happens to come first and not on account of its subject matter, is a random sample—cannot be relied upon to the same degree [as a public opinion poll] unless the sampling is conducted upon statistically valid principles. (Duggan *SR* 19; cf. Lord *HOP* 29, citing G. Kirk; Russo *CLHF* 246)

Still, Monroe's approach does have the advantage of taking up the question of formularity for poetic samples in the *four* meters that by far prevailed in classical Arabic poetry,[7] whereas I have given predominant consideration to evidential material in the *ṭawīl* meter alone, corresponding to the *ṭawīl* of *MuIQ*. I am fully in agreement with Monroe as to the capacity of given formulas or formulaic elements for accommodation to verse contexts of differing metrical values by means of slight shifts in word-order, modulations of word morphology, or word substitutions through synonymy (*OCPP* 27–32). But in my analysis, I have made only occasional reference to such "allomorphic" occurrences of formulas outside of *ṭawīl* verse, chiefly because the available material in *ṭawīl* afforded me ample evidence of formularity for the whole of *MuIQ*. Systematic adduction of evidence from verse in other meters would simply corroborate the findings offered here and, in fact, would most likely increase the percentage of formulaic density observed.

I do not, however, concur with Monroe's view that "it is the order of formulas that determines the meters of Arabic poetry," that "formulas are prior to the different meters," or that "the oral poet uses preexistent formulas to create meter" (*OCPP* 28, 29, 35). Such a view neglects the incontestable fact that formulas—indeed, the very formulaic technique itself—would have originated in the need and desire of generations of oral poets "to articulate sweet sounds together" (to borrow William Butler Yeats's phrase) in the measured and non-casual speech-form that everywhere distinguishes poetry from ordinary discourse. Parry's own definition of the formulas—"a group of words which is regularly employed *under the same metrical conditions* to express a given idea" (see chap. 1, § A.1, above; my italics), upon which Monroe bases his study (*OCPP* 7–10)—stresses its *usefulness* in enabling a performing oral poet to produce verse after *isochronous* verse (see *SET* I 125–34 = *MHV* 307–14).[8] For a meaningful understanding of oral-formulaic theory, therefore, one has to realize that some sense or even *choice* of meter would necessarily underlie and, to a great extent, condition the generation of formulaic phrases, which then become articulated in the uttered verse of a poem. Certainly, for Arabic poetry, such would be true with respect to rhyme, a second major determinant of the form of each line of classical verse. Although I am not prepared to address myself to the problem of the origin, character, and stylistic significance of the various meters of classical Arabic poetry, it seems clear to me that formulas can never be viewed as *prior* to the meters in which they function. Monroe quite rightly observes "that the formulas are in the poet's mind (however subconsciously) before he actually utters a line of poetry." It is not correct, though, to argue therefrom that "with the aid of rhythm [?], he then organizes them so as to produce a specific meter" (*OCPP* 29). What the poet does produce is an uttered realization of the formula, suitable for a *specific metrical context*—an allomorph, as it were, of a pre-verbal *Gestalt* conditioned by, and adapted to, the meter/rhyme template to which he would have been habituated, inclined, or constrained or which he might himself have chosen (cf. Nagler *TGV*; also chap. 1, § A.1, above).

My approach differs from Monroe's in a second respect. The mechanics of the technique of formulaic analysis developed by Parry and followed, with occasional modifications, by subsequent oral-formulists entails underlining, within a verse of the sample under consideration, those words or word-groups to which verbal or syntactic corresponsions are found in the evidential referent. Parry describes this technique as follows:

> I have put a solid line beneath those word-groups which are found elsewhere in the poems [i.e., the *Iliad* and *Odyssey*] unchanged, and a broken line under phrases which are of the same type as others. In this case I have limited the type to include only those in which not only the metre and the parts of speech are the same, but in which also at least one important word or group of words is identical. . . . (Parry *SET* I 117 = *MHV* 301)

As noted above (chap. 1, § A.1,), J. Russo proposed extending the sense of "formulaic" to include "localized phrases whose resemblance goes no further than the use of identical metrical word-types of the same grammatical and syntactic pattern, as truly representing certain more general types of formulaic systems" (*CLHF* 237).[9] Yet such phrases would presumably still be marked with a broken line according to Russo (or at least visibly differentiated from "formulas" proper); and I have followed his lead in my analysis (see following section).

Monroe, however, marks with a solid line both verbal formulas *and* what he calls "formulaic systems"—i.e., "larger groupings of different formulas related to one another in that they share at least one word in common in the same metrical position" (*OCPP* 17; cf. Parry, *SET* I 84–89 = *MHV* 275–79; Lord *ST* 35–36, 47–48). In no sense do I dispute his judgment as to the "formulaicness" of such systems. But in choosing not to differentiate between phrases repeated wholly or almost wholly verbatim and those related structurally, but sharing only a single common lexical item, Monroe has rather side-stepped some of the fundamental arguments that have shaped the oral-formulaic theory that his study advocates and may have obscured the phenomenon of oral-formulaic composition itself. Furthermore, it would appear from his analyses that phrases marked with a solid line do not always meet his own specified condition of being either formulas or formulaic systems. The following discrepancies in the use of solid underlining in the lines from *MuIQ,* for example, are among those that can be noted throughout all four analyses:

1. L. 1*b*: *bi siqṭi l-liwā*. Supporting evidence: *bi mun*^{c}*ariji l-liwā* (*Muf* 2:6); *fa l-liwā* (*Muf* 42:3; *DZuh* 6:9). In *MuIQ* 1, this phrase stands at the *beginning* of the second hemistich (*b*5),[10] whereas the instances adduced by Monroe all *end* the first hemistich of a *ṭawīl* line. Thus, if in these phrases *al-liwā* is the one word shared in common, it certainly does not occur "in the same metrical position." In fact, the evidential referents are actually instances of what Monroe calls "conventional vocabulary," and should have been marked with a broken line according to his own stipulation (*OCPP* 44).
2. L. 2*a: fa Tūḍiḥa fa l-Miqrāti* (*a*8). The only evidential citation for this solidly underlined phrase is *sa*^{c}*dānu Tūḍiḥa* (*DNāb* 5:28; m. *basīṭ*), which again represents, at most, "conventional vocabulary."
3. For 11. 3–4, two verbally identical lines are cited from *DIQ* (Ahl) Appendix 26:3–4 as evidence. However, as can be seen from Ahlwardt's critical apparatus (*Divans* 101, English), these two lines are nothing more than the very same lines of *MuIQ,* which normally occur at that point in the *qaṣīda*, but which were not included in the version published as *DIQ* (Ahl) 48. Hence, as cited evidence of "formulaicness," they are inadmissible, as well as misleading.
4. L. 7*a*: *min Ummi l-Ḥuwayriṯi qabla-hā* (*a*14). Of the cited evidential phrases, only one—*ummu ṣ-ṣabīyayni* (*Muf* 34:17)—has a shared word in common (*umm*) in the same metrical position. But that phrase occurs in a context (*wa qad* ^{c}*alimat ummu ṣ-ṣabīyayni anna-nī*) so structurally differ-

ent from the underlined phrase in *MuIQ* as to make it quite inconclusive as evidence of formulaicness.

5. L. 8*b*: *nasīma ṣ-ṣabā jā'at bi rayya l-qaranfulī* (*b*14). Although the entire hemistich is solidly underlined, only one of the evidential phrases—*rayya l-muxalxalī* (*b*14; *MuIQ* 30)—conforms to the criteria established for formulas and formulaic systems, so only the last six syllables qualify for solid underlining on the basis of the adduced evidence.[11]

Unfortunately, similar inconsistencies and imprecisions sometimes crop up in the other analyses[12] and mar the efficacy of Monroe's otherwise very vital contribution. As he himself acknowledges, and as I also would readily admit in my own analysis, "an element of subjectivity no doubt entered into the identification of some marginal formulas" (*OCPP* 32). But such subjectivity as occasionally seems to enter into some of the identifications of formulas put forward in *OCPP* goes even beyond more extreme forms of the "soft Parryism" that M. Nagler has mentioned (*TGV* 270–71, citing T. G. Rosenmeyer). Taking a somewhat "harder" position as to what constitutes "formulaicness" (see following section), one would have no trouble finding sufficient evidence for the pervasiveness of formulas and formulaic elements in *MuIQ* and elsewhere—evidence that both meets the criteria for admissibility that almost half a century of generally scrupulous scholarship has established for a number of diverse poetic traditions and also reflects the special features of language, genre, and cultural environment that have conditioned classical Arabic verse.

Monroe's study also breaks new ground in undertaking to test the formularity of verse by classical poets as compared with that of later literate poets. Potentially, this would be a most worthwhile undertaking, since analogous operations for other traditions have yielded results that conclusively demonstrate a marked reduction in the percentage of discernible formulas and formulaic elements in poetry known to have been composed in writing.[13] However, the analysis in *OCPP* 35–36 and 52–53 is conceived and carried out along lines that afford little prospect of demonstrating anything conclusive for the later literate poets in question. Monroe's hypothesis, which is quite acceptable in itself, is as follows:

> The best way to prove [that there is "a higher formulaic frequency among oral poets than among their literate colleagues"] . . . is to select a poet, or a group of poets, with regard to whose literacy there is no doubt whatsoever, and to determine whether he or they use formulas with as great a frequency as do oral poets. (*OCPP* 35)

To verify the hypothesis, Monroe took the "formulas" identified in *MuIQ* 1–10 and in Labīd's *mu^{c}allaqa,* ll. 1–10, and "checked [them] against the work of other Arabic poets to determine the extent to which they constituted a collective repertory" (*OCPP* 35). This was done first for two samples of verse, in *ṭawīl* and *kāmil* meters respectively, by six classical poets and then for two similar samples by "modern" poets, dating from the early ^{c}Abbāsid period to the late nineteenth century and geographically distributed from Baghdad to Spain.[14] It was determined that IQ's formulas constituted an average of 33.24 percent of the total text of *ṭawīl* lines of classical poetry, and Labīd's formulas made up an average of 30.46 percent of the total text of *kāmil* lines[15] (*OCPP* 35–36, 52–53). Now, such a procedure has a definite validity for poets of the classical period, since their relative contemporaneity and homogeneity of cultural and linguistic circumstances permit us to expect a substantial core of what Lord describes as "regional formulas" (*ST* 48–54; *HOP* 29–34). In testing for the formularity of a tradition, Lord says, "one must always begin with the individual and work outwards from him to the group to which he belongs, namely to the singers who influenced him, and then to the district, and in ever enlarging circles until the whole language area is included" (*ST* 49). And elsewhere, he phrases his opinion somewhat differently:

> A tradition is made up of all the singers in it, not of only one man. Nor is a tradition usually so limited in area that it would belong to only one region. There are bound to be both regional differences in the formulas, although there would be a very large stock that would be common to the entire singing area. (*HOP* 32)[16]

Inevitably and however imperceptibly, changes in the stock of formulas and in the formulaic diction creep into an oral tradition, in response to changes in the cultural, historical, and linguistic situation of the language community over the passage of time (Lord *ST* 43–45). As Parry has written,

> Whatever change the single poet makes in the traditional diction is slight, perhaps the change of an old formula, or the making of a new one on the pattern of an old, or the fusing of old formulas, or a new way of putting them together. An oral style is thus highly conservative; yet the causes for change are there, and sooner or later must come into play.
>
> These causes for change have nothing to do with any wish on the part of the single poet for what is new or striking in style. They exist above the poets, and are two: the never-ceasing change in all spoken languages, and the association between peoples of a single language but of different dialects. (*SET* II 9 = *MHV* 331; cf. 11–12 = 332–33)

None would dispute the magnitude of the changes that affected the Arabic-language community, beginning during the first/seventh century with the codification of the Qur'ānic text, the expansion of the Arabs over an area extending vastly beyond the Arabian peninsula, and their subsequent settling and urbanization in groups of mixed dialectal composition and in close contact with speakers of quite different languages altogether.

Thus, even were it possible to assume a continuity in the oral tradition from pre-Islamic times to the periods—some two to twelve centuries later—of the literate poets whose verse Monroe refers to, the expectation that *any* formulas used by the classical poets, Imra'alqays and Labīd, might show up in that verse would appear to be wholly unwarranted.

Monroe's investigation of the two referential bodies of verse written by later literate poets yields 9.22 percent IQ formulas and 9.88 percent Labīd formulas respectively (with "structural" or syntactic formulas constituting by far the majority of coincidences). But infrequent occurrence—even non-occurrence—of formulas used by Imra'alqays and Labīd in the later poems considered by Monroe can prove *only* that Abū Nuwās, Ibn Zaydūn, Shawqī, and the others did not use the *same* formulas as those two classical poets. And that is no more than a practical understanding of the oral-formulaic theory should lead us to expect. The later "modern" poets were active in environments that were enormously removed—chronologically, geographically, culturally, and linguistically—from that of their peninsular predecessors; and if their work were to be found formulaic to any substantial degree (though I doubt that it ever will be) and if the theory under discussion is sound, such formulas as would be found would correspond to those disparate environments, rather than to that of Imra'alqays and Labīd.

Thus, the percentages of IQ formulas and Labīd formulas found in the two referential bodies of "modern" verse have little meaning. They surely can in no way be used, as Monroe uses them, to substantiate his claim that "a pre-Islamic poet . . . uses slightly over three times as many formulas as a modern poet" and that, assuming a pre-Islamic poet's work to be 100 percent formulaic,[17] "this would mean that a modern poet's total use of formulaic constructions is somewhat less than 33.3 percent" (*OCPP* 37)—regardless of how correct such a claim may eventually turn out to be!

I am, nevertheless, reasonably certain that Monroe is correct in suspecting that the measure of formularity in works of later literate poets would be significantly less than that in the bulk of classical poetry. I also agree that *functional literacy* is probably the decisive reason for the difference. But to measure the formularity of a later poet's works and to compare the measurement *validly* with measurements of formularity in classical verse, one would have to conduct the analysis *primarily* on the basis of a referent drawn from the works of that poet and of his coevals.[18] Monroe has not done this; and there is no question that it would be an arduous and time-consuming operation with the means at our disposal. Neither is it my intention to do it in this context, even though such an analysis, as Monroe realized, could provide us with conclusive evidence as to the difference between the oral and the written way of making Arabic poetry.

It is because, above all, I fully share Monroe's conviction that pre- (and early) Islamic poetry was the product of a tradition of oral-formulaic composition and rendition that I have here taken issue with some particulars of his approach and findings. Precision and meticulousness are required, as regards both introducing and applying the theory and also selecting and interpreting the data. Since Parry's first studies were published (1928–32), the oral-formulaic theory has given rise to a complex and highly nuanced body of literary scholarship and has been applied to a number of diverse traditions (see chap. 1, above). We must, I feel, accept the responsibility, not only for accurately and coherently communicating to our colleagues that theory, together with its important ramifications, but also for recognizing and carefully taking into account the distinctive features of the early Arabic tradition that can affect the applicability of the theory to classical Arabic poetry.

A.3.a The analysis itself, which is to be found in Appendix A of this study, is based almost entirely upon my own reading of the *mu*^{c}*allaqa* of Imra'alqays (*MuIQ*) and a comparative examination of a referential body of verse in the same *ṭawīl* meter. This evidential referent, in excess of 5,000 lines, is drawn from the collected poems (*dīwān*) of IQ himself and those of several other poets from the early period; from the two famous anthologies, the *Mufaḍḍalīyāt* and the *Aṣma*^{c}*īyāt;* from the tribal *dīwān* of Huḏayl; and from such other miscellaneous sources as will be specified (for abbreviations used, see Bibliography, section II). Where particular phrases and words or striking syntactic patterns have been observed to occur both in a verse from *MuIQ* and in a verse from one of the other poems examined, this co-occurrence has been taken as evidence for a formula or formulaic element.

These recurrent, or *formulaic,* features are indicated in the analysis (Appendix A) by underlining them where they occur in verses of *MuIQ*. In substance, the analysis uses the system described and employed by Culley:

> The underlining may appear as a solid line, a series of dashes, or a series of dots. A solid line is placed under all the morphemes that are lexical constants in a group of phrases. The positions in phrases where normal substitution occurs (that is, where different lexical items from the same word classes are substituted) are underlined with a series of dashes. A series of dots is placed under positions in phrases where free substitution occurs (that is, where different word classes and different structures are substituted). Thus a formula will be un-

> derlined completely with a solid line. A formulaic phrase will have a solid line under the lexical constants but a series of dashes under positions where normal substitution occurs. If free substitution is found in a system, then this would be underlined with a series of dots (Culley *OFL* 33).

Three of the five principles for identifying formulas set forth by Lord have also been followed here.[19] Lord writes:

> In addition to exact repetitions of words in a group in the same order in the same posite line, I have also considered the following as formulas with solid underlining:
>
> 1) Declension or conjugation of one or more elements in the phrase, providing the metrical length of the phrase remains unchanged.
> 2) Metathesis, or inversion, or, in general, any change in the order of the words in the phrase as long as the metrical length is preserved and the meaning remains unchanged.
> 3) Repetition of a formula, even if it be in another part of the line from that of the verse being analyzed. . . . (*HOP* 25–26)

A.3b As suggested above, this analysis also gives special attention to recurrences of "striking syntactic patterns"—the "structural" or "syntactic" formulas described by Russo (see chap. 1, § A.1, above). Although the value of syntactic formulas as criteria for "formulaicness" has been questioned for the Greek epic tradition (e.g., Nagler *TGV* 271; Lord *HOP* 15–16 and references), in the case of classical Arabic poetry such repetitions of patterns and pattern sequences simply cannot be ignored, given the schematic morphology of the Arabic language (cf. chap. 1, § B.2, above). *MuIQ* offers a number of examples of phrases whose morphemic composition is metrically and functionally equivalent, element for element, to phrases occurring in other poems (often in circumstantially analogous passages).

The coordination of a sequence of place-names after a preposition such as *bayna* (or elsewhere) by means of a conjunction *fa* (see chap. 4, § C.3.a, below) exemplifies the importance of such syntactic formulas (see App. A, 1. 1, n. f and comment). The complex formulas of comparison introduced by *ka-anna* (see App. A, 1. 4, n. b), *ka-mā,* and so on, formulas of negative comparison (see App. A, n. 5), and similar syntactic devices connected with poetic imagery and rhetorical effect are encountered in the poetry with great frequency and merit a special study because of their evident indispensability in the formation of numerous lines. Jacobi has identified and discussed several such instances in some detail; and, though her observations are not at all directed to the question of formularity, they offer an excellent point of departure for future investigation (*SPAQ* passim, esp. chaps. 2–3).

As an example of "striking syntactic patterns," consider the close correspondence between the first hemistich of *MuIQ* 12:

fa ẓalla l-^{c} aḏāra yartamīna bi laḥmi-hā

and the following syntactic analogues (cf. App. A, 1. 12, n. a):

wa ẓalla ṣiḥābī yaštawūna bi na^{c}matin—*DIQ* 30:33;
fa ẓalla l-akuffu yaxtalifna bi ḥāniḏin—*D^{c}Al* 1:42;
taẓallu l-imā'u yabtadirna qadīḥa-hā—*DNāb* app 24:5;
fa ẓalla l-imā'u yamtalilna ḥuwāra-hā—*DṬar* 4:92.

In each of these examples, the formulaic element can be schematized, on the basis of the fourteen-syllable *ṭawīl* hemistich, in the following manner ($\circ$ = short syllable; — = long syllable):

i	*ii*	*iii*	*iv*
$\circ$ — $\underline{\circ}$	$\circ$ — $\underline{\circ}$	— $\circ$ — $\underline{\circ}$	$\circ$ — $\circ$ —

(14)

i. (a) conjunction + perf. of *ẓalla,*[20] or
(b) imperf. of *ẓalla;*
ii. pl. noun (human, usually fem.)—subj. of sentence;
iii. verb—pl. imperf. (usually fem.);
iv. (a) indir. obj. (prep. + noun), or
(b) direct obj. (noun in accus.).

A somewhat simpler, but more frequent, pattern may be observed in the first hemistich of *MuIQ* 34 (see App. A, 1. 34, n. a):

wa far^{c}in yazīnu l-matna

Formulaic correspondences include the following:

wa baytin yafūḥu l-misku—*DIQ* 30:14 = *DIQ*(Ahl) 40:14;
wa ġayṯin marat-hu r-rīḥu—*DIQ* 60:8;
wa xarqin yaxāfu r-rakbu—*DIQ* 79:12;
wa ṣadrin arāḥa l-laylu—*DNāb* 1:3.

Here is the schema for this syntactic formula:

i	*ii*	*iii*
$\circ$ — —	$\circ$ — —	— $\circ$

(8)

i. *wāw* (*rubba*)[21] + noun—gen. sing., undefined;
ii. verb (sometimes with attached pronominal obj.)—
introducing relative clause;
iii. noun—subj. or obj. of verb.

A third syntactic pattern is exemplified in *MuIQ* 40 and 67*a* and is always to be found as the second half of a *ṭawīl* hemistich:

bayna dir^{c}in wa mijwalī;
bayna ṯawrin wa na^{c}jatin.

Other examples of this pattern follow:

bayna ^{c}idlin wa muḥqabī—DIQ 3:52 = *DIQ*(Ahl) 4:64;
bayna ^{c}idlin wa mušnaqī—DIQ 30:34 = *DIQ*(Ahl) 40:34;
bayna ḏāmin wa jālibī—DNāb 1:15;
bayna ḥāfin wa nā^{c}ilī—DNāb 20:18;
bayna burdin wa mijsadī—DṬar 4:48;
bayna xabtin wa ^{c}ar^{c}arī—DLab 8:32;
bayna quffin wa ramlatin—Muf 41:12*a*;
bayna ẓi'rin wa xādimī—DḤass 24:10.[22]

These examples are all related isomorphously according to the following schema:

i	*ii*	*iii*	*iv*
— ○	— —	○	— ○ —

(14)

i. preposition *bayna;*
ii. undefined noun (or substantival adjective);
iii. conjunction *wa;*
iv. 2nd undefined noun (or adjective), usually—but not necessarily—contrasting in meaning with the first.

Variations on the above schema do sometimes occur in other verse or prose contexts, involving nouns of different metrical values, sequences of more than two nouns, and—occasionally—defined nouns (see Reckendorf *SVA* 225–26, 455; *AS* 195, 242–43). But the schema as given here by far prevails, so far as I have been able to determine, and only phrases that conform to it have been adduced as formulaic. Although syntactic formulas of this pattern are frequently used to complete the first hemistich of a *ṭawīl* line, their most important function is to provide the rhyming closure of the line, where a rhyme-vowel (*ṣilat ar-rawīy*) of *-ī* would permit a final noun in the genitive (i.e., with desinence *ī*).[23] What is particularly notable about this formulaic construction is that its relatively simple syntactical sense (viz., "between A and B") came to signify a rather complex semantic relationship. *Bayna* here must be understood as "governing nouns which occur as generic substantives (including also adjectives used as generic substantives); so it denotes an entire entity which wavers between both classes, belonging sometimes to one class, sometimes to the other; or partly to one and partly to the other; or to one as well as to the other'' (Reckendorf *SVA* 225). The neat and simple phrases from *MuIQ* quoted above each convey, then, nuances of some subtlety and sophistication: respectively, a maiden of an age and stature such that, though she fits the dress of a grown woman, she can still wear a child's smock, and a hunting-horse whose single charge can encompass both a strong, swift bull and a slower ewe (i.e., that runs circles around both or either).

Like the earlier examples, this syntactic schema, which occurred predominantly in poetry (if it did not indeed originate there as well), reflects the verbal economy and sheer usefulness that is the earmark of formulas and formulaic elements in every oral tradition. The fact is that in Arabic to deploy the schematized morphemic configurations of the language into equally schematized syntactic configurations—schematized *because conditioned by meter and rhyme*—can virtually generate a meaning, or an anticipated meaning, which merely awaits the utterance of appropriate lexical constituents to become realized semantically. It is because of this fact, first and foremost, that I hold the ''syntactic'' or ''structural'' formula to be intrinsic to the oral-formulaic tradition of Arabic poetry. In the above and many similar instances,[24] the recurrence of a recognizable syntactic pattern, composed of metrically and grammatically equivalent morphemes in the same metrical position from line to line and poem to poem, should leave no doubt regarding the functionality of such patterns in Arabic verse composition. Such syntactic formulas have been indicated, as mentioned previously, by a broken line for the variable elements and a solid line for the invariable elements (such as prepositions, conjunctions, particles, but including verbs and substantives where repetition of them has been observed).

A.3.c At this point it may be worthwhile to turn for a moment to the question of ''economy'' or ''thrift,'' as it relates to an oral-formulaic tradition.[25] Parry has used the term ''thrift'' with reference to the system of formulas, saying that a system's thrift ''lies in the degree in which it is free of phrases which, having the same metrical value and expressing the same idea, could replace one another'' (*SET* I 86 = *MHV* 276). Parry shows, in demonstrating Homer's ''thrift,'' that where different words or phrases have been used to express the same quality or idea, such variation is almost always determined by varying metrical requirements (see *MHV* 173–89).[26] ''Generally speaking, whenever Homer has to express the same idea under the same metrical conditions, he has recourse to the same words or the same group of words'' (*MHV* 22). In the Arabic tradition, however, it is not infrequent that one finds syntactical formulas like those described above, which contain metrically equivalent synonyms or near synonyms in the same position in the line. It is also possible to find synonyms, or at least words that perform identical thematic functions, that have different metrical values and whose usage is obviously conditioned by differing requirements of meter or rhyme. What, then, can we say about "thrift" or "economy" with respect to the Arabic tradition? Nothing substantial, it would appear, until the same sort of painstaking analysis has been undertaken for a relatively homogeneous body of classical Arabic poetry—either by a single poet or by a controlled group of poets (such as, e.g., the Huḏalī poets)—that Parry undertook for the Homeric epics.[27]

For the present, my opinion is that, although structural (or syntactic) formulas perhaps do not have the sure apodictic force of straight verbal formulas in establishing formularity to a significant degree, they must be accorded an exceedingly strong corroborative value. As was stressed earlier, the *qaṣīda* at its longest is considerably shorter by far than the Homeric poems, and this fact greatly reduces the urgency of the poet's need for a rigidly economical system of formulas to enable him to go steadily on producing verse through hundreds—even thousands—of lines. As Bowra has suggested, "it is easier for a poet to invent freely when he knows that only a short performance is expected of him" (*HP* 232). Thus, the very presence in the *qaṣīda* of such a discernible quantity of structural formulas, patterned after such readily discernible schemata, is evidence of their continuing *usefulness* to the poet. By means of them, or rather by means of the mental template or schema on the basis of which they were generated, lines could be composed and rendered that would be related analogously and isomorphously to other lines in a manner perhaps more compatible with the experience of a shorter poem than would be the verbatim repetitions that pervade longer oral narrative verse. And since Arabic's schematic morphology allows for a high degree of interchangeability of lexical parts (higher, perhaps, than do languages formally less regular and structured), verbatim repetitions as such, by themselves, may not hold quite the decisive authority in determining "formulaicness," and hence orality, for the early Arabic tradition that they have been granted for some other traditions. Even for the Greek tradition, Nagler has shown (as cited above, chap. 1, § A.1) "that it is at least a possibility that the prevailing concept of the fixed and determinable structure, be it superficial (the completed phrase) or relatively deep (e.g., the localization of a metrical sequence), is not *a priori* the only working model for the production of phrases in oral epic composition" (*TGV* 284). Lord himself, at one point, has cautioned against making too much out of the principle of "oral economy" applied indiscriminately and impressionistically outside the Homeric tradition, advising "that we would do well to continue to investigate and *to document with exactness* the comparative rigidity of formulas in Greek and South Slavic oral epic'' (*HOP* 33–34; my italics)—and, he would add, in other forms of oral verse. How important it becomes for us, then, that we seek to understand and demonstrate the ''formulaicness'' of early Arabic poetry *in its own terms,* as dictated by the texts at our disposal, rather than by too many assumptions and impressions imposed from outside.

A.3.d Acting upon hints derived from Nagler's study (*TGV*), I have sometimes indicated single words as formulaic elements for the purposes of the analysis. A repeated word has been solidly underlined, though, only if it occurs in the same metrical position in the line (or hemistich) and if either (1) the repetition occurs within the eighty-two lines of *MulQ* (on the assumption that the factor of mere coincidence is thereby somewhat reduced); or (2) the word seldom or never has been noted in any other position throughout the referential verses. Ordinarily, it seems, such one-word ''formulas'' are to be observed at the beginnings and ends of hemistichs.[28] Similarly, I have marked with a broken line particular kinds of morphological patterns recurring as rhyme-words. These patterns serve to fill the most crucial slot in the metrical line at a point where the traditional praxis absolutely insisted upon and required lexical variation.[29]

Nagler, of course, does not expressly deal with such words as ''formulas'' or as ''formulaic,'' chiefly because he is seeking ''to focus on the real nature of the formula as a mental template in the mind of the oral poet, rather than on statistical aspects of 'repetition' found among phrases in the text'' (*TGV* 269). For Nagler, some words or phrases (or even sound-patterns) can be observed to link together, in a not precisely definable way, a rather wide variety of superficially disparate verse contexts that are perceptibly ''corresponsional'' to one another, but that very often do not express one ''given essential idea'' (as Parry's definitions of the formula and formula-system stipulate). Thus, in underlining only these repeated words or morphological patterns, I am aware of oversimplifying a phenomenon the importance and complexity of which are made evident through Nagler's study. But I do not think that our present scholarly understanding of classical Arabic poetry and its tradition is yet either articulated or comprehensive enough to allow us to make distinctions as fine as those made by Nagler or arrive at conclusions as solidly documented and generally valid as his. With not even a concordance to the poetry or a similar *Hilfsmittel* of any kind at our disposal, we are practically reduced to reliance upon our individual powers of concentration and observation and are more or less obliged to take our formulas where we can find them and in the forms we can discern. The main point is to be informative and precise about what it is we are doing.

Parry (*SET* I 84 = *MHV* 225, "Note on Method") and Lord (*HOP* 26) omit individual words shorter than five syllables from their study of formulas. But considering the strategic position and function of these words or patterns in the line of classical Arabic poetry and considering, too, that relatively few words in Arabic exceed *four* syllables, I do not consider it improper to include such one-word "formulas" in the results of the analysis given below. Furthermore, inasmuch as the computations that follow are based upon the number of *syllables* found to be formulaic (rather than upon the number of hemistichs or lines containing formulaic material), to treat occasional single words as either verbally or structurally formulaic will not materially distort the final percentages presented, should my view on these repeated words and patterns be found unacceptable. In fact, one could argue that such a procedure might even give a more accurate picture of the true "formulaicness" of *MuIQ* than would be had with ignoring the recurrences altogether.

A.3.e There is one consideration that emerges from the analysis that offers remarkable confirmation of Nagler's thesis, insofar, at least, as it has applicability to the Arabic tradition. Of "formulaicness" in the Homeric epics, he writes:

> Within any set of identical noun-epithet combinations, complex phrases, whole lines, or even whole passages, absence of variation from one another need by no means imply a fixity in the tradition which hampered the poet's creative urges, or, for that matter, made his creativity unnecessary. The real "variation" is in the process which transmutes pre-verbal Gestalt into utterable phrase, line, or scene, and compared to this process the resemblences among given allomorphs are, again, quite secondary. (*TGV* 289)

A glance at the analysis itself (Appendix A) will show many verses in which verbal and syntactic formulas overlap or coincide.[30] In *MuIQ* 33, for instance, the phrase

wa jīdin ka jīdi r-rīmi (or *ri'mi*)

recurs verbatim in *DIQ* 2:7*b* = *DIQ* (Ahl) 52:7*b* and *DQays* 6:3. But its syntactic schema may be represented thus (cf. Jacobi *SPAQ* 118–23):

i	*ii*	*iii*	*iv*
o ___ ___	o	___ ___	___ o (8)

i. *wāw (rubba)* + noun (sing., undefined);
ii. preposition *ka*;
iii. noun;
iv. (a) 2nd noun (in construct), or
(b) modifier.

And this syntactic formula recurs three times in *MuIQ* alone (11. 33, 44, 50), not to mention its frequent recurrence elsewhere (see App. A, l. 33 n. d).

In the same way, the phrase *ila l-^{c}ulā* (*a*14; *MuIQ* 35) is repeated identically in *DNāb* 6:17, and the phrase *^{c}ani ṣ-ṣibā* (*a*14; *MuIQ* 42) recurs in *DIQ* 63:2 and *DŠamm* 11:10. But structurally both phrases are isomorphous with each other, with *MuIQ* 57, *^{c}ala l-wanā*, and with a large number of other examples such as the following:

mina l-wajā—*DIQ* 2:41 = *DIQ* (Ahl) 52:46
mina l-fatā—*DIQ* 60:3; *ila l-xanā*—*D Ṭar* 4:95;
ma^{c}a l-kulā—*DIQ* 79:28*b*; *ma^{c}a l-bilā*—*D Ṭar* 12:4;
^{c}alā ^{c}amā—*DIQ* 79:40*b*; *^{c}ala ṣ-ṣibā*—*DNāb* 17:8;
^{c}alā qilā—*DIQ* 79:41*b*; *mina l-malā*—*DBišr* 3:10;
mina l-liwā—*DZuh* 3:29; *mina n-nawā*—*DḤass* 4:15;
^{c}alā hawan—*DZuh* 20:24; *ila l-waġā*—*DḤass* 10:29;
^{c}ala l-wajā—*DHass* 2:11 / 12:5;
ilā Minan—*DḤass* 103:3/*DḤum zāy-mīm*:1

The schema for this phrase—a rather simple one—is as follows:

i	*ii*
o ___	o ___
	(14)

i. (a) preposition of the form *CVCā/a* (eg., *ilā*, *^{c}alā*, *ma^{c}a*) with or without a following def. art.;[31]
   (b) preposition of the form *CVC* (e.g., *min*, *^{c}an*) + short helping vowel + following def. art. (e.g., *mina l-*);

ii. noun of the form *CVCā/an* (where *-ā* = the *alif al-maqṣūra*; see Wright *AG* I 11B), defined or undefined if i,a; defined only if i,b.

As a result of such co-occurrences of verbatim repetitions together with structural anaphora, the distinction between verbal and syntactic or structural formulas will not always be sharp, and many phrases in the analysis of *MuIQ* will be found underlined more than once. But, though there may have been some hesitation at times as to whether the line should be drawn solid or broken, there was seldom any hesitation as to where the line should be drawn. In other words, we can add a major dimension to our understanding of oral-formulaic poetic composition and rendition among the early Arabs if we recognize that the poet formed his verses upon a foundation, not only of phrases remembered and repeated more or less verbatim, but also of syntactic patterns absorbed with the very language and diction specially reserved to poetry (see chap. 3 below). The individual lexical components of such patterned phrases (or individual patterns) might vary, but they would vary within well-defined metrical and morphemic boundaries. That these syntactic or structural formulas frequently coincide with, and indeed underlie, many of the more strictly verbal formulas and that they seem to have been equally or nearly as essential as verbal formulas to the production of classical Arabic poetry should lead us to include them without reservation in our sense of what is "formulaic" about that poetry.

A.4.a In computing, then, the proportion of formulaic material that went into the composition of *MulQ*, I have sought to determine three separate percentages: first, that of *verbal* formulaic material; second, that of *syntactic* or *structural* formulaic material; third, that of all *formulaic* material as such. Recalling the fact of the frequent overlap of verbal and syntactic formulas, one should realize that the percentage of *combined formulaic* material in no way represents the sum of the other two percentages. These percentages, incidentally, were arrived at individually, by calculating the portions of formulaic material (i.e., the underlined items) that each of the eighty-two lines has been determined to include—the determination for each line having been based on the number of syllables that a given verbal or syntactic formula comprised. (To avoid conveying an impression of finality, I would also add that the results of an analysis of the same poem through the aid of concordances or computer methods would probably change my figures, most likely increasing them to some extent. Further, needless to say, these figures do hold good only for *MulQ*, and they would undoubtedly vary somewhat from one early poem to another—offering, perhaps, a good index of the likelihood of a poem's oral or written origin.)

Besides computing the proportions of formulaic material for the entire *qaṣīda*, I have also broken down the analysis so as to reflect the proportions for its individual passages as well. The passages as I see them correspond roughly to those determined by M. Bateson in her linguistic study of the odes (*SCP* 41–45), with such differences in line numbering as are occasioned by use of a different recension (i.e., Ibn al-Anbārī's vs. az-Zawzanī's; see App. C). In addition, my view of the thematic division of the *qaṣīda* differs from hers in the following respects:

1. the division between I.B.1. and I.B.2. is made at 1. 15 instead of 1. 17;[32]
2. the four lines 49-52 (=Z 48–51), which Bateson omits from her analysis on the grounds that they "are generally attributed to Ta'abbaṭa Sharrā" (*SCP* 42; cf. chap. 4, §B, below), are included here as I.C.2.;
3. to achieve a slightly more exact degree of differentiation, the longer middle passage II has been divided between ll. 63 and 64, on the basis of discernible thematic particularities.

Here, then, in outline form, are the passage divisions of *MuIQ* that have been adopted for this analysis:

- I. *Nasīb* and development (1–52)
  - A. *Nasīb* proper: halting at abandoned camp-site and weeping (1–6)
  - B. Episodic and descriptive development (7–43)
    - 1. Reminiscences (7–15)
      - a) of two former attachments (7–9)
      - b) of the virgins at Dārat Juljul and the slaughtered camel (10–12)
      - c) of sharing a ride with the reluctant ᶜUnayza (13–15)
    - 2. Remembered encounters (16–22)
      - a) with pregnant "one like you" (*miṯli-ki*) (16–17)
      - b) with Fāṭima (=*miṯli-ki* ?) on the "sand-hill's back" (18–22)
    - 3. Leisurely seduction of the well-guarded matron (23–30)
    - 4. Extended idealized description of "beloved," ending with the poet's infatuated recalcitrance to any reproach or advice (31–43)
  - C. Long night and poet's alienation (44–52)[33]
    - 1. Portrayal of lonely night as a camel ponderously settling down and the stars as mountain-tethered horses (44–48)
    - 2. Poet's solitude, with a wolf as his only companion (49–52)
- II. Poet's horse and hunting scene (53–70)
  - A. Description of the horse's appearance and qualities (53–63)
  - B. Narration of the hunt and its aftermath (63–70)
- III. Description of rainstorm and its effects on the physical environment (71–82)

In the following chart, the absolute figure in each of the three right-hand columns represents the number of formulaic syllables—verbal (A), syntactic (B), and combined (C)—in the given set of lines, and the percentage figure represents the measure of formularity in the passage, section, or entire poem.

In the figure opposite, one may examine an even more detailed and illustrative representation of the three kinds of observed formularity in the eighty-two lines of *MuIQ*. There, the vertical bars in each of the three graphs indicate the number of syllables per twenty-eight syllable line that have been found to be composed of verbal formulas (A), syntactic formulas (B), and combined verbal and syntactic formulas (C), respectively. The horizontal broken bar indicates the *average* number of formulaic syllables per line in each category.

Of the three determinations, undoubtedly the least stable and the most subject to revision (probably upward) is that of syntactic formularity (B). To retain more or less intact the verbatim formulation of the entire poem and, at the same time, to keep in mind its more salient morphological and syntactic

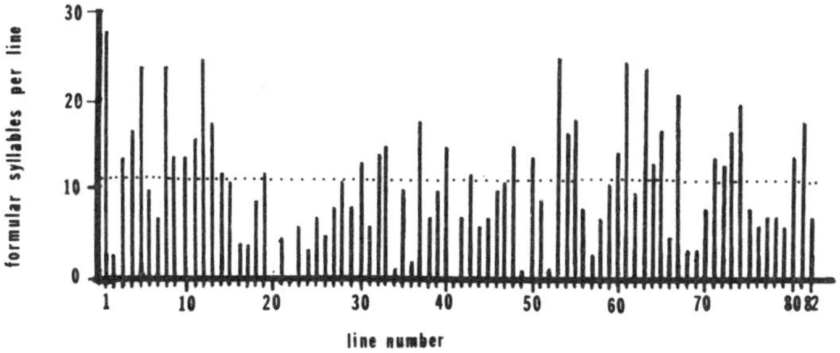

Verbal Formulas (A)

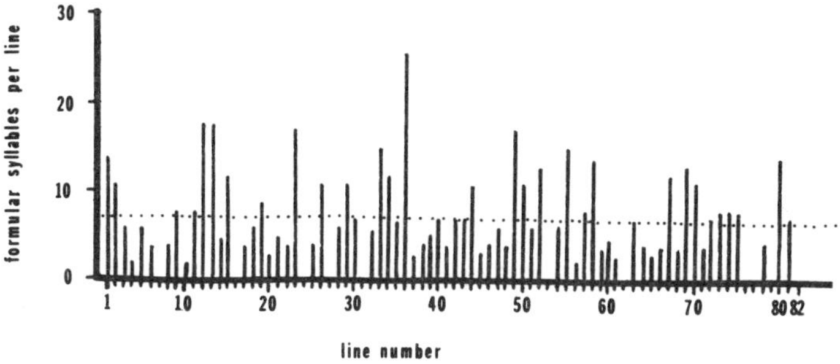

Syntactic Formulas (B)

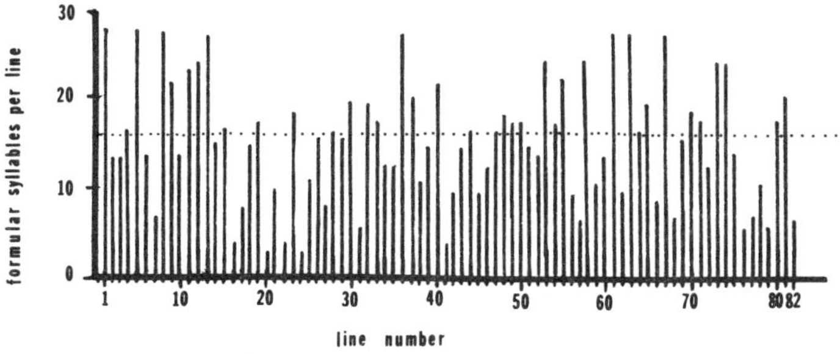

Combined Verbal and Syntactic Formulas (C)

FORMULAR DISTRIBUTION IN Mu. I.Q. (82 lines)

	LINES	SYL-LA-BLES/PAS-SAGE	FORMULARITY		
			Verbal (A)	Syntactic (B)	Combined (C)
I. A.	1–6	168	96—57.1%	43—25.6%	115—68.4%
B. 1.	7–15	252	141—56.0%	75—29.8%	180—71.4%
2.	16–22	196	34—17.3%[34]	31—15.8%	62—31.6%[34]
3.	23–30	224	61—27.2%[34]	56—25%	110—49.1%[34]
4.	31–43	364	117—32.1%	103—28.3%	196—53.8%
C. 1.	44–48	140	49—35%[34]	28—20%	76—54.3%[34]
2.	49–52	112	25—22.3%	47—42.0%	65—58.0%
Subtotal	(1–52)	1,456	523—35.9%	383—26.3%	804—55.2%
II. A.	53–63	308	162—52.6%	64—20.8%	198—64.3%
B.	64–70	196	70—35.7%	51—26.0%	116—59.2%
Subtotal:	(53–70)	504	232—46.0%	115—22.8%	314—62.3%
III.	71–82	336	137—40.8%	60—17.9%	171—50.9%
Total	(1–82)	2,296	892—38.9%	558—24.3%	1,289—56.1%

patterns, while running over as many lines of verse as this study has consulted, presented simply too many opportunities for subjectivity, inattention, fatigue, and human error. In addition, I may have had a tendency to be more aware of syntactic formulas for lines that had exhibited little or no verbal formularity. Nevertheless, the data on syntactic formularity seem for the most part valid inasmuch as they reflect a margin of deviation from the average considerably narrower than that observed for verbal formulas; and, further, although they augment the figures for combined formularity, those figures still remain generally parallel to the lower and more concrete figures for verbal formularity.

A.4.b What may be of particular consequence for the comparative study of oral tradition is the figure of 38.9 percent verbal formularity for the poem as a whole. This percentage agrees to a remarkable extent with the percentages of repeated hemistichs (hence, verbal formularity) in the oldest *chansons de geste*, as determined by Duggan: between 29 percent and 39 percent, including 35.2 percent for the *Chanson de Roland* (*SR* 23–26, 30, 34).[35] If subsequent analyses of other classical Arabic *qaṣīdas* were to yield percentages of verbal formularity somewhere in that range, as this one has, it could lead us to conclude what has only, so far, been a matter of speculation: namely, that there are modes of thought and operation underlying the process of oral composition and rendition that are basically the same from tradition to tradition and from people to people, regardless of vast differences in culture, language, and genres of poetry produced. The analysis of one *qaṣīda*, of course, proves no such thing. But the results obtained here do offer some grounds for guarded optimism and an incentive to continue investigation along these lines.[36]

In regard to another matter, a glance at both the statistical chart and the graphs makes it readily apparent that the first ten lines of *MuIQ* give no reliable indication whatever of the density of the poem's formularity throughout. According to my calculations, the percentages of verbal, syntactic and combined formulaic material in ll. 1–10 are respectively 55.4 percent, 20.4 percent, and 66.4 percent.[37] Indeed, only if one were to choose as a ten-line sample ll. 11–20, for instance, would the densities of verbal and combined formulaic material—39.6 percent and 56.1 percent—reflect the over-all average densities of the whole poem, though one would have to go to the following ten-line segment (ll. 21–30) to find a syntactic formulaic density—23.2 percent—as close to the average. But however randomly one selects a sample for formulaic analysis, the irregularity of formulaic distribution makes it practically inevitable that any similarity between percentages of formularity in that sample and those in the poem as a whole would be purely coincidental.[38] Lord's dictum that "one should really analyze an entire poem in order to have as true a picture as possible" (*HOP* 29), which becomes operative in Duggan's study as a fundamental working principle (*SR*, esp. 19–21), seems distinctly compelling in the present case. Considering that the average length of the *qaṣīda* brings such an analytic approach quite within the realm of feasibility (difficult as it might be to implement it in particular instances), and considering, too, how likely any random sample is to be misleading, we would be rather ill-advised to build a theory of oral tradition in classical Arabic poetry upon analyses of any samples that are not complete poems.

Later, in chapter 4, I shall put forward some conjectures, based upon the percentages of formularity and the graphs, about the processes of oral composition and rendition in the Arabic tradition. It must be emphasized that the considerations which will be raised at that time *are* conjectures. They are primarily supported only by the evidence derived from the analysis of a single poem and require corroboration through similar analyses of other classical *qaṣīdas* before they can be accepted as other than provisional. Still, they do receive strong secondary reinforcement from the few pieces of solid information that have been transmitted to us by the medieval literary and philological traditions about the poetical processes of the pre- and early Islamic Arabs. The fact is, therefore, that these conjectures, along with the formulaic data that has prompted me to advance them (however tentatively), are consistent with what can be learned both about the early Arabic tradition and, to a certain degree, about other oral traditions that have been better investigated. It is this fact that gives some assurance that the approach to formulaic analysis followed here can carry us closer to understanding the character and implications of the oral tradition of classical Arabic poetry.

A.5 There is a further consideration that helps to corroborate the formulaic nature of classical Arabic verse. Medieval literary theorists who discussed the subject of plagiarism among poets seem to have disregarded almost entirely literal verbal recurrences as such. This they did despite the fact that for a cursory reader such recurrent phrases would be by far one of the most readily observable forms of correspondence among the works of various classical poets and, hence, one of the most obvious kinds of "plagiarism," in the theorists' sense of the word. The reasons for this disregard are complex, but the important considerations seem to have been the following.[39] (1) The theory of plagiarism was applied predominantly to the works of "modern" (i.e., post-classical) poets and (2) was founded on the assumption that virtuosity, originality, and invention on the *verbal* level were the prime requisites of poetic achievement. Hence, since (3) simple verbatim "thefts" (*sariqāt*) of another poet's verses were to be deplored and scarcely to be acknowledged, (4) interest and criticism were centered on the modern poet's more or less skillful treatment or variation of "stolen" elements on the *thematic* level. How remote this theory was from the realities of *classical* Arabic poetic praxis can be gathered by noting that the theorists hardly dealt at all with the frequent verbal repetitions that cropped up in the poems of one classical poet after another, and that, except for a few celebrated examples, their censures of plagiarism as they saw it were seldom directed to coincidences in Jāhilī and Islamic (ca. 50–110/670–728) poetry, much less in Jāhilī poetry itself. One can only suspect that the framers of the theory, like their Hellenistic predecessors, predicated and upheld an aesthetic of more or less conscious variation, avoiding verbal formulas, repetitions, and the like—an aesthetic at once both contrary to that of the early Arab poets and, if Parry, Lord, and others are correct, indicative of the fundamentally literary (rather than oral) orientation of the theorists and of the later poets as well (see chap. 3, § D.4.c, below).[40]

B. It may be granted, then, that formulaic diction is intrinsic to the compositional technique of many, if not all, of the poets to whom are attributed the works of early Arabic poetry that have been recorded and preserved. Of the second characteristic of "orality"—the general absence of necessary enjambement—there can be no doubt. That enjambement (Arabic: *taḍmīn*), in its widest sense of the continuation of a sentence from one verse into another, occurs relatively seldom in the works of classical Arab poets has often been noted.[41] Nevertheless, the occurrence of enjambement—of certain kinds, at least—was frequent enough for an early scholar and litterateur, Ibn ᶜAbdrabbih (d. 328/940) to remark on the fact in setting down *taḍmīn*, or rather the *muḍamman* (enjambed line), among faults to be avoided in handling the rhyme (*min ᶜuyūbi l-qawāfī*).[42]

B.1 Like most of his fellow critics and literary theorists among medieval Arabic writers, Ibn ᶜAbdrabbih's immediate interest, in the context of his remarks, was to set forth rules and prescriptions for the proper fashioning and evaluating of verse. These critics generally based their doctrines upon an exhaustive, but often impressionistic, reading of the classical poets, in preference to all later ones; and they established principles of poetic praxis that, if they did not always derive from the highest or most unique achievements of those poets, at least represented a sort of statistical norm of phenomena encountered in that poetry. Thus they maintained that the poet's finest works would result from his proficient formulation of a series of well-conceived, well-executed, self-contained, end-stopped verses (*muqalladāt*).[43] And we may be sure that, in so maintaining, they were guided by a certain statistical, if not aesthetic, reality. Some among them, Ṯaᶜlab (d. 291/904) for instance, found evidence enough to convince them that the best verses were those in which each hemistich was fully independent of the other.[44]

Yet, even while classifying *taḍmīn* as a poetical fault, Arabic literary theoreticians felt obliged to make certain reservations that indicate both their uncertainty with regard to the precise degree of the phenomenon's "faultiness" and their sense of the difference in its use by "modern," as contrasted with "ancient," poets. Indeed, one of the earliest and most prominent prosodists and grammarians, Abu l-Ḥasan al-Axfaš al-Awsaṭ (d. 215/830 or 221/235), held that *taḍmīn* was no fault at all, although it would better be avoided.[45] Al-Axfaš's opinion, however, conflicted with that of his more eminent predecessor and mentor, al-Xalīl b. Aḥmad (d. 175/791, 170/786–87, or 160/776–77), credited with being the founder of the Baṣran philological school and of Arabic lexicography and prosody, if not of Arabic grammar as well. The *muḍamman* verse, in al-Xalil's view, was decidedly a poetical fault,[46] and the consensus among Arabic literary theorists seems to have followed him, rather than al-Axfaš.[47] But enjambement was considered a really serious defect only when "the one verse be wholly destitute of meaning if separated from the other; as when èn-Nābiġa says

[humū waradu l-miyāha ᶜalā Tamīmin
wa hum aṣḥābu yawmi ᶜUkāẓa innī]
They water their herds at the wells in spite of Temīm,
and they are the victors of the day of Okāẓ; verily I

which is unintelligible, because the *ḫabar* of [*inna*] is unknown, till we hear or read the next verse:

[šahidtu la-hum mawāṭina ṣāliḥātin
aṯabtu-humū bi waddi ṣ-ṣadri minnī]
have seen them fight many a good fight, (for which) I
reward them with my heart's whole love."[48]

Ibn Kaysān (d. 299/911 or 320/932)[49] has provided us with one of the earlier extant discussions of prosody, and in his section on *taḍmīn*, he admits that "it is not a gross defect. But the most eloquent style is that in which each verse of the *qaṣīda* stands by itself and when recited separately, wholly comprises the motiv (*maᶜnā*) which it was composed to express" (*KTQ* 57). Imra'alqays was considered one of the most skillful at composing individual verses into which he would incorporate, not just one, but two or more motivs (*KTQ* 57–58; cf. Brockelmann *GAL Suppl* 126 n. 3). But even he was obliged sometimes to carry over the sense of his utterance into a following verse, so that "the first verse was implicated in (*ḍummina*) the second, and the second one in the first" (*KTQ* 58). One must, though, make a distinction between Imra'alqays' use of enjambement that, as cited by Ibn Kaysān,[50] resulted from the circumstance that a word in the first verse was explained (*mufassara*) by the verse that followed— "and had (the poet) omitted the second verse, the sense (of the word) would have been obscure" (*KTQ* 58)—and between the much uglier enjambement of an-Nābiġa, cited above.

Ibn Rašīq (d. 456/1064 or 463/1070) is somewhat more precise in his treatment of *taḍmīn*. Defining it as "the dependence of the rhyme-word or a word which precedes it upon what comes after" (*Umda* I 171: *an tataᶜallaqa l-qāfiya aw lafẓa mim-mā qabla-hā bi-mā baᶜda-hā),* he cites the standard example of an-Nābiġa. He adds, however, that "whenever the word which depends upon the second line stands at some distance from the rhyme-word, it is less harsh a fault than *taḍmīn* (as such)." Two lines of Kaᶜb b. Zuhayr approach an-Nābiġa's in their use of enjambement:[51]

diyāru llatī battat ḥibālī wa ṣarramat
wa kuntu iḏā-ma l-ḥablu min xullatin surim
faziᶜtu ilā wajnā'a ḥarfin ka-anna-mā
bi aqrābi-hā qārun iḏā jildu-ha staham (m)

"(There are) the lodgings of her who cut my bonds (with her) and snapped them apart. And I was wont, when the bond by a friend was severed,
to resort to a lean, high-cheeked (camel), with leathern flanks, sweat-darkened, like pitch."

But less serious a fault are the lines of Ibrāhīm b. Harma (*Umda* I 172);

immā taray-nī šāhiban mutabaddilan
ka s-sayfi yaxluqu jafnu-hū fa yaḍīᶜū
fa la-rubba la<u>dd</u>ati laylatin qad niltu-hā
wa ḥarāmu-hā bi ḥalāli-hā madfūᶜū

"If you think me haggard and shabbily clad, like a sword whose sheath becomes worn and lost,
well, I've had many a night's delight—its illegitimate (result) averted by the legitimate (one)."

And the following lines of Mutammim b. Nuwayra, though they present some enjambement, are hardly at all to be thought of as *taḍmīn* (*Umda* I 172):

la-ᶜamrī wa mā dahrī bi ta'bīnī hālikin
wa lā jazaᶜan mim-mā aṣāba fa awjaᶜā
laqad kaffana l-Minhālu taḥta ridā'i-hī
fatan ġayra mibṭāni l-ᶜašīyāti arwaᶜā

"By my life!—though I am unused to elegizing one dead or bewailing misfortune or pain—
al-Minhāl indeed has shrouded beneath his cloak a splendid youth, no glutton who gorged himself at dinner."[52]

Ibn Rašīq concludes by saying: "Several verses may sometimes come between the two enjambed verses, as many as may allow the sentence to follow its course to completion and allow the poet to enlarge upon (his) motivs; but that [i.e., such enjambement] will not be held against him, if he does it skillfully" (*Umda* I 172; cf. Rāḍī *STX* 377).

Ibn Manẓūr (d. 711/1311) cites as authorities in his discussion of enjambement and enjambed verses both al-Axfaš al-Awsat (see p. 64 above), and Ibn Jinnī (d. 392/1002). He suggests that enjambement should be judged a fault only in proportion to the dependence of the first verse upon the second for completion of its sense and to the strength of the syntactical (or semantic) bond that joins them: the more necessary the dependence and the stronger the bond, the more objectionable would be the *taḍmīn* (*LA* XVII 128 ll. 18–19). The following lines are cited as an example of enjambement even more extreme than an-Nābiġa's (which is also cited):

wa laysa l-mālu fa ᶜlam-hū bi mālin
mina l-aqwāmi illā li llaḏīyī[53]
yurīdu bi-hi l-ᶜalā'a wa yamtahin-hū
li aqrabi aqrabī-hi wa li l-qasīyī

"Wealth does not—and know this!—belong to all: (it is) his only who
through it strives for eminence; let him exhaust it in service to his closest intimates and to those far removed."

Ibn Manẓūr's point here is that the syntactical bond between the inchoative particle, plus its subject, and its predicate (e.g., between *in-nī* and *šahidtu*, as occurs in the lines of an-Nābiġa) is not as strong as that between the relative (conjunctive) pronoun (viz., *allaḏī*[*yi*]) and the relative clause it introduces (viz., *yurīdu*, etc.) (*LA* XVII 129 l. 1).

More recently, Muḥammad Ḥusayn al-Qazvīnī, known as Kīšvān, composed a long *muzdawij* poem on the subject of prosody, accompanying it with extensive notes. In dealing with *taḍmīn* (Rāḍī *STX* 374–77), he refers to several earlier authorities and cites, besides the standard lines of an-Nābiġa, enjambed lines by Bišr b. Abī Xāzim.[54] Quoting the analysis of Abu l-ᶜIrfān Muḥammad b. ᶜAlī aṣ-Ṣabbān (d. 1206/1792),[55] Kīšvān contends that enjambement is considered a fault "because one ought to pause and make a break at the end of a line and if the sense of the rhyme-word requires something following it, stopping at that point would not be admissable. But (in that case) the rhyme-word would not be functioning as it properly should" (*STX* 375). As did Ibn Rašīq, Kīšvān also holds that the farther removed the enjambed word stands from the end of the verse the less objectionable is the enjambement. He cites a case in which the (negated) subject stands at the beginning of one line, the rest of which consists of a relative clause modifying that subject; then the second line presents the predicate, introduced by the preposition *bi* (conforming to an accepted usage of the negative in Arabic), and further elaborated by subordinate clauses.[56] Such a case is not, he states, *taḍmīn*, but is rather to be thought of simply as a "semantic dependence" (*taᶜlīq maᶜnawī*).[57] Kīšvān continues:

> Al-Maᶜarrī mentions, together with *taḍmīn*, *iġrām*,[58] saying: "It is less serious than *taḍmīn*. The need [for the sense of one verse to be completed by another] in *taḍmīn* is as it were much stronger than in *iġrām*, since *taḍmīn* occurs, for example, in an-Nābiġa's verse, "*wa hum aṣḥābu yawmi ᶜUkāẓa innī*—." Now "*innī*" very much requires its following predicate (*xabar*), while with *iġrām* the necessity (for a following verse) is not quite so great; as, for instance, in the lines of an-Nābiġa:[59]

wa law kānū ġadāta l-bayni mannū
wa qad rafaᶜu l-xudūra ᶜala l-xiyāmī
ṣafaḥtu bi naẓratin fa ra'aytu min-hā
bi janbi l-xidri wāḍiᶜata l-qirāmī

"Had they been generous, the morn of departure after they had raised the (woman-segregating) curtains of their tents,
I could have glanced about and glimpsed her (face) beside the partitioning curtain, bare of her bright-figured wool veil"
(Rāḍī *STX* 396).

B.2.a There emerges from this short survey of some traditional discussions of *taḍmīn* and from a certain familiarity with classical Arabic poetry a decided awareness that the character of enjambement in that poetry is, in many respects, every bit as "distinctive" as that in Homeric verse, so well described by Milman Parry. (*EHV* = *MHV* 251–65). Drawing upon the essay *On the Ordering of Words* by Dionysius (Denis) of Helicarnassus, a literary critic of the Augustan age, and upon Aristotle's *Rhetoric* (mainly Book III 9:1ff./ 1409a-b), Parry analyzes enjambement in the following terms:

> Broadly there are three ways in which the sense at the end of one verse can stand to that at the beginning of another. First, the verse end can fall at the end of a sentence and the new verse begin a new sentence. In this case there is no enjambement. Second, the verse can end with a word group in such a way that the sentence, at the verse end, already gives a complete thought, although it goes on in the next verse, adding free ideas by new word groups. To this type of enjambement we may apply Denis' term *unperiodic* [i.e., *aperiodos*]. Third, the verse end can fall at the end of a word group where there is not yet a whole thought, or it can fall in the middle of a word group; in both of these cases enjambement is *necessary*. (*EHV* 203–4 = *MHV* 253; cf. Lord *ST* 284 n. 17).

If we grant a degree of accuracy to the normative sense of the traditional Arabic critics and to the findings of more recent scholarship, we must notice how applicable, in general, Parry's analysis is to the phenomenon of enjambement in early Arabic verse. Since I cannot here undertake the kind of exhaustive study of a large body of verse such as Parry's,[60] I would propose that the character of enjambement as these secondary sources present it be accepted only tentatively, in lieu of a more thorough and conclusive analysis of its occurence in both classical and later Arabic verse. Nevertheless, two facts are quite clear, which correspond very closely to Parry's findings for Homer. First, as already mentioned, the end-stopped line is considered by early critics to represent the classical norm, and the statistical validity of their view is borne out by the researches of later scholars. Similarly, "in Homer nearly one half of the verses finish where the sentence ends" (Parry *EHV* 205 = *MHV* 254). Second, *necessary* enjambement, of the kind where a word or particle in one verse can have no meaning until joined to a word or word group in the next verse, is exceedingly rare in *early* (and particularly *earliest*) Arabic poetry, just as it is in Homer (*EHV* 218 = *MHV* 264). We have seen that the cases of *taḍmīn* deemed most objectionable are those in which the enjambed word (1) stands at or very near the end of the verse and (2) is itself a word or particle that functions primarily as an inchoative or conjunctive element, and hence requires, by its very nature, to be followed by something. It is easy to realize, then, first, how seldom this most necessary form of enjambement was in classical Arabic verse, and, second, how completely it seems to have been a function of the rhyme-scheme: i.e., such instances, seldom as they might be indeed, may never have occurred at all had it not been that the particles' final sounds coincided (or could be adjusted to coincide) with the rhymes of the poems.[61]

B.2.b As to the other forms of enjambement discussed by Parry, *unperiodic* and the more common forms of *necessary,* it would need a special and painstaking study to determine to what extent, if any, the categories of enjambement used by Homer resemble those used by early Arab poets. It cannot be denied that Arabic poets, composing within strict conventions of meter and rhyme, had to approach the problem of creating and mastering a poetic diction from a point of departure quite unlike that of poets such as Homer, for whom the consideration of rhyme was nonexistent.[62] For example, one only occasionally sees the same rhyme-word used twice in a single poem, at least not in the same sense or not without several verses intervening.[63] This fact, of itself, could stand against our expecting to find in Arabic verse repeated verse-end formulaic combinations identical or similar to those that Parry shows to be so characteristic of Homer's use of unperiodic enjambement (*EHV* 206–15 = *MHV* 255–62). Again, the Arabic language itself is lacking in much of the syntactical diversity present in Greek, especially with regard to modes of expressing subordination and complex sentences.[64] In Arabic, outside of the sometimes clause-like verbal usage of participles and infinitive nouns, the syntax of nearly all clauses (in the classical poetic language particularly) is essentially alike, whether they are independent simple propositions or members of a complex sentence; apart from context, only variations in the subordinating particle (if one is involved) or in the morphology of the verb indicate the fact and the kind of subordination.[65] Arabic also does not permit as much fluidity of word position within a verse as do more highly inflected languages. Although the classical Arab poet was by no means as restricted in ordering the words he used as is, say, a modern English poet, the syntactical exigencies of the language were such that he was more limited in his choice of word-forms to end a clause (hence, a verse) than Homer or Virgil would have been. It has been said that "word-order in classical Arabic is at once both *syntactical* and *expressive*. *Syntactical*, because the appearance of certain words or certain particles at the beginning of the sentence determines in advance the sequence of the expressions which are going to follow. *Expressive*, because one nearly always can choose freely the term that he wishes to emphasize at the beginning of the sentence" (Blachère/G.-D. *GAC* 386).[66]

Nevertheless, the phenomenon that Parry calls *unperiodic* enjambement, and to which he attaches much importance as a distinctive feature of Homeric, as opposed to later (i.e., literary) verse, is unquestionably and demonstrably a frequent occurrence in early Arabic poetry. Taking only the "seven long pre-Islamic odes"—the famous *Muᶜallaqāt*[67]—which, as a group, may justly be acknowledged representative of the "classical" style, one finds a really remarkable correlation between the modes of unperiodic enjambement differentiated by Parry and those encountered in the Arabic poems. Even considering the reservations expressed in the previous paragraph and taking into account the difference between Greek and Arabic syntax, the fact remains that, as with Homer, "one may group under four headings the various means by which [the poet] . . . can continue beyond the end of a verse a sentence which, at that point, already gives a whole thought" (*EHV* 206 = *MHV* 255). Of Homer, Parry says, "First, he can add a free verbal idea, using a dependent clause, a participial phrase, or a genitive absolute" (ibid.). If we substitute for the Greek genitive absolute the Arabic circumstantial accusative *(ḥāl)* and accept the other two constructions in terms of their Arabic equivalents, we may observe that this form of unperiodic enjambement occurs probably more often than any other, in these particular *qaṣīdas* at least:[68]

diyārun la-hā bi r-Raqmatayni ka-anna-hā
marājiᶜu wašmin fī nawāširi miᶜṣamī
bi-ha l-ᶜīnu wa l-ārāmu yamšīna xilfatan . . .

"Dwellings she has at ar-Raqmatayn, like tracings tattooed across
wrist cords,
whereat wend the dark-eyed kine and, in succession, white
antelope . . ." (Zuhayr 2–3)

"The second means of unperiodic enjambement is the addition of an adjectival idea, that is, one describing a noun in the foregoing verse" (Parry *EHV* 206 = *MHV* 255). Here in the Arabic poem one comes across instances of the "adding" style of an oral poet at its most conspicuous:[69]

ka-anna ḥudūja l-Mālikīyati ġadwatan
xalāyā safīnin bi n-nawāsifi min Dadī
ᶜadawlīyatun . . .

"The litters of the Mālikī camels that morn in the broad water-
course of Wadī Dad were like great schooners
from ᶜAdawlā [i.e., great ᶜAdawlī schooners] . . ." (Ṭarafa 3–4;
trans. Arberry *SO* 83)

"Third, the added idea may be adverbial, dwelling more fully on the action named in the foregoing verse. This idea is usually expressed by a phrase, sometimes by a simple adverb" (Parry *EHV* 206 = *MHV* 256). In the Arabic examples, the prepositional phrase, in particular, is by far the most frequent; possibly because the adverb, as a separate and significant part of speech, hardly exists in Arabic, which relies instead upon accusative and certain fixed forms of nouns and a few particles:[70]

wa ammā yawma lā naxšā ᶜalay-him
fa nuṣbiḥu fī majālisi-nā ṯabīnā
bi ra'sin min banī Jušama bni Bakrin . . .

"On the day we do not tremble for them, we sit about in knots
in our tribal assemblies,
(led) by chiefs of the Banū Jušam b. Bakr . . .
(ᶜAmr 42—43; trans. Arberry *SO* 206)

The "last means is that of adding by a coordinate conjunction a word or phrase or clause of the same grammatical structural as one in the foregoing verse" (Parry *EHV* 207 = *MHV* 256):[71]

qifā nabki min ḏikrā ḥabībin wa manzilī
bi siqṭi l-liwā bayna d-Daxūli fa Ḥawmalī
fa Tūḍiḥa fa l-Miqrāti . . .

"Halt, friends, both! Let us weep, recalling a love and a lodging
by the rim of the twisted sands between ad-Daxūl and Ḥawmal,
Tūḍiḥ and al-Miqrāt . . . (Imra'alqays 1–2; trans. Arberry *SO* 61).

Perhaps significantly, the last two means of enjambement are "less usual than the two given before" (Parry *EHV* 207 = *MHV* 256)—in the *qaṣīdas*, just as in Homer.

Parry says of *necessary* enjambement in Homer, "Those cases in which the reader must go to the following verse to complete the thought are of two sorts. First are those in which the poet ends the verse at the end of a word group. . . . The second sort . . . is that in which the word group is divided between two verses" (*EHV* 216–17 = *MHV* 263). Examining the instances of necessary enjambement in the *Muᶜallaqāt*, as well as those included in the examples adduced by Bräunlich (*VLB* 263) and Blachère (*HLA* 365 n. 1), one may observe that they too fall into two classes roughly corresponding to Parry's. In the first case, enjambement results from the extension of a temporal or conditional complex sentence[72] into a following verse. When this occurs, the sentence is almost invariably divided in such a manner that the protasis, with its related members, would form a completed clausal proposition at the end of one verse, and the apodosis would be introduced only in a following verse:[73]

fa lammā ajaznā sāḥata l-ḥayyi wa ntaḥā
bi-nā baṭnu xabtin ḏī qifāfin ᶜaqanqalī
madadtu bi ġusnay dawmatin fa tamāyalat
ᶜalay-ya haḍīma l-kašḥi rayya l-muxalxalī

"After we crossed the tribe's enclosure and a spacious,
dune-twined vale veered us down,
I spread out both (her) fronded (tresses); then she swayed
over me, slender (her) waist, supple and full (her) beringed ankle"
(Imra'alqays 29–30)[74]

The second case, involving the division of a word-group between two lines, seems limited, in the examples considered, to the separation of the subject of a sentence from its predicate, by means of an intervening dependent clause (usually adjectival or adverbial) or attributive phrase:[75]

fa aqsamtu bi l-bayti llaḏī ṭāfa ḥawla-hū
rijālun banaw-hū min Qurayšin wa Jurhumī
yamīnan la-niᶜma s-sayyidāni wujidtumā
ᶜalā kulli ḥālin min saḥīlin wa mubramī

"So I swear, by the Holy House about which circumambulate men
of Qurayš and Jurhum, whose hands constructed it,
a solemn oath (I swear)—you have proved yourselves fine masters
in all matters, be the thread single or twisted double"
(Zuhayr 17–18; trans. Arberry *SO* 115)

What is perhaps most distinctive about these cases of necessary enjambement in Arabic poetry, and is probably as well a function of the syntax of complex sentences in the Arabic language, is the following: in almost every observable case where "the reader must go to the following verse to complete the thought of the sentence," the verse itself ends with a syntactically complete clausal proposition of some kind. That is to say, when enjambement results from the continuation over two or more lines of a conditional-temporal complex sentence, the dependent clause (i.e., that which is introduced by the subordinating conditional or temporal particle) will itself only very rarely extend beyond the end of a verse; or if it is continued into the following verse (by means of modifiers, relative clauses, coordination, and so on), it is expanded to the verse-end; and only then will the main clause be introduced—*at the beginning of a new verse*. Likewise, when subject and predicate of a sentence are enjambed, the elements interposed between them, in the vast majority of cases, take the form of a dependent (relative, circumstantial, and so on) clause (or clauses), which will also scarcely ever go beyond the end of a verse; and the enjambed predicate will stand *at the beginning of a new verse also*. Thus, we see that, perhaps even more than Homer, classical Arabic poetry is distinguished by verses the ends of which coincide with the ends of syntactically complete clauses and that even if the sense of a sentence requires an additional verse or verses, the poet instinctively ensures an aesthetically suitable and syntactically justifiable closure at the end of every verse.[76] Here is to be found the underlying reason for the objections to such cases of absolutely necessary enjambement as those mentioned above. And here, too, can be sensed the consideration that prompted the critics to treat *taḍmīn* more as a matter of the degree of dependency of the first verse upon the second and of the distance of the enjambed word from the verse-end, than as a downright poetic fault (cf. Parry *EHV* 202 n. 8 = *MHV* 253 n. 1).

B.3 It has been to afford a measure of support for my conviction—namely, that classical Arabic poetry can be approached as an oral-traditional poetry—that this discussion of enjambement has been undertaken. Parry has concluded from his comparison of Homer's use of enjambement with that of Apollonius of Rhodes and Virgil that an essential difference between the *Iliad* and *Odyssey*, on the one hand, and the two later epics, on the other, lies in the manner in which the sense is drawn out from line to line. For Parry, the various forms of unperiodic enjambement, "more than anything else, give the rhythm in Homer its special movement from verse to verse" (*EHV* 207 = *MHV* 256). They occur twice as often in Homer as in the other two, whereas necessary enjambement is found only about half as often in the earlier epics. Most important, however, is the "fact that the use of set phrases [i.e., formulas] by Homer is closely bound up with the way in which his verses join" (ibid.). Parry thus characterizes the divergence in technique and style which had to exist between Homer and the epic poets of a later, literate age:

> Both Apollonius and Virgil, bent each upon making his own kind of epic, wrote out their verses without haste, forming their styles carefully from their wide knowledge of many forms of literature, from their memory of the words of many centuries. But Homer put all his trust in a technique of formulas which he accepted without thought of change: it was the traditional style and by it he could put together rapidly and easily his spoken verses. It may be doubted if he ever dreamed that in doing so he was cutting off from his poetry any new shades of style which would be his very own: that is not an ideal to which the poet who composes long tales without paper has any reason to be drawn, for new words and phrases in any number would jar badly the working of his formulas. What Homer sought in his style was to reach a traditional idea of perfection, not one that he had shaped himself, and it is only in this spirit that a poet can fit his

> thought to a purely formulaic diction, just as it is only by the ear that such a diction can be learned and only by the voice that it can be used.
>
> Moreover Homer was ever pushed on to use unperiodic unjambement. Oral versemaking by its speed must be chiefly carried on in an adding style. The Singer has not time for the nice balances and contrasts of unhurried thought: he must order his words in such a way that they leave him much freedom to end the sentence or draw it out as the story and the needs of the verse demand. . . . This need of the oral poet to order his thought unperiodically . . . has made unperiodic enjambement twice as frequent, necessary enjambement twice as infrequent, as in the writers of the literary epic. (*EHV* 214–15 = *MHV* 261–62)

Whether the same or similar figures would hold good for Arabic verse throughout the course of its history cannot be determined with certainty in this study. One would, for instance, have to ascertain clearly how much the bulk of poetic composition during post-classical times was *actually* determined by the generally recognized aesthetic principle of avoiding enjambement of any kind (see above). With the efforts of later *literary* poets directed for the most part by this and other principles (which themselves were arrived at largely through deduction from the classical models), and with these models probably the products of techniques and attitudes typical of *oral* poets, it is hard to imagine that post-classical poetry would fail to show some effect of the established preference for "a series of well-conceived, well-executed, self-contained, end-stopped verses" (§ B. 1 above; cf. below).

At any rate, it can be said that already in the later classical period (ca. 50/670–107/725) enjambement in general was noticeably more frequent than it had been previously (Blachère *HLA* 555–56, 683). It need not be thought merely coincidental that the Arab poet's increased use of enjambement, associated by Parry and others with the literization of poetical composition, came about more or less at the same time that education and literacy among the Arabs (and speakers of Arabic) were making tremendous advances, with active encouragement from both religious and secular authorities.[77]

Moreover, it may not be unrelated that during this same time, *rajaz* verse[78]—that is, verse composed in the *rajaz* meter—underwent a phenomenal metamorphosis. Before and shortly after the advent of Islam, it appears that *rajaz* "had been the meter habitually utilized in the popular poems of the bedouins" (Nallino *LAOU* 168), associated only with a kind of "popular doggerel" (*volksthümliche Knittelvers*—Goldziher *AAP* 78). *Rajaz* verses were ordinarily excluded from "poetry" proper (*šiʿr, qarīḍ, qaṣīd*), and instead of being employed in dealing with traditional "classical" motivs, they had been relegated to expressing only certain specialized or more commonplace themes.[79] No one in the pre-Islamic period composed a *qaṣīda* in *rajaz*, and *rajaz* played no part in the works of the great professional poets of the Jāhilīya (Ullmann *UR* 18, 26).[80] Just the opposite became true in the Islamic period, when *rajaz* came to be used not only for conventional (though linguistically recherché and extraordinarily "baroque," even "grotesque")[81] *qaṣīdas*, but also for various kinds of quite learned historical and didactic poems of considerable length.[82] *Rajaz* poets would have to be acknowledged by far the most active participants in the gradual elaboration of form and extension of motiv that began under the early Umayyads.[83] Add to all this the fact that enjambement, often very necessary enjambement, was a relatively frequent occurrence in *rajaz* verse and that long periods, of as many as ten or more verses, were by no means rare (Ullmann *UR* 65–67), and it is hard to ignore the obvious correspondence to Lord's description of the effects of literization on an oral-poetical tradition (*ST* chap. 6).

It is certainly possible, on the basis of such secondary information as the preceding, that a close comparative analysis of enjambement in "classical" and "modern" poetry might well lead to solider conclusions along Parry's lines. We would be again, at least, supported by the opinions of the medieval theorists, who evince a definite sense of a difference between *taḍmīn* as it presented itself in the works of the classical poets and *taḍmīn* as it was used by the moderns. According to Ibn Kaysān, "Sometimes a modern poet intentionally employs *taḍmīn* throughout his poem, succeeding if he is quite capable" (*KTQ* 58). Adducing an example then of seven lines in *sarī*ᶜ meter (interestingly, a variant of *rajaz*—Ullmann *UR* 16–17), exhibiting throughout the most necessary kind of enjambement,[84] Ibn Kaysān continues: "That which occurs intentionally is not the same as that which we have [previously] discussed, because the composer intended it thus, so he cannot be faulted on account of it. [*Taḍmīn*] is a fault only when it is found in [the poems of] one who strives to make all of his verses like epigrams (*amṯāl*), each standing alone, self-contained and independent" (*KTQ* 59). Several centuries later, Ibn Xaldūn (d. 808/1406), probably one of the most perceptive and well-versed students of Arab-Islamic culture and civilization ever to have lived, devoted the final portion of his famous *Muqaddima* to a discussion of the nature and development of the Arabic linguistic sciences, as well as to an excursus on Arabic poetry and versification. Here he defines poetry as "an effective discourse, based on metaphor and descriptions, divided into parts [i.e., verses] agreeing with one another in metre and rhyme, each one of such parts being independent in scope and aim of what precedes and follows it, and *conforming to the moulds* [or styles] *of the Arabs appropriated to it*" (*Muq* IV 1295).[85] The emphasis, already provided by the translator of the passage, E. G. Browne, is very much to the point in this context, for Ibn Xaldūn here means by "Arabs" specifically "the pre-Islamic pagan poets of the Arabs" (Browne *LHP* II 87), as well as those early Islamic poets whose works are closely (perhaps even naturally) affiliated with those of their predecessors. Hence, when he offers this definition of poetry, stressing as it does the avoidance of enjambement and based upon classical usage, and when he has already noted earlier how difficult it was for later poets to compose poems made up of such independent parts or verses (*Muq* IV 1290; Rosenthal III 374–75), then we may accept his testimony, I believe, together with that of Ibn Kaysān, as evidence that *something* had been introduced into the formations or dispositions of poets during or just after the second/eighth century. This *something*—whether it was literacy and the existence of a sizable *reading* audience (which is the most immediate and attractive conclusion) or some other factor[86]—led to significant changes in later poetic attitudes and techniques; and surely one of the easiest of these to perceive, if medieval and modern scholars alike have informed us rightly, would have been a poet's more common reliance upon necessary enjambement to draw out the sense of his verses.

C. The last of the three tests that Lord proposes for determining the possible orality of a text or body of texts is that of thematic analysis. The need of the oral poet for "well-established themes for rapid composition" (*ST* 131) gives rise in his poetry to a significant number of recurrent motifs, images, situations, episodes, relationships, and contexts—all of which can certainly be considered "formulaic" on the conceptual, if not verbal, level (cf. Bowra in Wace/Stubbings *CH* 30–31; Nagler *TGV* passim; Duggan *SR* passim).

C.1 Obviously, themes and thematic elements of this kind operate in written literature, as well as oral.[87] But there is in oral tradition a close functional relationship between a poem's themes and its formulation—between its thematic and its formulaic content—that does not seem to stand out so sharply in written tradition. Parry describes the operation of this relationship at its most characteristic in the following terms:

> The verses and the themes of the traditional song form a web in which the thought of the singer is completely enmeshed; there is some strand of words to bind up his lightest thought. His major theme can be made up only of minor themes, his minor, only of lesser, and his lesser, only of the verses and phrases which he has heard from other singers. The old romantic notion of the poetry as a thing made by the people is by no means a completely false one.[88] The poetry does stand beyond the single singer. He possesses it only at the instant of his song, when it is his to make or mar. Make it or mar it he will as he is able or unable to tell a story well, but well told or poorly told a song must be made of the traditional themes and traditional verses. (*MHV* 449–50)

Of course, Parry does not suggest that the expression of a theme is limited just to a *single* formulation. Lord, who has given much attention to the question of themes in oral poetry,[89] makes this point:

> There is nothing in the poet's experience (or in ours if we listen to the same song from several singers and to the same singer telling the same song several times) to give him any idea that a theme can be expressed in only one set of words. Those singers whom he has heard have never reproduced a theme in exactly the same words, and he has no feeling that to do so is necessary or even normal practice. The theme, even though it be verbal, is not any fixed set of words, but a grouping of ideas. (*ST* 69; cf. 285 n. 2)

Nevertheless, for the oral poet ''building themes,'' like building verses, is ''a technique inherited from generations of singers before him'' (*ST* 81).

> To [the singer] the formulas and themes are always used in association one with another; they are always part of a song. To the singer, moreover, the song has a specific though flexible content. (*ST* 95)

Again we find that there is a problem raised if we try to apply Lord's approach to thematic analysis immediately and directly to Arabic poems. In the oral epics with which he deals, both formulaic techniques and themes ''serve only one purpose. They provide a means for telling a story in song and verse. The tale's the thing'' (*ST* 68). But, although verbal formulas and formulaic structures can be seen as serving a poet in his creation of phrases and formation of lines (*ST* 43–45) not only for a narrative poem but for other forms as well, the *theme*, as described by Lord, would have relevance only as an element in a narrative (see below).

Yet, if we realize that structure and theme are hardly unique properties of narrative; that a lyric, an ode, a hymn, a psalm, an elegy, a prayer, or any other non-narrative form of verbal art may equally be composed orally or for oral rendition; that a poem, simply by virtue of being a poem, obviously would involve motivs, images, relationships, and the like—whether recurrent or not; that ''the tale's the thing'' only if the object of the poet and the function of the poem is to tell a tale: if we realize these things, we need readjust our sights but slightly to see that classical Arabic poetry is permeated with themes and thematic elements that are intrinsic both to the form of the poem and, it would seem, to the mode of its composition. There can be no doubt, besides, that these themes, just as those described by Lord with regard to the oral epic, constitute a large, though by no means unlimited, fund upon which classical Arab poets would draw quite freely for the making of their poems and outside of which they seldom took recourse—not because they were bound by a set of arbitrary conventions that dictated the form and scope of their productions, as many of their later successors may have come to be, but rather because it was through re-creating these traditional themes and reawakening them in the minds of their hearers that their poems achieved success at all.

C.2 In an article entitled "*Qaṣīda*," Alfred Bloch has summarized the most important earlier attempts at analysis of the classical ode's thematic structure—notable those of Ibn Qutayba,[90] I. Guidi,[91] and G. Richter[92]—followed by a presentation of his own. It is not my purpose here to discuss these analyses, but simply to point out the fact that they all agree in insisting that the traditional *qaṣīda* was composed of a few (usually three or four) major thematic divisions, which could easily be seen as analogous to thematic divisions in a narrative. These divisions reappear, more or less in the same sequence,[93] in ode after ode; and, at the same time, they are themselves made up of a number of secondary themes or thematic units that also recur from poem to poem (and even sometimes within the same poem) and that form the basic repertoire of variations upon the larger structural themes of the *qaṣīda* that every Arab poet had to have at his command.[94] Bloch's sensitive analysis, to which I have by no means done justice, has been too much neglected by students of Arabic literature, and deserves recognition as, in my opinion, the first really successful attempt to project—without condescension, tendentiousness, or oversimplification—something of the thematic, structural, and generic complexity of the *qaṣīda*.

Today, however, it must be acknowledged that all previous attempts at elucidating the *qaṣīda* and resolving questions of its thematic repertoire and structure have been superceded by the 1971 monograph of R. Jacobi, *Studien zur Poetik der altarabischen Qaṣīde*. (It must be acknowledged, also, as Jacobi readily and graciously does, that Bloch's participation and influence can be sensed at many points in the work—and, indeed, are sometimes explicitly indicated.)[95] F. Sezgin has justly commended this "distinguished" study as one that "carries us an essential step forward in connection not only with the perplexive character of the *qaṣīda*, but also with many other aspects of Arabic poetics" (*GAS* II 9 and n. 1).[96]

Jacobi's work is based upon a minimum of 174 poems (including 61 whole *qaṣīdas*) that make up the *dīwāns* of the six classical poets, an-Nābiġa, ᶜAntara, Ṭarafa, Zuhayr, ᶜAlqama, and Imra'alqays (= Ahlwardt *Divans*). In her investigation into the formal, thematic, and stylistic properties of this body of poetry, and of the *qaṣīdas* in particular, Jacobi carefully sets forth the recurrent "motifs, images, and stylistic figures of speech [that] disclose the common tradition," maintaining that "only on the grounds of a poetic that held for everyone [*allgemeinverbindliche Poetik*] is it possible to characterize adequately the work of a school of poets or of an individual poet" (*SPAQ* v-vi; cf. 196). Her sensitive and thorough analyses of this "poetic," in its diverse manifestations, should do away once and for all with the centuries-old sterotype of the classical *qaṣīda* as a simple tripartite organization of larger more or less unrelated thematic units: reminiscence at the deserted campsite (*nasīb*), journey by camel or horse (*taxalluṣ*), and concluding eulogy (*madīḥ*). Not only do her identification and delineation of major and minor thematic units reveal the presence of considerably more variety, complexity, and internal coherence than most earlier accounts would lead one to believe; in addition, in practically every phase of her analysis she links modes of thematic and stylistic expression directly to patterns of verbal expression that underlie them. Thus, specific syntactical usages and verbal techniques—such as particle-governed comparisons (with *ka, mitla, ka-mā*, and so on), particular sentence types, direct or indirect discourse, adjectives used metonymically, kinds of paranomasia and anaphora, interjectory and other affective constructions, and the like—regularly accompany, facilitate, make possible, and in effect actuate certain thematic and stylistic developments.

Jacobi's orientation toward the poetic texts differs from mine chiefly in that orality, for her, appears to have been a circumstance that was only accidental to the true nature of the poetry. At most, she seems to suggest, the effects of orality could be discerned in the poems in the form of certain techniques that the poets "would have developed to preserve the sequence of verses from disruption [*Zerstörung*] in the course of oral transmission [*mündliche Tradierung*]. . . . The frequent use of many rhetorical figures is motivated by the endeavor to tighten the bond between the separate verses" (*SPAQ* 11; cf. 16, 172, and esp. 182–96). Yet these techniques, involving as they do various forms of repetition and parallelism, can be considered just as productive on the generative and associative level of oral composition as they might be preservative or stabilizing on the level of oral transmission. Interlinear structural reinforcement from that point of view, therefore, would be a *result of,* not a *reason for*, such techniques. Indeed, Lord portrays such structural patterns in South Slavic oral poetry as primarily springing from the singer's "strong sense of balance" that guides him during the process of live composition and rendition (*ST* 55–58), and as only secondarily serving to preserve the wording and order of the verses:

> A perfectly natural *consequence* of building passages by syntactic parallelisms and acoustic patterns is that passages so built tend to have a comparative stability, or better, a continuity in time both in the habit of the single singer and, to a lesser degree, in the current of a tradition. Just as formulaic lines with internal rhyme or with a striking chiastic arrangement have a long life, so couplets with clearly marked patterns persist with little if any change. (*ST* 57; my italics)

The difference between the two points of view is fundamentally a genetic one, not merely one of aspect.

Nevertheless, the thematic and stylistic features that Jacobi describes and interprets in such a comprehensive, original, and perceptive fashion are altogether consistent with those that have come to be expected in a tradition of oral composition and rendition. Moreover, Jacobi declares that the very point of departure [*Ausgangspunkt*] of her work is "the conviction that early Arabic poetry is a collective poetry [*Kollectivdichtung*] and that its motifs, images and stylistic resources can be described in terms of a poetic that held for everyone" (*SPAQ* 196; cf. above). This point of departure is virtually identical with that of Alfred Bloch (*KWAV* 236–38) and, to a certain extent, that of K. Petráček (*VAL* 46–47; *DSSV* 10, 78–80; *QAAL* 405). In seeking to explain the distinctive, yet shared, elements of classical Arabic poems, they too had recourse to the notion of a "collective" or "folk" poetry—a notion that had the advantage of long tradition of scholarship and an elaborate theoretical apparatus behind it. I have discussed this approach elsewhere (*BFOT*) and have proposed there that, not only does the notion of "oral tradition" quite satisfactorily deal with all the obscurities and idiosyncracies of early Arabic poetry that the notion of "collective" or "folk tradition" was thought to illuminate, but also it comes to grips far more effectively with the essence and etiology of the phenomenon of that poetry itself (cf. Finnegan *OLA* 21, 36–37 and passim). When, therefore, I adduce Jacobi's work in this context as definitive and conclusive evidence that the thematic make-up of most classical Arabic *qaṣīdas* and other poems confirms, along with formularity and absence of necessary enjambement, their origin in an oral tradition, such an adduction in no way impugns the validity of her findings nor compromises the position as regards "orality" that is advanced here. I do not think we need any more convincing proof than Jacobi has provided us that, in the *qaṣīda* as in Homeric or South-Slavic poetry, "the verses and the themes of the traditional song form a web in which the thought of the singer is completely enmeshed" (Parry *MHV* 449–50; cf. above).

C.3.a Another consideration can also be raised at this point. There is some reason for believing that the *qaṣīda*'s major thematic divisions—such as the erotically reminiscent *nasīb*; the poet's description of his mount and his journey; his praise of self, patron, or tribe, and (so on)—may well have existed at one time as separate genres, as did elegy (*riṯā'*) or "satire" (*hijā'*). Such thematically unified passages then would have been sometimes composed at different occasions and perhaps subsequently joined together to form the larger ode. A state of affairs like that would be consistent with the existence of so many "unfinished" *qaṣīdas* and "fragments" (*qiṭa*^{c}; pl. of *qiṭ*^{c}*a*) and, also, with the survival of many *qaṣīdas* concentrating preponderantly on the elaboration of a single theme, while attending only perfunctorily to others.[97] It would accord as well with the early emergence of anthologies devoted to presenting such specimens of verse classified according to considerations that seem to have been, in general, more generic than thematic—namely, the various *ḥamāsa* collections.[98] Lord's remarks on the oral poet's approach to his thematic material may be pertinent to this aspect of early Arabic poetry and its textual state:

> Although the themes lead naturally from one to another to form a song which exists as a whole in the singer's mind with Aristotelian beginning, middle, and end, the units within this whole, the themes, have a semi-independent life of their own. The theme in oral poetry exists at one and the same time in and for itself and for the whole song. This can be said both for the theme in general and also for any individual singer's forms of it. His task is to adapt and adjust it to the particular song that he is re-creating. It does not have a single "pure" form either for the individual singer or for the tradition as a whole. Its form is ever changing in the singer's mind, because the theme is in reality protean; in the singer's mind it has many shapes, all the forms in which he has ever sung it, although his latest rendering of it will naturally be freshest in his mind. It is not a static entity, but a living, changing, adaptable artistic creation. Yet it exists for the sake of the song, and the shapes that it has taken in the past have been suitable for the song of the moment. In a traditional poem, therefore, there is a pull in two directions: one is toward the song being sung and the other is toward the previous uses of the same theme. The result is that characteristic of oral poetry which literary scholars have found hardest to understand and to accept, namely, an occasional inconsistency, the famous nod of a Homer. (*ST* 94; cf. 285–86, nn. 15, 16)

C.3.b Themes of a secondary kind, too, recur again and again in Arabic verse—so frequently, in fact, that medieval Arabic philologists and critics produced a substantial number of florilegia devoted solely to cataloguing them and recording their treatment at the hands of different poets. These "Books of Poetical Motivs" (*kutub ma^{c}āni š-ši^{c}r*),[99] as we can see from those that have been published,[100] provide quite convincing evidence of the existence of a common stock of themes and motivs among even the earliest poets. The evidence has also been well supported by various Western scholars, whose analyses have, as Bloch's and Jacobi's, often given greater precision to the kinds and contents of Arabic thematic material.[101] Nor can one ignore the rather left-handed corroboration afforded by those orientalists who have expressed, in von Grunebaum's words, "the long prevailing conviction of the stagnating uniformity of classical poetry" (see p. 5 above and chap. 1 n. 9).

It must be added though, as was already indicated in the case of verbal repetitions (§ A.4 above), that the medieval theoreticians confined a large share of their observations, criticisms, and judgments more particularly to the works of post-classical poets: they attached to the earlier masters a fundamentally paradigmatic value and seldom applied to classical verse the brunt of their critical views, since it had been out of classical verse that their views had largely been derived. Thus, while the philologists and critics, faced with the phenomenon of recurrent themes and motivs, chose to deal with it in terms of plagiarism or "thefts" (*saraq/sariqa*, *ax<u>d</u>*), they admitted two important reservations. First, a great many "commonplace" themes, images, and so forth, which naturally occurred to all—poet or not—were left out of consideration as a matter of course. Joined closely to these commonplaces, as being unworthy of critical attention, were "a great number of themes which, at the outset, were indisputably created. These themes were afterwards so often reused that they would enter into everyone's speech, just as the commonplaces themselves. That amounts to saying that a theme is of itself excluded from the realm of 'plagiarism' the moment that it becomes part of the common poetical heritage. Such is the case, for instance, of those themes one meets with at each step in early poetry" (Trabulsi *CPA* 197; cf. von Grunebaum *CPAT* 237–74, 241 and n. 71, 243, 244 = *KD* 105–6, 111 and n. 71, 114, 116).

Second, in the matter of plagiarism itself, one was obliged to recognize important differences between the *sariqāt* of the Ancients and those of the Moderns.

> The "plagiarisms" of the Moderns differ from those of the Ancients as regards the way in which they are carried out. The Ancients "plagiarized" more frankly or naively. Their "plagiarisms" present themselves to the eye and critics have no trouble unearthing them. As for the Moderns, they "plagiarize" with more subtlety and refinement—dissimulation, in fact. They have their methods, often skillful ones, of recreating the themes they borrow from others. This is why the "plagiarisms" of the Moderns were the more interesting to critics the more they offered them the chance for subtle and difficult examination. (Trabulsi *CPA* 199–200; cf. von Grunebaum *CPAT* 238 n. 30 = *KD* 106 n. 30)

Now, if one realizes again that Arabic critical doctrines were not arrived at haphazardly and that they reflect at least a certain statistical reality, it becomes clear that, as with enjambement, "modern" (i.e., ᶜAbbāsid and later) poets had become conditioned to regard the thematic elements of their poems quite differently from their "ancient" forebears. A contingent of them set out to introduce into their verse substantive innovations in themes and motivs:[102] some sought to change the established motiv-patterns of the traditional *qaṣīda* and adapt them to contemporary urban demands; others parodied the old themes and forms or rejected them outright for new ones.[103] Another group of poets, who subscribed to the "motto of most literary lawgivers''—viz., ''imitation of accepted predecessors'' who were ''admitted as classical''—focused all their attention ''on the best rather than the first expression of a given motiv'' (von Grunebaum *CPAT* 248 = *KD* 121). Both they and the ''lawgiving'' theorists shared with the Hellenistic Greek and Roman theorists before them the feeling ''that subject matter was common property and that it was sufficient vindication of originality or independence to present the traditional subject in a new and preferably better garb'' (*CPAT* 251 = *KD* 125).

Yet in every case, the later poet was deliberately trying for a kind of variation—of theme, expression, or whatever—that was alien to classical Arabic poetry as it was known to him and his contemporaries and as it is known to us. Moreover, it was a kind of variation that is equally unknown to the oral-traditional poet as Lord has portrayed him. The circumstances that define the situation of Arabic poetry and poets during the ᶜAbbāsid period and after, and that clearly divide most of the verse of that period from the earlier classical verse, correspond remarkably to those that, in Lord's view, accompany the transition from an oral to a literary tradition of poetry. ''The oral poet,'' Lord says,

> needs well-established themes for rapid composition. . . . Eventually, however, writing will free him from the need of the themes for purposes of composition. This will mean not only a freer opportunity for new themes, but also greater freedom in consciously combining and recombining themes.
>
> Writing as a new medium will mean that the former singer will have a different audience, one that can read. Psychologically, he may at first be addressing himself for some time to the audience of listeners to whom he has always been accustomed.[104] But the new reading public, though it will be small at first, will undoubtedly have different tastes developing from those of the traditional nonliterate audience. *They will demand new themes, or new twists to old themes.* (*ST* 131; my italics)

There is, therefore, a reasonably firm basis for proceeding further on the question of the *oral tradition* of pre- and early Islamic poetry. This poetry manifests, to an unmistakable degree, the essential characteristics of oral verse—formulaic diction, avoidance of necessary enjambement, and well-established themes and motivs. There is, besides, indication that later developments in Arabic poetic praxis and theory followed the course outlined by Lord for the transition from oral to written composition of verse. What remains, then, is to see whether external literary, historical, and biographical sources offer corroboration of this internal evidence. How was the oral tradition carried on among the pre- and early Islamic Arabs?

D. I have spoken of the conventional theory of ''oral tradition'' as it is usually applied by scholars of Arabic literature to the classical poets and their works (see pp. 13–14 above). We can find, however, that its elementary statement, as phrased by Kosegarten and, on the whole, accepted by most others, has occasionally undergone certain refinements. Most discussion has centered—as it ought to—on the nature of the occupation of the *rāwī* and the institution of *riwāya*.

D.1 The word *rāwī* (or the intensive form *rāwiya*), in its original sense, seems to have been used in reference to a water container, a water-bearing beast, or a human water-carrier, although it could equally have been understood as one who bound something (a water bag, a man, or the like) to a camel with a *riwā'* (rope or thong). It could also mean "one who contemplated or reflected upon (something)." Its application was extended to include those who bore, or bound upon themselves, burdens in a more figurative sense, including especially *rāwī*—or *rāwiyat—ad-diyāt* "(a chieftain) who takes upon himself (payment of) bloodwits." The usage with which we are concerned, however, is that of *rāwī/rāwiya* as a "bearer" (*ḥāmil*) or "transmitter" of poems and traditional narratives (*axbār*) (See Lane *Lex* I:iii 1194c, 1196c; Asad *MSJ* 187–89).[105]

Nāṣiraddīn al-Asad has written the most thorough and best documented study of the *rāwī* (*MSJ* 222–54).[106] He distinguishes two stages in the evolution of this semi-profession. In the first stage, extending from the pre-Islamic period to about the middle or end of the first/seventh century, the words *rāwī* and *riwāya* appear to have been restricted almost entirely to the sphere of poetry and, to a lesser extent, *axbār*. Later, when the collection and study of poems became established on a more systematic basis, *rāwī* came to designate, from the second/eighth century, the transmitter of traditions from an earlier authority and even the compiler of written recensions of poetical works (Asad *MSJ* 189–90). This later development in usage was, in my opinion, probably still more closely tied up with the evolution of the profession or office of *qāri'*, "reciter, reader (of the Qur'ān)" and the science of *qirā'a*.

During the earlier period, though, the usage of the term *rāwī* was by no means so unambiguous as Kosegarten and others might lead us to believe. All evidence points to the fact that the *rāwīs of* pre- and earliest Islamic times were not merely "reciters . . . who got by heart numerous songs of their poets, and recited them occasionally, in public assemblies and private parties." I. Goldziher has already noted the early use of the term to indicate the rendition of one's own verses as well as those of another (*AAP* I 99 n. 1). Elsewhere he adds that "the *rāwīs* were not simply echoing the poets; rather they contributed to the perfection of those works which they were to transmit from others. Here is the reason why we can find famous poets serving as *rāwīs* of their fellows' works'' (*MS* II 8 n. 2). Such *rāwīs*, who ''revise'' or ''improve'' the poems that they render, are considered specially by Asad (*MSJ* 241–44).

The frequency with which the characters of poet and *rāwī* were combined during this early period in a single person has often been pointed out (e.g., Lyall *AAP* xxxv; Nicholson *LHA* 131; Gibb *ALI* 19–20).[107] Ṭāhā Ḥusayn observed that the early Islamic poet Kuṯayyir ᶜAzza was the *rāwī* of Jamīl, who was the *rāwī* of al-Hutay'a, who in turn was *rāwī* to Kaᶜb and his father Zuhayr b. Abī Sulmā, the latter himself having been Aws b. Hajar's *rāwī*, with Aws having served as *rāwī* to Ṭufayl al-Ġanawī. Based on this observation, Ṭāhā Ḥusayn advanced the hypothesis of the existence of 'poetical schools'' (*madāris šiᶜrīya*) to account for these facts (*FAJ* 266–68).[108] G. E. von Grunebaum, after a close examination of poetical texts and literary-historical evidence, has differentiated six such ''schools'' or ''groups'' of pre-Islamic poets (*CFD* esp. 342–44), each marked by a distinct technical and stylistic praxis observable over successive generations of poets. These poets apparently accepted service as *rāwīs* to established poets within their ''schools'' during the initial phase of their careers (*CFD* 329–37).

Even earlier the accepted definition of a *rāwī* as one who learned and published his poet's verses was criticized and, for the pre-Islamic period under discussion, largely rejected by E. Bräunlich. Rather, Bräunlich contended, the relationship between *šāᶜir* and *rāwī* should be recognized as that of teacher and student. It cannot be thought merely coincidental that the several series of poets and their *rāwīs* (who themselves became poets), traceable from generation to generation during this period, belonged generally to single tribes,[109] or even to single families.[110] ''We must assume that, for the young *rāwī*, the main thing was to acquaint himself with the traditions and literary productions of his own tribe—in short, to prepare himself for the profession of *šāᶜir*'' (Bräunlich *VLB* 220–21). Bräunlich, then, with Ṭāhā Ḥusayn before and von Grunebaum after, holds the view that one is able ''to trace poetical schools within early Arabic poetry,'' growing out of an affinity of the *rāwī* for his master, which is, as it were, a function of their mutual consanguinity (*VLB* 221).[111] This view is subsequently confirmed by an analysis of various stylistic and technical usages found to be peculiar to certain poets, who could thus be said to constitute a ''school.'' After examining in considerable detail the poetry of poets of the tribe of Huḏayl in particular and demonstrating its shared and distinctive features, Bräunlich gives us good reason to accept his judgment

> that the *rāwī* of a poet would originally have been not so much the transmitter of the latter's works as rather the poet-to-be who would be tutored by the master in the art of poetry. Hence it is only natural that both [poet and *rāwī*] also exhibit general characteristics in their works through which they are distinguished from others. (*VLB* 265)

This view of poetical schools, made up of poets and their *rāwīs* (the latter to be seen then as *apprentice poets*), has since been adopted by a number of scholars,[112] although, as Blachère has cautioned, one must avoid the inference of a "cénacle" or of subscribers to a literary manifesto (*HLA* 336). Yet it is important to see further the implications of such a view for our understanding of the nature both of poetic composition and rendition during the Jāhilīya and the first century of Islam and of the textual tradition of the poetry ascribed to that period. The similarity is self-evident between what we know about the activity of the early *rāwī*, his "apprenticeship" to an older poet within the tribe, and his own emergence as an accomplished poet in his own right, and between Lord's description of the training of an oral poet (*ST* 17–26).

Consider, for example, the anecdote—remarkable even if apocryphal—that tells of Zuhayr b. Abī Sulmā's reaction to his son Ka^{c}b's premature efforts at poetizing.[113] Zuhayr went to the extent of beating Ka^{c}b to prevent him from versifying before he was suitably prepared, lest his verses be poorly fashioned and worthless poems be circulated under his name and rendered abroad. When the beatings proved ineffective, Zuhayr confined Ka^{c}b and, finally, sent him out alone to herd the stock. Even from the pastures, however, Zuhayr heard reports of his son's poetic attempts.[114] The father, incensed, saddled his camel and rode off to find his son in hopes of both exposing and embarrassing him as a faulty versifier and ascertaining just what poetic ability Ka^{c}b might actually possess. To this end, he mounted Ka^{c}b before him upon his camel, pronounced a verse containing a traditional description of a camel (set in the *ṭawīl* meter most favored by classical poets), and then proceeded to beat his son until the latter had satisfactorily improvised a complementary verse. When Ka^{c}b succeeded in capping not only Zuhayr's first verse but each of his successive three as well, the father openly acknowledged his son's proficiency and gave him permission to continue composing poetry, accepting him also (we learn elsewhere—*Ag* XXI 264:12–13) as his own *rāwī*.

Although the incident as narrated may well embody fictional elements,[115] the situation portrayed itself reflects in a way the three stages in the training of an oral poet as Lord has outlined them. The second and third stages—those of application and practice and of rendition before a critical audience—are clearly represented. The first stage—of listening and absorbing—is unquestionably presumed necessary, even though it is not explicitly mentioned, if only because Zuhayr is depicted as so vehemently opposed to his son's poetizing without adequate preparation or formation.[116]

We have good reason, therefore, to revise substantially our idea of the early *rāwī* and of the manner of composition and transmission of early Arabic poetry. We have too long allowed our judgment in these matters to be swayed by the unintentionally biased reports of medieval literary scholars steeped in a bookish tradition and by our own literarily grounded biases and expectations. Circumstantial evidence, such as the story of Zuhayr and his son, merely lends external support to the testimony of the existing poetical texts themselves. Our records of pre- and early Islamic Arabic poems, as discussed above and in Appendix A below, clearly demonstrate those features deemed most typical of "oral"—rather than "literary"—texts. Their renderants, then, must be understood in that context; and the accusations leveled against them—of misattribution, interpolation, and fabrication—must be considerably modified, if not retracted altogether, as I hope to show in the final chapter.[117]

1. I use this term in the sense generally intended by Bateson in *SCP*, esp. chap. 5.

2. On the difficult and, as yet, unresolved question of what constitutes a "significant" proportion of formulaic material, see, e.g., Lord *HOP* 19–24; Culley *OFL* 113–13; Duggan *SR* chap. 2.

3. The lines are *DIQ* (Ahl) 48: 1, 17, 18, 44 = *A* (i.e., *MuIQ*) 1, 19, 20, 46. Note that l. 18 = 20 does not really qualify, since *qātilī*, at the end of the first hemistich (i.e., the *ᶜarūd*-word), is not in conformity with the *rawīy* pattern of the *qasīda* (-*CVCCVCV̄*) and thus cannot be considered a genuine rhyme; cf. Abu-Deeb *TSA* II 40.

4. Monroe does not specify which recension of *MuIQ* he uses. It would appear to be, for these verses, the same as I have used: i.e., that which is common to *A* = *T* = *Z* and others through the first ten lines. *DIQ* (Ahl) is cited for all other references to IQ's poetry, but the *muᶜallaqa* in that recension—*S* = *DIQ* (Ahl) 48—omits ll. 3–4 of the passage analyzed in *OCPP* 44–46. See also the partial list of discrepancies (no. 3 on the list) below; also App. C, n. e.

5. For a review of this approach to formulaic analysis, see Duggan *SR* 16–21.

6. Here Duggan has in mind, I believe, samples of 10–30 or so lines, not whole poems whose total number of lines does not exceed a two-digit amount.

7. Citing Bateson *SCP* 30, Monroe give the following statistics for the use of meters in "all pre-Islamic poetry": *ṭawīl*—50.11%, *kāmil*—17.53%; *wāfir* and *basīṭ*—24.77%; all others—6.37% (*OCPP* 34).

8. Cf. also Parry, *Les Formules et la métrique d'Homère* (Paris: Société des Belles Lettres, 1928); translated in *MHV* 191–239.

9. For some, Russo's "structural formula" has represented too "soft" an approach, and objections to it have been raised; cf. Lord *HOP* 15–16 and references cited.

10. I.e., the phrase *ends* with the fifth syllable of the second (*b*) hemistich; see p. 235 below.

11. But cf. further evidence for the formulaicness of this line in Appendix A of this study.

12. One of the enigmas of Monroe's study is how, precisely, he arrived at the striking two-decimal-place percentages of formulaic material in the four passages analyzed. On the basis of his charts (*OCPP* 44–45, 47, 48, 50–51), I have computed the percentages of underlined material, reckoning in turn the portions of hemistichs underlined, the number of words (sometimes an arbitrary figure for Arabic), and the number of syllables. I have not once been able to match the percentage figures given in *OCPP* 34–35 (nos. 2–5), to which much significance is subsequently attached. It would seem proper to make explicit the nature and constitution of the proportions represented by these percentage figures.

13. See, e.g., Lord *HOP* 12–29; Duggan *SR* 21–38, 60, 220–21.

14. The referents used are specified in *OCPP* 35 nn. 1–2, 36 nn. 1–2. Classical poems in *ṭawīl* and *kāmil* are taken from the works of an-Nābiġa, ᶜAntara, Ṭarafa, Zuhayr, Imra'alqays, and Labīd. "Modern" poets referred to are Abū Nuwās, al-Mutanabbi, Ibn Zaydūn, al-Bārūdī (*ṭawīl* only), and Shawqi (*kāmil* only).

15. Cf. n. 12, above, on the question raised by Monroe's percentage figures.

16. Cf., with reference to the early Arabic tradition, the highly suggestive study by von Grunebaum, *CFD*.

17. Here Monroe remarks parenthetically, "Although theoretically correct, this assumption cannot be proved owing to the lack of a sufficiently large referent" (*OCPP* 37). The theoretical correctness of the assumption for the Arabic tradition, however, remains to be proved.

18. Lord, for example, in his analysis of a passage from the pseudo-Homeric *Batrachomyomachia* (which he finds has markedly fewer actual formulas than the *Iliad* and the *Odyssey*), expresses reservations about his findings because he used as a referent, not only the poem itself, but also the two considerably earlier Homeric epics. "From the point of view of the purist," he writes, "only the material from a single singer should be used in the analysis of oral poetry" (*HOP* 28).

19. Cf. Lord *HOP* 26. I have not attempted to take into consideration divisions within hemistichs, although one can find many formulas that cross over from one hemistich to another (e.g., line 5, note a; line 8, note a; line 29, note b; line 65, note a; line 74, note b; etc). The nature of the caesura in classical Arabic verses has by no means been definitively investigated to my knowledge; cf. Monroe *OCPP* 26–27; Jacobi *SPAQ* "Sachindex," *s.v. Zäsur*.

20. Cf. here the anomalous forms *ẓiltu*, etc., discussed in chap. 3, § B.5.c, below.

21. Or sometimes simply a one-syllable preposition; cf. *MuIQ* 55 and *DNāb* 1:22.

22. Note also that the second phrase from *MuIQ*—*bayna ṯawrin wa naᶜjatin*—is repeated verbatim as part of a full hemistich formula in *DIQ* 2:48 = *DIQ* (Ahl) 52:53v; 3:43 = 4:53v; and *DᶜAl* 1:39; cf. the discussion of overlapping verbal and syntactic formulas below.

23. Of course, a final *-ā* would also be possible if a diptote occurred at position iv as a rhyme-word. There is no reason why, in theory, a diptote should not occur in the formula at that position: diptotes ending in *-a* (> *-ā*) occur as rhyme words as a matter of course in other constructions. It is just that I have not so far encountered them in this schema.

24. E.g., line 23, note a; line 26, note a; line 36, notes a–b; line 40, note d; etc.

25. See on this question esp. Lord *HOP* 29–34, responding to G. Kirk "Formular Language and Oral Quality," *Yale Classical Studies* 20 (1966): 155–74. Cf., also, Adam Parry in Parry *MHV* xlii–xliii.

26. See also Parry's work cited in n. 8, above.

27. But cf. Monroe *OCPP* 28–29, who claims, on the basis of a minimum of evidence, that "a meter-by-meter formulaic analysis reveals . . . that as a general rule certain synonyms tend to recur in particular meters, while other do not." His only example of this phenomenon, however, is the alternation of *ṭalalun* or *dimanun* in *wāfir* and *ṭawīl* meters with *ad-diyāru* in *kāmil*.

28. E.g., line 3, notes a and d; line 4, note e; line 9, note b; line 18, note b; line 29, note a; line 55, note c; etc.; but cf. line 12, note c; line 14, note b.

29. E.g., line 11, note e; line 12, note f; line 14, note e; etc.

30. E.g., line 1, notes e–f; line 10, notes b–c; line 33, notes b and d; line 55, notes a–b; etc.

31. It should be recalled that in liaison with the definite article *CVCā* > *CVCa l-*, and that *ma*^{c}*a* would only occur in conjunction with a defined noun.

32. As Bateson says, "It is difficult to find appropriate sub-divisions in [Z] 7–47 [=*MuIQ* 7–48], because it is never quite clear when the poet is speaking of the same woman" (*SCP* 42). Nevertheless, ll. 16–17, which Bateson connects with the preceding passage as IQ's boasting "of his success with other women to overcome her [*sc.*, ^{c}Unayza's] objections" (*SCP* 42–43), I have taken as the beginning of an extended catalogue of amorous conquests, and hence as the beginning of a new passage.

33. There are a number of reasons why I would prefer to consider ll. 44–52 as a separate major division, distinct from the *nasīb* and its development. However, for purposes of formulaic analysis, I must agree with Bateson's judgment and with Jacobi's opinion about ll. 44–48, which "zwar nicht in Nasīb stehen, aber ohne Zweifel in seinem Motivkreis gehören" (*SPAQ* 200).

34. In computing these particular percentages, I have omitted from consideration those verbal formulas marked as questionable—i.e., with (?)—because the referent smacked of literary allusion rather than formulaic recurrence.

35. If the relatively higher figure of 38.9% yielded by *MuIQ* should come to present any problems, it could be rationalized by considering that my calculations were based on the total number of verbally formulaic *syllables*, whereas Duggan's were based on the number of repeated *hemistichs* (hence he omits formulaic material covering less than a hemistich or extending beyond a hemistich).

36. Pertinent to this important question, see, e.g., the studies by B. Colby and M. Cole and by R. Finnegan in Finnegan/Horton *MT* 63–91, 112–44.

37. For the same lines Monroe (*OCPP* 34) "discovered that at least 89.86% of Imru' al-Qais's text is formulaic." The problematic character and uncertain derivation of Monroe's percentages, however (n. 12, above), make it impossible for me to reconcile his figure with any of those yielded by my analysis.

38. Some attempts at random division of the poems into samples for analysis have included the following: (1) six ten-line segments followed by two eleven-line segments; (2) eleven segments composed of six and seven lines alternately; (3) two eight-line and eight seven-line segments consisting of every tenth line (i.e., 1, 11, . . . 81; 2, 12, . . . 82; 3, 13, . . . 73; etc.). For the various segments so produced, the deviations of the percentages of formularity from the average percentages ranged rather widely, as indicated by the following table:

	Verbal	*Syntactic*	*Combined*
(1) 10/11-line segs.			
Highs:	55.4% (1–10)	30.4% (31–40)	66.4% (1–10)
Lows:	23.6% (21–30)	18.2% (72–82)	44.3% (21–30)
(2) 6/7-line segs.			
Highs:	59.8% (8–15)	35.2% (31–7)	71.2% (8–15)
Lows:	17.3% (16–22)	12.8% (76–82)	31.6% (16–22)
(3) 8/7-line segs.			
Highs:	58.5% (3,13 . . . 73)	34.8% (3,13 . . . 73)	76.8% (3,13 . . . 73)
Lows:	22.3% (6,16 . . . 76)	14.7% (7,17 . . . 77)	44.6% (6,16 . . . 76)

39. See von Grunebaum *CPAT* = *KD* 101–29; Trabusli *CPA* 192–213; cf. Monroe *OCPP* 38–39.

40. When R. Pfeiffer (*HCS* 25 n. 1) rejects as "misleading" Parry's "negative check" (see E. Dodds in *FYT* 13) of the *Argonautica* (i.e., his findings that "no such system of metrically controlled epithets as in Homer is to be found in pen-poets like Apollonius Rhodius" [Dodds], he

does so simply on the basis that "Apollonius Rhodius followed the Hellenistic theory of variation and consciously avoided formulae, repetitions, and the like." This seems to indicate a somewhat unnecessarily rigid attitude on Pfeiffer's part, for Parry's and Lord's point, overlooked or ignored by Pfeiffer and hardly refuted by his statement, is precisely that such a "theory of variation" is a function of a literate and literarily inclined culture, as opposed to the culture of Homer and his contemporaries.

41. See, e.g., Brockelmann *GAL Suppl* I 27 (continuation of p. 26 n. 3); Blachère *HLA* 364--65. *Taḍmīn* as an element of prosody is distinct from *taḍmīn* as a rhetorical figure—viz., that of inserting into one's own work quotations taken from other poets, from the Qur'ān or Ḥadīṯ, or from proverbs: cf. Rāḍī *STX* (the author is actually Muhammad Ḥusayn al-Qazvīnī, known as Kīsvān [d. 1356/1937], ar-Rāḍī being editor and annotator) 375 n.x. On the latter usage of *tadmīn,* see von Grunebaum *CPAT* passim, esp. 245 n. 98 = *KD* 101–29 passim, 117 n. 98. But, most importantly, see Bloch *KWAV* 220–22 n. 15, for the best classification of types of enjambement in early Arabic poetry.

42. *IF* V 508:14–15: *wa huwa* [sc., *al-muḍamman*] *kaṯīr fī š-šiᶜr.*

43. See Brockelmann, *GAL Suppl* I 26 n. 3 and references cited there. Cf. Boileau's praise of Malherbe (*L'Art poétique* I 137–38), because, thanks to the latter's efforts,

Les stances avec grace apprirent à tomber
Et le vers sur le vers n'osa plus enjamber.

Von Grunebaum, who quotes these lines (*KD* 138 n. 22), adds: "Kein arabischer Theoretiker hätte seiner Abneignung gegen das *taḍmīn* besser Ausdruck geben können" (not in the earlier English version, von Grunebaum *AFAL*).

44. Ṯaᶜlab *QS* 70–76: *al-muᶜaddal min abyāt aš-šiᶜr.* Cf. Trabulsi *CPA* 173–74; Monroe *OCPP* 27.

45. In *LA* XVIII 127–28. Al-Axfaš's reasoning is quite interesting to follow, as it indicates a willingness to deal with the poetry on its own terms, rather than according to some abstract standard of theoretical excellence (an attitude not necessarily typical of al-Axfaš): "Were everything to be [judged] ugly just because there existed something more beautiful, then the poet's verse [*DTar* 4:102 (a line often held up as one of the finest in the language)] 'The days shall disclose to you what you knew not; and one you did not provision shall bring you news,' would be [held] inferior (*radī'*) if a finer verse were to be found. But inasmuch as this verse is not an inferior one, so neither is enjambement [to be thought] a fault."

46. According to Abū Zayd *KNL* 209:10.

47. See references cited in Bräunlich *VLB* 263 n. 1. Cf. Ibn ᶜAbdrabbih *IF* V 508; Ibn Kaysān *KTQ* 56–59; al-Xwārizmī *MU* 96; Ibn Rašīq *Umda* I 171–72; *LA* XVII 127–29 (s. r. *ḍ-m-n*); Rāḍī *STX* 374–77.

48. Wright *AG* II 358. The lines (= *DNāb* 29:16–17, with variants) are frequently cited as an example of *taḍmīn* in its most flagrant form. Bräunlich-Fischer *SI* 258b:5 and 259a:19, indicate rhyme variants of *in* and *min* (for *in-nī* and *min-nī*), but these do not eliminate the enjambement. Rāḍī *STX* 375 n. xxx notes that, according to al-Aṣmaᶜī, the two enjambed lines are falsely attributed to an-Nābiġa; cf. Abu Zayd *KNL* 209:11–15: . . . *wa zaᶜama l-Aṣmaᶜī anna-hu manḥūl.*

49. See Brockelmann *GAL* I 110; *Suppl* I 170, where the earlier date is preferred.

50. = *DIQ* 14:18–19 = *DIQ*(Ahl) 17:16–17 = *Ag* VIII 71 (with variant):

wa taᶜrifu fī-hī min abī-hī šamā'ilan
wa min xāli-hī wa min Yazīda wa min Ḥujur
samāḥata ḏā wa birra ḏā wa wafā'a ḏā
wa nā'ila ḏā iḏā ṣaḥā wa iḏā sakir

"In him you will recognize virtues of his father, of his mother's brother.
of Yazīd, and of Hujr—

One's magnanimity, one's probity, one's loyalty, and one's attainment—
whether he is sober of drunk."

Interestingly, al-A^c^lam aš-Šantamarī (quoting al-Aṣma^c^ī?), without mentioning any *taḍmīn*, observes that the second verse, "despite its extreme concision, is the most comprehensive treatment of this motiv" (*DIQ* 14:18 sch.).

51. = *DKbZ* (Dār) 62:8 and 63:5 = *DKbZ* (Kowalski) 4:3–4.

52. Cf. Nöldeke *BKPA* 97 and 104; Lyall *Muf* I 57:1–2. Enjambement, in fact, results only from the interposition of a *ḥāl-clause* (*wa mā dahrī . . .*) between the oath (*la-^c^amrī*) and its complement, which requires to be introduced by *laqad*: see Wright *AG* II 175–76.

53. The final vowel of the relative pronoun is strengthened (*mušaddad*) as a poetic licence; see Ibn al-Anbārī *IMX* 281: 17–20 (Weil) = 675:14–17 and n. 426 (^c^Abdalḥamīd).

54. = *DBišr* 39:10–11 (with variant). The rhyme-word in the first line is *iḏāmā*, a conditional particle that requires the second line as a following proposition.

55. See Brockelmann *GAL* II 288, *Suppl* II 399; cf. Weil *GSAM* 54; idem, "^c^Arūḍ," *EI*² I 668.

56. The anonymous lines are as follows:

wa mā wajdu a^c^rābīyatin qaḏafat bihā
ṣurūfu n-nawā min ḥayṯu lam taku ẓannatī
bi akṯara minnī law^c^atan ġayra annanī
uṭāminu aḥšā'ī ^c^alā mā ajannatī

"Nor has a distraught bedouin maid, flung off and
sent to unsuspected destinations,
more anguish than I; yet I suppress my inner pangs,
though they drive (me) mad."

57. Blachère *HLA* 365, citing a similar example, remarks that some such clichés or comparisons, extending beyond a single verse, are occasional exceptions to the technical practice typical of earlier (i.e., before 50/670) Arabic poetry as regards avoiding enjambement in general as a "fault." Cf. Bräunlich *VLB* 263 n. 8; and esp. Bloch *KWAV* 221 n. 15 (under example *f*).

58. Rāḍī *STX* 376:10 and 13 reads *aġrām* (or *uġrām*) with *hamza* above the *alif*, quoting from al-Ma^c^arrī, *al-Fuṣūl wa lġāyāt fī tamjīd Allāh wa l-mawā^c^iẓ* (ed. M. Ḥ. Zanātī), p. 446. I have not seen al-Ma^c^arrī's work in order to check the form of this word there. However, I suggest that *iġrām* (verbal noun of Form IV *ġ-r-m:* to make someone fond, desirous of; hence, as it were, a "fond attachment" between two lines) is the more likely reading both on analogy with other such poetical terms (*ikfā', taḍmīn, īṭā'*, etc) and because the morpheme *af^c^āl* has no sense in Arabic that would be appropriate in the context.

59. = *DNāb* 27:3–4 (with variants).

60. Six one-hundred line passages from each of the four great epics, *Iliad, Odyssey, Argonautica,* and *Aeneid*; see *EHV* 204 n. 9 = *MHV* 254 n.1.

61. Equally interesting as the cases of enjambement involving such introductory or conjunctive particles are cases where such particles form rhyme words, but where, to avoid enjambement, their complements, which ought necessarily to have come in the next verse, are omitted as being understood from, or implied by, the context; see, e.g., Bräunlich-Fischer *SI* 43b:25 (*wa llatī*) / 221b:20 (*wa in lam*) = 243a:18 (*lamī* [for *lam*]) / 248b:4 (*aynamā*) / 281b:8–9 (*innah* [for *innahu*]), and the sources indicated there. That such ellipses as these, often very jarring, were preferrable to enjambement seems to show how strongly conditioned the poet was both to avoid such "prosaic" connections and, more importantly, to produce an effective pause at the end of a verse. Cf. Parry *EHV* 218–19 = *MHV* 264–65. (I owe thanks to Professor Anton Spitaler for correcting my earlier misinterpretation of the significance of the Bräunlich-Fischer citations.)

62. Cf. chap. 1, n. 81. A. Bloch, in his painstaking and sensitive study (*VSA* 31–34, 51, 84),

has determined that the prosodic requirements of Arabic verse—the meters and particularly the unchanging rhyme—rather than stylistic tendencies constituted the most decisive factor influencing word-order, verse-ends, and other aspects of Arabic poetic diction. Unfortunately, there have been few attempts to undertake a really comprehensive analysis of Arabic poetic diction, as such, aside from the work of Bloch and a handful of other scholars (e.g., P. Schwarz's discussion of the language of ^{c}Umar b. Abī Rabī^{c}a, in *DUbaR* IV 94-172; or M. Ullmann's analysis of the linguistic and stylistic features of *rajaz*-verse, *UR*, esp. 9. Kapitel). Cf. chap. 3 below.

63. Some authorities held that seven was the proper number; see Wright *AG* II 357.

64. On this subject see esp. Bloch *ADZ*.

65. See, e.g., Blachère/G.-D. *GAC* 415–16.

66. Cf. Fleisch *AC* 159–60. For more detailed discussion of word-order in Arabic see, e.g., Wright *AG* II 250–88 and passim; Reckendorf *AS* 8–9, 10, 72–74, 133–39, 227–32, 287–88, 303–4, 446–47, 553–59; Bloch *VSA* IV. Abschnitt and 154–55.

67. The text used here is that established by Abu Bakr Muḥammad b. al-Qāsim al-Anbārī (d. 328/940), *Šarḥ al-qaṣā'id as-sab^{c} aṭ-ṭiwāl al-jāhilīyāt* (ed. ^{c}Abdassalām M. Hārūn) (= Ibn al-Anbārī *SQS*), it being the earliest extant recension of the poems as a distinct collection that has been published.

68. Examples (cited by line; a dash between line numbers indicates consecutive occurrences of the same kind of enjambement; a comma, the presence of intervening lines between the two enjambed lines)—Imra'alqays (= IQ): 1,5 / 10f / 31f / 57f. Ṭarafa (= Tar): 1f / 8f / 26f. Zuhayr (= Zu): 24f / 27f / 44f. ^{c}Antara (= An): 3f / 11f / 11,13 / 15f / 16,18 / 20f / 24–26 / 42f / 44–46 / 67f / 75f. ^{c}Amr b. Kulṯūm (= AbK): 2f / 18f / 31f/ 80f (there are, however, many discrepancies recorded in the line-sequence of ^{c}Amr's *qaṣīda*; see chap. 1, n. 78, above). al-Ḥāriṯ b. Ḥilliza (= HbH): 10f / 15–17 / 23f / 32f (could be included in the following category, adjectival, as description of *ayyāma*) / 37f / 59f / 65,68. Labīd (= La): 27f / 37f / 43f / 45f / 48f / 50f / 64f.

69. Examples—IQ: 30f / 32–36 / 40f / 53–63. Tar: 6f / 11f / 21f / 31f / 33f / 48f / 83–85 / 93f. Zu: 1f / 21f / 34f / 42f. An: 22f / 24,27 / 29f / 53f / 53,58. AbK: 1f / 39f / 48f / 71f / 82f. HbH: 19f / 25f / 38f / 65–67 / 68f / 75f. La: 2f / 12f / 16f / 31f / 34f / 36f / 55f / 71f / 78–81.

70. Examples—IQ: 6f / 76–79 / 80–82. Tar: 51f / 70f / 70,75 / 98f. Zu: 4f / 41f. An: 16f / 38f / 49f / 64f. AbK: 30f / 38f / 92f. HbH: 1f / 41f / 69f. La: 4f / 12,14 / 21f / 79f.

71. Examples—IQ: 76f. Tar: 8,10 (reading *wajh* in the genitive following *šarḥ, SQS* 149:2f) / 18 / 21, 29–31, 33 / 57–59. An: 14f / 18f. AbK: 15f / 52–54 / 74–77. HbH: 2–4 / 12f / 70f. La: 1f / 8f / 17f / 24f.

72. On the arabic *"phrase double"* see Blachère/G.-D. *GAC* 450–72.

73. Examples—AbK: 37f / 63f. La: 23f / 28f / 49f / 65f / 67f. From Bräunlich (numbers in parentheses refer to the corresponding pages and lines in the Cairo ed. *SAH*), Sā^{c}ida: 1:54f (1118f:54f) / 2:13,15 (1126f: 13,15) / 10:9f (1176:9f) / 10:19f (1178:19f) / 10:23f (1179:23f) / 11:2.4 (1181f:2,4). Abū Ḏu'ayb: 2:13f (47f:13f) / 5:20f) (77f:20f) / 13:9f (? 149f:7f) / 15:10f (162f:10f). Abū Xirāš: 5:3f (1208:2f) / 11:1f (1226:1f) / 19:1,4 (1240:1,4). al-Mutanaxxil: 1:32f (1261:32f) / 2:2,7 (1263f: 2,7). From Blachère, *DXan* p. 16:4,6 (not 5,7 as in *HLA*).

74. Some grammarians rather unnecessarily assert that *wa ntaḥā binā* actually introduces the apodosis, the *waw* being merely "inserted" (*muqḥama*) to express wonder (*li ma^{c}na t-ta^{c}ajjub*); see Ibn al-Anbārī *SQS* 55:10 ff.; cf. also chap. 4 § C.3.c, below.

75. Examples—An: 33f. Abk: 6f / 9f,11,12 / 73f. HbH: 9f / 52. From Bräunlich, Sā^{c}ida: 1:25f (1107f:25f) / Abu Xiraš: 8:4,9 (1218f:4,9; cf. n. 57, above) / 15:1,4 (1232:1,4). al-Mutanaxxil: 2:10f (1265:10f). From Blachère, *DNāb* 5:44,47 / *D, ^{c}An* 2:3f / *DA^{c}ša* 5:62,4.

76. Cf. the remarks of aṣ-Ṣabbān, cited by Kīsvān, p. 67, above; also n. 61, above.

77. See, e.g., Goldziher *EM* 199ab; Hell *AC* 51–52.

78. For details on the subject of *rajaz*-verse see, e.g., Goldziher *AAP* 78–83; Nallino *LAOU* 146–70; Bloch *Qas* 116–17; Blachère *HLA* 361, 364, 369–73, 380; and esp. M. Ullmann *UR* 1–3, 18–59, 214–17 and passim.

79. For the themes usually treated in pre-Islamic *rajaz*-verse, see e.g., Blachère *HLA* 364; Ullmann *UR* 380.

80. Ullmann *UR* 24 indicates that the celebrated pagan poets avoided composing in *rajaz* because it was employed only for "Volkspoesie, Vulgärpoesie"; and that it is for this reason that only very seldom would a short *rajaz* selection be found in the *dīwāns* of those poets. It is thanks just to the zeal of the medieval philologists for collectanea of that nature that we have so many "kunstlosen Verse" from this early period. Without questioning Ullmann's view, I would suggest that, since practically all recorded pre-Islamic poetry has come to us through the intermediary of the professional *ruwāt* and the early editors and philogists, the traditional formation and conditioning of the former, not to mention the classicistic and puristic predilections of the latter, may have had something to do with the exclusion of *rajaz* verse from the *dīwāns* of eminent Jāhilī poets. The poets could have composed longer *rajaz* verse: in fact, *rajaz* might easily have served for their first poetical flights—as their initiation into the intricacies of Arabic versification. In any event, I do not think we can ever forget about those oral and literary middlemen who themselves—and not, so far as we can determine, the poets—were ultimately responsible for the configurations of the classical Arabic poetical tradition as we know it; not necessarily for the poetry itself, that is, but for the shape that it is in. Consider, for example, the loss to our understanding of the classical tradition occasioned simply by the prevelant tendency, noted by al-Asmaʿī (in Ibn Qutayba *KSS* 162; Marzubānī *Muw* 104), to ignore the poetry of ʿAdīy b. Zayd and Abū Du'ād al-Iyādī, two pre-Islamic poets of Hīra, on the seemingly arbitrary grounds that their linguistic usage did not conform to that of Najd (*li-anna alfāẓa-humā laysat bi najdīya*); cf. Ahlwardt *BAAG* 74; also Brockelmann *GAL Suppl* 1 58–59; Fück *Ar* 45; von Grunebaum *NAU* 15 and n. 1.

81. See Ullmann *UR* 214–17.

82. Ullmann *UR* 46–59. On versified history, in particular, see Rosenthal *HMH* 179–85.

83. See von Grunebaum *GSAP* 129–34 = *KD* 23–27; Blachère *HLA* 681-716; Ḍayf *TTSU* passim and esp. chaps. 3–4; Haddāra *ISA* (very important).

84. Each hemistich carries the rhyme *-mā*, which is variously used as a relative, conjunctive, negative, or conditional particle, always requiring a following word or proposition. The attribution of the lines is discussed in Rāḍī *STX* 377.

85. Trans. by E. G. Browne in Browne *LHP* II 87 (Browne's italics and brackets).

86. In this connection see chap. 3, § E, above.

87. Adam Parry has written: "It is uncertain how far the *theme*, as Parry and Lord use the term, can be said to be unique to oral poetry. It would not be difficult to illustrate 'composition by theme' in the 19th-century English novel; or still more in the modern detective story. Anyone who has read more than two or three of the works of Rex Stout or Ross MacDonald will recognize that these writers compose more completely in standard scene types, most of them fairly traditional at that, than either the *Iliad* or *Odyssey*" (in Parry *MHV* xlii n. 1).

88. Cf. Zwettler *BFOT* 203.

89. See §§ 15 and 18 in Holoka *HOS*; cf. A. Parry in Parry *MHV* xlii nn. 1–2. For additional references to relevant works by other authors, see Holoka *HOS* §§ 123–36.

90. Ibn Qutayba *KSS* 20–22 (ed. De Goeje, p. 14); cf. Gaudefroy-Demombynes *ILPP;* trans. in ibid., Nicholson *LHA* 77–78, Jacobi *SPAQ* 3 (quoted *in toto* by Sezgin *GAS* II 9 n. 3); other references in Blachère *HLA* 141.

91. "Il 'nasīb' nella *qaṣīda* araba," *Actes de XIVe Congrès des Orientalistes* (Algiers, 1905) III 141.

92. "Zur Entstehungsgeschichte der altarabischen Qaṣīde," *ZDMG* 92 (1938): 552 ff.

93. But cf. also Bloch *Qas* 129; Jacobi *SPAQ* 3–4 and passim.

94. Cf. Blachère *HLA* 378–79. Blachère, who himself offers a most sensitive exposition of the *qaṣīda's* thematic elements (*HLA* 368–453, 561–91), seems not to have seen Bloch's study

(dated 1948) at the time of writing *HLA* (published 1952–66), although he alludes to the three analyses that Bloch considers. It would be most valuable to have had his impressions of the earlier presentation by Bloch.

95. Jacobi writes, acknowledging Bloch's contribution to her work, "Einige Hinweise and Übersetzungsvorschläge, die ich verwertet habe, sind durch (B.) gekennzeichnet" (*SPAQ* vii).

96. See judicious assessments of Jacobi's *SPAQ* by, *i.a.*, W. Heinrichs (*Islam* 51 [1974]: 118–24) and G. Windfuhr (*JAOS* 94 [1974]: 524–33).

97. Cf. Krenkow "Ḳaṣīda" *EI*^{1} II 796; idem "Shā^{c}ir" *EI*^{1} IV 286; Brockelmann *GAL Suppl* 29–30; Serjeant *PPH* 56–57; Bräunlich *VLB* 214–15; Bloch *Qas* 116–18; Jacobi *SPAQ* 6.

98. See Brockelmann *GAL Suppl* 39–41; Blachère *HLA* 150–52; Trabulsi *CPA* 26–28; Ch. Pellat "Ḥamāsa" *EI*^{2} III 110–12; and esp. Sezgin *GAS* II 66–75 and references cited. The *Ḥamāsa* of Abū Tammām, for instance, has several chapters that correspond to the various major thematic divisions of the traditional *qaṣīda:* e.g., *an-nasīb, al-hijā, al-madḥ, as-ṣifāt, as-sayr wa n-nu^{c}ās, al-marāṯī*, etc.

99. On this genre of literary-philological compilation, see von Grunebaum *CPAT* 236 n. 18 = *KD* 105 n. 18; Trabulsi *CPA* 22–24; and esp. Sezgin *GAS* II 57–60. To the thirty-odd titles listed in these three sources one may also add, by Abū ^{c}Aṣīda Aḥmad b. ^{c}Ubayd b. Nāṣiḥ, *az-ziyādāt min ma^{c}āni š-ši^{c}r li Ya^{c}qūb* [*b. as-Sikkīt*] (Ibn an-Nadīm *Fih* 73:23). Other works might be added if books entitled only *kitāb al-ma^{c}āni* were also thought to deal with poetical motifs; see, e.g., *Fih* 48:9, 52:14; cf. *Fih* 56:10, *kitāb abyāt al-ma^{c}ānī* (Flügel *GSA* 81 renders this last title "Über sententiöse Verse"; but perhaps in the context something like "thematic verses" or "one-line motifs" might be more apt; cf. Trabulsi *CPA* 187).

100. E.g., Ibn Qutayba *Kitāb al-ma^{c}āni l-kabīr* (Heyderabad, 1368/1949); al-Ušnāndāni *Kitāb ma^{c}āni š-ši^{c}r.* (Damascus, 1340/1922); Abū Hilāl al-^{c}Askari *Dīwān al-ma^{c}ānī* (Cairo, 1352).

101. Detailed and revealing analyses of themes employed in classical Arabic verse have also been undertaken by, e.g., I. Lichtenstädter "Das Nasīb der altarabischen Qaṣīde"; M. Bravmann (see chap. 1, n. 73, above); Bräunlich *VLB* 222–36; von Grunebaum *CFD*; and others (cf. Sezgin *GAS* II 13 n. 2). Bräunlich's and von Grunebaum's studies are particularly relevant to the discussion at hand, for they demonstrate the likelihood of poetical "schools" from the recurrence of specific themes and motifs in the works of certain poets; but cf. Jacobi *SPAQ* 205 n. 1.

102. On the complex question of this, the thematic front of the "Battle of the Ancients and Moderns," see Goldziher *AAP* 122–76; Nicholson *LHA* 285–91; von Grunebaum *GSAP* 131–-34 = *KD* 24–27; Gibb *APAP*; Trabulsi *CPA* 187–92; Gabrieli *LT* 90–93; R. Blachère in *CDC* 279–86; Haddāra *ISA*, esp. chap. 2.

103. Even so classically oriented a poet as Abū Tammān "emphasizes his avoidance of *sarq* and asserts that he is keeping away from any oft-repeated *ma^{c}nā*" (von Grunebaum *CPAT* 248 n. 120 = *KD* 121 n. 120).

104. On the problems of the "transitional text," whose possibility Lord does not accept, see chap. 1, § A.4, above.

105. A tempting, but somewhat speculative, etymology would be to see the *rāwī* as one who "binds" each verse to the *qaṣīda* by means of a properly prepared for and enunciated *rawīy*; cf. chap. 3, § B.3.d, below. If one accepted an otherwise unsatisfactory interpretation of the term *qaṣīda*, relating it to a fat, well-marrowed camel, this etymology would not be out of the question.

106. H. Lammens's discussion of "La Corporation des 'Rāwia'" (*Etudes sur le siècle des Omayyades*, 263–64) is not very helpful and refers primarily to a later period than the one here considered. See also, however, Sezgin *GAS* II 14–33.

107. Gibb (*ALI* 19–20) claims, without apparent substantiation, the *rāwī* who became a poet

did so "with an almost inevitable diminution of spontaneity and substitution of conscious art." But both al-Jāḥiẓ (*BT* II 9:12, citing Ru'ba b. al^cAjjāj) and Ibn Rašīq (*Umda* I 197–98) place the poet-*rāwī* in the first class of poets. Ibn Rašīq explicitly states that the ancient and naturally unaffected (*al-maṭbū^cūn*) poets were preeminent through their rendition (*riwāya*) of poetry, their knowledge of traditional narratives (*axbār*), and their apprenticeship (*talmaḏa*) to poets who were superior to them (*Umda* I 197:6–8).

108. Blachère (*HLA* 335 n. 5) holds, however, that Ṭāhā Ḥusayn based his thesis "sur des données plus vraisemblables qu'établies." Cf. n. 101 above.

109. Zuhayr and Ka^cb, despite their patrilineal connection with Muzayna, seem to have become affiliated, through the action of Zuhayr's father Abū Sulmā, with the poetically prolific tribe of Ġaṭafān. They maintained their relationship with this tribe on the side of Zuhayr's grandmother and were generally associated with Ġaṭafānī poets. See *Ag* X 309–10 = Būlāq IX 156; *DZuh* (Dār) pp. 1–3, 326; Ibn Sallam *TFS* 89, 92–93; Caskel *GN* II 10–11, 611 (*s. n.* Zuhair b. Rabī^ca); W. Robertson Smith, *Kinship and Marriage in Early Arabia,* p. 182.

110. Bräunlich (*VLB* 218–19, 221) mentions several such instances. Other "dynasties poétiques" are noted by Blachère *HLA* 335, 484; cf. idem, "Influences héréditaires et problèmes posés par la recension de la poésie archaique," *Studies . . . Gibb* 141–46.

111. K. Petráček (*QAAL* 404–5) stresses the close bond between the national poetry of the Arabs in this early phase and the kinship-based society out of which it was produced.

112. See, e.g., F. Krenkow, "Sha^cir" *EI*¹ IV 285–86; Gaudefroy-Demombynes *ILPP* xxxi ff.; von Grunebaum *GSAL* 125–27 = *KD* 20–21; Blachère *HLA* 333–34 and Index (*s.v.*, École); Asad *MSJ,* esp. 222–31. But cf., also, Jacobi *SPAQ* 205 n. 1.

113. The account is in *Ag* XV 147–48 and *DZuh* (Dār) 256–59. Both Bräunlich (*VLB* 221) and Blachère (*HLA* 336 n. 2) allude to the incident (with the *Ag* passage inaccurately cited and without reference to *DZuh*), but neither pursue it beyond the allusion. The lines that form the point of the anecdote may also be found in *DZuh* (Ahl) App. 10.

114. Interestingly, the verses reported are *rajaz*; cf. n. 80 above.

115. Blachère (*HLA* 336 n. 1) asks: "Quel cas faire . . . de l'anecdote . . . ?"

116. Lord (*ST* 21) relates a firsthand account of the formation of the Yugoslav oral poet that bears a certain resemblance to that of Ka^cb. Cf. also al-Aṣma^cī's account, set in the early third/ninth century, of a critical "seminar" in which a taciturn old *shaykh*, well-versed in poetry and the historical traditions of the Arabs (*ayyām an-nās*), sits in judgment upon the poetical productions recited to him by young poets of his and a neighboring tribe (al-Qālī *Am* II 264–65). Blachère (*HLA* 336 n. 2) questions the value of such anecdotes as information on the training of the early poets. The only valid hypotheses, he maintains, are based on examination of the texts and on the intellectual attitudes they may evoke. If, however, as has been shown, the texts in themselves do bear witness to the oral nature of their composition and rendition, then it would seem quite obtuse not to regard accounts such as these as corroborative evidence at least.

117. Cf. p. 14 and chap. 1, no. 40, above. Sezgin (*GAS* II 14–33 and passim), most recently, has collected an impressive body of primary and secondary evidence that makes it practically impossible to doubt that "die schriftliche Fixierung von Gedichtsammlungen im Vor-und Frühislam bereits *in gewissem Umfang* üblich gewesen sein muss' (*GAS* II 36, my italics). I think it essential to repeat that this fact does not materially affect the arguments advanced here. As C. H. Whitman has said, with reference to the fact "that the Greek epic, oral though it is, belongs almost surely to a period when literacy existed": "The problem of Greek writing, however, affects in reality only the preservation of Homeric poetry, and not its creation. Despite attempts to disprove or modify it, Parry's thesis remains cogent, that the *Iliad* and the *Odyssey* are products of a purely oral technique of composition" (*Homer and the Heroic Tradition,* p. 5).

*

Chapter Three

The Classical ^{c}*Arabīya* as the Language of an Oral Poetry

A. Besides calling attention to the *volkstümlich* nature of classical Arabic poetry, Petráček did raise another important consideration. When he described the language used in the early poems—the poetic *koinē*, the classical ^{c}*arabīya*—as a *stylistic* rather than *dialectal* phenomenon, he did so in the opinion that the presumably established *Volkstümlichkeit* of the poetry would permit comparison with other "folkloristic and ethnographic analogies."[1] Petráček's vagueness and imprecision in this regard, to which I have previously alluded, should not blind us to his fundamental insight, especially if we concentrate upon oral-traditional—i.e., oral-formulaic—rendition as the earmark of folk poetry (cf. chap. 1, §C, above).

A.1 Classicists, and Homeric scholars in particular, have devoted much attention to the language of the epics and have for some time acknowledged that, in M. Bowra's words, "Homer's language can never have been spoken by men" (in Wace/Stubbings *CH* 26). The Homeric *Kunstsprache* is characterized by "the availability of alternative forms of differing value for metrical purposes, which originated in different dialects and periods. It cannot be doubted that these alternatives were a feature of the mixed and artificial dialect in which the *Iliad* and the *Odyssey* were originally composed" (Edwards *LHTC* 122).[2] It is, comments P. Chantraine, "as if the late bards (*aëdes)* had at their disposal a double set of forms, some more archaic, the others more recent'' (in Mazon *Intro* 104). Many scholars have found in the oral-formulaic theories of Parry and Lord the most satisfactory explanation for this linguistically heterogeneous state of affairs. M. Bowra, for instance, gives the following interpretation of the Homeric *Kunstsprache*:

> Homeric language is then the fruit of a long tradition which preserved relics of Mycenaean times. It was able to do this because it was formulaic. Its copious formulae were devised to assist the bard in the task of oral composition. Since he composed for hearers and much of his work was necessarily improvised, he needed a large number of formulaic phrases to help him. . . . All oral poetry needs and uses formulae, and indeed cannot exist without them. If the poet has them in full control, he can produce a poem on almost any subject at short notice. . . . We cannot doubt that when Homer learned his craft what he mastered was a rich store of formulae connected with heroic legends and ready to meet almost any emergency. Once a phrase met a need and was found to have an appeal to the poets' audiences, it might come to stay, while others less worthy were abandoned and replaced by new phrases. This is how an oral tradition works, and we may assume that this is what happened before Homer found the art in existence and made his own magnificent use of it. The formula makes the Homeric style what it is and is fundamental to any understanding of it. (In Wace/Stubbings *CH* 28)

And L. R. Palmer, too, who recognizes interdialectal and archaic features as ''*characteristic of the language in which the Homeric poems were actually composed*'' (Palmer's emphasis), thinks it ''likely'' that such an artificial language

> was the product of a long tradition of oral poetry, which passed over from an Achaen to an Ionic milieu, whereby certain Achaean elements, preserved particularly in stereotyped formulae, were transmitted from one generation to another of professional bards as picturesque, traditional elements in ''poetic diction.'' (Ibid., p. 100)[3]

A.2 The key work on this subject still remains, however, Parry's study ''The Homeric Language as the Language of an Oral Poetry.''[4] In this fundamental essay Parry traced the history of ancient and more recent attempts to account for the peculiar chronological and dialectal mixture that made up the language and diction of the epics.[5] These prior theories have had their corresponding parallels in Arabic linguistic and literary scholarship. The ancient view of the Homeric language, for instance, was that ''Homer himself chose various forms and words from the dialects which he had heard in his travels around Greece'' (*SET* II 2 = *MHV* 325–26). This view, Parry declares, ''while it seems the simplest, is likewise the furthest from the truth'' (*SET* II 1 = *MHV* 325).[6] Deprived of its itinerant rationalization, it is closely analogous to that of the traditional Muslim philologists with regard to the origins of the classical *ᶜarabīya*: for them, the *ᶜarabīya* was the dialect spoken by the

Qurayš at Mecca, who had culled the best linguistic features from the dialects of the many tribes who visited the city annually on pilgrimage to the *Ka^{c}ba*, then a pagan sanctuary (see § B.5.b, below).

It is, as already suggested, Parry's idea of the formula that underlies his understanding of the Homeric language. In the epics, the individual line and the extended poetic passage are formed through molding together linguistic materials (words, word forms, and word groupings) mainly heard and absorbed as formulas by the poet from other poets during his formative period, but also sometimes generated during composition on the analogy of known formulas. Into the make-up of oral poetic language as Parry sees it go four basic elements. These are elements of the archaic, the new, the foreign, and the artificial: all of which emerge naturally because of the circumstances involved in oral poetical rendition with an inherited traditional diction, yet without the stabilizing factor of a text.

Parry's discussion of these elements and how they may become incorporated into the language of oral poetry (*SET* II 6–19 = *MHV* 329–39) should be read for itself and for its relevance to any understanding of the poetic *^{c}arabīya*. Here, though, it will only be emphasized that from among these elements the choice of a poet, in rendering a line or passage, would be guided above all by considerations of how faithfully it re-created what he had heard or uttered before and of how conveniently it fit into the specific metrical context and so advanced the rendition itself. Neither verbal originality, on the one hand, nor verbatim reproduction, on the other, are recognized criteria for judging the success of an oral poet or the excellence of his rendition. As Parry says, the "whole art" of the traditional poet is "to make a poem like the poems he has heard" (*SET* II 12 = *MHV* 334). And this might entail his repeating an element of diction that had been heard long ago and reused in poems because of its acknowledged appositeness; or modifying or adapting his traditional diction to produce a new element, thus maintaining an accord with changes in his own or his audience's conditions; or adopting a word or usage from a speech group other than his own because it was especially apt, had no metrical equivalent in his own speech, or was already part of his inherited diction; or even, under the pressure of a particular metrical need, generating an otherwise nonexistent form to fill out a line, which then becomes accepted as part of the already uncommon diction of poetry and is passed on with the rest. If oral rendition were to entail, as it does, any or all of these eventualities, none of them would arise as a result of willful striving after an archaic, original, exotic, or artificial effect. Rather, they would arise as a result of the inherent conservatism, immediacy, and fluidity—in a word, orality—of the tradition itself.

Parry enumerates eight traits that he finds characteristic of an oral formulaic diction (*SET* II 20–23 = *MHV* 339–42).[7] These, too, in many cases find parallels in the Arabic tradition and will be referred to in context, although no attempt has been made to work out a one-to-one correspondence. The most important contribution of Parry's study, however, can be epitomized in the following passage:

> Oral poetry is altogether made up of traditional formulas and series of formulas, each of which is an artifice for making the verse and the sentence. The singer has learned these formulas by hearing them in the mouths of older singers, and he makes his own poetry out of them from beginning to end, since the only way he can compose is by thinking in terms of the formulas. Thus while the poems of an oral poetry are ever each one of them in a neverceasing state of change, the diction itself is fixed, and is passed on with little or no change from one generation of singers to another. (*SET* II 43 = *MHV* 358)

Parry's conclusions as to the all-pervasiveness of formulas in Homer, the high degree of variability to which an oral poem is exposed, and the absolute necessity of the set formula for successful improvisation have been somewhat revaluated and modified in recent years.[8] The possibilities of a certain amount of verbatim recitation and of later textual emendation have not always been sufficiently brought out in his studies.[9] But on the whole, as evidenced in the earlier discussion, modern scholarship has largely accepted his view of the language of the Greek epics as the function of an inherited and formulaic diction formed to the needs of oral poetical rendition. In this light one can see that such a diction ensures a continuity of verbal form and usage over a fairly long period that, in conjunction with a limited repertoire of traditional themes, would make it relatively easy to preserve intact the essential distinctive features of a given memorable poetic utterance, despite numerous variations of detail—especially when the utterance was no more extensive than the average *qaṣīda*.

B. Can we, then, similarly account for the origin of the classical poetic *ᶜarabīya* that found its unique realization, primarily, in the poems of the pre- and early Islamic Arabs and, secondarily, in the Qur'ān? Before venturing to explore this question, one would be well advised not to expect any conclusive answer, recalling A. Spitaler's caution that, with regard to the *ᶜarabīya* and related issues, "there is hardly today [i.e., in 1961] a *communis opinio* on any one of the numerous separate problems. Controversy exists, for instance, over the basic question of the interrelationship (*gegenseitiges Verhältnis*) of the language of early Arabic poetry, the Qur'ān, and the Bedouins; the problem of the *iᶜrāb;* the nature and origin of the classical *ᶜarabīya* of later centuries; etc." (in Levi Della Vida *LSPF* 124).[10] Furthermore, in the field of

Arabic philology we have nothing even approaching the statistical tools—concordances, word-counts, *Parallele-Homer,* comprehensive analyses of particular features, and such—that have been available to Homeric scholars for some generations. Thus, of necessity, much of what follows will seem rather impressionistic. Yet, should it encourage serious investigation of classical Arabic poetry, if only for the sake of refutation, it will have served some purpose.

B.1 There is certainly good authority for presuming that the Arabic language as it appears in the classical poetry "as far back as the late sixth century . . . was, apparently, a super-tribal language, absorbing lexical and at this time presumably also phonetic, morphological, and syntactic features of various tribal dialects" (Blau *ELB* 3). This language or linguistic configuration, which has often been labeled the "poetic *koinē,*"[11] constituted precisely that *ᶜarabīya* which was to be found, as al-Bāqillānī (d. 403/1013) specifies, in "the poems of the pre-Islamic pagans, the utterances of fluent and wise Arabs . . ., those of the seers and of composers of *rajaz*-verse and rhymed prose (*sajᶜ*), and other eloquent and stylistically pure forms of Arab expression."[12] And whether it may originally have derived from an existing tribal dialect or would have been from the beginning a formal or poetic diction separate from all the dialects, most scholars (with the notable exception of medieval Muslim philologists and J. Fück) seem now to concur that it never formed as such the spoken vernacular of any Arabic-speaking group, either before or after Muḥammad[13] (although one cannot dismiss the possibility, particularly in post-Islamic times, of highly educated court or scholarly circles speaking, or trying to speak, the *ᶜarabīya* as a conventional idiom). "The literary language of Arabia," as C. Brockelmann writes, "is a language of poets, made for the poets and comprehended by themselves above all" (in Fleisch *IELS* 100 n. 1).

As to the relationship of the language of the Qur'ān to the poetic *ᶜarabīya*, this question has occasioned a good deal more debate than that of the non-vernacular nature of the *ᶜarabīya* itself. At this stage, at any rate, it seems safe to say that the Qur'ān was revealed and first uttered in a linguistic form that was, if not identical with the language of poetry, close enough to it to be distinguished rather sharply from the spoken dialects (including that of Qurayš, contrary again to Fück and Muslim tradition) and to make feasible the inclusion of Qur'ānic usage with that of classical poetry as basic source material for the early philologists' standardization of the Arabic language.[14] The deviations from the poetic idiom are probably still best understood, though, especially from the point of view to be developed here, in accord with J. Fück's sensitive judgment:

> In the Qur'ān, for the first time in the Arabic language, a monotheistic ideal is revealed, for which the enigmatic, studied, and rhymed language of the ancient seers offered a model only for the external features of stylistic praxis—figures of speech and of thought; while the arduous task of finding a mode of expression befitting an entirely new content represents an unprecedented achievement by Muḥammad, an achievement undiminished by the fact that the Prophet himself saw it just as the reproduction of that which he had received, during his ecstatic moments, from on high. (*Ar* 3)

Or, viewed somewhat less appreciatively, "the Qur'ān has been written [sic] in the language of poets, by a man who was not a poet and who left in his work traces of his Meccan dialect" (Brockelmann in Fleisch *IELS* 100).[15]

B.2 We have not yet been provided with any kind of comprehensive diachronic study of classical Arabic such as exists for Homeric Greek or such as J. Fück has undertaken for post-classical Arabic and J. Blau for Christian and Judeo-Arabic. It may indeed be that a study of this kind would be impossible, given the scarcity and varying reliability of available material relating to the linguistic evolution of pre-Islamic Arabia. Even Ch. Rabin's basic work *Ancient West Arabian* gives a description of the dialectal situation and its significance for the classical *ᶜarabīya* from an essentially synchronic point of view—an approach that understandably was determined, for the most part, by the nature of the sources themselves. In these circumstances it is often difficult, not to say impossible, to identify and chronologically assign elements of diction that could rightly be considered "archaic" from the standpoint of a normal speaker of Arabic at, say, the time of Muḥammad. If, however, the findings of Homerists in this regard hold any value for Arabists, it lies in their having shown how intimately connected is the preservation of archaic or dialectal forms in the Homeric language to the fact that those forms, at some earlier stage in the tradition, were incorporated into formulas by poets during the course of oral rendition. These formulas afforded satisfactory ways of dealing with specific metrical and thematic contingencies and successfully aided in advancing the on-going poetic rendition. Once these formulaic "archaisms" and "dialectisms" had proved acceptable to both poets and audiences, the inherent conservatism of the oral poetic tradition ensured their retention as part of the traditional poetic diction that every would-be poet absorbed during his formative years and throughout his career (cf. Parry *SET* II 9–12 = *MHV* 331–33).

Although the relative homogeneity of the *ᶜarabīya* has been noted by a number of scholars,[16] it is certain that the poets had a wide spectrum of lexical, morphological, and (to a lesser extent) syntactical alternatives to choose from in coping with a particular poetic exigency. It is equally certain that, in many cases, these alternatives were introduced into the common vocabulary and diction of the poets at different periods and from different tribal or local groups. Moreover, these so-called archaisms and tribalisms or provincialisms were no less frequently employed in poems ascribed to early seventh-century poets than in those dated 100–150 years earlier (not to mention many of those dated as late as the second/eighth century).

Of course, caution must be exercised in identifying such elements and in explaining their occurrence in each given instance. A. Spitaler, for example, partially on the basis of Alfred Bloch's study of the syntactical accommodations that differentiated classical Arabic poetic diction from prose, has strongly emphasized that irregularities of syntax and word-order that are conditioned solely by the requirements of meter and rhyme ought not to be classed or analyzed as discrete linguistic phenomena.[17] Nevertheless, there remain among the poet's compositional resources many identifiably archaic or dialectal features that although certainly filling certain prosodical needs, seem otherwise to be equivalent with similar forms or expressions of later or more generic vintage.

The antiquity of several of the most integral themes of the *qaṣīda* is attested by the pre-Islamic (first century B.C.–seventh A.D.) Ṣafaitic, Ṯamūdic, and Liḥyānic inscriptions and graffiti, which often allude to traces of former encampments, yearning for absent or deceased companions, and dream visitations, and also frequently give descriptions of camels and other animals (using a nomenclature already quite profuse and diverse).[18] Whether verbal forms like those in the inscriptions in any way corresponded to, or could have been adopted as, the formulaic expressions for such themes in the classical *qaṣīda*[19] I cannot say. The formulaic vocabulary for the *nasīb* and *taxalluṣ* (mount-description) segments of the *qaṣīda* is quite well established in those specimens of poetry designated as among the earliest; and the selection of similar, not to say identical, subjects, both for epigraphic notation and in the classical poetry, can hardly be mere coincidence (cf. Caskel in von Grunebaum *SICH* 41), although the linguistic difference would probably leave out of the question any verbatim borrowing of proto-Arabic forms as such. (One can, though, conceive of the possibility of their direct translation or natural assimilation into the *ᶜarabīya* by poets who were also familiar with the inscriptional languages.)

B.3.a Rhyme in classical Arabic poetry, the feature that at once most clearly distinguished and most decisively determined its formal expression, also provides one of the most striking and pervasive examples of linguistic archaism in the poetic *ᶜarabīya*. The essential element in Arabic rhyme (*qāfiya*) is the final consonant in the line (*rawīy*) which remains constant throughout the poem for as many as 80–120 lines (often more for *rajaz* poems). Two basic types of rhyme seem to have been recognized by the poets: one in which the *rawīy* alone was the last sound pronounced in reciting each verse, i.e., verse-end *consonance;* the other, by far the more frequently attested, in which the *rawīy* was pronounced with a final long-vowel *-ū/-ī/-ā*, i.e., verse-end *consonance and assonance*. The first was called *qāfiya muqayyada* "fettered rhyme;" the second, *qāfiya muṭlaqa* "loose rhyme." The final long vowel (*majrā*) of the *qāfiya muṭlaqa*, lengthened through what seems to have been an artificial poetic convention called *tarannum* ("singing, cantillation, intonation,")[20] was properly to be, like the *rawīy* itself, constant throughout the poem. Where called for, it was uttered both for the short-vowel inflectional suffixes of verbs and determined or diptotal nouns and for the *tanwīn* suffixes of undetermined triptotes *-un/-in/-an*.[21] The Arabic grammarians gave much consideration to the form and articulation of words in rhyme-position, classifying their remarks under the more general heading of speech phenomena at the termination of utterances or word groups, i.e., in *pause* (*waqf, wuqūf*). For them, there were notable differences between the pausal forms encountered in poetry (*šiᶜr*), specifically at the rhyme, and those encountered both in the Qur'ān and in prose (*kalām*);[22] and the primary difference lay in poetry's having been rendered most typically with final long vowels in pausal (=rhyme) position (*waqf bi t-tarannum*), whereas prose was characterized by pause on consonants or long vowels only (*waqf bi l-iskān*).[23]

H. Birkeland has found these two classes of pausal phenomena to give evidence of different chronological stages of the Arabic language. The poetic language, as it was predominantly manifested in the *qāfiya muṭlaqa* (i.e., with long vowels in pause), "reflects a linguistic stage where in pause, just as in context, short final vowels had not yet been lost. Of course, [the language] was no longer spoken that way. In that respect, the grammarians may be right if they differentiate *kalām* from *šiᶜr* for this reason" (*AP* 14; cf. 104). A further implication, since the *majrā* vowel was expected to be the same throughout the poem and since this usually required the final word to be inflected with that vowel-desinence, was that in the linguistic stage reflected by the poetic *ᶜarabīya*, the *iᶜrāb* system (see chap. 3, §C, below), complete with short vowels and *tanwīn*, was fully operative both at the point of pause and in context (*AP* 18). That such a situation was far removed from the linguistic norm that generally obtained during the sixth and early seventh centuries is indicated, above all, by the relatively high incidence in the classical poetry of the so-called poetic fault called *iqwā'*, involving the variation of the *majrā* vowel (especially between *-ū* and *-ī*). This frequency of *iqwā'* shows that final vowels in pause were no longer differentiated audibly in the poets' living speech, if they were not in fact already dropped altogether (*AP* 13–14; cf. Corriente *FY* 37 n. 26).[24] In the *qāfiya muqayyada*, the Qur'ān, and the grammarian's "*kalām*," on the other hand, one can discern a different stage of the language. Pause with *iskān*, as it is found in these three speech forms and preeminently in the Qur'ān, is reckoned to be unquestionably the prevailing usage in the *ᶜarabīya* in general; for even poetry composed with *qāfiya muṭlaqa* was recited as a rule with the *majrā* left unpronounced (i.e., with *iskān*) or considerably reduced (*AP* 7–8, 18–19, 22–26). Implicit here is a condition in which the actual usage, already well established in the spoken language, entailed the apocopation in pausal position of all final short vowels of inflection (*-u*/*-i*/*-a*) as well as of *tanwīn* suffixes *-un*/*-in*, only *-an* being preserved in the form *-ā*. Naturally this condition would not have come about all at once, nor would it have advanced everywhere at the same rate. The synchronic and frequently "casuistic" pausal systems elaborated by the Muslim grammarians[25] have recorded at least three different vocalic or semi-vocalic accommodations to consonantal pause (*iskān*), which appear to have been essentially phonetic compromises between a synthetic poetic language with (long-vowel) inflectional suffixes at verse-ends and a much more analytic spoken language without them.[26] Nevertheless, what is reflected by such entirely undifferentiating and non-inflectional accommodations to consonantal pause is "a stage where there was still no sharp distinction made, with regard to final vowels, between pause and context" (Birkeland *AP* 104). For the *ᶜarabīya*, of course, this means that these pausal vocalic compromises recalled the more archaic (and difficult-to-adhere-to) system of fully inflected forms with desinence in pause and echoed the final-vowel inflections that regularly occurred in context (cf. Fischer *SVA* 51). But for the spoken dialects of those who employed the *ᶜarabīya* in poetic and formal prose utterances, it means something quite different. Since for the synthetic purpose of designating syntactical relationships these "poetic licenses" were no more helpful than complete apocopation of final vowels (*iskān*), their use at the point of pause, like complete apocopation itself, marks at least "the incipient breakdown of the *iᶜrab* system which was becoming more and more afunctional. Word order gradually displaces the function of the inflectional vowels. This is particularly clear for the genitive, the *-i* of which in general no longer really had a function" (*AP* 47). One even suspects that the breakdown of the *iᶜrāb* system and the disappearance of final short vowels in context was well underway in some, if not most, spoken dialects at the outset of the seventh century. "This development is already signaled in the *ᶜarabīya* where [apocopated] pausal forms could sometimes occur in poetry even in context"

(*AP* 105; cf. 100–102; also Nöldeke *BKPA* 40 and n. 2; Gaudefroy-Demombynes *ILPP* 31–32, 85 nn. 125–26 and references). Although the philologists normally referred to this phenomenon as a poetic license (*darūra*),[27] Birkeland's judgment in such instances must, I think, be upheld: "The so-called poetic licenses are . . . actually not as a rule plucked out of thin air. In most cases they have a basis in the living language" (*AP* 29; cf §§ B.4 and B.5.c, below). Thus, we must presume that the potentiality of using apocopated pausal forms in context, in contrast to standard usage of the *ᶜarabīya*, existed precisely because such was the general practice in one or more spoken dialects upon which the *ᶜarabīya* was founded. And if these "licenses" or "faults" are attested almost entirely in poetry, rather than prose (*AP* 100–102), such a circumstance is perfectly in accord with what has been said with regard to an oral-poetical language: namely, that the introduction of apparent linguistic anomalies and anachronisms into a poetical rendition is largely in response to the prosodic demands at the moment of a given utterance.[28]

B.3.b In confirmation of the preceding view, one can observe the real extent to which the poetic *ᶜarabīya*, despite its apparently archaic pausal tendencies, had been very much affected by the later more general use of pausal apocopated forms. That it was even greater than Birkeland suggests is evident from consideration of the occurence of final consonant clusters (or rather pairs: i.e., *CVCC-*, *katb-*, *kitb-*, *kutb-*) in rhyme position. Disregarding the case where the paired consonants came about simply through gemination (Wright *AG* II 373C; Birkeland *AP* 53; Fleisch *TPA* 175), one finds that the treatment of such pairs in absolute pause presented several problems in pronunciation, which were resolved in nearly all instances (with the debatable exception of accusatives) by interposing some sort of epenthetic or anaptyctic vowel between the two consonants. The "rules" governing the introduction of this vowel were rather complex and perhaps over-elaborated somewhat by the early grammarians in their striving for completeness and systematization. They were applied, in due course, to apocopated pausal forms in both poetry and *kalām* (see Wright *AG* II 372A; Birkeland *AP* 53-60; Fleisch *TPA* 177–78; Fischer *SVA* 45–46). Now, one finds no instances in classical poetry where the apocopated form *CVCC* occurs as such at rhyme-pause in a *qāfiya muqayyada* (Wright *AG* II 354D; cf. 355D; Fleisch *TPA* 191) and only few in the Qur'ān, where *-Cr* makes up the consonantal pair in the great majority of rhymed *āyas* (e.g., LXXVII: 32–33; LXXXIX:1–5; XCVII: 1–5; CIII: 1–3) and *-Cl* in the next proportion of any significance (e.g., LXXVII:13–14; LXXXVI: 13–14) (cf. Vollers *VSA* 167; Nöldeke/Schwally *GQ* I ; Fischer *SVA* 55).[29] There was, though, no objection whatever to such a form

(*CVCC*) in a *qāfiya mutawātira mujarrada*. In this case the poet would add at the end of each verse the long inflectional vowel of pause with *tarannum*: e.g., *CVCC*+ *-ū/-ī/-ā* (Wright *AG* II 354A, D, 355C). Theoretically, all roots for which words of this form exist,[30] as well as all those having forms *CVCVC* that could be reduced to *CVCC*-,[31] could, therefore, be used for rhyme-words in this *qāfiya*, as in any other *qāfiya muṭlaqa*. As a matter of fact, however, the *qāfiya mutawātira mujarrada* (i.e., where the *rawīy* is preceded by an unvocalized consonant rather than by a long vowel or a diphthong) was rarely used in the classical poetry and even more rarely for poems of any significant length. A survey of close to a thousand *qaṣīdas* of nine or more verses turned up only fifty-two where the rhyme-word was of the form *CVCC$\bar{V}$*; and out of these fifty-two, the *rawīy* consonant in over 60 percent of the poems was *-r* or *-l*, and *-m* was a distant third, accounting for only 11.5 percent.[32]

Undoubtedly there were a number of factors restricting the use of *CVCC* forms as rhyme-words. Certainly their monovocalic pattern, limited chiefly to abstract, infinitive, and plural substantives, offered fewer morphological possibilities for verse-end (and hence clause-end) position than even the simple bivocalic forms *CVCVC*-, which included most verbs as well as many nouns. The question of lexical availability—i.e., just the *number* of such forms that existed for final radicals, other than *-r* and *-l*—would have to be answered also. I do not know of any reliable statistics on how often the various consonants occur in rhyme position, much less how often they occur as final radical in words of *CVCC* pattern. But a very general and quite inconclusive estimate, based on the relative number of pages devoted to each letter in the *Qāmūs* (entries arranged according to the last radical), suggests that the overwhelming preference for *rawīys -r* and *-l* in *qāfiya mutawātira mujarrada* results, in part at least, from a probably greater selection of roots with these consonants as final radical.[33] *Rawīy -m*, the next runner-up, also ranks third after *-r* and *-l* in number of pages allotted. Yet there the correspondence seems to cease. Other much-dealt-with consonants, such as *-b*, *-ᶜ*, *-f*, or *-n*, are very seldom found as *rawīy* in classical poems whose verses end in *CVCC* forms (although they do occur more frequently in later *literate* poems).

The phonological basis of rhyme and its relation to the phonetic structure of the language are well beyond the scope of this study.[34] Yet it is evident, I think, that the predominance of *-r* and *-l* in the situation under discussion is not simply due to their greater lexical availability.[35] If it were, then why would there not be a proportionate number of rhymes with the other consonants? One might, indeed, expect fewer, but hardly the utter paucity that we find for most of them. I believe the explanation is suggested by the Qur'ānic usages of *CVCC* forms in pausal rhyme, mentioned above. Final *-l* and, above all, final *-r* occur in well over 80 percent of the rhymed *āyas*. Now, since it has been established that pause with *iskān* was basic to rendition of the Qur'ān, probably from its earliest revelation on, we can be sure that, e.g., *al-qadri* was regularly pronounced by many reciters with some sort of anaptyctic interconsonantal vowel—*al-qadVr* (cf. Vollers *VSA* 167; also above). This becomes doubly certain when we recall that such anaptyxis (*CVCC*>*CVCVC*) was precisely one of the most characteristic features of Ḥijāzī speech and would have been conditioned, for the most part, by the absence of final vowels (see Vollers *VSA* 16–17, 97–100; Rabin *AWA* 3, 97–99; Blachère *HLA* 74). Moreover, in Arabic (as in English), the articulation of resonantal *r* and *l*, immediately preceded by another consonant and especially at the end of an utterance, required a sort of quasi-vocalic accommodation, even with a following vowel.[36] Hence, their resonance already inclined them to an anaptyxis that just became vocalically completed through pause with *iskān*.

B.3.c Applying these observations to the language of poetry, I would submit the following points for consideration. The poetic *ᶜarabīya* displayed as its most conspicuous archaic feature—with respect to the Qur'ān, "*kalām*," and the spoken dialects—the retention of pausal forms with *tarannum* (i.e., final long vowels standing in pause for the short-vowel and *tanwīn* desinences reflecting a much earlier stage of the language). There are several indications that the poets actually spoke, or were closely acquainted with, linguistic usages that no longer employed final short vowels or *tanwīn* (except, perhaps, for a generalized undetermined accusative *-an*; cf. below). Furthermore, if the poets responsible for most of the recorded classical poems had actually spoken and thought in a language in which words were regularly articulated with final vowels or if their poetry had regularly been composed and rendered with a complete sense of such a language, then there should have been nothing to prevent the use of *CVCC* forms as rhyme-words in *qāfiya muṭlaqa,* subject only to the limitations imposed by lexical availability.[37] But the poets whose works remain tended very much to avoid such rhyme-words because, in all likelihood, *CVCC* just did not commonly occur as a pausal form in their spoken language or, in many cases, as a contextual form, except perhaps where liason (*waṣl*) or genitive construction (*iḍāfa*) may have permitted addition of an intervening auxiliary vowel of indeterminate quality (e.g., *al-uḏn-V ṣ-ṣaġīr, ᶜumr-V Muḥammad*; otherwise: *uḏVn*, *ᶜumVr*). If *CVCC* patterns with final *-r* and *-l* were employed as rhyme-words with comparative frequency, that was because such words could most easily and unobtrusively fluctuate between a *de jure* pause with *tarannum* and a *de facto* pause with *iskān*.

Fleisch (*TPA* 191) readily acknowledges that the non-occurrence of rhyme-words with final paired consonants in *qāfiya muqayyada* indicates dialectal influence on the poetical language. I would hold, further, that their rare and highly select occurrence in *qāfiya muṭlaqa*, where one could expect much more freedom of choice, is just as much an indication of dialectal influence. The poetic *ᶜarabīya* did indeed preserve the indisputable archaism of pause with *iᶜrāb*. But at the stage reflected by most of our poems, it was heading, albeit gradually and far behind the spoken language, away from this synthetic usage toward that of the Qur'ān and toward the analytic usage of modern Bedouin poetry. It may be of interest that most of the poems with *CVCC* rhymes, where the *rawīy* is other than *-r*, *-l*, or *-m*, have been ascribed to very early poets and so may retain through successive renditions a feature more characteristic of a bygone period of more widespread competence in formulating verses with pausal *iᶜrāb*.[38]

B.3.d Whether any definite connection can be established between a higher or lower frequency of *CVCC$\bar{V}$* rhymes and the much-discussed East-West dialectal cleavage, I am not prepared to say. One thing is certain, though. The poetic *ᶜarabīya* was, even more than Birkeland has pointed out, in a state of transition from a linguistic form that was synthetic to a high degree and whose synthetic character was *everywhere* manifested by final inflectional vowels, into one that kept that synthetic archaism of assonantal rhyme under the conditions of formal intonation or cantillation, but that actually was better suited for producing simple consonantal rhyme without the complication of case and mood endings.[39] That some poets developed greater skill than others in adapting their more analytic speech patterns to this synthetic diction so essential to poetry was only natural and undoubtedly often a result of their stricter formation in the *rāwī* apprenticeship (see chap. 2, § D, above). In fact, given the absolute indispensability, for really successful Arabic versification, of rendering each verse with an identical and invariable rhyming sound (*rawīy* in the sense of consonant *plus* vowel), it is hardly surprising that the entire process of so rendering, and of learning how to so render, poems (*riwāya*) would have been felt as one of properly reiterating the *rawīy*. And to do this the *rāwī*, following the poet (*šāᶜir*: one who knows how, is aware), had to master those desinential inflections (*iᶜrāb*) that set off the *rawīy*, that constituted the hallmark of the poetic *ᶜarabīya*, and that required considerable reflection and deliberation (*rawīya*) for consistent and meaningful formulation into one fine verse after another from beginning to end of a poem (cf. chap. 2, n. 105).

The feature that has been considered here—the paucity of CVCC-rhymes where the *rawīy* would require a vowel for proper articulation—is merely another index, perhaps more striking than many, (1) of how very remote from most of the spoken forms of Arabic was the diction of the classical poetry; (2) of what hurdles of language and style the aspiring Arab poet had to overcome; and (3) of how applicable to the classical poetic *ᶜarabīya* is Parry's "first principle" for understanding the traditional language of an oral poetry: "The spoken dialect of the author of an oral poem is shown by his poetic language wherever he has no metrical reason to use an older or foreign word or form or construction" (*SET* II 20 = *MHV* 340). In the Arabic tradition there was a compelling reason to use the older synthetic inflections in pausal position. But it is exactly through the virtual elimination from this position of nearly all the (theoretically quite acceptable) *CVCC* forms, except such as could be easily articulated without final vowels, that we are made most aware of the essentially analytic and predominantly noninflectional character that seems to have prevailed in the speech underlying the poetry.

B.4 Among other archaic or dialectal features peculiar to the *ᶜarabīya* of the poets were a good number of "poetic licenses"—*ḍarūrāt aš-šᶜir,* "necessities" or "constraints" of poetry, as they were called. Rabin states that "we know that poetic license often reflects archaic or dialect usage" (*AWA* 89; cf. 131 and passim; also Birkeland, cited p. 106, above). And the result is often such that we can say, as has G. Jacob, that "poetry employs new linguistic material alongside of the old" (*AB* 199; cf. Chantraine's remark, pp. 97–98, above). Jacob's examples include the often-recurring instances of *-ū* suffixed to the second- and third-person masculine plural pronominal forms (*humū*, *antumū*, *katabtumū*, and so on) and of a vocalic form of the first-person singular suffix (*-iya*/*-niya*). Both of these suffixed vowels occur in poetry in situations where they are unnecessary for purposes of liaison with *alif al-waṣl* (Jacob *AB* 199). These forms are seen without question to be retentions of a much older Semitic pronominal usage (ibid.; cf. Fleisch AC² 136, 138); and the facts that they are virtually nonexistent in prose[40] and that they vary freely in poetry with the standard pronominal forms (*-um* and *ī*/*-nī*), their occurrence being determined only by the needs of prosody, suggest them to be at least similar in nature and function to analogous features in the Homeric language (see nn. 2, 3). W. Wright offers a more comprehensive list of such licenses, one of which in particular is "the employment of ancient uncontracted forms instead of the more modern contracted ones" (*AG* II 374–90, esp. 378–79). W. Caskel has noted as another archaic feature of the classical poetic diction "the fact that diptota and triptota are not yet strictly distinguished" (in von

Grunebaum *SICH* 37; cf. Birkeland *AP* 48–52; Fleisch *TPA* 277–80). Yet, once again, the distinction in the inflections is made sheerly on the basis of metrical position.[41] Alfred Bloch, too, has indicated one of the few syntactical anomalies apparently unique to poetry: namely, the interposition of a substantive in temporal *iḏā* clauses between the conjunction and the verb. For Rabin this construction "appears to be an archaism preserving the emphatic demonstrative character of the particle" (*BCA* 30).

B.5.a The widely diverse tribal dialects proved an even richer source of alternative forms suited to every possible metrical position and providing many a critical rhyme-word. It is to the poets' freely drawing upon dialectal usage whenever their rendition necessitated that one can often trace a large share of the morphologically distinct, but semantically identical, expressions so typical of the classical poetic language. Such expressions would include, for example, the various more or less equivalent forms of demonstrative pronouns (Fleisch *AC*² 139–43; Rabin *AWA* 120, 152–54), of verbal nouns (Fleisch *AC*² 91 and n. 1, 109–10; idem *TPA* 351–52, 354 n. 1), and of broken plurals (Fleisch *TPA* 471–72). Differences in dialectal usage incorporated into the *ᶜarabīya* have also been felt to lie behind the origin of many of the so-called *aḍdād*, words with two (real or imaginary) opposite meanings.[42] Jacob (*AB* 199–201) and Rabin (*AWA* 73, 77, 90, and passim) give several other instances of dialectisms that were in current use by the classical poets, irrespective of their own tribal affiliation in many cases; and these instances could undoubtedly be multiplied.

One might add further that much of the often-mentioned stock of synonyms and near synonyms that are to be met with in classical Arabic poetry, covering a wide range of objects, activities, and concepts, can be presumed to reflect individual tribal usages as they came to be absorbed into the common poetic vocabulary of Arabic-speaking poets (even though such words might still be found more often among the tribes in whose dialects they originated).[43]

B.5.b That the interdialectal (or perhaps transdialectal) nature of the *ᶜarabīya* was fully recognized by the early Muslim philologists and Qur'ānic authorities (who would have been, after all, in a much better position to judge than we are) can be seen in their fairly general acceptance of the syllogistic fiction that became the traditional explanation for the language of the Qur'ān. This explanation, which seems first to have found currency among the Kūfan scholars and *qurrā'*, was framed to account for both the pious assumption of the linguistic excellence—even superiority—of the Qur'ān[44] and the undeniable presence of various dialectisms in the Qur'ānic language.[45] The tradition that arose has it, first of all, that the language of the Qur'ān, being identical with that of the poetry, forms together with it the basis of the ^{c}*arabīya*. The Prophet, who was Meccan by origin, would of course have received and delivered his Revelations only in his own dialect, that of Qurayš. Thus, the classical ^{c}*arabīya* is what the Meccan Qurayš spoke naturally (cf. Blachère *Intro* 157; Rabin *BCA* 22).

Now, the infiltration of other dialectisms into this super-dialect of Qurayš was rationalized by al-Farrā' (d. 207/822) as an index of its very preeminence over other vernaculars. For just as Qurayš chose for wives the finest of women from among all the Arabs who regularly made pilgrimage to Mecca during the Jāhilīya, and thus

> gained superiority besides those qualities by which they were [already] particularly distinguished, . . . [i]n the same way they were accustomed to hear from the tribes of the Arabs their dialects; so they could choose from every dialect that which was the best in it. So their speech became elegant and nothing of the more vulgar forms of speech was mixed up with it. . . . Correctness came to them in their selection of pronunciation just as they selected their wives. (Trans. in Kahle *ARK* 70)[46]

Although we can acknowledge that al-Farrā' has evoked here a fair superficial picture of the classical ^{c}*arabīya* (though, of course, not of the actual dialect of Qurayš), we can also see that, as an etiological theory, his rationale has no more validity than the ancient view that Homer acquired his language through his travels to different dialect-areas where Greek was spoken (see pp. 98–99 above). The supposition that either a single man or even a single group of men could spontaneously create a poetic language is, in Parry's opinion, simply without foundation: "A poetic language, it is clear, is poetic only by a convention shared by the poet and his hearers, so that the growth of a poetic language must be gradual" (Parry *SET* II 2; cf. 7–8 = *MHV* 326; cf. 330).

B.5.c With reference to both the archaistic and dialectal elements in the poetic ^{c}*arabīya*, it cannot be emphasized too much that these "retentions" and "borrowings" existed and were used in the poetic diction precisely because they adequately and quite satisfactorily functioned in specific prosodic contexts. As features of an intertribal oral-traditional mode of expression, such forms often lost the particular semantic or morphological nuances they may have enjoyed at one time or within one tribe. They became, in many instances, conventionalized—one might say, "homogenized." As a result, constructions peculiar to a certain dialect could show up in works attributed to poets of quite different speech-groups, the precondition of their occurrence being, of course, their functionality in the poetic verse. Vollers (*VSA* 132), for example, adduced the ^{c}Uṯmānic Qur'ānic reading *ẓalta/u* (in XX:97,

LVI:65; for *ẓaliltalu*) as a Ḥijāzī vernacular residue missed by those who allegedly redacted the text of the Qur'ān along Eastern dialectal lines. But, as R. Geyer has made quite clear (rev *VSA* 14), not only does an uncontracted form (*ẓalilna*) occur in poems by such genuine Ḥijāzīs as Ḥassān b. Ṯābit, but also a contracted form (*ẓaltu*) is attested in a line of the Eastern Asadī, ᶜAbīd b. al-Abraṣ. Moreover, "the ᶜUqail, who often appear together with the Qais [= Eastern] tribes Ghanī and Kilāb, are said to have used *ẓiltu* in poetry, though it was not of their dialect" (Rabin *AWA* 163). Considering how frequently the third-person *ẓalla* (or *fa/wa-ẓalla*) stands as a verse-opening formula (see pp. 51–52 above), it is not surprising to find its metrical equivalent (*ẓaltu/a*) taken over from the Western dialects to fill the same slot for the first and second persons. Similar instances, Geyer feels, could be produced in fairly large number, warning us against too readily assuming a definitive cleavage between tribal dialects (rev *VSA* 14–15; but cf. Rabin *AWA* 1–5). Warning us, too, I would add, that factors other than purely linguistic may have been operating in the selection of speech forms and constructions—factors closely connected with the processes and requirements of oral-poetic rendition.

One more possible result of this "homogenization" of dialectisms may have been that fine distinctions in meaning could be overlooked or set aside in choosing one near-synonym rather than another to fill a certain metrical or rhyme position under the pressures of rendition. G. Wiet has written:

> The synonyms for animal names . . . represent specific terms borrowed from a tribal linguistic atlas, and the same perhaps holds for features of the terrain or the characteristics of watering places. This diversity of vocabulary has given rise to the supposition that the Arabic language was extremely rich in substantives for designating topographical prominences, rainstorms, or the qualities and defects of things. But, apart from this fact that certain words were of dialectal origin, they were sometimes shifted from their overly precise denotations where called for by the meter or the rhyme; they then became generic terms (*ILA* 23; also Wild *KA* 50–51 and n. 139; but cf. Fleisch *TPA* 327–28).

Perhaps an illustration of this phenomenon is to be seen in Abū ᶜUbayd al-Qāsim b. Sallām's[47] "Treatise on Dialect Words in the Qur'ān" (*Risāla fī mā warada fi l-qur'ān min luġāt al-qabā'il*). Of this work Rabin remarks, "The dialect meanings recorded in the Risāla hardly ever fit the passage they are supposed to elucidate" (*AWA* 7). Although I have not myself been able to examine Abū ᶜUbayd's *Risāla*, Rabin's observation seems to give evidence of a trend toward generality or homogeneity of meaning, or at least away from an originally greater specificity.

A somewhat similar phenomenon can be noticed in the case of the many place-names mentioned throughout the classical poetry. This wide-ranging poetic toponymy was without doubt founded on the nomadic Bedouin's intimate knowledge of his Arabian homeland and corresponded to the reality of his migratory itinerary. Accordingly it can be—and has been—utilized in geographical studies and descriptions of the peninsula and in tracing the movements of the pre-Islamic tribes.[48] But the impression that emerges from reading a fairly large number of *qaṣīdas* is that many, perhaps most, of these toponyms are to a great extent interchangeable, depending very much upon the prosodic function to be fulfilled in a given verse. C. Lyall noted the tendency of pre-Islamic Taġlibī poets, whose terriotory lay mainly in Mesopotamia, Iraq, and the Syrian desert, to refer to sites located primarily in East Central Arabia: "It is not improbable that the poets of Taghlib used the names of these old settlements in the preludes to their *qaṣidahs* as part of the old poetic convention" (*Muf* II 156, n. to XLII:8). Alfred Bloch, proceeding from his highly original analysis of the *qaṣīda* structure,[49] thinks that the series of place-names "perhaps arise out of ancient mnemonic verses (*Merkverse*), by means of which one reminded oneself (or the sender of the message reminded his messenger) of the way-stations along the route that was to be followed; these places, then, were readapted, in conformity with the sustaining fiction of the *qaṣīda*, to signify encampments abandoned by the beloved's tribe: one pretended to journey toward them out of yearning for the [lost] love" (*Qas* 126). Thus, these toponyms, as well as those used in the sequences describing rainstorms (*ibid.*), served essentially as thematic devices whose precise signification, like that of many other quasi-synonyms in the classical Arabic of poetry, was qualified by, or subordinated to, their function in the poetic line. Not that they would have been used indiscriminately or without due regard to patent geographical absurdities; on the contrary, most of the passages where place-names appear show a noticeable sense of accuracy, appositeness, and evocative power in the choice of such names (see, e.g., Thilo *OAP* 9–12; Blachère *HLA* 44–42). But toponyms were intrinsic to one of the most conspicuous formulaic usages in the *qaṣīda*: the sequential listing of campsites anomalously coordinated with *fa*, rather than *wa* (see App. A, l. 1 comment). Morphologically, they offered a variety of alternatives for filling particular metrical or rhyme positions. The imprecisions, errors, and even "falsifications" of toponymy that U. Thilo speaks about (*OAP* 14–15) would not have been due, therefore, just to "mistakes in oral and written transmission"; nor should they, as Goldziher seems to imply, be taken at face value for indices of a poem's genuineness, insofar as one could ascertain "whether the places actually lay in the territory of the tribe to which the traditionally designated composer belonged'' (*AAP* 128). Within an oral-formulaic tradition of poetry, such as the sixth and seventh century Arabs were likely to have had, a certain homogeneity of usage in the sphere of toponymy must have prevailed, just as it did in other nomenclatural spheres; and such a homogeneity, growing out of a fairly standardized inherited and (to a great extent) intertribal system of formulas, would quite naturally engender some uncertainties, confusions, and inconsistencies of a geographical kind similar to other kinds that seem to be typical of oral poetry almost wherever found.[50]

B.6 How to interpret the stabilization of *a* in the imperfect preformative of classical Arabic (*yAkta/i/ubu*) presents an especially interesting problem in this context. It is difficult to regard the *a*-preformatives, as Rabin does (*AWA* 61, 90, 206), as an old, inherited archaism in Arabic that was retained after the later importation of *i*-preformatives from the Canaanite area had come to predominate in the Eastern dialects and possibly in some of the Western ones as well. Ariel Bloch has argued convincingly that in the old Arabic dialects ''*i*-imperfect is not secondary but existed side by side with *a*-imperfect, the forms being distributed according to Barth's Law [i.e., one form with *i*-preformatives and *a* in the stem (*yiktabu*) and another with *a*-preformatives and *i* or *u* in the stem (*yakti/ubu*)], and that dialectal *i*-imperfect is the result of a generalization'' (*VIP* 28).[51] Because the *i*-imperfect was also attested in the West, specifically among a part of the Hu̱dayl (Rabin *AWA* 61, 90), if not among other groups as well, Bloch assumes the known prevalence of *a*-imperfect in other parts of the Western dialect-area (especially the Ḥijāz) to ''have been generalized, like in Classical Arabic'' (*VIP* 27 n. 18); but he gives no suggestion as to which generalization—that of the dialects or that of the classical, if either—may have been prior. It is important to remember, however, that the linguistic evolution that led to the formation of Middle and Modern Arabic dialects seems to have affected the Bedouin dialects too—both ''originally'' Eastern and ''originally'' Western ones—in certain generally homogeneous ways, and that one of the most characteristic of these became the practically universal occurrence of *i*-imperfect as standard dialectal usage.[52] Now, the language of the poets may not already have been standardized with *a*-preformatives in the imperfect by Muḥammad's time: the vaunted linguistic—or more correctly, stylistic—superiority of Hu̱dayl (many of whom employed the *i*-imperfect in their speech),[53] the existence of a number of Qur'ānic readings with *i*-preformatives attributed to Eastern *qurrā'* (Vollers *VSA* 129; cf. Rabin *AWA* 158; Bloch *VIP* 25),[54] and the fact that ''basically the Eastern dialects are the same as the Classical Arabic of the poets'' (Rabin *AWA* 1, 96 and passim)—all suggest, though they do not prove, that these particular vowels may have been pronounced in accordance with the poet's native dialect, thus *i* and *a*, alternating according to Barth's Law (with *i* gradually prevailing), in the East and *a* alone in the Ḥijāz.[55] If, then, Rabin is correct in saying that "the pronunciation of the literary [!] language in the mouth of the Ḥijazis was of course largely accommodated to their native dialect" (*AWA* 3–4; cf. Nöldeke *NBSS* 3–4; also Parry's "first principle," above), then it would follow that the imperfect with *a*-preformatives could be a typical feature of Qur'ānic *ᶜarabīya* (but *not necessarily* of the poetic *ᶜarabīya* as a whole). Subsequently this usage, confirmed and reproduced by at least a first generation of Ḥijāzī *qurrā'*, could in turn have been assimilated to the language of poetic rendition in general; both because of the steadily increasing prestige of the Book itself among Arab Muslims, as well as their growing familiarity with its literal wording, and also (perhaps more importantly from our point of view) because so many of the more prominent patrons of poets during the first decades of Islam were themselves Ḥijāzīs (Qurayš, Ṯaqīf, the Anṣār, and so on) and hence liable to expect—even to insist upon—poetical renditions embodying their own (*and* the Qur'ānic) pronunciation. Such a development, leading to a general adoption of the *a*-imperfect in the poetic *ᶜarabīya* of the early Islamic period, could have been somewhat accelerated or reinforced out of a stylistically induced polarization in reaction to the drift prevalent in the urban, and ultimately in the Bedouin, vernaculars toward a stabilized *i*-imperfect.

Admittedly these remarks are largely conjectural. Yet it remains true that the generalized *a*-imperfect in classical Arabic, ordinarily considered an anomalous feature with reference to other Semitic languages (cf. Nöldeke *NBSS* 3 n. 1) and with reference to all living Arabic dialects, has not so far been explained in linguistically satisfactory terms. Seen as an element of a traditional oral-poetic diction unconsciously readjusted and adapted by oral poets to startlingly new sociolinguistic and geopolitical conditions and to audiences become perhaps rather more aware of dialectal differences, the *a*-preformative in the imperfect might be more legitimately accounted for than upon purely linguistic grounds (cf. Blachère *HLA* 79 n. 3).

C. There has never been any question, from the earlist Muslim era (if not before as well) to the present day, that the single most essential and distinctive feature of the poetic *ᶜarabīya* is its capacity for synthetic expression through desinential inflection—i.e., the *iᶜrāb*. Aḥmad b. Fāris (d. 295/1005), calling poets the "princes of speech" (*umarā' al-kalām*) and listing a number of linguistic or stylistic liberties they may permit themselves, then adds emphatically: "But as for faults in handling the case- and mood-endings (*laḥn fi* *l-iᶜrāb*) or improper usage of a word, they may not do that!'' (*SFL* 275; also in Suyūṭī *Muz* II 471).[56]

There has, however, been a great deal of question—most of it during this century—as to whether the *iᶜrāb* was a phenomenon unique to the poetic *ᶜarabīya* or whether it existed among the spoken vernaculars as well. Muslim tradition, as was seen, held that the *ᶜarabīya* of the poetry and the Qur'ān—complete with its *iᶜrāb* vowel- and *tanwīn*-suffixes—was identical with the dialect regularly spoken by Qurayš and, to a similar degree, the dialects spoken among most of the Bedouin tribes, particularly those of Najd and Eastern Arabia. During the flourishing age of Arabic philological activity (second/eighth–fifth/twelfth centuries), anecdotes proliferated on the subject of the Bedouin's natural linguistic superiority and correctness and his disinclination—even inability—to err in using the case- and mood-endings.[57]

C.1.a In 1906 K. Vollers published his epoch-making (cf. Geyer rev *VSA* 12) treatise *Volkssprache und Schriftsprache im alten Arabien*, in which he concluded that the Qur'ān was first uttered by the Prophet in a Ḥijāzī vernacular that lacked many of the features we normally associate with the classical *ᶜarabīya*. Chief among these missing features were the articulated glottal stop (*hamza*), various nominal and verbal forms, and, above all, the desinential inflections—the *iᶜrāb*.[58] With reference to the latter particularly, Vollers expressed (with emphasis) the following opinion:

> Far from being a self-evident binding observance (*Pflicht*), growing out of the common linguistic usage, *iᶜrāb* already at the Prophet's time was perhaps the special property of certain tribes; for the rest, it was only the prerogative of more elevated discourse—to be more specific, probably just of the strict, metrically based poetry. (*VSA* 169)

Vollers questioned, too, whether a given suffix ever had the grammatical function so confidently assigned to it in the standardized *ᶜarabīya* of a subsequent age, since ''there seem to have been dialects that recognized only two suffixes or indeed only one'' (*VSA* 169–70). Still, the true character of *iᶜrāb* might be sought in the etymology of the world itself, which means (according to J. Wetzstein) ''to bedouinize'' (*Beduinisierung*)—i.e., to translate into the nomadic idiom from another one (*VSA* 171).[59] So, given the social geography of pre-Islamic Arabia, one ought, Vollers contends, to understand what is implied by the near coincidence of the division between users and non-users of *iᶜrāb*, on the one hand, and the East-West cleavage between Tamīm and the Ḥijāzī tribes, on the other. It was, he states, ''not that *iᶜrāb* was altogether missing in the West, nor that in the East there was no speech without *iᶜrāb*;

but rather that the East was preeminently the land of the nomads and their own unique language" (*VSA* 172). Thus, Vollers seems to say that the *i^{c}rāb*, so essential to the poetic *^{c}arabīya*, was to be found as a feature of a spoken vernacular only among the Bedouin tribes (where it was to be found at all) and, hence, mainly in the East; whereas in the more sedentarized West, it was retained simply as an element of "more elevated discourse"—of an *^{c}arabīya* borrowed from the Bedouins for poetic and other highly formalized purposes. Muhammad, then, as well as his fellow Ḥijāzīs (both urbanized and urban-influenced), spoke an idiom that lacked precisely that feature most characteristic of their poetic *^{c}arabīya*—the *i^{c}rāb*.

C.1.b I do not follow Vollers in his conclusion that the Qur'ān itself was initially delivered in this *i^{c}rāb*-less and, in other respects, generally colloquial speech, and that it was only later redacted on the basis of forms, constructions, and principles deduced from the language of poetry. The arguments of Geyer (rev *VSA*), Nöldeke (*NBSS* 1–5), Blachère (*HLA* 75–79; *Intro* 159–69), Rabin (*AWA* 3–4; *BCA*; "Arabiyya" EI^2 I 565b-66a), Bell/Watt (*Intro* 82–85), and others have practically demolished any validity this aspect of Vollers's work may ever have had. The important studies of P. Kahle (CG^2 141–49, 345–46; *QA*; *ARK*), who adduces a body of traditions and a passage by al-Farrā' purporting to prove that the Qur'ān was recited at the earliest period without *i^{c}rāb*, have not been notably successful in rehabilitating Vollers' main thesis (see, e.g., Rabin *BCA* 25–29), although they do provide valuable material on the sociolinguistic situation during the early Islamic period, relative to the Qur'ān and native speakers of Arabic (see chap. 3, §C.6, below; cf. also Corriente *FY* 38–40).

C.2 A good deal of the discussion on all sides, however, has been colored by sociological, ethnological, and aesthetic preconceptions similar to those outlined previously in the case of folklore scholarship. (chap. 1, §C, above, and Zwettler *BFOT*).There has too frequently been an assumption—usually implicit but sometimes, as with Geyer, quite explicit—that a really prestigious *Dichtersprache* (a literary *Hochsprache* or *Kunstdialekt*) necessarily went hand in hand with superior social status and/or more advanced (literary) culture and education. Thus, on the one hand, the poetic *^{c}arabīya* would have to be accepted more or less as the naturally spoken language of the Bedouins because, in their primitive and culturally homogeneous environment, one could scarcely expect the poetic idiom to have been very far removed from the vernacular; and so, both would of course have shared the typical feature of *i^{c}rāb*. If anything, Geyer says (in a passage that requires no comment),

> we may consider the *Dichtersprache* quite as having played an intermediary role between the dialects of the tribes and the personal idioms of individuals, though without a consciously and artfully set-up distinction existing between it and the spoken language. Besides, there could never have been a *Literatur-* or *Schriftsprache* proper among the Bedouins of early Arabia: the written fixation of "literature" was missing, as was the use of a select and special language by a caste of nobles or an upper social stratum (*Oberschict*) separated in some other way. (rev *VSA* 15; cf. nn. 15, 60, 93 to this chapter)

That some sort of stylized and artifical speech form might arise without the use of writing and out of what would be called the *Volk* did not occur to Geyer, whose argument is founded upon highly questionable and superficial premises and an overriding conviction that *Literatur* is inseparable from *Schrift*.

On the other hand, Geyer continues, this same *ᶜarabīya* would have been adopted by the urban "patrician" classes of the Ḥijāz as their distinctive idiom because of its close association with their aristocratic Bedouin heritage (rev *VSA* 15–19, 54). For Muḥammad and the Meccan Qurayš the use of *iᶜrāb* would have been acquired along with the other elements of an upper-class *Schriftsprache*,[60] the *ᶜarabīya*, which they would have spoken in evidence of their social and cultural superiority. Hence (according to Geyer), contrary to Vollers's thesis, Muḥammad would of course have "written"[61] the Qur'ān (which as his "*kitāb*"—scripture—was "primarily a literary product") using the *ᶜarabīya* with its full *iᶜrāb* system, since "whoever wished to achieve a literary effect in Mecca could use no other language but the *ᶜarabīya*" (rev *VSA* 18). No one who set out to influence the "patricians" of Mecca, by means of a work of such a sacred and artistic character, would have considered using the *iᶜrāb*-less *Vulgärsprache* (so well described by Vollers), spoken by the urban "plebians" of the Ḥijāz.

C.3.a Geyer's solid refutations of Vollers's views on the language of the Qur'ān, and particularly his complete revaluation of the evidence from Qur'ānic rhyme (rev *VSA* 20–54), are quite conclusive, and were, on the whole, accepted as such by Th. Nölkeke (*NBSS* 1-5). Nöldeke, however, very rightly does not agree with Geyer's dubiously founded judgment

> that Vollers may at least have proven that at Mecca there existed a language of the common man (the *ᶜāmma*), diverging sharply from the *Hochsprache* of Muhammad and his compeers. Something of the like might be supposed on general grounds, but it still remains to be seen whether it is correct, were more to be understood thereby than that the slaves imported from Africa or other foreign lands may not have expressed themselves quite properly or may have had their own idioms. (*NBSS* 4; cf. Spitaler rev *Ar* 145b)

On the subject of any serious dislocation of the poetic speech (and that of the Qur'ān) from the spoken language, Nöldeke expressed himself quite clearly in a prior study (also directed against Vollers' theory in its preliminary form). There, in opposition to Vollers' denial that the classical *^{c}arabīya* was a living language in Muḥammad's Mecca and his doubts with regard to the Bedouin dialects as well, Nöldeke writes:

> On the contrary, it is for me very unlikely that Muḥammad would have employed in the Qur'ān a form of speech utterly different from that which was customary in Mecca—that, in particular, he would have brought into play the case- and mood-endings (*i^{c}rāb*) with as much care as possible if his compatriots had not used them. And similarly I take it for granted that the poetry of that period represents the language which the Bedouins spoke then and for quite some time thereafter. (*BSS* 2; cf. Blachère *HLA* 77)

Elsewhere Nöldeke is even more specific on the question of the Qur'ānic language: the linguistic form visible in the consonantal text of the Qur'ān exhibits no outstanding influence from an actually spoken language that differed substantially as to desinential inflection. Such influence is usually to be expected in the case of an artificially framed hieratic language, but none—other than formalized departures from everyday speech typical, Nöldeke alleges, of "the Oriental"—can be found. Hence, he concludes, "it may be said with assurance: *had the Prophet and the faithful of his time uttered the Qur'ān without* i^{c}rāb, *the tradition thereof would not have disappeared without a trace*" (*NBSS* 2).

In *BSS* 2–7 and passim, Nöldeke adduces evidence from comparative Semitics, Islamic cultural history, and modern (i.e., late nineteenth-century) Arabic dialects, with the intent of verifying the presence of *i^{c}rāb* suffixes in spoken Arabic of the seventh century. In *NBSS* 4 and note 3, referring to the ^{c}Uṯmānic text of the Qur'ān, he points to the only two definite instances, "alongside of numerous 'correct' forms," of the oblique case of the sound masculine plural [*īn*] being written where the nominative [*ūn*] would be expected according to the *i^{c}rāb* norm (II:177/2; IV:162/0).[62] All that is proven there, he says, is simply "that in Mecca, and in Yaṯrib [= Medina] as well, the strict *^{c}arabīya* had already begun to devolve into the later *Vulgärsprache*."

C.3.b I do not think that Nöldeke's evidence for *i^{c}rāb* in the spoken language is at all conclusive.[63] The one clear statement of his opinion (see above) is in essence an assumption, which the findings of P. Kahle have shown to be unfounded to a considerable degree (see §C.6, below). On the other hand, Nöldeke's correction of Vollers' view regarding the "non-canonicity" of the Qur'ānic variants adduced in *VSA* (*NBSS* 1–2); his pointing out that many phenomena attested by the variants, such as the *idġām kabīr* (assimilation of two identical or similar consonants with the omission of an intervening vowel), were not uncharacteristic of conventional modes of recitation (*NBSS* 2); and his notes on the "correctness" of the *iᶜrāb* showing through the Qur'ānic orthography—all refer to traits associated precisely with *formal oral or written rendition of the Qur'ān*. If the Qur'ān had first been delivered in a semi-artificial language evolved out of the exigencies of oral poetry (as will be maintained here)—if, that is, its linguistic usage, together with that of the poetry, had differed markedly from regular casual usage by virtue of its formular and traditional qualities; then these and other traits observable through the text and the "variants" before all else would have to be taken as representing what was deemed essential to *as accurate a transcription as possible* of the verbal form of Muḥammad's message. Of course, in many areas the language of the poems and the Qur'ān would have reflected the spoken language of those who uttered them—or more exactly, from our present point of view, of those from whom they were recorded (cf. Parry *SET* II 20–21 = *MHV* 340). Yet, what these areas were—where the traditional *ᶜarabīya* and spoken idioms overlapped and where they diverged— can be determined only (if, any more, at all) through careful comparative and statistical analysis of all available evidence. Colloquialisms and scribal errors must certainly be taken into account as well. But to conclude the presence of a feature such as *iᶜrāb* in a spoken vernacular from its presence in works that may well have been composed in a traditional formulaic language would seem to be circular reasoning at best, especially if one had set out to prove the identity of both speech-forms in the first place (cf. §C.4.b, below).

I must agree with Nöldeke that the presence of *iᶜrāb* in the classical *ᶜarabīya* cannot have been due to a later theoretical regularization imposed by the Muslim philologists and that the short-vowel desinential inflections undoubtedly reflect the living language as it must have been spoken *at some stage*. But it seems to me unjustified to generalize from a final short *a* of the third-person sing. masc. perfect, as preserved in modern Amharic, to a full system of vowel-suffixes for case and mood in early spoken Arabic, particularly when, as Nöldeke himself acknowledges, the Arabic dialects have not shown this feature for at least several centuries (*BSS* 2–3). And so, when he asks, "Why should we now doubt that the poets, for whom the form *faᶜala* was terminated with *-a*, used the form still actually common at their time?" (*BSS* 3), one is tempted to respond, "Why should we not doubt it?"

The statements of the ᶜAbbāsid philologists as to the purity and correctness of Bedouin speech, to which Nöldeke attaches "the greatest weight of all" (*BSS* 4–5), can by no means be taken at face value, as Blachère (*SIIB*) and

Blau (*RBA*) have shown, at least insofar as *iᶜrāb* and other grammatical questions are concerned (see below).

C.4.a What one can validly predicate concerning the state of the ancient dialects from examination of the modern ones, beyond simple continuity of usages, must always remain uncertain. Nöldeke (*BSS* 5–7) and, more recently and in much more detail, Blau (*ELB* App. III, esp. 167–70, 187–212) have given attention to vestiges of *tanwīn* (the desinential suffixes of undefined triptotes: *-un*/*-in*/*-an*) in the modern Bedouin dialects, with the more or less explicit assumption that such vestiges are indicative of an earlier state of full inflection. Yet the facts as gathered from both scholars are (1) that this *tanwīn* feature is recorded, and seems to occur by far the most frequently, in poems and other non-casual utterances of the Bedouins (stories, proverbs, and so forth), borrowings or retentions from the *ᶜarabīya* (usually adverbial), and "fossilized" (*ELB* 191) exclamations of various kinds; (2) that it is almost invariably the suffix *-an*, corresponding to the accusative of the classical, which is to be heard, regardless of the noun's actual grammatical function;[64] and (3) that its *casual* use is always optional.[65]

Given this contemporary state of affairs, it is to be wondered whether anyone would ever have considered proposing that the dialectal *tanwīn* had originated in a three-vowel desinential system, had he not previously been aware that such a system had operated in the classical *ᶜarabīya*. Certainly, by itself this feature of the modern dialects is in no way evidence that Arabic was casually spoken with full *iᶜrāb* at the time of Muḥammad.[66] Rather, there may in fact be reason for believing it represents a continuous usage, at least as regards the language spoken in the Ḥijāz during the early seventh century.

C.4.b It is fairly well established that the writing system in use at Mecca and Medina at the time of Muḥammad, as represented with all its shortcomings in the *scriptio defectiva* of the ᶜUṯmānic Qur'ān text, had been adapted from a Nabatean (or Syro-Aramaic) prototype for the purposes of expressing the Arabic dialect spoken in the Ḥijāzī urban settlements. This is most obvious, without question, from its lack of any provision for indicating the glottal stop (a sound that we know to have been absent from the Ḥijāzī dialects in general) and from other features as well.[67] Now, from one point of view, it will be agreed that the Qur'ānic skeletal text cannot give an accurate picture of the language *exactly* as spoken or recited, since it indicates only consonants and some long vowels (Brockelmann in Spuler *Sem* 216), with words usually written as they were pronounced in pausal form (Nöldeke *BSS* 7; Bergsträsser/Pretzl *GK* 27–31; esp. Birkeland *AP* 10, 19–21; but cf. Fischer *SVA* 53–60). But, from another point of view, one must also consider that, if the Qur'ān were to have been delivered in a traditional language conforming to poetic and other kinds of mantic, non-casual utterances, and if such a language were to have differed from the ordinary speech of Mecca and Medina in important features like the use of *hamza* and *iᶜrāb*, the original transcribers of Muḥammad's delivery (or of his delivery as rendered by those with recognized authority to do so) still would have had no alternative but to employ the only appropriate orthographic system at their disposal: that which was geared to reproducing various forms of expression in the dialectal speech. The several orthographic inconsistencies of the Qur'ānic text, such as the haphazard indication of ā in medial position by *alif* (Bergsträsser/Pretzl *GK* 31–33), of final ī (*GK* 33–35), and others (*GK* 51–53), not to mention again the various scribal compromises associated with representing the *hamza* (n. 67 to this chapter), all suggest that one or the other—perhaps both—of the following circumstances obtained. Either, on the one hand, no orthographic conventions had yet been adopted on any wide-scale basis (a not inconceivable possibility, given the very nature of the *scriptio defectiva*); and hence, no established orthographic procedure existed for consistent and faithful transcription of speech phenomena in extensive works like the Qur'ān. If this had been so, however, it would hardly have accorded with the commercial, political, and religious[68] importance of the Ḥijāzī cities (of Mecca, above all) that had been increasing steadily since about the early fifth century,[69] entailing as well, in N. Abbott's opinion, a concomitant rise in writing activity (*RNAS* 12–14).

The other possible circumstance is, quite simply, that the language in which the Qur'ān had been rendered was, in several conspicuous regards, sufficiently differentiated from the spoken language so that the effectiveness of the available dialectally based orthography was quite limited when it came to transcribing accurately this disparate linguistic form. H. Wehr, in a crucial review of Fück's *ᶜArabīya*, has cogently raised this issue, precisely in the course of arguing for a distinct poetical language separate from the Meccan and most tribal vernaculars. Wehr writes:

> The orthography of the Qur'ān is no valid argument [against Muḥammad's having delivered the Qur'ān in a poetic *Hochsprache* divergent from his own idiom]; for the written form must not be considered in any way identical with Muḥammad's pronunciation, as it often tacitly is. We know that, long before the Qur'ān was recorded, writing was already in use at Mecca and Medina for everyday as well as commercial purposes; and of course one hardly wrote in the poetic language, but rather in the way one spoke. Where writing is carried on, there is a more or less fixed orthography. The essential colloquial features of the Qur'ānic orthography—the absence of nunation and also of the glottal stop within words and at the ends of syllables (*bīr, mūmin, nāyim*, etc.)—no doubt

> result from this earlier orthography which reproduced the dialect; and they were carried over when the problem arose of setting down the pronunciation of the *ᶜarabīya* by means of the orthography available at the time. (rev. *Ar* 184)

C.4.c One will concede, with Wehr, the speculative nature of these remarks. But surely it is not unreasonable to look at the ᶜUṯmānic text as a "compromise solution" to the problem of having to use an orthographic system conforming to the spoken vernacular in order to transcribe utterances delivered in a linguistic form that could have differed from it considerably in phonology and morphology. This is certainly just as reasonable as assuming, for instance, that later scholars could have gotten away with such a wholesale "improvement" of Muḥammad's pronunciation as arbitrarily introducing the glottal stop, if they had not had reliable information that, e.g., when *s-y*(unpointed)-*l* had first been written *su'ila* had been heard (Nöldeke *BSS* 11; but cf. Fleisch *TPA* 100 n. 4). The usual argument that the *hamza* was introduced later in accordance with the usage of the poetic *ᶜarabīya* could scarcely be maintained when one considers that that very *ᶜarabīya*, with the selfsame feature (which would have been, for the Ḥijāz, an archaism; cf. *BSS* 11), could well have constituted the original speech-form of the Qur'ān. Even the reports of some early opposition to introducing the *hamza* into the Qur'ānic text and recitation[70] are not very convincing, while those favoring the addition of *hamza* quite clearly present Qur'ānic usage in that regard both as a very real phenomenon and as an anomaly that contrasted sharply with the normal speech of the Ḥijāz and even with the Prophet's own idiom (Rabin *AWA* 144–45).[71]

Similarly, there are the seemingly unregulated orthographic treatment of final long-vowels *-ī*/*-ū* and the total non-representation of final *tanwīn* *-in*/*-un*.[72] These, too, could have resulted from failures of the conventional writing system to cope with word-end articulations, for the transcription of which it had not been designed. I am aware that such orthographic traits are usually attributed to the presumed custom of dictating each word or short word group in its isolated pausal form (see above); and thereby most of the omissions of *waw* and many of *yā'*, when they would have been shortened through liaison (*waṣl*), can certainly be understood, as can several other apparent inconsistencies (though by no means all). But how is one to understand the unaccountable irregularity with which final *-ī* is indicated sometimes by *yā'*, as would be required by its pausal pronunciation, but also quite often by no orthographic sign at all—and this even apart from liaison- or rhyme-positions (Bergsträsser/Pretzl *GK* 33–35)? Bergsträsser and Pretzl rationalize this "orthographic instability" (*Schwanken*) as reflecting "the actual instability in pronunciation" of the Qurašī dialect (*GK* 34–35). Birkeland objects to this view, though, on the grounds that, though the many shortened forms would have been founded in Muḥammad's ordinary speech, one can hardly speak of "instability of pronunciation" in a regularly spoken, socially accepted vernacular (*AP* 20). It need not even be supposed, as it is by Birkeland, that this instability resulted from Muḥammad's own mispronunciations of the *ᶜarabīya* under the influence of his Meccan dialect. But one can still accept the validity of his conclusion: namely, that "the retention of so many forms which were incorrect as regards the later orthography very likely proves . . . that the originally long final vowel *-ī* had been shortened throughout in Meccan speech" (*AP* 20) and that, correspondingly then, originally short final vowels would have been apocopated (*AP* 21). Contrary to Birkeland, however, and on the basis of the foregoing discussion (and his own conclusions), I do not feel that instances of final *yā'* in the Qur'ānic text should be seen as due so much "partly to fluctuations in Muḥammad's pronunciation and partly to the pervasive influence of the later orthography" (*AP* 20). Can they not just as plausibly be set down in the primary stage to the inadequacies of a Meccan (or Medinan) script and the uncertainties of a Ḥijāzī scribe, both called upon to render in writing familiar words with unfamiliar terminations (cf. Fischer *AA* 815–16)?

C.4.d Looking now to the question of modern dialectal *tanwīn* and its value as evidence for *iᶜrāb*-suffixes in seventh century dialectal usages, how far are we justified in accepting such evidence, on the basis of determinable features of the language as it was spoken at that time?

As a first point, it may be noted that this dialectally based writing system, which had demonstrated so much irregularity and imprecision in representing final long-vowel or *tanwīn* sounds with *-u*/*-i*, appears to have been well suited to indicating final *-ā* or *tanwīn -an*. The remarkable consistency with which *alif* is written for *-ā* and *-an*, both in context and in pausal position,[73] as well as at points of liaison (*waṣl*),[74] seems the more surprising when one recalls how unpredictable in general was its use for *ā* in word-medial position (Bergsträsser/Pretzl *GK* 31–33; Blachère *Intro* 152–53). Even the rhyme-pausal lengthening of short *-a* to *-ā* at the end of both verbs and nouns is shown by *alif* in the ᶜUṯmānic text (Nöldeke/Schwally *GQ* I 37 and n. 4; Bergsträsser/Pretzl *GK* 52; Beck *UKK* 367–68). To seek no explanation for this circumstance other than that it reflects the already mentioned custom of dictating words in their pausal forms (*-an* suffixes being pronounced *-ā*, while *-in*/*-un* suffixes were not pronounced) does not go far enough; for it ignores two further important questions.[75] First, why should the desinential complex *-a*/*-ā*/*-an* have received such preferential treatment from the pausal convention of the *ᶜarabīya* that seems to have predominated at Muḥammad's time—i.e., pause with *iskān* (Birkeland *AP* 7–8, 18–21; Fleisch *TPA* 173–90, 194–95)? After all, final articulations involving *u* and *i* were dropped invariably when they were short or nunated and frequently even when they were long (always at verse-ends). Second, why should the Meccan orthography, quite woefully deficient in representing other vowel phenomena (especially desinences), have been so conspicuously well equipped for transcribing final *a*-sounds?

The answer to the first question lies obscured in the pre-history of the Arabic language. But what is at least clear from the very fact of this early differentiation between *-a*, on the one hand, and *-u*/*-i*, on the other, is the following, as stated by Birkeland: "We can only affirm that in the *ᶜarabīya* *-an* developed differently than did *-un* and *-in*; and [that] this corresponds to the special phonetic position of *a*, which as a rule was kept longer than *i* and *u*" (*AP* 46, cf. 17–18, 36–37, 47–48, 82–83). Apart from his own evidence, Birkeland's observation can also be verified by noting that this vowel opposition, *a* versus *u*/*i*, finds its counterpart in the sphere of rhyme-phenomena where, for example as *ridf* vowel (i.e., as long vowel preceding the final consonant in a verse) *ā* remained invariable throughout a poem, while *ū* and *ī* were used interchangeably (Wright *AG* II 353D). More analogies may be cited as well (ibid. 354D, 355A, 356C, 357A). Birkeland points out that a parallel development can be detected in the dialects (*AP* 103–6). But whereas the *ᶜarabīya* as we know it in the Qur'ān and the poetry apparently kept both the short vowels and the nunation of *iᶜrāb* in contextual forms, this was not the case in the dialects and has not been for some time. Here, as the pausal phenomena of the *ᶜarabīya* suggest and the actual usages of the dialects manifest, forms of final *-i* initially disappeared, followed by *-u*, with *-a* the last to go. Again, the occasional substitution of pausal (apocopated) forms for contextual ones in poetry hints that a state of the spoken language was already in existence where such substitutions prevailed far more generally, if not entirely (*AP* 100–101, 105). Yet, just as in the *ᶜarabīya*, final *-ā*/*-an* was always preserved in context, and *-ā* almost always preserved in pause, so too in the dialects forms of final *-a* have shown a similar tenacity (*AP* 105).

Furthermore, a most important confirmation of Birkeland's point of view lies in a fact that he did not bring out clearly enough: for the contextual forms with *tanwīn* that he notes as still occurring in several dialects, especially central Arabian ones, are precisely those that were discussed at the beginning of this excursus—those that have lost all inflectional significance and remain only as generalizations of the final morpheme *-an*. That such a generalization of final *-a* forms was already under way in the sixth and seventh centuries is again visible in certain recorded traits of the *ᶜarabīya*: specifically in such affective usages as exclamations (*yā ᶜajabā/an, wā ᶜAbdalmuṭṭalibā/āh*), the vocative (*yā abatā/āh, yā ahlāh, yā rajulan*), free variations between accusative and nominative (*waylun/an*), some so-called adverbial forms (*ahlan wa sahlan*, etc.), and the like (Wright *AG* I 294B–296A; Reckendorf *SV* 324–31; Blachère/Gaudefroy-Demombynes *GAC* 375–80; Rabin *AWA* 168). Even among those Qur'ānic reciters of the first/seventh and second/eighth centuries, who have been closely identified with upholding Bedouin usage as the most correct, there had been a noted and sometimes disparaged tendency to use final *-a/-an/-ā* (i.e., *naṣb*-forms) freely, when any doubt arose as to the proper usage (see. Beck *ASA* 195–208 passim).[76]

Thus the existence of *tanwīn* in the modern dialects cannot be considered on the primary level, if at all, as evidence that a three-vowel case- and mood-system had been operative at any time in either urban or Bedouin dialects of Arabic.[77] Rather, the generalization of final *-an* seems to have resulted from a process rooted deep in the morphophonemic structure of the language, having little to do with the "morpho-syntactic," or synthetic, function that, as a case-marker, it performs in the *ᶜarabīya*, and having much more to do with its somehow stabler phonological quality and its value as a marker of indetermination and/or affective states. It is, then, more in keeping with the analytic trend of the spoken dialects in general.

But I would contend further that this generalization of the *-an* morpheme was already in full force at the beginning of the seventh century, at least in the Ḥijāz but possibly elsewhere as well. A number of non-inflectional uses of *-ā/-an*, as well as a pronounced (Ḥijāzī?) tendency to expand its inflectional use,[78] point to such a conclusion; and the strongest evidence for its validity is provided by the well-established and highly standardized orthographical technique of representing final *-ā/-an* by means of *alif* throughout the ᶜUṯmānic Qur'ān. After the foregoing considerations, it cannot be maintained as a counterargument that *alif* consistently written as a termination for words that function syntactically as accusatives gives no proof of a generalization of the *an* suffix beyond its inflectional meaning. That the *alif* was written "correctly" just demonstrates that it was the *ᶜarabīya*, and not the spoken dialect, that the scribe heard. However, more to the point, a scribe would and could consistently transcribe with an *alif* the sound *-ā* (or *-an*) at the ends of words, because the writing system with which he was familiar, and which had been adapted and developed on the basis of his spoken language, made quite easy and natural such an operation; whereas with the other inflectional and long-vowel terminations he may have heard dictated, no such ease and naturalness of transcription obtained, since they were not a part of that spoken language, but belonged to the *ᶜarabīya* alone.[79] The use of *alif* also to transcribe the non-inflectional final *-an* (>*-ā* in pause) of the energetic form of verbs and of the particle *iḏan* (Birkeland *AP* 99–100) only serves to confirm the impression that it was a conventional orthographic technique answering to a widespread and widely heard phenomenon, which was not the case with the other two vowels.[80]

C.5 Some space has been devoted to responding to Th. Nöldeke's arguments against the existence of a non-casual linguistic form proper to works of verbal art and mastery and distinct from the everyday speech both of those who uttered it and of those who heard it. Nöldeke was undoubtedly correct in affirming, as against Vollers, the practical identity of the language of the Qur'ān and the poets' *ᶜarabīya* and also in refusing to see that *ᶜarabīya* either as an artificial hieratic *Schrifsprache* or as an upper-class *Hochsprache* cultivated and spoken by a Ḥijāzī urban patriciate. But when he recognizes no essential disparity between the *ᶜarabīya* and the Bedouin dialects, on the one hand, or between the *ᶜarabīya* and the language spoken at Mecca and Medina, on the other, he appears to admit a homogeneity of linguistic usage among sixth- and early seventh-century speakers of Arabic (at least so far as *iᶜrāb* was concerned) that goes well beyond what determinable facts can allow us to accept. And here again, it is a question of that underlying presupposition about the nature of verbal creativity that we have met before: this is what, it seems, has inclined Nöldeke to formulate and defend such a position. "After all," he says, "it is inconceivable to me that, for one thing, the vocalic richness within [poetic lines] as assured by the meter and, [for another,] the grammatical consistency as acknowledged by the tradition and, to a very great extent, warranted by meter and rhyme would have run wholly counter to actual usage in the verse of a primitive people (*Naturvolk*) who could not have been imitating any ancient literature" (*BSS* 4).

Thus, like Vollers, Geyer, and many others, Nöldeke too leaves out of serious consideration the possibility that between the speech of Muḥammad, citizen of Mecca and tribesman of Qurayš, and that of Muḥammad, inspired renderant of the Word of God and vocal adversary of poets and seers, there might have been an important and perceptible difference—one occasioned simply by virture of the profound difference between the two spheres of activity themselves and manifested precisely and preeminently in the manner of verbal expression. And likewise for the poets: that in their capacity of traditional masters of language they might *ex opere operato* have given way to verbal usages quite—even profoundly—distinct and distinguishable from their normal dialectal speech seems not to have been taken into account. Yet we know now that such, in fact, is and has been the case among peoples of the very kind that Nöldeke would probably have classed *Naturvolk:* Todas, Somalis, Uzbeks, Kara-Kirghiz, and so on (see n.3 to this chapter).

And so, Nöldeke and other scholars who have contributed to the earlier discussion of the *ᶜarabīya* all appear to have shared in some degree the assumption that sixth- and seventh-century Arabs (like Muhammad and the classical poets), in producing verbal works of high artistry and import, would not have departed significantly from the linguistic idiom that prevailed in their daily lives. Thus, Vollers, finding strong evidence for an *iᶜrāb*-less *Volkssprache* in Western Arabia and certain traces of that vernacular in the Qur'ānic orthography and variant readings, leaped to his unjustified conclusion regarding the language in which the Qur'ān was delivered. Geyer realized that Vollers was wrong to suppose an uninflected vernacular original for the Qur'ān: its style was too artistic, its purpose too "literary," its message too solemn. So his alternative was an aristocratic *Hochsprache* that Muhammad, as a Qurašī addressing Qurašīs, would naturally have spoken and in which he would have formulated his "Book." The untenability of this position was recognized by Nöldeke. He, however, judged that the Qur'ān offered a fairly accurate and comprehensive representation of linguistic usage in seventh-century urban Ḥijāz: there the *ᶜarabīya* was spoken with its full *iᶜrāb*, as we have it in the Qur'ān, though in a state of incipient decline. For these and many other scholars, as well as for the Muslim philological tradition in general, the Bedouins presented no problem in this respect: they (the *ᶜarab*, more precisely *aᶜrāb*) of course regularly both spoke and composed poetry in a language (the *ᶜarabīya*) that, despite undeniable dialectal features peculiar to certain tribes, was remarkably uniform throughout the peninsula—a language that included, particularly, the full system of desinential inflections (*iᶜrāb*).[81]

C.6 This assumption that the linguistic form used in daily speech would have been taken over, substantially unchanged, for the highly non-casual[82] utterances represented by classical poetry and the Qur'ān has also determined the emphases and conclusions of three studies written by P. Kahle that deal specifically with the question of *iᶜrāb* and the Qur'ānic language (see n. 14 to this chapter). Following the traditional view, Kahle has no doubt that "the language spoken by the Bedouin" and the language in which "the famous pre-Islamic poetry was composed" are identical (*CG*² 142; also *QA* 181). But the case of Muhammad and his companions is not so clear. On the basis of a previously unknown text by al-Farrā' and a large number of sayings attributed to the first generations of Muslims urging proper usage of the *iᶜrāb* in reciting the Qur'ān, Kahle concludes that, contrary to Nöldeke's belief (see §C.3.a, above), a tradition that the Qur'ān was uttered without *i^{c}rāb* by the early Muslims *had been preserved*. The reported sayings show by their large number and urgent tone that, at least in the second/seventh century and possibly somewhat earlier, *i^{c}rāb* was missing from the vernaculars of most, if not all, Muslims. As for the early eighth century A.D., Kahle exemplifies in his reasoning the assumption already spoken of:

> There are two alternatives. First, the Prophet and his companions read the Koran according to the rules of classical Arabic. In this case we have to suppose that the language spoken by the Ḳuraish in Mecca . . . was in the main identical with it. . . . The other alternative is that, in the language spoken by the Kuraish in Mecca, the rules of classical Arabic were not observed; that the Prophet and his companions did not use classical Arabic in reading the Koran, the language now connected with the Holy Book. (*ARK* 69)

Our awareness of the inconsistency shown by al-Farrā' in claiming linguistic superiority for Qurayš while seeking it among the Bedouins should, Kahle feels, point to the probability of the second alternative.

Rabin has effectively countered the theses advanced by Kahle; and in terms of a poetic *^{c}arabīya* separate from any spoken language, he has demonstrated where they "founder completely" (*BCA* 24–29; cf. also Fück *Ar* 3 n). I wish only to call attention to the fact that the devotional reading or reciting of a revealed Qur'ānic passage, once it had been delivered, could not but have been an operation wholly distinct from its original delivery by Muhammad, or even from its rendition by someone qualified and authorized to do so. Even if the traditions adduced by Kahle actually went back to the early decades of Islam, they would provide additional evidence that, indeed, *i^{c}rāb* was omitted from the normal speech of the Companions and of Muhammad himself, but not that it was absent from the Qur'ān as solemnly delivered by the inspired Messenger of God. Quite to the contrary, such insistent and repeated exhortations to render the Qur'ān with correct *i^{c}rāb*, had they any foundation in historical fact, would have to have had in view a very real, if hard-to-achieve, objective: namely, the reproduction of an actual and perceptible linguistic phenomenon that marked the speech of Muḥammad's Qur'ānic delivery, but not that of his conversation. The same, according to the position of this study, would hold true for the poets. Thus, all that we can be sure of from accounts of solecisms (as opposed to dialectisms or other anomalies) in Qur'ānic or poetic recitations is that the reciter lacked the special linguistic formation of a poet or the inspiration of a prophet.

C.7 As was mentioned above (§ B.1), the view "that Classical Arabic was not the spoken language of the poets who used it for their poetry . . . has been accepted by practically all more recent European writers who discussed the matter at all" (Rabin *BCA* 23). Writing those words in 1955, Rabin added: "In recent years it has become usual to call it [i.e., the classical *^{c}arabīya*] the 'poetic *koinē*'—not an entirely happy term, since the Greek *koinē* was, after all, a spoken language, and Classical Arabic, on this view, resembles more closely the status of Homeric Greek" (*BCA*; cf. n. 11 to this chapter). Earlier (in 1947),[83] H. Fleisch, R. Blachère, and Rabin himself had concurred in admitting the totally non-vernacular character of the language of the poets; and they had, moreover, "apparently independently . . . arrived . . . at the conclusion that the language of the Koran, far from being pure Meccan either subsequently revised (Vollers) or slightly adapted to the poetic idiom, was none other than the poetic *koinē*" (*BCA* 24; cf. nn. 13–14 to this chapter). Yet, strangely, none of these scholars chose to express a clear opinion on the role of *i^{c}rāb* in the pre-Islamic linguistic picture: none explicitly broached the question, so important to previous discussions, of whether *i^{c}rāb* was unique to the poetic "koinē" alone or whether it was shared by some or all of the spoken dialects.

Fleisch in *IELS*, at this time, did not even allude to the *i^{c}rāb* except in quite general terms, as a feature distinguishing Arabic from other Semitic languages (e.g., *IELS* 113). Subsequently, however, he has been much more definitive, affirming its presence in the Bedouin dialects, at least (see § C.9, below). Nor did Blachère, in *Intro*, consider the distinctiveness or non-distinctiveness of *i^{c}rāb*, although, in *HLA* 77–78, he specifically notes that Nöldeke's remarks on the presence of the desinential inflections in Meccan and Bedouin speech (*BSS* 2; see above) failed to get to the heart of the matter. Rabin in *AWA* was also inconclusive in this regard, but the weight of his opinion tends toward accepting a general weakening and disappearance of final short (i.e., *i^{c}rāb*) vowels in the spoken dialects by the early seventh century (*AWA* 12, 56–57, 81, 119–20).[84] Nevertheless, all three scholars unreservedly maintain that the language of the classical poetry and the Qur'ān was not the spoken vernacular of any tribe; and Blachère and Rabin, particularly, would seem inclined to see preservation of desinential vowels as one feature differentiating that language from the various dialects. I must disagree, however, with their (not uncommon) assumption that a parallel to its emergence as an intertribal poetic idiom is to be sought in the development of languages such as German, Spanish, French, or Italian out of particular dialects that achieved some sort of *literary* ascendency (e.g., Fleisch *IELS* 99; Blachère *HLA* 66–67, 79; Rabin *AWA* 3).[85] The situation of classical Arabic, had it been an oral poetical idiom arbitrarily adopted and later standardized as a *Schriftsprache* at a certain point of time, would have been fundamentally different.[86]

C.8.a With the publication of J. Fück's learned and wide-ranging treatise, *^{c}Arabīya* (1950), the problem of *i^{c}rāb* in the spoken vernaculars again comes to the fore. Fück recognized in the desuetude of the *i^{c}rāb* suffixes, attested even during the first/seventh century, a sure sign of post-classical "middle" Arabic (although the converse—the use of *i^{c}rāb* as an index of classical *^{c}arabīya*—could not at all be assumed). In answer to the question of how long the *i^{c}rāb* was retained in the living language, he makes the following assertion:

> The pre- and early Islamic Bedouin poetry shows us the desinential case- and mood-endings still fully in operation; and the fact that, at least down into the IVth/Xth century, the grammarians would betake themselves to the Bedouins to study their language indicates that the outer morphemes were still in full flower at that time (*Ar* 2; cf. 69, 89–91).

As for the Qur'ān, the synthetic character of its syntax, and hence its compositional reliance upon complete *i^{c}rāb*, is confirmed "with absolute certainty" by the free placement or interchange of subject and predicate in several passages. "Such clausal constructions are possible (as *matrem amat filia*) only in a language where case-declension is still living" (*Ar* 2). Calling attention to the Qur'ān's insistence that it had been phrased in "a clear Arabic tongue" (*lisān ^{c}arabīy mubīn*), Fück concludes: "Evidently, for Muhammad and his compatriots, there existed no essential difference between the language of the Qur'ān and that of the Arabs, i.e., of the Bedouin tribes" (ibid.).

Thus, in Fück's opinion, classical poetry and the Qur'ān were composed using practically the same linguistic form in both cases; and this linguistic form, the *^{c}arabīya,* was characterized by the utterance of case- and mood-desinences for syntactical differentiation. Furthermore, it also constituted the normal speech of the Bedouins, who continued to speak in this fashion, pronouncing the *i^{c}rāb*-suffixes, for some centuries to come. The disappearance of the desinential inflections, which led to the formation of "Middle Arabic," was due to the introduction into the Arabic linguistic community of innumerable non-Arabs whose native languages retained none of their original inflectional systems. These non-Arabs, having then to speak Arabic, found it difficult to follow the complicated rules of classical Arabic syntax. "They moved more freely in the periphrastic forms of expression to which they had been accustomed in their mother tongue, and they generally dropped the final vowels which they encountered only within phrases and never in isolated words" (*Ar* 9).

C.8.b It is plain to see that Fück, like many others before him, either did not consider the possibility of a linguistic form separate from any spoken vernacular and peculiar to the non-casual verbal expressions of poetry and prophecy, or he did not consider such a possibility a valid alternative. Yet no fewer than three scholars, writing between 1952 and 1953, expressed strong reservations to Fück's assumption that the *ᶜarabīya* of the poetry and the Qur'ān was essentially identical with the Bedouin vernaculars; and they objected, above all, to his assertion that the *iᶜrāb* was "in full flower" in living speech either at the time of Muḥammad or down into the fourth/tenth century. H. Wehr (rev. *Ar* 180–84), A. Spitaler (rev. *Ar* 144b–147b), and F. Rosenthal (rev. *Ar* 309–10), arrived apparently independently at agreement in finding this line of Fück's argument quite unjustified on the basis of available reliable information concerning the linguistic situation of the time.

Spitaler and Wehr, particularly, deal extensively with this question in their reviews, and both seem to concur fully in the following conclusions. There can be no doubt (1) that, among the Arabs of the sixth to the early ninth centuries, there existed a language or linguistic form, the *ᶜarabīya,* whose most outstanding feature, it has been almost universally agreed, was the inflection of verbs and nouns through final short-vowel suffixes; (2) that this *ᶜarabīya* was to be heard and sought preeminently in the formal elocutionary utterances of the poet, orator (*xaṭīb*), and seer (*kāhin*); and (3) that the Qur'ān, too, itself a formal elocution beyond any question, had been rendered in the same inflected *ᶜarabīya* (although this last fact cannot be validly demonstrated, as Fück had held, from syntactical displacements in sentence word-order).[87] There is no basis for accepting Fück's assumptions, however, (1) that during that same period the *ᶜarabīya* was ever actually encountered as a spoken vernacular; (2) that the expansion of the Bedouins with the Islamic conquests would have resulted in a "common Bedouin language" spoken in the garrison cities with full *iᶜrāb;* and (3) that the linguistic predisposition of the subjugated non-Arabs for analysis and periphrasis would have led them originally to drop the case- and mood-suffixes for the sake of simplification.

In the first place, the evidence of the modern dialects, practically every feature of which has been directly or indirectly attested for both Bedouin and urban dialects of the first/seventh century, confirms a general continuity, rather than discontinuity, of usage for at least the last 1,200 years (cf. also § C.4.d, above); and no feature is more typical of dialectal usage as a whole than the absence of final short vowels in casual speech—a feature shared, incidentally, by almost all Semitic languages from their earliest literary periods on (cf. Corriente *FY* 41–50; idem *FY*2 156). Moreover, nothing stands in the way of our supposing that such a continuity of linguistic usage extended back into Muḥammad's period and even before: both the special distinction and prestige accorded to the language of pre-Islamic poetry "and other eloquent and stylistically pure forms of Arab expression'' (cf. p. 101 above) and the nearly total and exclusive reliance of the earliest philologists upon these same sources make a supposition like that not unwarranted. And, further, if the philologists still into the fourth/tenth century sought linguistic correctness and heard the case- and mood-endings among the Bedouins of their time, it must be recognized that what they were after was precisely the *ᶜarabīya* that they knew from the classical poetry and that the Bedouins alone could provide—because, I hope this study will convincingly show, *they alone maintained, as they have until today, a tradition of oral poetry out of which the ᶜarabīya had been generated and derived to begin with.* And since it was the *ᶜarabīya* that the philologists went out into the desert to seek, it was the *ᶜarabīya* that they got. The products of formal elocution (poetry, oratory, etc.) were what interested them: so whether the colloquial speech of the Bedouins was identical with the *ᶜarabīya* or whether, as seems now more likely, it was substantially different, in both morphology and syntax, we cannot definitely ascertain from the accounts and examples that have been recorded (cf. esp. Corriente *FY* 26 n.8). As to the theory of a ''common Bedouin language'' (a ''koinē'' in the more proper sense of the word), this is an idea that presupposes a greater dialectal homogeneity among the pre-Islamic tribes and a greater evenness of tribal distribution among the conquering and colonizing Arab armies than reliable sources permit us to accept (cf. n. 84 to this chapter). Besides, if *iᶜrāb* cannot be proven to have been in use in the individual Bedouin dialects, it could scarcely be presumed to have existed in a ''common Bedouin language,'' which would, if anything, have been necessarily something of a linguistic common denominator.

Finally, to hold the non-Arabs responsible for the abandonment of the outer morphemes of case and mood by suggesting that because of them those synthetic devices, the short-vowel suffixes, were dropped from the ''common Bedouin language'' to be replaced by a syntax of analysis—to maintain this view, all three scholars emphasize, would be to presume a capacity for linguistic abstraction and an ear for morphological subtleties in circumstances where such qualities could hardly be expected and to ignore the fact that the disappearance of final short vowels corresponds to a much more profound process of linguistic evolution through which other Semitic languages had already passed at a much earlier period. As Spitaler says in this regard, ''This phenomenon, rather, would most naturally be explained simply by assuming again that the peoples in question did hear Arabic [spoken] in its uninflected form and that also, as a result, they were able to adopt nothing else'' (rev. *Ar* 147b; cf. Corriente *FY* 39–40 and n. 30).

In conclusion, Spitaler and Wehr would argue that we have no real basis for thinking that the classical *ᶜarabīya* has been, at any time during the past 1,300–1,400 years, identical either with the spoken dialect of any Arab tribe or group of tribes or with a hypothetical early Islamic "common Bedouin language," the existence of which must be deemed questionable, at best. Quite the contrary: the *ᶜarabīya* would have functioned solely as an artistic *Hochsprache* or a *Kunstsprache,* unique to the formal and elocutionary utterances of practiced and practicing word-smiths—poets, orators, soothsayers, and prophets—who alone would have had mastery over it. To this extent, their opinion is in accord with a consensus of present-day scholarship (cf. § B.1 and pp. 130–31). But even further, they would contend, proper and unbiased interpretation of the evidence strongly indicates that, just as the use of the *iᶜrāb* suffixes for case- and mood-markers has been the single most characteristic feature of the *ᶜarabīya* since its earliest known appearance, so too,during the same period, their use would have been just what most strikingly and decisively distinguished the *ᶜarabīya* from the various dialectal forms of the language. In other words, the Arabic vernaculars spoken at the time of Muhammad and thereafter would, as regards final short vowels, already have reached the stage where such vowels were generally eliminated in casual speech—the same elimination that both urban and Bedouin dialects are acknowledged to have undergone many centuries ago and that represents a normal linguistic development for Semitic languages in general. In this view, therefore, the presence of *iᶜrāb* in the poetic and Qur'ānic *ᶜarabīya* is to be recognized as nothing less than the retention of a linguistic feature that would have been lost from vernacular speech. And this vocalic archaism would have been retained precisely because it served an indispensable prosodic function in formulating Arabic quantitative rhymed verse and cadenced prose (cf. §B 8.3.c-d, above) and because it was heard as an intrinsic property of the "hallowed language of poetry" (M. Hartmann, quoted in Spitaler rev *Ar* 146 n. 14; cf. H. Fleischer, cited in n. 11 to this chapter).

C.9 More recently, H. Fleisch and J. Blau have come to the defense of Fück's claim that *iᶜrāb* was "in full flower" in the Bedouin dialects down to the fourth/tenth century.[88] To be sure, both admit—indeed, insist upon—the completely non-vernacular nature of the *ᶜarabīya* and stress that it cannot be identified, as Fück had done, with any spoken dialect. As Fleisch says, "It is a question of an artistic and traditional language . . . developed and perfected through the agency of poets" (*ACAD* 35, 36). Furthermore, Blau utterly rejects Fück's theory of a post-conquest "common Bedouin language" (cf. n. 84 to this chapter; also Blau *IMAD* 224–28).

Yet, though Fleisch and Blau evince awareness of the objections raised by

Spitaler and Wehr, nevertheless both continue to assume that the Bedouin dialects shared with the poetic *ᶜarabīya* the synthetic features of short-vowel case- and mood-endings. As expressed by Fleisch, their view is essentially as follows:

> These Bedouins, on the whole, at the time of the [early Islamic] conquests . . . , were speaking an Arabic which bore all the *iᶜrāb*-vowels, with the variations peculiar to their dialect and with the other particularities of their dialect. This *iᶜrāb* was not a relic left over from the past, retained by the poets in the tradition of poetry. It was not a kind of more or less artificial appendage added to the word. It constituted an integral part of the everyday language, and the young Bedouin would learn it naturally, simply through repeating the language of his family and his milieu, as does every child. Certain groups can already have lost the use of *iᶜrāb,* but that would not change the general impression. This situation must have lasted for quite some time thereafter. (*ACAD* 42)

As proof of the last statement, Fleisch adduces the testimony of al-Azharī (d. 370/980), who claimed to have heard, while a prisoner among the Bedouin Carmathians of east-central Arabia, "hardly any solecism or flagrant error" in speech (*ACAD* 42–43; cf. Fück *Ar* 91). "It is inconceivable," Fleisch notes, "that al-Azharī would have made such a statement had the Arabs in question spoken an Arabic without *iᶜrāb*" (*ACAD* 43 n.1).[89]

Blau, too, has quite uniformly held the opinion that the Bedouin dialects "maintained a structure that was on the whole synthetic, thus remaining akin to Classical Arabic, as against the more analytic urban Middle Arabic dialects" (*IMAD* 225). Although substantial differences did exist between the various Bedouin dialects and between classical Arabic and the tribal vernaculars, these differences

> must not be overestimated. Typologically, they were closely akin, all of them being languages of the synthetic type, tending to express several concepts in a single word and possessing similar systems of declension and conjugation, so that it was relatively easy to switch from one language to another. (*ELB* 2)

For both scholars, then, the disappearance of desinential inflections and the general analytic trend, which for many centuries have characterized all forms of dialectal Arabic and which can be discerned through papyri evidence in the earliest post-conquest urban dialects (cf. esp. Blau *IMAD* 220–24; *ELB* Appendix I), were due after all to the contact of the Arabs with native populations whose languages had lost their inflectional endings long before. Fück's hypothesis in this matter—that the non-Arabs dropped the endings in their speech to avoid the syntactical complexities of the inflective Classical language (cf. § C.8.a, above)—is accepted but applied with reference to the allegedly synthetic Bedouin vernaculars instead of classical Arabic itself. A development of this nature, it is held, leading to the reduction or elimination of *iᶜrāb* suffixes in the dialects spoken in the conquered territories, need not have required so unimaginably precocious a capacity for morphemic analysis as Spitaler and Wehr (and Rosenthal) indicated. The non-Arabs could have come to adopt an Arabic without *iᶜrāb*, Fleisch and Blau contend, not because their Bedouin conquerors would already have arrived among them speaking in such a manner, but because they would have been used to hearing the uninflected word-forms prominently placed at the ends of breath-groups or longer phrases, due to the established practice of pause with *iskān* (Fleisch *TPA* 282; idem *ACAD* 43; idem *AC*² 30; Blau *ELB* 3).

Although this argument would be difficult to deny categorically, it still leaves the fundamental question unanswered. It does not seem very plausible that a widely spoken and socially accepted Arabic dialect of the analytic type could have been produced solely—or even mainly—on the basis of the final words in phrases uttered by speakers of a synthetic form of the language—and produced, moreover, in an incredibly short period of time and, at least in the settled areas, among both native subjects and Arab overlords (cf. Blau *ELB* 4–8). Such a hypothesis overlooks the fact, so incisively demonstrated by Fleisch earlier, that for the undeniably inflective classical Arabic (and hence, for the allegedly inflective Bedouin dialects as well) the word in pause is only a single grammatical facet of the true significative base of the language—namely, the clause or sentence. The pausal form in the classical Arabic clause simply acts, on the one hand, as one constituent terminating a unified series of constituents tightly bound together through liaisons and assimilations "bordering on geminates," and, on the other, as the final "syllable" in "this new lexical unity which could emerge as an autonomous word, playing a grammatical role" (*ALP* 94). Viewed thus, apocopated pausal forms could hardly have been abstracted from coherent utterances in an inflective spoken idiom and redistributed as constituents in another, non-inflective, idiom. One must, I think, with Spitaler and Wehr, predicate a more concrete and immediate prototype for the analytic dialects spoken in the earliest Islamic cities and wherever Arabic is a living language today.

Discussing the inner morphology of classical Arabic nouns, Fleisch calls particular attention to the existence of forms $C_1VC_2VC_3C_3$ (two short vowels with geminated third radical). "Without the final declensional vowels," he writes, "the appearance of this . . . class [of nouns] would have been morphologically impossible in the Arabic language. This example clearly shows that these vowels are not a more or less artificial appurtenance, but belong to the structure of the language" (*TPA* 357 n. 2; *AC*² 51 n. 1). No one, however, would ever seriously doubt that the inflectional suffixes belonged to the structure of *classical Arabic, the ᶜarabīya of poetry and of prophecy.* But whether the suffixes belonged to the structure of the spoken dialects at the time of Muḥammad and later is another question. And precisely Fleisch's further observation—that these extremely rare forms are representative of the ancient Bedouin vocabulary, attested thus in verse and collected by the philologist as *ġarīb* expressions (*TPA* 358; *AC*² 52)—can be taken as evidence that such nouns were uttered, as a rule, only under conditions of formal rendition of poetry and certain kinds of prose, where final short vowels would be heard. Such an explanation is at least as plausible as taking these uncommon noun-forms to show that final vowels were present in *ordinary* Bedouin speech and only subsequently disappeared through non-Arab influence.[90]

For Blau, further, "the lack of pseudo-correct features in the Qur'ān demonstrates . . . that Classical Arabic was not, structurally at least, different from the idiom of Mecca" (*ELB* 3 n. 1; cf. idem *PSSL* 57–58). That is to say, the Arabic spoken in Mecca also was an inflective language; for had it been otherwise, more pseudo-corrections reflecting the absence of final inflections, of the kind that can be found in the earliest post-Islamic Arabic texts, ought to have appeared. Yet, I do not believe this *argumentum e silentio* satisfactorily refutes the point raised by Wehr about the evidence to be derived from the Qur'ānic orthography (rev. *Ar* 184; cf. pp. 123–24, above). One must consider that, on the one hand, the Qur'ān consists of the careful transcriptions, through available scribal and orthographical means, of *heard* utterances couched in the special inflective idiom of poetry and conceived of as emanating directly from God by way of His Messenger. These transcriptions subsequently were compiled and established in text under probably the most scrupulous and stringent control conditions ever applied to an Arabic work, either before or since (see, e.g., Nöldeke/Schwally *GQ* II 47–119; Blachére *Intro* 52–65). The fact that so few pseudo-correct features are to be encountered in the Qur'ānic text and the fact that the orthography does indicate the presence of *iᶜrāb* vowels (e.g., *abā' unā*/*abā' inā* with *wāw* and *yā'* respectively, etc.) show us actually no more than that the transcribers were successful, within the limitations imposed by a vernacular-based script, in transcribing *what they heard*—namely the inflective *ᶜarabīya* (cf. Fischer *SVA* 59– 60).

On the other hand, one is not entitled to expect from a work thus rendered, thus recorded, and thus transmitted the sort of scribal lapses that Blau so penetratingly analyzes in early Arabic documents and texts.[91] These were composed, written, and copied by lettered men who evidently spoke a non-inflective form of Arabic and whose grasp of the inflective *ᶜarabīya,* however perfect or imperfect, came from school training in reading and writing, not from training in the oral formulation of "just measures of isochronous verse" (Magoun *BSC* 52, quoted on p. 9 above).

To support the opinion that Muḥammad's spoken dialect could not have been too far removed from the formal ^{c}*arabīya,* Blau makes the following surprising statement:

> One will not claim that Muhammad imitated the language of the *kuhhān,* the soothsayers, so well that he did not deviate from Classical Arabic; Muhammad, though influenced by the *kuhhān,* did not belong to their guild; cf. e.g., his saying (quoted by R. Parent, *Muhammad und der Koran* [p 51], . . . from Ibn Sa^{c}d, Vol. I, Part I, p. 130) that he was afraid to be a soothsayer. (*PSSL* 58 n. 15)

Aside from a doubt about the existence of any "guild" of *kuhhān,* an examination of the relevant passages reveals that Muhammad expresses loathing for the soothsayers and that it was precisely the nature of what he had experienced and the tenor of what he had heard that led him to fear lest he become one of them. In other words, according to the received narratives, the similarity between Muḥammad's first revelations and the *jinn*-inspired utterances of the *kuhhān* and poets[92] was so striking that the Prophet himself at first—not to mention his Meccan compatriots later—could not immediately distinguish between the two (see §D, below).

C.10.a Some months after I had completed the final draft of this chapter, two items came to my attention that provide strong corroboration for the view advanced here regarding noun- and verb-desinences (*i^{c}rāb*) in the classical ^{c}*arabīya.* It has seemed advisable to include them in my discussion at this point.

The first in fact consists of three articles published between 1971 and 1973: an initial study by F. Corriente, "On the Functional Yield of Some Synthetic Devices in Arabic and Semitic Morphology" (*FY*); a counterstatement by J. Blau, "On the Problem of the Synthetic Character of Classical Arabic as against Judaeo-Arabic (Middle Arabic)" (*PSC*); and a reply to Blau by Corriente (FY_2).

In his primary study Corriente addresses himself principally to two problems: (1) the importance of *i^{c}rāb* as a functional synthetic device in the ^{c}*arabīya* and later forms of apparently inflected literary Arabic, and (2) the role that final mood- and case-endings might ever have played in the history of Semitic languages in general. For the purposes of this study, I shall concentrate on Corriente's handling of the first problem, though it is possible that his findings with regard to the second may be linguistically of greater significance.

Corriente argues that, first, it may be granted that the *i^{c}rāb* suffixes of verbs and, particularly, nouns (and adjectives) are conspicuously operative in the classical ^{c}*arabīya* of the early poetry and the Qur'ān and just as conspicuously inoperative—indeed, absent altogether, now and for several centuries at least—in Middle Arabic and all living forms of spoken Arabic (*FY* 20–22,

40–41); yet it may also be granted that, in connection with the earliest epigraphic and onomastic appearances of Old Arabic[93] and with many of the earliest *ᶜarabīya* texts (occasional lines of poetry and a number of canonically established readings [*qirā'āt*] of the Qur'ān),[94] there is evidence of an *iᶜrāb*-less form of Arabic already coexisting both chronologically and locally with the *iᶜrāb* form, thus precluding, it seems, a simple and exclusive assignment of the two forms to "two successive states in the evolution of one and the same (diachronically speaking) language" (*FY* 23; cf. 22–23, 33–34). But how could the *ᶜarabīya,* supposedly "a highly synthetic linguistic structure" (*FY* 24) that would have relied principally upon the *iᶜrāb* suffixes to convey meaningful logical and grammatical relationships, be uttered at the same time, in the same area, and often (from all indications) by the same speakers as the *iᶜrāb*-less speech-form, characteristic of Middle Arabic and the younger dialects? For Corriente, "this most frustrating problem in the historical grammar of Arabic[95] could be clarified by means of a survey of inflectional forms, based upon the principle of functional yield here applied . . . to morphosyntactical oppositions" (*FY* 25). To perform this survey, Corriente "selected texts, both prose and poetry, from diverse epochs, and applied to each case morpheme[96] in them the commutation test,[97] in order to find out whether or not the case ending used is indispen[s]able to ensure the integrity and identity of the logical content" (*FY* 34).[98] What emerges from the survey is confirmation for Corriente's impression that the desinential inflections, which are so characteristic of the *ᶜarabīya* and differentiate it from Middle Arabic and younger dialects, in fact "have a negligible functional yield," since the precise sense of the passage in question can be determined almost always without recourse to the inflections through reference to such analytic features as word-order, "morph-words,"[99] and the like (*FY* 25). The inflectional endings, therefore, "instead of being compared to the Indoeuropean markers of nominal and verbal flection, should be demoted to the category of secondary ones: the language can very well do, and does, without them, occasionally already in Old Arabic, regularly in what we call Middle Arabic" (ibid.; cf. 32–33f, 40–41, 44–45, 49–50).

Corriente's statement of his thesis as to the linguistic situation in early Arabia and later Arabic-speaking territories reads as follows:

> We are therefore inclined to believe that in agreement with the native tradition, early poetry, the Qur'ān, and even the daily speech of many Bedouin tribesmen (used as a source of reference by much later urban grammarians), possibly also of some urban dwellers, was indeed characterized by the presence of the *Iᶜrāb*. On the other hand, linguistically this amounted to very little, except perhaps the social prestige attached to such forms. Their functional yield was equal or very

close to zero already in the oldest samples of Arabic that we can find, and this happened because the prevailing structure of the language was rather analytical, as Middle Arabic shows clearly after it has gone one step further by dropping the secondary morphs which have now become completely idle, thus substituting not a new structure for an older one, but just one linguistic form for another, within the same structural frame. As for the Classical Literary Arabic of later periods, which was no more than a mere vehicle of written communication, and for the extent to which its *Iᶜrāb* was or is today read at all, our impression, subsequently confirmed by statistical count, pointed to a completion of the aforementioned trend toward analytical expression: the functional yield of the *Iᶜrāb* in prose texts tends to equal zero. (*FY* 25–29)[100]

Thus, although it would be impossible to date the point at which any group of speakers would have ceased using the desinential morphemes in daily speech (*FY* 25, 40–41; but cf. § C.10.d, below), their disappearance was inevitable, because their insignificant functional yield indicates, Corriente holds, that "we are dealing at best with a mere secondary set of morphs, at worst with a linguistically irrelevant legacy of the past, a dead system, the formal survival of whose terms is hardly surprising in such a conservative social institution as language tends to be" (*FY* 32).[101] According to this view, then, there would have been little or no problem of mutual compatibility or mutual comprehensibility between those who spoke an *iᶜrāb*-form of Arabic (however few they might have been) and those who spoke an *iᶜrāb*-less form, because the two linguistic forms in effect shared a single, predominantly analytic structural frame, the apparently synthetic case-endings serving merely as "secondary morphs" attached to "the morphological word . . . in order to confirm, rather than affirm" its grammatical function in a logical relationship (*FY* 47; cf. 29).[102]

In the second part of his study, Corriente calls attention to the several Semitic languages that, with "amazing unanimity," wound up "in dropping many an old system of synthetic [desinential] morphemes, or reducing their functional yield to insignificant levels (with eventually the same result)" (*FY* 43; cf. 41–43). To follow this part of his argument would be out of place here. Suffice it to say that his judgment as to the dispensability of the synthetic *iᶜrāb* devices in classical Arabic is borne out by his examination of ancient Semitic languages, where "synthetic devices . . . (even in Proto-Semitic, as far as we can infer) were much less prominent than most scholars tend to assume" (*FY* 46; cf. 44–50).

J. Blau's article (*PSC*) takes issue with Corriente on several points, most of which the latter subsequently defends or clarifies, while admitting the justice of Blau's critique in some instances (FY_2). Corriente does, for example, "acknowledge the validity of Blau's remarks in [objection] a), i.e., the peculiar and slightly deviant usage . . . of the term 'analytical' " (FY_2 154) In (a) Blau points out that "word-order as such, determining the functions of the constituents of an utterance, is neither synthetic nor analytic"; although, he continues,

> one will readily admit that analytical languages evince a marked tendency to distinguish, for example, between subject and direct object by means of fixed word order . . . Nevertheless, the interdependence between analytical lingual type and fixed word-order is by no means automatic. (*PSC* 30)

It seems curious to me, however, that having expressed this quite valid reservation to Corriente's rather facile identification of analytic linguistic structure with fixed word-order, Blau would proceed to argue in (e), adducing "a rich display of Middle Arabic examples" (Corriente FY_2 161),[103] that "the different structure of classical Arabic is also exhibited by the freer word-order in classical Arabic" (*PSC* 33, with a *pace* to Corriente *FY* 38), and that "the freer word-order in classical Arabic clearly exhibits a structure different from that of Middle Arabic and the modern dialects" (*PSC* 36). On the face of it, the two positions argued in (a) and (e), however they might be qualified or refined, strike me as simply incompatible and irreconcilable.[104] On the whole, as Blau himself makes plain (*PSC* 29–30), allegations of analytic or synthetic status for a given speech-form cannot validly be made solely—or even to a large extent—on the grounds of fixed or free word-order. Thus, when Corriente argues for the underlying analytic structure of classical Arabic and the essential otiosity of the inflectional morphs, neither the presence of radical word displacements in classical nor the absence of such displacements in Middle or dialectal Arabic can effectively disprove his case.

We might, for the sake of analogy, refer to sentences in literary English such as the following:

And him thus answered soon his bold compeer . . .
(*Paradise Lost* I:127)

. . . therefore as far
From granting he, as I from begging, peace.
(*P. L.* IV:103–4)

Him who disobeys
Me disobeys.
(*P. L.* V:611–12)

> And me perhaps each of these dispositions, as the subject was whereon I entered, may have at other times variously affected; and likely might in these foremost expressions now also disclose which of them swayed most, but that . . .
>
> (*Areopagitica,* 1st paragraph)

Would we for a moment claim that, on the grounds of his aberrant word-order, Milton spoke a highly synthetic language; that the undeniably inflective nominative- and objective-case pronouns, which are so violently wrenched out of their "normal" positions, constitute evidence of his language's synthetic structure; or that indeed Milton's displacements of subjects and objects are less radical than those to be encountered in classical Arabic? Such displacements and deviations from "normal" order, whether they occur in basically analytic or basically synthetic languages, must be recognized for what they, in fact, are: namely, cases of "stylistic reordering" that, as N. Chomsky maintains, are generated according to rules which "are not so much rules of grammar as rules of performance."[105]

Blau also criticizes Corriente's approach to "the practical problem of determining the functional yield of cases in various languages," pointing out a number of instances, omitted from Corriente's calculations, where commutation of cases would be possible, but either "gives rise to a sentence which is perfectly grammatical, yet insofar as its meaning is concerned, rather ill-adjusted for the context," or "gives rise to a different construction, which is, however, almost identical in sense with the first one" (*PSC* 36).[106] The question asked by Blau, "Where is the limit beyond which such a commutation must be considered impossible?" (ibid.), is justifiable; and Corriente, in response, willingly expresses "some misgivings . . . about the soundness of the counting system used there [*sc.*, in *FY*] in order to find out the proportion between noun cases with and without functional yield" (FY_2 154), suggesting also certain refinements that would improve the accuracy of the computation (FY_2 154–55). But the computation arrived at in *FY*, he feels, "anyhow . . . reflected the phenomenon with at least relative accuracy rather than absolute precision, and that was sufficient for our purposes" (FY_2 155). The other objections raised by Blau (*PSC* 30–33; cf. 38) are, in my opinion, adequately dealt with in Corriente's reply (FY_2 155–63). And, for the present, I will subscribe to the judgment delivered there, that

> one should regard the redundancy in Semitic inflexional systems, especially in Arabic, with a more critical eye [than does Blau *PSC* 31], in view of the frequent cases of absolute irrelevance, and, despite the higher incidence of free word-order, consider the structural and typological evolution from Old to Middle Arabic as less significant, in agreement with the just slight decrease of the true rates of functional load observed between both forms of the Arabic language. Once we [do] justice to the real linguistic value of case and mood endings in Arabic, and consider that most instances of free word-order display reference pronouns (*ḍamīr ᶜā'id*), very little is left in Old Arabic to justify the current belief that this one is "much more" synthetic than Middle Arabic. (FY_2 160– 61)

C.10.b I part company with Corriente, however, on the question of the status of the inflected *ᶜarabīya* in sixth- and seventh-century Arabia (see above and n. 100 to this chapter). His solution to the "dilemma" presented by "the very fact that *Iᶜrāb* seems to be at the same time present . . . and absent" is restated when he postulates

> the co-existence of *Iᶜrāb* and *Iᶜrāb*-less dialects in an epoch as early as the VII and possibly the VI century at least (sometime before that and genetically, of course, one cannot forgo the inescapable conclusion that *Iᶜrāb* Arabic was the *terminus a quo*), and this as a result of a dialect split after which some dialects developed more quickly and some less so. But . . . [the fact of negligible functional yield of the *Iᶜrāb*-devices] provided the similar structural frame that allowed the mutual intelligibility of both types of dialects as well as the identification of inflected and uninflected forms within one and the same body of linguistic material. Among those two types of dialects, one would have generated most features of what became the Arabic koiné[107] and, then, the Classical and written language of the Arabs, while the other abutted upon the spoken Arabic of later epochs. (*FY_2* 157–58)

For Corriente, then, not only did *iᶜrāb*-Arabic before and during the early years of Islam constitute the linguistic vehicle of classical poetry and the Qur'ān (an opinion with which I am heartily in accord), but it also served as "the prestige forms in the cities, and even standard speech among many Bedouin tribes" (*FY* 38; cf. *FY_2* 159). It is this second assumption—that at the period in question the *ᶜarabīya*, with its *iᶜrāb*-suffixes, or some analogous form of desinentially inflective Arabic would have been normally *spoken* by any group or groups (Bedouins included) and that *iᶜrāb* itself "could have remained in some forms of spoken Arabic until the Abbasid period . . . as a mere symbol of high class style or of Bedouin aristocracy" (*FY* 39)—that I find to be quite unnecessary.[108] Given an originally desinentially inflective proto- or prehistoric Arabic, [109] there may indeed have been a good deal of diachronic variation among different groups of Arabic-speakers in the dysfunction, disuse, and disappearance of *iᶜrāb* suffixes (cf. Corriente *FY* 40–41). W. Diem's article, discussed below (§C.10.d), suggests that this is so and suggests also that the process of eliminating the case-endings was well under way in the North Arabian-Nabataean area before the first century B.C., hence considerably reducing—if not precluding—the likelihood of their *natural* retention in Central Arabia down to the sixth-seventh centuries A.D. But to understand the phenomenon of *iᶜrāb* in the classical *ᶜarabīya*, there is no need to postulate a "thesis of coexistence . . . of both types of dialects within a single structural frame" (Corriente *FY_2* 159; cf. n. 100 to this chapter). I believe that the phenomenon can be better explained by applying the theory advanced here, which, unorthodox as it might be, corresponds more closely to known linguistic, historical, and cultural facts of pre- and early Islamic Arabia.

In terms of that theory, therefore, the *iᶜrāb* system, *as it is encountered in classical poetry and the Qur'ān*, is to be seen—and, I think, it was then seen[110]—as a palpable linguistic anomaly, an anachronism or archaism with respect to *all* spoken dialects (even such dubious few as may still have held on to some residual propensity toward desinential inflection). The case- and mood-endings were retained, above all in poetry, as a functional and vital element of skilled poetic rendition because (1) they had been unquestionably a functional and vital feature of the proto-language itself at the earliest, formative stages of the oral-poetic tradition, whenever that might have been;[111] (2) they inhered in the received traditional formulary of phrases and phrase-patterns that complied with the rhyme/meter demands of oral verse, as far as preserved records of it permit us to judge; and (3) they were intrinsic to the generative diction of that verse, assimilation and mastery of which was an essential coefficient of production and reproduction of poems that were identifiable and certifiable as such by a poet, his colleagues, and his audiences.

How such a diction itself might have come into existence and how it might have evolved prior to the first poetic and Qur'ānic textualizations of it are questions whose answers can only be speculative. Parry writes, in this connection:

> Actually . . . this birth of a diction is beyond observation, and unless it can really be shown that a people reverting from written to oral poetry created anew a formulaic diction we must suppose that it took place in a very distant past, since the poetry of an unlettered race has as much claim to age as have any of its other institutions. But if the birth of a formulaic diction is only to be described theoretically, we can see in living oral poetries how such a diction is passed on from one age to another, and how it gradually changes. (*SET* II 8 = *MHV* 330)

Corriente himself seems to have sensed something of the intimate, interdependent relationship between the inflective *ᶜarabīya* and the classical poetry, for he frequently feels compelled to account for the significantly higher functional yield of case-endings in early poetry by appealing, for instance, to "the traditional character of Arab aesthetic taste and the rhetorical background of such literary types" (*FY* 28 n. 12)—phrases whose explicatory value leaves something to be desired. Poetry is more dependent upon the *iᶜrāb* system because, he says, it "*follows old patterns more closely*; but for the same reason it is less true to linguistic reality, farther away from the spoken forms and language structure of the epoch, more artificial and less interesting" (*FY* 29 n.16, my italics). With this statement I can agree totally, on condition that "old patterns" be construed as the formulaic phrases, schemata, and diction that enabled an early Arab poet to produce a poem that reflected the cumulative and old-inherited consensus as to what a poem was, and "interesting" construed as applying to the poetic language from a structural linguistic, rather than a cultural linguistic, point of view. This "cleavage between poetry and prose" (*FY* 30 n.16), as evinced by poetry's greater capacity for contrastive use of the inflectional suffixes, seems to have troubled Corriente to some extent, else I do not think he would have made the following claim, which is, in my judgment, so close to the facts of the matter, but so far from adequately explaining them:

> The higher rate of the functional *I^{c}rāb* in poetic contexts of all periods is directly related to the almost servile imitation of ancient models which prevailed throughout the history of Arabic literature in ways not limited to the aesthetic background but even reaching the point of actual borrowing of complete sentences. (*FY* 40)[112]

C.10.c Corriente's contributions have indisputably improved and augmented our understanding of the structure and early history of the Arabic language and of Semitic languages in general. I have found almost all his observations and conclusions to be directly pertinent to the position taken in this chapter, and I do not hesitate to adduce in support of that position his findings as to the non-inflective character of the spoken forms of Arabic underlying the inflective *^{c}arabīya*. However, instead of Corriente's "thesis of coexistence" of both *i^{c}rāb* and *i^{c}rāb*-less dialects "within a single structural frame" (*FY*$_2$ 159), I would propose a different hypothesis to account for the peculiar linguistic situation of Arabic during the sixth and seventh centuries (and thereafter). There occurred no prehistoric dialect "split" into inflective and non-inflective speech-forms. *I^{c}rāb* vowels have been universally eliminated from all forms of spoken Arabic for several centuries at least, and it is far more reasonable to assume that the drift away from the three-case desinential system of proto-Arabic toward the analytic non-inflective structure of Middle Arabic and the living dialects proceeded along more or less uniform lines among *all* groups of Arabic-speakers, though not necessarily at a uniform rate (cf. Corriente *FY* 40–41). Some groups, very probably city-and town-dwellers (as Corriente indicates), would have dropped the case-endings earlier than others. Yet, as the Nabataean Arabs had done so apparently well before the beginning of the Christian era (see following section), it is doubtful whether, by the time of Muḥammad, any group—Bedouins included[113]—would have uttered the *i^{c}rāb* vowels as part of their standard speech in any but a most atrophied and dysfunctional form, if even that (cf. Cohen *KLD* 111).

But *iᶜrāb* was indubitably "alive and well" in pre-and early Islamic poetry, as is attested by practically every verse of it that has come down to us. The isochronous metrical schemes that generated the regular cadence of each line constantly required word-final short vowels in key positions as a matter of course, while the rhyme schemes, with their convention of vocalic pause (*waqf bi t-tarannum*), maintained the pressure consistently to provide distinct and contrastive qualities (*-ū/ī/ā* >*-u/i/a*) for those vowels. And these conditions obtained, even had such final vowels not been uttered in the poet's standard speech.

Parry's is still the best description of how such a "cleavage" (if we should want to use the word) might come about between a poet's spoken language and his poetic diction and of how the language of oral poetry could readily come to preserve sounds, words, constructions, and even whole systems, when necessary, that had long since ceased to be used in standard speech—preserve them not for "rhetorical" or "prestige" reasons, as Corriente asserts of the *iᶜrāb* suffixes, but simply because no other way of making verse was accessible or acceptable (above all, see Parry *SET* II 6–23, esp. 9–12 = *MHV* 329–42, esp. 331–33, and passim). Parry says of the archaic element in oral-formulaic diction:

> As the spoken language changes, the traditional diction of an oral poetry likewise changes so long as there is no need of giving up any of the formulas. . . . But when a change in the form of a word must also change its metrical [and, for Arabic, its rhyme] value . . . , the poet, if he then wished to keep up with the spoken language, would have to put up with a phrase which was metrically false [or which resulted in a discordant rhyme], or give it up altogether and make himself a new one. But neither of these two choices is pleasing. . . . Each formula . . . is the long-proven choice of a long line of singers, and it is not possible that a phrase which is useful in oral composition could be made in any other way than by a singer who, making his verses through his sense of the scheme of the formulaic diction, created, in the stress of the moment, a new phrase more or less like an older one. For otherwise the new phrase would not fit into the scheme of the diction, and since it could be used only with an effort it would not be used at all. . . . Thus by no willful choice, but by the constraint of his technique of verse-making, the singer keeps the formula though its language has become archaic. . . . When the formula can be changed it sooner or later will be, and the cleavage between the old and the new in the style depends on whether it is easy or hard to change the formula. . . . Thus the language of oral poetry changes as a whole neither faster nor slower than the spoken language, but in its parts it changes readily when no loss of formulas is called for, belatedly when there must be such a loss, so that the traditional diction has in it words and forms of everyday use side by side with others that belong to earlier stages of the language. (*SET* II 9–12 = *MHV* 331–33)

There is no need to dwell, any more than we have already, upon the applicability of Parry's words to the state of the pre-literary (i.e., poetic and Qur'ānic) *ᶜarabīya*, with all its oft-noted archaisms, anachronisms, parallel forms, inflectional lapses, and other anomalies. That *ᶜarabīya* had as its most prominent archaic feature the *iᶜrāb* vowels, and certainly no linguistic feature was more deeply embedded in the prosodic constitution of classical Arabic verse—and hence in its diction—than those same *iᶜrāb* vowels. That *ᶜarabīya*, moreover, can never[114] have served any group as their standard speech—neither in the form in which it appears in classical poetry and the Qur'ān nor *a fortiori* in the form later deduced, codified, and expounded by the philologists and grammarians as *al-ᶜarabīya al-fuṣḥā*. Nor, by the same token, can it be taken to represent a *stage* of the language in any linguistically admissible sense of the term. Several *stages* of the language, however, are unquestionably represented in the *ᶜarabīya*, most important of which would naturally be the earlier prehistoric stage when a three-case inflectional system was regularly operative.[115]

In my view, therefore, Corriente's "thesis of coexistence" and many of his observations about what he describes as the "*iᶜrāb*-dialect" still can be read to provide an effective exposition of the linguistic situation in sixth- and seventh-century Arabia, with the reservations expressed above and with the following understanding: the coexistent "*iᶜrāb*-dialect" that he describes was normally spoken by no group or groups at that time either as "standard speech" or "as a mere symbol of high class style or of Bedouin aristocracy" (*pace* Corriente *FY* 32–33).[116] Rather, it constituted the special speech-form routinely mastered by poets and *rāwīs* as an automatic consequence of mastering the art of making and rendering Arabic verse and occasionally employed (with a marked reduction in its already limited synthetic yield) for certain highly formal, non-casual prose or semi-prose elocutions, preeminently the Qur'ān.

According to this theory, furthermore, the vestiges of nunation and the inflectively meaningless final short vowels which are met with sporadically in modern Bedouin or rural renditions of poetry, tales, and such (cf., e.g., Corriente *FY* 23 n. 5, 41 n. 32) would not reflect the dialectal usage of the present or any determinably earlier time. The decisive consideration is that they are to be encountered almost exclusively in poetry, where they only serve to fill certain metrical slots, or more rarely in highly non-casual prose. They must, therefore, be recognized as functioning in those contexts merely as prosodemic counterparts of the three-case *iᶜrāb* suffixes once operative in the early poetic *ᶜarabīya*. And the diction of present-day Arabic-speaking oral poets and storytellers, in which these elements play a prosodemically significant but grammatically insignificant role, would be the distant descendant, after some thousand years of linguistic evolution not of any erstwhile spoken dialect but of that same oral-formulaic inflective *ᶜarabīya* intoned by the pre-Islamic poets and the Prophet of the Qur'ān.

C.10.d With the second item I wish to consider, W. Diem's study "Die nabatäischen Inschriften und die Frage der Kasusflexion im Altarabischen" (*FKA*), we move to some extent outside the realm of protolingual speculation. Diem offers the first substantive evidence that I am aware of for actually dating, with more precision than heretofore, the breakdown of the three-case inflectional system in a major dialect of Arabic. Diem, like Corriente and many other scholars, repeats the observation that "quite the most important feature which differentiates classical Arabic from the present-day Arabic dialects consists in its having held on to the ancient Semitic case-inflectional system, while the present-day dialects are familiar only with a single noninflective [*kasusindifferente*] form of the noun" (*FKA* 227). For him the significant question is, "At what point in time did Arabic abandon the case-inflectional system?" (Ibid.)

To bring us closer to an answer, he subjects to careful examination the forms of the many personal names occurring in the body of inscriptions left by the Arab Nabataeans, who dominated the area from Damascus to what is now Saudi Arabia for a period beginning in the later second century B.C. The inscriptions themselves were written in Aramaic with an Aramaic script. But since Arabic was the spoken language of the Nabataeans, many Arabic elements show up, especially in personal names. There one often finds the Arabic definite article *'l* (=*al*), the Arabic word *'bn*/*bn* (=*ibn*) "son," and so on.[117] Diem writes:

> What is of significance for the problem of the case-inflectional system is that the written forms of these Arabic names exhibit letters on the end which in Semitic languages commonly serve to indicate vowels. The letters in question are [*w*/*u*], [*y*/*i*], and [*'*/*a*]. Coming upon these three letters, one immediately thinks of the three case-endings *u, i, a* of the singular noun, as deduced for Semitic languages in general and preserved in Akkadian, Ugaritic, and classical Arabic—though not in Aramaic. (*FKA* 229)

Considering several alternative explanations for these final vocalic letters (*FKA* 229–30), Diem proposes to analyze the forms on the basis of a division into simple names (ᶜAmr, Jušam, etc.) and compound names (ᶜAbdallāh, Abū Aws, Ibn Qawm, etc.). He determines for the simple forms that better than 95 percent of them were written with a final *w*/*u* (the rest having either a final *y*/*i* or *'*/*a* or no such letter at all)—a circumstance that "justifies considering the written form with [final *w*/*u*] as the rule" (*FKA* 231). This final *w*/*u* in the conventional orthography of simple personal names reflects nothing less than the *u*-suffix of the Arabic nominative originally incorporated into the spelling of the name to represent a sound once heard in that position and retained as a grapheme long after the sound was no longer uttered. It was retained, moreover, because of the conservative character of any orthography— especially Aramaic (ibid.; cf. p. 235).

For compound names, which are all of the genitive-construct type, two determinations are made: one for theophoric names (Amatallāh, Wahballāh, Samsalba^{c}l, etc.) and the second for names with *abū* "father," *ibn* "son," and so forth, and other non-theophoric construct-type names (^{c}Abd ^{c}Amr, Mar['] al-malik, etc.). Theophoric names are written with a final *-y/i* in by far the majority of cases, otherwise with no final vocalic (e.g., *^{c}bd'lhy*[118] over fifty times versus *^{c}bd'lh* only five) In the other group of non-theophoric compound names, the second (genitive) noun is written sometimes with, not final *-y/i*, but final *-w/u*, and sometimes without any final vocalic.[119]

With respect to their last letters, then, compound personal names fall into two categories: (1) theophoric names with final *-y/i* and (2) *abū-*, *ibn-*, and other non-theophoric constructs with final *-w/u*, both categories including written forms without any final vocalic letter whatsoever (*FKA* 233–34). Since the theophoric names composed a "lexical unity," they would have been uttered as genitive constructs from their earliest use as personal names and recorded as a single entity when first set down in writing. Thus, the final *-y/i* shows itself to be as it were the graphemic echo of a once regularly uttered and heard genitive suffix *-i*, which, like the final *-w/u* in simple names corresponding to the nominative *-u*, was preserved by the exceedingly conservative Aramaic orthography. Non-theophoric names, however, forming no such lexical unity and constructed "according to need" and in order to *characterize*, not just to *designate*, particular individuals (i.e., a "father" whose son was "Aws" versus "the slave of God"), merely annexed the simple form, with its orthographically established final *-w/u*, to the first member of the compound. Such names, of course, had nowhere near the antiquity of origin of the theophoric names and were produced on a person-by-person basis at or around the time when the inscriptions themselves were written.

Diem sees but *one* conclusion to be drawn from these circumstances:

> The written forms with final letter [*y/i*] in the compound theophoric names and those with final letter [*w/u*] in the simple names must stem from a time when Nabataean Arabic still had a case-inflectional system, and when the written forms with final [*-w/u*] and final [*-y/i*] expressed a nominative *-u* and genitive *-i* respectively, (both) present in the language. However, already by the time of

> the inscriptions, [i.e., late second century B.C. and thereafter,] . . . Nabataean Arabic must have abandoned the case-inflectional system, a development that had to have been connected with the loss of the short case-vowels. (*FKA* 234)

This is proven by the discrepant spelling of compound names: the writing of final *-w/u* in non-theophoric names where *-y/i* is written in old-established theophoric names "can only mean that the ancient case-system no longer existed and [that] the written form with [*-w/u*] had been kept merely as an orthographic peculiarity" (*FKA* 235).

Needless to say, the occasional forms written without any final vocalic letters reflect the actual linguistic situation throughout the period of the inscriptions: namely, one in which *no* final case-vowels were uttered and simple and compound names were both pronounced alike in that respect, regardless of their different graphemic representations in the conventional Aramaic orthography (ibid.).

Diem's final remarks, touching upon the implications of the fact that Nabataean Arabic had abandoned the Semitic three-case inflectional system before the first century B.C., are of singular importance to the position argued throughout this chapter. He acknowledges that conditions ascertained for the Nabataean dialect—something of a marginal or peripheral one (*Randdialekt*) geographically speaking—should not be predicated directly for the dialects of Central Arabia "out of which classical Arabic emerged [*hervorging*]"[120] (*FKA* 237). Nevertheless, he contends, there is some basis for conjecture:

> If Nabataean Arabic no longer had a case-inflectional system at such an early period, then it is hard to conceive that the bordering Central Arabic dialects would still have kept the full inflectional system until the VIIth century—i.e., eight centuries longer. Even presuming that peripheral dialects like Nabataen first proceeded to abandon the inflection system, this development has to have involved all Arabic dialects [*muss . . . von allen arabischen Dialekten mitgemacht worden sein*] already long before the VIIth century. *Only the language of early Arabic poetry preserved the ancient conditions any longer.* (Ibid.; my italics)

C.11.a Let us return now to the contention that *i^{c}rāb* was "in full flower" in the Bedouin dialects during Muḥammad's lifetime and for about three centuries thereafter. In the final analysis, even for Corriente (see above and n. 113 to this chapter), this hypothesis derives its chief support from the reports of the Muslim philologists regarding the linguistic faculties and grammatical correctness of the Bedouin of their own era. But these reports, which Nöldeke and Fück, among others, accepted more or less at face value (cf. pp. 121–22, 132, above), must be approached with grave reservation and caution. Rabin, for instance, frames his judgment of them in the following terms:

> It seems that this view of the linguistic superiority of the Bedouins was the corollary of the theory which attributed everything that was incorrect to the influence of foreign languages on the speech of the settled population. This was part of the general idealization of early Islamic society and corresponds to the romantic hankering after the primitive in other urban societies. To some extent it was justified by the rich speech of the Bedouin and his natural rhetorical ability, and by the fact that a tradition of Classical poetry still continued among the tribes for some centuries, as is proved by the Dīwān of Hudhail. (*AWA* 18)

Elsewhere, he remarks:

> Even the respect for Bedouin usage must be taken with a grain of salt. The "native assistants" of the [grammatical] schools were most probably professional *ruwāt*. It was the *rāwī* who transmitted literary Arabic usage from generation to generation. Early philologists . . . clearly drew their information from the *ruwāt*, if they did not, as is quite likely, start their own career as *ruwāt*. (*AWA* 23; cf. 12–13)

Rabin's judgment is, on the whole, upheld by Blachère (*SIIB*), who adds that, besides being *ruwāt*, the Bedouin informants whose names have been preserved were known poets as well. Blau (*BBA*) also follows Rabin's judgment along general lines, but feels "that he went too far in his scepticism" (*RBA* 43 n. 2). Blau agrees that "the stories in which every ordinary Bedouin poses as an expert in every fine shade of Classical Arabic must be considered as apocryphal" (*RBA* 45). Moreover, he very perceptively notes that, of the justifications given by Rabin for the high linguistic reputation of the Bedouins, the only one "of real importance" is that "a tradition of Classical Arabic poetry still continued among the tribes for some centuries" —and that was due to their largely unchanged conditions of life (ibid.). Also to be acknowledged is the leading role played by the *ruwāt* in maintaining this poetic and linguistic continuity.[121] "But besides these sociological reasons," Blau adds, "there was also a linguistic consideration that not only facilitated the survival of Classical Arabic poetry among the Bedouins but, in our opinion, also contributed to the emergence of these apocryphal stories" (ibid.). This consideration lay in the dichotomy (which, so far as I can determine from Blau's writings, is largely assumed) between the non-inflective, analytic Middle Arabic urban dialects, on the one hand, and the synthetic Bedouin dialects and classical Arabic, with their case- and mood-endings, on the other.[122]

> Because of the chasm between Middle Arabic dialects and Classical Arabic, the urban speakers had to overcome considerable difficulties when they tried to use Classical Arabic, whereas even ordinary Bedouins, speaking, as in the *Djāhiliyya,* synthetic dialects closely akin to Classical Arabic, could do so relatively easily and were less apt than the urban populations to make mistakes.

> It was therefore much easier for a *rāwī* of Bedouin stock to transmit Classical Arab poetry. Moreover, even an ordinary Bedouin, speaking his own dialect, may have appeared to speakers of Middle Arabic vernaculars of the lower strata of the town population to be speaking some kind of Classical Arabic, since he used case endings, the most conspicuous outward sign of the literary language. Against this background, the emergence of stories extolling the linguistic faculties of Bedouins becomes quite understandable. (*RBA* 46)

Yet Blau does acknowledge (1) that the stories about the linguistic superiority of the Bedouins that do have some historical basis "refer to Bedouins who acted as *ruwāt* and were therefore masters of Classical Arabic" (*RBA* 47), although they did not speak it as their natural language;[123] (2) that ordinary Bedouins might be questioned on matters of lexicography, but probably little, if at all, on matters of phonology, morphology, and syntax, about which the philologists were much stricter; and (3) that "all the stories about Bedouins who simply could not speak anything but 'correct' Arabic are to be regarded as apocryphal" (*RBA* 47–48). Arriving at a similar conclusion and stressing that the *ᶜarabīya*, not a tribal vernacular, was the philologists' object in consulting the Bedouins, Spitaler had already written:

> Seen thus, the fact cannot be surprising that the philologists actually did encounter *iᶜrāb* among the Bedouins. But to conclude therefrom that there would not at all have been a language without *iᶜrāb* among the Bedouins would be an inadmissible *argumentum e silentio*. (rev *Ar* 146a; cf. esp. Corriente *FY* 26 n. 8)

Thus, it is hard to understand how Blau, in a response to Spitaler's review, could make the assertion, "As to the Bedouin dialects, their synthetic character is, in our opinion, sufficiently established by the stories about the linguistic superiority of the Bedouin" (*ELB* 3 n. 1).[124] Given what seems to be originally an assumption that the dialects were synthetic, such reasoning appears ambiguous, if not circular.

C.11.b The philologists, however, especially the early ones, were by no means unanimous in granting linguistic precedence to the Bedouins and in considering their usage naturally correct. The poetical fault *iqwā'*, already noted above (pp. 104–5), was recognized as the consequence of an incapacity for handling the relatively more synthetic poetic language with its *iᶜrāb* inflections. The second/eighth-century Šīᶜite poet, as-Sayyid b. Muḥammad al-Ḥimyarī, for instance, quite explicitly identifies *iqwā'* (variation of the desinential vowel of the rhyme-word) with *laḥn* (faulty use or neglect of *iᶜrāb* suffixes) (al-Marzubānī *Muw* 3:9; cf. Fück *Ar* 52).[125] On the authority of Yūnus b. Ḥabīb (d. 182/798 or 152/769), the philologist and critic

Muḥammad b. Sallām al-Jumaḥī (see chap. 4, n. 82) observes (1) that *iqwā'* was fairly common in poems of the desert Arabs (*al-aᶜrāb*); (2) that it was more common among minor than among major poets; (3) that modern poets had to avoid it because they knew better; and (4) that the Bedouin in general did not care if it occurred, so it was (more ?) excusable in his case (*TFS* 58–59; al-Marzubānī *Muw* 17).[126] If I have interpreted this passage correctly,[127] it would seem to imply that Ibn Sallām, and his source Yūnus b. Ḥabīb, accepted certain facts about Arab poets and about the idiom in which they poetized. First, even the best of the classical poets did not have sufficient mastery over the synthetic properties of the poetic idiom to ensure consistent placement of the proper rhyming inflection. Second, "modern"—and hence, educated and literate—poets, because of their linguistic formation and rhetorical training, must be considered culpably negligent if they committed *iqwā'* in their verses. Third, the rule of avoiding *iqwā'* simply could not be applied to the Bedouin poet in general, because he made no serious attempt to provide the rhyme-words of his poem with a constant *and correct* desinential vowel throughout. Whether we are to infer from this that among the Bedouins poetry was commonly rendered (as it is today) pausing at verse-ends either with *iskān* or with one of the non-inflectional vocalic accommodations alluded to above (cf. p. 105 and n. 26; also Fischer *SVA* 51) cannot be determined. The observation recorded by Ibn Sallām, however, makes it quite doubtful that poetic rendition by "the Bedouin" (*al-badawīy*) gave any indication of a natural ability on his part for dealing with an inflective and more synthetic language.

One of the earliest statements we have on Bedouin linguistic usage, made before the romanticization and classicization of the Bedouin tradition had become an Arab-Islamic cultural dogma, specifically denies the capacity of the common Bedouin to handle properly the inflective aspects of the poetic *ᶜarabīya*. In the *Naqā'iḍ* of Jarīr and al-Farazdaq, Abū ᶜUbayda (d. ca. 210/865), recounting the "Day" of Tiyās, includes six verses by Ḏu'ayb b. Kaᶜb, a Tamīmī poet. One of the verses (*Naq* 1026:3) is rendered thus:

jānī-ka man yajnī ᶜalay-ka wa qad
tuᶜdi ṣ-ṣiḥāḥa mabārika l-jurbū

"Who gathers you gain will do you harm,[128] for there may infect healthy (camels), through resting-places, those with the mange."

In a scholium (*Naq* 1026:5–6), Abū ᶜUbayda notes: "Dā'ūd, one of Ḏu'ayb's descendants, and others recited it to me [*anšada-nī*] thus: *aṣ-ṣiḥāḥa mabāriku l-jurbi*—putting *mabārik* in the nominative and *al-jurb* in the genitive. But that would constitute *iqwā'*." Then he quotes the quite frank opinion of Abu l-Xaṭṭāb al-Axfaš al-Akbar (d. 177/793),[129] a contemporary of al-Xalīl and, next to him and Yūnus b. Ḥabīb, one of Sībawayh's chief authorities:

> Common Bedouins neither understand the poet's intent nor have they any skill at interpreting (it). *Iqwā'* in this (verse) came about just because those who rendered it lack understanding. The poet simply meant: "And the mangy (camel) may infect the healthy one through a resting-place." But when they encountered the verse with displacements in word-order, they were unable to deliver it intelligibly. And they came upon *mabārik* as a diptote: and then they lost sight of the meaning altogether. (*Naq* 1026:6–9)[130]

The early date, unimpeachable authority, and precise wording of this comment mark it as one of the more reliable and germane testimonies on this subject that we possess. Abu l-Xaṭṭāb's reputation for piety, trustworthiness, and philological acumen (e.g., *Muz* II 74:18–19), together with his personal familiarity with the Bedouins (ibid.) and his noted penchant for never omitting the *iᶜrāb* suffixes in his speech,[131] all give his opinion here additional weight. Moreover, the great scholar Abū ᶜUbayda, who had studied with al-Axfaš, without hesitation adduces his mentor's judgment on a matter that subsequently would be looked at from a far less disinterested point of view. And so we can safely assume that nothing asserted by al-Axfaš contradicted anything in Abū ᶜUbayda's own not inconsiderable experience. Further, given (1) the later emergence and suspect character of the stories about Bedouin linguistic superiority, (2) the extreme likelihood that it was precisely the *ruwāt— trained in the oral tradition of poetry*—who served as authorities on the *ᶜarabīya* for the philologists (*not* "the common Bedouin"), and (3) the other considerations raised in the course of this discussion, I feel we are justified in accepting the word of these scholars, at least, as valid evidence for the general conditions of the Bedouin dialects during most of the second/eighth and early third/ninth centuries, if not earlier as well.

What al-Axfaš's statement reflects is a linguistic situation in which the majority of Bedouins, unversed in the praxis of poetry and, specifically, unable to deal effectively with its syntactic and inflectional complexities, spoke an idiom that could scarcely have been either identical with or "closely akin to" the synthetic *ᶜarabīya* proper to the poets. And if this proposition is sound, then the idea that the *iᶜrāb* was "in full flower" in Bedouin speech as late as the fourth/tenth century can no longer be taken for granted. Languages do not become transformed from non-inflective to inflective and back to non-inflective again in somewhat less than two centuries while circumstances in which they are spoken undergo no significant change.

C.11.c In addition, it has been the presumed synthetic character of the Bedouin dialects during the Islamic literary period to which modern writers have attached "the greatest weight of all" (see p. 121 above) as proof of *i^crāb* in living Arabic speech at an earlier period. If, therefore, such a synthetic character cannot validly be presumed or proven, then one can no longer reject the possibility—indeed, probability—that most or all of the vernaculars heard in Arab territories during the seventh and perhaps the sixth centuries A.D., among nomads and urbanites alike, had already lost the use of final short-vowels as case- and mood-markers and that these desinential vowels were retained, and very likely recognized, as the unique property of poetry and formal elocutionary prose (as Vollers had proposed some years ago; cf. §C.3.b, above). It requires little proof to verify how deeply rooted these final short vowels were in the very phonological texture of every classical Arabic verse (cf. Nöldeke *BSS* 3–4) and how indispensable their differential values were to the production of the consistent and traditional verse-end rhyme (cf. §B.3.d, above). To utter eloquent verses such that the words bearing these archaic suffixes would fall into accommodating metrical positions and to structure the syntax of each verse of a poem so as to provide throughout the same verse-end vocalic desinence (not to mention the same consonant)—to do this might well have required a skill in the oral rendition of poetry and a familiarity with its synthetic linguistic peculiarities such as was, al-Axfaš, Abū ^cUbayda, and others attest, beyond the range of "the common Bedouin," and such as may have been possible to acquire only as part of the oral poetical tradition inherited, assimilated, and regenerated by the practicing *rāwī* in the course of becoming a proficient poet. (cf. also Spitaler rev *Ar* 145b; Cohen *ELA* 183).

D. What we are able to determine about early attitudes toward Muḥammad and his Qur'ānic message may also be understood to lend support to this hypothesis—namely, that full, regular, and syntactically meaningful *i^crāb* inflections were uttered almost solely during the rendition of poetry and other highly non-casual elocutions, and usually by those whose formation in such a tradition of oral rendition had endowed them with this peculiar linguistic aptitude. The Qur'ān, as is well known, most insistently denies that Muḥammad was either a poet or a *kāhin* and seeks to dissociate itself from the verses of the former or the vaticinations of the latter.[132] One is made aware that comparisons—invidious or otherwise—had been drawn by Muḥammad's Meccan detractors between his revelations and the familiar utterances of poets and soothsayers; and one generally and, I believe, correctly assumes that such comparisons had their basis in some sort of perceived similarities of form and style and, to unsympathetic observers, source of inspiration as well.[133]

D.1.a That formal and stylistic similarities did exist between the rhymed prose of the early *sūras* and the *saj^c^* oracles of the *kāhins* is beyond doubt; although how close these similarities actually were is still a matter of question (cf. Blachère *HLA* 212). Yet, judging from the evidence in the Qur'ān, the charge that the Prophet was a *kāhin* seems not to have been thought so grave or to have required so vehement a refutation as the one that he was a poet. It is, to be sure, explicitly stated that Muḥammad is not "by thy Lord's blessing . . . a soothsayer—nor possessed (*majnūn*)" (LII:29), and that his utterances constitute "the speech of a noble Messenger, . . . not the speech of a soothsayer (little do you recall)" (LXIX:40, 42). But both statements occur in immediate connection with equally emphatic denials of imputed poetic abilities (cf. LII:30–31; LXIX:41). Moreover, the Qur'ān makes specific allusion to the circumstance that the Prophet's revelation had been dismissed by the Meccans as merely the words of a poet (XXI:5; XXXVII:36/5). And in another context one finds the express declaration: "We have not taught him [*sc*. Muḥammad] poetry; it is improper for him (*lā yanbaġī la-hu*). It is only a reminder and an articulate recitation" (XXXVI: 69).

This same theme of the *proper* or *suitable* genre for prophetic, as opposed to poetic, expression recurs in the *sūra* of *The Poets*. There the charges that Muḥammad was a poet possessed by *jinn* (*šā^c^ir majnūn*)

> were answered by the affirmation that the Koran is inspired by God, is not the work of human beings, is inimitable, and *sui generis*. To prove its divine origin and uniqueness it became necessary to distinguish it from the discourse with which it had been confused by the Meccans, namely, poetry. The most effective way of demonstrating this contrast and the mutually exclusive essences of the two was by contrasting their respective sources; God, the source of the Koran, and the *shayāṭīn* [demons], the source of poetry. (Shahīd *CKE* 570)

Thus, we meet the unequivocal denial:

> Not by the demons has it [*sc*. the Qur'an] been
> brought down.
> *It is improper for them*, nor are they able.
> Truly, they are removed from hearing.
> (XXXVI:210-12; my italics)

We are informed, rather, with polemical fervor,

> . . . upon whom the demons do come down.
> They come down upon every culpable liar [*affāk aṯīm*]
> who (all) give ear, while most of them speak falsely.
> And the poets!—Attending them (are) those who lead
> astray [i.e., the demons, *al-ġāwūn*]
> Have you not seen them wildering in every valley,
> and how they say what they do not do?
> (XXVI:221-26)[134]

It seems evident, then, that the public accusation that Muḥammad's utterances were identical with those of the *kāhins* and, more seriously, with those of the poets impaired his prestige as the Messenger of God to his people and severely threatened the success of his mission. Yet, we might ask, wherein lay that similarity between the Qur'anic revelations and pre-Islamic poetry upon which such an accusation had presumably to be based? What precisely did the early *sūras* have in common with the classical *qaṣīdas* and other poetic genres that would have justified the assertion of Muhammad's detractors that he was a poet and his preaching poetry? Relating the content and form of the early Meccan revelations to that of the poems we have come to accept as pre-Islamic, one cannot fail to observe that there is apparently only the most superficial ground for comparison. The complex of themes, figures of speech, and images emerging from the Qur'ān, for instance, is so far removed from that which prevailed in the poetry and each complex is so richly and diversely articulated within its own context that we cannot honestly suspect confusion of the two genres to have arisen because of any similarity of content. Formal differences, too, would have seemed just as pronounced to hearers who were at all acquainted with the classical poetic tradition. Apart from the obvious fact that the Qur'ān lacked any of the isochronic metrical regularity that made up the very fabric of Arabic verse rendition, even the rhymes terminating the *saj*ᶜ units (which many have assumed to have lain behind the confusion) represented a significant departure from the technique associated with poetry. The Qur'ānic rhyme convention, entailing pause with *iskān*, must have sounded in noticeable contrast to the long final vowels of pause with *tarannum* usually heard in formal poetic rendition. The difference between consonantal rhymes and vocalic rhymes could scarcely have escaped a people oriented so predominantly toward the spoken word as the Arabs of the early seventh century A.D.—even those settled at a commercial center like Mecca.

And we can guess that such disparities did not escape the Meccans, for Ibn Isḥāq records the authoritative judgment attributed (perhaps tendentiously) to one of Muḥammad's strongest early opponents, al-Walīd b. Muġīra. Al-Walīd argued against the opinions current among his Qurašī compatriots, to the effect that the Prophet fit none of the formal (or behaviorial) categories of mantic experience known to them:

> They said, "He is a *kāhin*." He said, "By God, he is not that, for we have seen the *kāhins*, and his (speech) is not the unintelligible murmuring (*zamzama*) and rhymed prose (*saj*ᶜ) of a *kāhin*." "Then he is possessed (*majnūn*)," they said. "No, he is not that," he said. "We have seen and known the possessed state, and here is no choking, spasmodic movements, and whispering." "Then he is a poet," they said. "He is not that," he replied. "We have known poetry in all its

> forms and meters, and this is not poetry." "Then he is a sorcerer," they said. "No he is not that," he said, "for we have seen sorcerers and their sorcery, and here is no spitting and no knots." (Ibn Hišām *Sīra* 171:6–11; trans. adapted from Guillaume *LM* 121)[135]

Another pagan chieftain and opponent of Muḥammad, ᶜUtba b. Rabīᶜa, is said to have expressed (more concisely) a similar opinion (*Sīra* 186:18–19).

D.1.b Thus, the following considerations can be raised. The Qur'ān bore no sharp resemblances, either in form or content, to the poetry composed among the pre-Islamic Arabs as we know it.[136] This fact can be ascertained by simple comparison of the two genres and seems to have been recognized by discerning auditors of the Prophet's time as well. Nevertheless, the confusion persisted almost throughout the Meccan period, furnishing Muḥammad's enemies with (apparently) one of their most potent polemical weapons against him—one which drew down an emphatic Qur'ānic denunciation and a profound differentiation between the two sources of mantic inspiration, the God of Muḥammad and the *jinn* and demons of the poets and *kāhins*. And so, as Margoliouth wrote half a century ago:

> We are confronted with a slight puzzle: Mohammed, who was not acquainted with the art [of poetry], was aware that his revelations were not in verse; whereas the Meccans, who presumably knew poetry when they heard or saw[!] it, thought they were. We should have expected the converse. (*OAP* 418)

Margoliouth resolved this "slight puzzle" by advancing his famous theory that the poems we know as pre-Islamic were actually forgeries of a later, Islamic period, being largely "a development of the styles found in the Qur-'ān" (*OAP* 446). This theory, based upon often specious—not to say dishonest (cf. Arberry *SO* 238)—argumentation, can no longer be regarded as tenable. In addition to the refutations already referred to (chap. 1, n. 30), one can cite also a "final argument," adduced by H. A. R. Gibb, "that it would be as impossible to 'reconstruct' the poetry of the Jāhilīya from the poetry of the Umayyad period as it would be to 'reconstruct' Elizabethan from Caroline drama" (quoted in Shahīd *CKE* 564 n. 3; cf. Gibb *ALI* 21).

Still, the "puzzle" does remain, and in my opinion it admits of only one convincing solution. The single feature that we can be sure the Qur'ān shared with the mantic expressions of the *kāhins* and, especially, the poets was a feature that could have been so striking to ordinary Arab audiences that it obscured glaring disparities in form and content between the genres and was scarcely to be explained except as a product of supernatural (i.e., demonic) inspiration. This feature would have been the use of the non-vernacular classical *ᶜarabīya*, the language that had been created, conditioned, and cultivated through an old-inherited and seemingly pan-Arab tradition of poetic rendition. Granted that the association of Muḥammad with the *kāhins* was, to some extent, understandable, given a certain formal correspondence between his early revelations and their oracular incantations. Nonetheless, the accusation that he was a poet is in no way explicable unless we assume (1) that Arabic poetry, at least as it has come down to us, had simply not been known in pre-Islamic Mecca and the Ḥijāz, and poems and reports of poetry from that area were later fabrications (Margoliouth's position); (2) that the Meccan Arabs were utterly incapable of distinguishing between these two very disparate verbal art-forms (hardly a likely possibility—any more than the previous one—if there is any truth to the accounts concerning the fairs at ᶜUkāẓ); or (3) that the *linguistic idiom* employed in framing the Qur'ānic messages was, to the minds of Muḥammad's hearers (and of Muḥammad himself), inextricably and exclusively bound up with their total experience of poetry, so that they were quite unprepared to hear it enounced competently and coherently in any other genre of comparable length and artistry. (If the activities of the *kāhins* have not been grossly misrepresented to us by the sources, their short, enigmatic, and highly occasional utterances offered no real precedent for recurrent and sustained use of the poetic idiom outside the realm of poetry, as represented by the Qur'ān.)

No one would doubt that the inflective classical *ᶜarabīya* was integral, perhaps unique, to the very nature of pre- and early Islamic poetic production; and most have come to agree that the *ᶜarabīya* of the poets and the language of the Qur'ān are essentially identical and that this poetic idiom was not spoken by any group of Arabs as a vernacular tongue. It should not be surprising, therefore, if the Meccans and others who listened to the Prophet's formal preaching early in his career had been impressed by this man's ability to hold forth eloquently, correctly, and at considerable length, using a form of Arabic they had heretofore heard used so well only by poets. And their wonder could have been all the greater and their imputation of poetical powers to Muḥammad all the more ready, if the difference between their own spoken dialects and the speech of poets poetizing corresponded to a difference between noninflective and inflective linguistic forms. Such a situation, too, would account partially for the apparent failure of almost all of Muḥammad's contemporaries, even among the poets, to take up the Qur'ānic challenge to "bring a *sūra*" (or "ten *sūras*") like those that they had accused him of fabricating (II:23/1; X:38/9; XI:13/6: cf. XVII:10).[137] If the speech of Muḥammad's hearers was normally analytic, then the proper use of this inflective idiom of poetry at any time would have put a considerable strain upon the linguistic capacities of all but those nurtured in the tradition of oral poetic rendition of which it formed an indispensable and indistinguishable element. And even poets themselves could have been hard pressed to utilize their own idiom successfully for utterances in which the generative template of vocalically conditioned rhyme and meter was inoperative.

D.2 It is not difficult to understand why the Qur'ān would have been formulated in the inflective language of poetry, despite the confusion of the two genres this led to. The prestige that was attached to the "hallowed language of poetry" (see above) among the Arabs, together with its aura of supernormal virtuosity and its interdialectal intelligibility, left any other alternative practically out of the question, in view of the intent and scope of the Prophet's mission from the outset.[138] While the pre-Hijra program of that mission, as it emerges from the middle and later Meccan *sūras*, called for a decisive break with the poetic-*cum*-mantic traditions of the Arab past and the establishment of Muḥammad's authority and stature as the culmination of a long line of "national" prophets,[139] the linguistic connection with the repudiated poets was not merely maintained: it was transformed and, as it were, co-opted, like so many elements in the non-Islamic milieu, into the special and distinctive feature of the Islamic message. Hence, on one hand, the identification of Muḥammad as a poet or soothsayer was to be rejected in no uncertain terms, and both the style and the subject-matter of the *sūras* of this period move farther and farther away from any formal similarity to their utterances: "The traces of the poetic spirit which often show up in the earliest *sūras* become indeed ever more scarce, though they do not disappear entirely" (Nöldeke/Schwally *GQ* I 119). On the other hand, however, it was precisely at this time, when the Qur'ān was pointing out and expounding on the magisterial relationship of a prophet to his national community, that the ethnic attributive *ᶜarabīy* was introduced into the revelations and applied to (among other things) the language in which they were enounced.

D.3 The term *ᶜarabīy* occurs three times applied specifically to *līsan* "language, tongue," and two out of the three with the additional qualifier *mubīn* "clear, distinguishing, articulate" (XVI:103/5; XXVI:195; XLVI:12/ 1). In seven instances it modifies (directly or indirectly) *qur'ān* (XII:2; XX:113/2; XXXIX:28/9; XLI:2/1, 44; XLII:7/5; XLIII:3/2); and once it is used with *ḥukm* "judgment, jurisdiction" (XIII:37). In the opinion of most authorities, all of these passages were revealed after opposition to Muḥammad had broken out and before his Hijra to Medina,[140] so one can legitimately seek the significance of the term *ᶜarabīy* within the context of the revelations and prophetic program of those years. And indeed *āya* XIV:4, revealed approximately in the middle of this period (no. 78 in Blachère's enumeration), establishes both the context and the sense in which the word is to be taken:

> We have sent no Messenger
> save with the tongue of his people [*lisān qawmi-hi*]
> that he might clearly expound to them.

Lisān ^{c}arabīy, then, to no one's surprise, is an "Arab (*or* Arabic) tongue," and *qur'ān ^{c}arabīy* is an "Arab (*or* Arabic) recitation." But what did this word mean to the Qurayš of Mecca; to the Aws and Xazraj of Medina; and to the several other tribes who heard Muḥammad's message? As a rule, the socio-political consciousness of each of these relatively self-contained tribal groups seldom had an effective extent beyond the limits of that group's operative sense of relationship through kinship or alliance.[141] D. Müller, in fact, has held that it was Muḥammad who *first* spoke about an "Arabic" language and an "Arabic" Qur'ān; although he, like his Arab contemporaries, did not know the word *^{c}arab* as an ethnic or national designation, but only the word *a^{c}rāb* as a name for the desert Arabs or Bedouins in general (in Pauly/Wissowa *RECA* II 344–45). Müller's position cannot be maintained as such, but it is clear that the Qur'ānic use of the word *^{c}arabīy* represented, in certain ways, an important departure from the usage that seems to have been current in the early seventh century A.D.

The word *^{c}arab*,[142] in one form or another, probably originated among *non-Arab* settled peoples of the Near East as a more or less generic appellative for either the desert itself or desert nomads of any kind, even including those of the Iranian plateau. First used by the Greeks, it seems, as a specific ethnic and geographical designation referring to the Bedouins of the Arabian peninsula and the Syrian desert, the words "Arabia" and "Arab" come to denote this area and its inhabitants (who were later called "Saracens" as well). Subsequently, "Arabia" itself was adopted as the official name of the Roman province whose sometimes fluctuating boundaries roughly corresponded to those of the old Nabataean kingdom centered at Petra. During the Christian era, this province (or the peninsula proper) was the birthplace of at least one declared heresy (*haeresis Arabicorum*) (see Aigrain in *DHGE* III 1163–66; A. Lehaut in ibid. 1339); and as a province of the Christian Byzantine Empire, it enjoyed a colorful, if somewhat wayward, ecclesiastical history.[143] There existed, then, at least among Eastern Christians, some precedent for speaking of "Arabia" and "Arabs" (or "Saracens") in terms of a reasonably identifiable geopolitical and religious entity.

The term *^{c}arab*, however, is not known to have been used by Arabic-speaking peoples as an ethnic designation for themselves before the mid-fourth and the fifth centuries A.D.; and then it seems to have denoted both sedentarized and nomadic residents of the area, as it had already come to do to an even greater extent in contemporary non-Arabic usage. Certainly, the form *ᶜarab* (or *ᶜurb*), in its few attested appearances in pre-Islamic poetry, does seem to have had this wider ethnic application and is generally to be found in opposition to the (linguistically based?) appellative *aᶜjam* (*ᶜajam*, etc.) "barbarian, non-Arab, non-Arabic speaking."[144] The quasi-plural form *aᶜrāb*, though, tended to occur only in the sense of "Bedouins (camel nomads)." There is no question that such is the sense of the word as used in the Qur'ān (von Wissmann "Badw" *EI*² I 884a–885a). Incidentally, the basically pejorative use of *aᶜrāb* in that context precludes any direct *intentional* derivation of *ᶜarabīy*, as an appellative for the language of revelation, from the term for Bedouins, as is often assumed.[145]

One can grant, therefore, that it is "scarcely tenable" to contend, as Müller had, "that the name 'Arab' was unknown to the natives of Arabia till Mohammed introduced it as a national designation" (Nöldeke in *EB* 274b). Before Mohammed's mission began, the name had been used widely and commonly by peoples both to the north and south with whom the peninsular Arabs were in close cultural and commercial contact, and it was known among the peninsular Arabs themselves. Also, the peninsula itself seems occasionally to have been called *ᶜArba* (or *ᶜAraba*), whence Ibn al-Kalbī (d. 204/819) finds the derivation of the term *ᶜarabīy* (Yāqūt *MB* III 634:8–11).[146] Whether such appellative uses of the root *ᶜ-r-b* had originated indigenously among the Arabs or whether they had been borrowed and Arabicized from an established terminology that was standard throughout much of the civilized Near East (including the South Arabian kingdoms; cf. M. Höfner in Gabrieli *ASB* 60–68), one thing is certain. Applying the term *ᶜarabīy* to the language of the Qur'ānic message and to the Qur'ān itself, three times in deliberate opposition to *aᶜjamīy* or *al-aᶜjamīn* (XVI:103/5; XXVI:195-8; XLI:44), meant to Muḥammad and his contemporaries neither more nor less that adapting an already existing semantic usage for the purpose (1) of identifying, with greater precision and in sharp contrast to previous non-Arabic scriptural revelations, the special and perhaps "inimitable" linguistic idiom of this new "Arab" revelation' and (2) of redirecting the Prophet's followers, all speakers of various Arabic dialects who had now to learn *to recite correctly* the message he preached, to think of this idiom in altogether new terms. No longer were they to conceive of it just as the "hallowed speech of poetry"—the exclusive property of poets and the primary vehicle for expressing all that was chauvinistic, divisive, overweening, and anti-authoritarian in tribal life (cf. Goldziher *MS* I chaps. 1 and

2, esp. 44–50, 54–60; Chelhod *ISI* 23, 41–42, 58). Rather were they to accept this idiom for what it more truly had become: in conjunction with the oral poetical tradition, from which theretofore it had been essentially indistinguishable and by virtue of which it had remained alive and in use among groups of varied dialectal and socio-cultural complexions, the linguistic form that was to be classical Arabic had come to provide the Arabic-speaking inhabitants of provincial Arabia and the peninsula proper, by the opening of the Prophet's career, with some feeling of identity and unity, at least as a *Kulturnation*, if not a *Staatsnation* (von Grunebaum *NAU*; Caskel in von Grunebaum *SICH* 37; idem *BBGA* 10–11).

This feeling could only have been intensified and solidified as a result of religious, economic, political, and military events of the preceding 50–100 years, especially Persian and Byzantine (i.e., *a^{c}jamīy*) interference in the northern Arab buffer kingdoms, Abyssinian incursions from the South, and Mecca's own consolidation and politico-economic hegemony over West Arabia. Furthermore, just as Mecca's position and prosperity owed much to a studied course of political neutrality with regard to her more powerful southern and northern neighbors, so in turn this course seems to have precluded the city's general adoption of either of the major monotheistic religions, Christianity or Judaism, because of the extent to which these religions, had been compromised in Arab eyes by association with the major rival powers (cf. Watt *MMec* 11–16, 27–28; idem *IIS* 13–14, 258–59). The preaching of Islam as a specifically "Arab" religion[147] (though not necessarily a "religion of the Arabs") avoided this complication. And as a monotheistic message in "the tongue of his people," Muḥammad's "Arabic recitation" would not only have afforded his compatriots an indigenous alternative to the linguistically alien (e.g., Aramaic, especially) liturgies and scriptures that they heard in use among even the Arab Christians and Jews of the time (cf. Paret *MK* 53–55; Abbott *RNAS* 13).[148] It also distinguished and exalted the primary and most readily perceptible bond joining the Arabs together as a cultural community—the language of their poetry—and it did so within the eastern Mediterranean environment where religion, nationality, and language have for millenia been hopelessly intertangled. Thus, the Qur'ān as a "scripture" in "an articulate Arabic tongue" brought to the Arabs who heard it an increasing sense of unity (as colinguists, at least), prestige (as possessors of the "last word" in revelation), and purpose (as strivers in "the way of God"). As events demonstrated thereafter, this shared sense soon obviated any further need for Meccan neutrality and carried the Arabs and their language over most of the civilized world.

D.4.a The effects that the Qur'ān had upon the cultural and linguistic consciousness of first/seventh-century speakers of Arabic are nearly impossible to overestimate, and they are equally impossible to estimate accurately. How extensive literacy had become among the Arabs before Islam is still uncertain. That it was much more widely spread than had been thought some years ago is clear, at least in the areas of southern Mesopotamia and Syria and the Ḥijāzī settlements. But, although it is possible that some poems were recorded before the second half of the first/seventh century,[149] this practice can hardly be said to have been the rule, nor can it be adduced as evidence of poetic *composition* in writing (cf. p. 14 above and chap. 2 n. 117).[150] A pertinent question also would be: What form of Arabic was transcribed as the written language at Ḥīra, the Laxmid city on the Euphrates often considered to have been the cradle of Arabic *literary* culture (cf. Abbot *RNAS* 5–8; Blachère *HLA* 347, 363–64 and passim; Rabin "ᶜArabiyya" *EI²* I 565a) and the site where Arabic poems may first have been set down in writing (see, e.g., Krenkow *UWP* 266; Asad *MSJ* 195)? If there is truth to the theory that the Arabic script in use in Mecca and the Ḥijāz before Islam had been adapted and was ordinarily employed to transcribe the vernacular spoken there (cf. chap. 3, § C.4.a, above), or at most a kind of commercial *koinē* distinct from the poetic idiom (cf. Geyer rev. *VSA* 13, 17; von Grunebaum *CI* 26; Corriente *FY* 27 n. 9), then we cannot disregard the possibility that an analogous situation had obtained at Ḥīra. Was the form of Arabic usually written there also a local vernacular, perhaps somewhat adapted for scribal use, as seems to have been the case at Mecca and Medina? Was it actually a *Schriftsprache*, in the more proper sense of the word? Or could the systematization and standardization of the poetic *ᶜarabīya* into a literary language already, before the Qur'ānic text was established, have been under way in this Christian Arab center, providing a precedent and a pattern for the later wholesale adoption of the oral poetic idiom as the language of literate culture wherever Arabic was spoken? Similar questions can now also be asked regarding the Arab Christian community at Najrān (see nn. 68 and 148 to this chapter). But none of these questions can at present be definitively answered. Yet regardless of how they might be answered, we have to accept that, for all practical purposes, the writing-down of the Qur'ān represented one of the earliest—if not the earliest—large-scale attempts to reproduce graphically the oral language of poetry.

But at the same time an entirely new attitude toward this language was fostered. For, as envisioned by Muḥammad, the idiom of the Qur'ān, so far from belonging preeminently to the poets "who were the prophets of tribal hatred'' (Goldziher *MS* I 80), assumed the role of ''the tongue of his people'' through which God's message was made known to them. Because of the religious and social requirements of the Islamic community, and above all because of the liturgical principle of public oral recitation and prayer, the capacity for using this idiom could no longer be reserved solely to poets, *rāwīs*, *kāhins*, and their like, but had to become the common acquistion of all who heard, understood, and accepted God's ''Arabic Qur'ān'' as delivered through his chosen Arab Messenger. This included, at first, all the members of Muḥammad's super-tribal Arab Muslim community and, later, the entire community of Muslims, Arab and non-Arab alike (only some of whom at any time would be endowed with notable poetic ability).

For even the earliest faithful to acquire this capacity, though, a radical departure would have to be made from the formative process through which it had been instilled in those acknowledged masters of the art of the word, the poets. One neither expected nor desired that the ordinary believer undergo the long, arduous, and relatively unstructured training regimen of a *rāwī* in order to develop an ability to handle the poetic language. Moreover, as far as the poets themselves and their audiences were concerned, this ''language'' (if such we may call it) had been simply an incidental concomitant of the poetic art, the distinctive medium of poetic rendition, indistinguishable and inseparable from the poem itself (and from analogous forms of non-casual verbal expression). It was the Qur'ān, with its uncompromisingly innovative and effective use of this medium for non-poetic purposes and its forthright claim to being ''an *Arabic* recitation'' in ''an articulate *Arabic* tongue,''[151] that perhaps for the first time gave recognition and significance to the poetic ''language'' as a quantity abstractable from the poetry and accessible to non-poets as well. It was the Qur'ān, too, as a self-consciously instituted ''scripture'' (*kitāb*), like those of the other prominent ''scriptuaries'' (*ahl al-kitāb*), that from the first laid the groundwork for the intellectual and educational revolution that was to come. The ''articulate Arabic tongue'' that was intrinsic to this ''Arabic recitation'' could be learned just as all true knowledge had ever been learned: through the written word of revealed scripture. This ''language,'' too, would be included in that ''true human knowledge . . . equated with religious insight'' (Rosenthal KT 29)[152] that God ''taught [man] by the Pen'' (XCVI:4), when He ''taught him articulateness (*al-bayān*)'' (LV:4/3),[153] and that can be acquired only through direct revelation or, the Qur'ān implies, through ''studying'' scriptural or religious texts (e.g., III:79/3; VII:169/8; XXXIV:44/3).

D.4.b As it turned out, however, although the Qur'ān had an overwhelming and decisive influence in orienting the Muslim Arabs, especially those living in urban surroundings, toward acceptance of the authority of the written word and the primacy of literacy among human intellectual achievements, it no more dislodged poetry (at least not for a few centuries) from its central position in Arab culture than had the Christian Bible three or four centuries earlier displaced Homer and the dramatists in Hellenistic culture. On the one hand, a living tradition of oral poetry was still carried on and patronized among the early generations of Muslims (and even later among the Bedouin tribes), and its aesthetic, social, and even didactic values continued for some time to be appreciated by important figures in the Islamic community (see, e.g., Goldziher *MS* I 29–31, 38–39, 50, and passim; Blachère *PC* 100–103; and esp. Asad *MSJ* 194–215). But, on the other, the poetry itself began to take on an altogether new significance within Arab and Arabic-speaking cultural life—not as verbal art or expression, nor even as the so-called "register of the Arabs" (*dīwān al-^{c}arab*), but rather as the principal repository and normative standard for the singular and specialized linguistic phenomenon the Qur'ān had called "an articulate Arabic tongue," the classical *^{c}arabīya*. For it was to the poetry that one turned in the first century and a half of Islam, not to the Qur'ān, in order to deduct, codify, and prescribe the "correct" usage to be followed, not just in reciting the scriptural text, but in composing and presumably uttering all subsequent forms of literary (i.e., written) expression quite apart from poetry (out of which that usage seems to have been generated to begin with). Thus was initiated pre- and early Islamic poetry's gradual transmutation from the primary *Bildungsgut* of a people—the Arabs—who cherished it as such while and wherever they prevailed in the Islamic world, into the primary *Sprachgut* of a society—Islamic society—dominated no longer by Arabs, but by Arabic. For this society, then, philological study became among the noblest and most seriously pursued intellectual activities, and acquiring proficiency in the *^{c}arabīya* became the necessary propaideutic to any intellectual activity at all.

That from the earliest Islamic period speakers of Arabic saw in poetry the source and model of "correct" usage and that this usage both corresponded to that of the Qur'ān and differed markedly from their own (especially as to inflection) is borne out in the collection of traditions translated by P. Kahle (*QA* 171–79: esp. nos. 30, 31, 53, 54, 67).[154] As Rabin has shown (*BCA* 25–26; see p. 130 above), these traditions prove nothing about either the *formal rendition* or the *original enunciation* of the Qur'ān itself; but they do indicate that the use of *i^{c}rāb* in reciting the Qur'ān seems to have imposed an unwonted burden upon the linguistic capacities of the Arabs in question. In addition, since even the earliest preserved papyri documents, both Muslim and Christian, contain enough "indications of the disappearance of the case endings . . . to show that . . . the copyists . . . spoke a language devoid of declension'' (Blau *ELB* 126; see p. 136 above), one can see there a reflection of the situation portrayed in the reported traditions.[155]

D.4.c When we recall how intimately linked were the productions of the pre- and early Islamic poets with their special linguistic medium and how completely the work of codifying the *ᶜarabīya* was based upon the poetry, we can understand how later literary poets also composed verses in this synthetic language that were ''correct'' in diction, meter, and rhyme. But this, of course, presents an entirely different phenomenon, analagous to the Hellenistic poets' mastery over the epic hexameter and many external features of the poetic language that had belonged to the oral tradition of Homer. These post-classical Arabic poets composed pen in hand or scribe close at hand, following grammatical and stylistic ''rules'' they learned and perfected in schools—rules that had been set down and standardized on the basis of what the philologists had read in recorded works of the classical masters and heard uttered by the skilled and orally trained poets and *rāwīs* of the Bedouins (cf. Gibb *ALI* 160–61). For, in reality, it was among the Bedouins, and almost only the Bedouins, that the overriding impulse to literacy—to read the sacred Book—that has dominated most of Islamic civilization was slowest in making inroads. Blau rightly declared:

> It seems evident that the tradition of Classical Arabic poetry continued among the Bedouins largely because their conditions of life, in contradistinction to those of the settled population, had not changed, and still, as before Islam, constituted the background to Bedouin poetry. (*RBA* 45)

But surely one of the most important of those unchanged conditions, one that accounts for the fact that even present-day illiterate Bedouin poets ''compose their poetry in archaic and often extraneous dialects'' (Rabin *AWA* 17), was the Bedouins' relative unfamiliarity with writing and written poetical composition and their concomitant reliance on oral rendition and public performance.

There was, perhaps, among early connoisseurs of poetry and linguistic experts a conscious or unconscious awareness of the decisive effect exerted by literacy, together with the expectations and predispositions that accompany it, upon an oral tradition of poetry. This at least would help to explain why the philologists and litterateurs tended to distrust and disparage the linguistic and stylistic purity of those early poets like ᶜAdīy b. Zayd and others who had been too closely associated with urban centers, and why, as it is said, the *rāwīs* declined to transmit their poetry (Brockelmann *GAL Suppl* I 59, 61; Blachère *HLA* 71; von Gruenbaum *NAU* 15). Furthermore, it may not only have been the urban and commercial aspects of life at Mecca but also the greater familiarity with writing and more pervasive influence of the written word that prevailed there which could have been responsible for the marked failure of Qurayš to produce any reputable poets until well into the more literate Umayyad period (e.g., *Ag* I 35:16–19; Nicholson *LHA* 237). At the same time poets, such as D̠u r-Rumma (d. 117/735–36), who had acquired literacy, often felt constrained to conceal the fact in order not to prejudice their poetic reputations (e.g., Suyūṭī *Muz* II 349–50; Goldziher *MS* I 111–12).[156]

Finally, we should recognize that hand in hand with the expressed preference for Bedouins as linguistic informants and as renderants of poetry went that profoundly "classicistic" tendency of the late second/eighth–fourth/tenth centuries. This tendency granted sole normative supremacy in the dual areas of linguistic usage and poetical composition to the pre- and early Islamic poets (the *jāhilīyūn* and *muxaḍramūn* respectively), almost without exception, and to many poets of the Umayyad period (the *islāmīyūn*)[157] (see, e.g., Lane *Lex* IV:1611, *s. v. šāhid*). And underlying it was, for the most part, a real and perceived disparity between the verbal art of these earlier poets, as it may have been recorded at that time and as it was still preserved in living rendition among the nomadic Bedouins, and between that being composed by their urbanized contemporaries. If the oral-traditional origins of classical Arabic poetry are accepted to any substantial degree, then one may therein find a new explanation for the deviations of many late Umayyad and ᶜAbbāsid poets from the formal, thematic, and linguistic standards established on the basis of recorded classical verse and living Bedouin practice—deviations associated with the so-called "Battle of the Ancients and Moderns" (cf. Goldziher *AAP* 122–74; Gibb *APAP*; von Grunebaum *CPAT* passim; Blachère in *CDC* 279–86). In part, at least, they may be understood as the attempts of poets (who themselves and whose audiences were often quite literate, not to say learned) to break away from the artificially deduced and imposed restrictions of a technique of poetic composition no longer accessible or appropriate to them. That is, poets who were educated to read and write, who read the poems of their predecessors and contemporaries and wrote their own or had them written down, would have had little or no opportunity to develop naturally the formulaic techniques of oral composition and rendition that had generated the poems that served as their models.[158] Thus, they could have had to choose between self-consciously imitating the classical masters, as most of the critics demanded, or more or less deliberately departing from the conventions peculiar to an oral style and diction so as to create a literary style and diction satisfactory to an audience of practised readers, as well as hearers. In either case (and unquestionably in the latter), certain deviations from the norms of oral-traditional poems might be expected, simply by virtue of the poets' inadequate command of the improvisatory formulaic techniques as such. Such deviations or a more noticeable infrequency of verbatim correspondences cannot just be attributed, then, to a "theory of variation" that "consciously avoided formulae, repetitions, and the like" (see chap. 2, n. 40), unless it is also understood that a theory of that kind would undoubtedly have arisen out of a *literary,* as opposed to *oral,* approach to poetical composition (cf. Wehr rev *Ar* 185).

E. The object of this chapter has been to demonstrate the need for a fresh approach to one of the oldest problems in the field of Arabic studies—namely, the origin and nature of the poetic ^{c}*arabīya*—and the value of forming such an approach around the insights provided by a theory of oral-formulaic poetic composition and rendition among the pre- and early Islamic Arabs. In pursuing this object, I readily and gratefully acknowledge my debt to the oral-formulists among the Homerists and especially to Milman Parry. Parry's treatment of the language of the *Iliad* and *Odyssey* as the language of an oral poetry has given philologists and linguists a key to understanding many otherwise inexplicable features of the Homeric *Kunstsprache*. As conceived by Parry, the language of an oral poetry could exhibit a wide range of anomalous features—such as archaic usages of various kinds and from various periods, intermixture of dialectal or even foreign elements, coexistence of parallel and equivalent grammatical forms, morphemic and syntactic peculiarities absent from the spoken vernaculars, and others. Such features, often apparently linguistically incompatible, could occur together in the work of an oral poet because, in the course of becoming an oral poet, he had taken over from other poets and absorbed a vast body of phrases and phrase-patterns upon which he drew in formulating and performing aloud his own verses. That these formulaic elements might be of the most varied chronological, geographical, and even linguistic provenance mattered not at all, so long as they satisfactorily filled out the metric line of the poem and adequately contributed to the success of the on-going performance. What resulted was not so much a *language* as a *diction* that was inherited by a younger poet from his masters simply as an *aspect*—an integral and inseparable aspect, to be sure—of a traditional technique of making non-written verse. "Thus," as Parry wrote, "while the poems of an oral poetry are ever each one of them in a never-ceasing state of change, the diction itself is fixed, and is passed on with little or no change from one generation of singers to another" (see p. 100 above).

A more conclusive demonstration of the formulaic character of classical

Arabic poetry—of its "orality"—is reserved to the preceding chapter. In this chapter, I have only tried to determine how far we may go in applying Parry's theory to the language of classical Arabic poetry. Can features of the *ᶜarabīya* deemed anomalous or peculiar to verse be better understood in light of that theory? In the case of such phenomena as the articulation of final vowels in rhyme-pausal position, the occurrence of many so-called poetic licences, the use of various dialectal forms on an interdialectal basis, the juxtaposition of many archaic words and morphemes with their more modern equivalents, the apparent generalization or "homogenization" of terms of place-names away from a once more precise and specific signification, the answer is an unequivocal "yes": the existence of these and related phenomena, like that of demonstrable analogs in the Homeric language, can be accounted for without exception in terms of the function they would have performed in meeting the prosodic and thematic demands of a verse produced under pressures of oral composition and rendition.

But even further, some of the most essential and intrinsic properties of the *ᶜarabīya* are quite consistent with what may be admitted to be its wholly non-vernacular character, and seem to flow mainly, if not solely, from its role as the medium for various modes of non-casual, elocutionary expression—particularly poetry. These properties include a generalized *a* as the vowel of the imperfect preformative, in the face of a practically universal drift toward *i* in the spoken dialects, and, above all, the retention of the morpho-syntactic archaism of short-vowel desinential endings indicating case and mood—the *iᶜrāb*-suffixes. Evaluating the evidence for and against the presence of *iᶜrāb* in the vernaculars of sixth- to ninth-century speakers of Arabic, we are forced, I think, to conclude that nowhere can this synthetic property be confidently presumed to have been heard as a regular feature of casual speech either of town-dwellers *or* of Bedouins. To the contrary, it can be strongly argued that what set the Arab poet apart from his fellow tribesmen or townsmen and enhanced their awe of him was precisely his ability to utilize this unusual inflective diction in formulating verses that thereby would be vocalically suited to isochronous measures and would be each conspicuously and correctly terminated with the same desinential vowel.

The linguistic situation thus projected would have involved an archaic and interdialectal synthetic or quasi-synthetic speech-form, the *ᶜarabīya*, restricted primarily to the rendition of poetry, in contrast with various urban and nomadic analytic dialects spoken generally in casual intercourse. Such a situation seems even more reasonable to assume when we consider that the fact that the Qur'ān utilized this distinctive poetic idiom would have removed it, too, along with poetry, far from the realm of everyday speech; and that this circumstance alone, rather than any supposed formal or thematic similarities, could have given the Meccans just the pretext they needed to identify and dismiss Muḥammad as a poet.

The same fact, that the Qur'ān had been delivered in the inflectional language of oral poetry, has been of overwhelming significance in the linguistic and cultural history of Arabs and users of Arabic. It meant that what had previously existed by and large only as a *heard and non-written* linguistic phenomenon, associated almost uniquely with the oral rendition of poetry and certain other forms of non-casual speech, was to appear in probably its first—and undoubtedly its most important—*written* manifestation of any scope, in the form of a "scripture" for the Arabs, an "Arabic recitation." Heretofore, mastery over this idiom, with its relatively unfamiliar case and mood desinences, had been acquired by poets and *rāwīs* as an automatic accessory to the art and technique of formulating unwritten verse. It could hardly have been conceived in abstraction from poetry and other such elocutionary utterances. Islam and the Qur'ān changed all that. Since recitation of the Qur'ānic message, available as a text within a generation of the Prophet's death, had become fundamental to Islamic religious practice, accurate reproduction of its linguistic form became not merely a desideratum but, more properly, an obligation incumbent upon all believers. This, together with the emergence of a deeper sense of cultural unity (even superiority) among the ruling Arabs and the resultant need for an intertribal, and later international, medium of expression and communication, led the early Muslims to take the seemingly inevitable, yet rarely precedented, step of systematically abstracting, describing, and standardizing the linguistic medium of an oral poetry. This medium was then adopted and prescribed as the language of literature and of literary and verbal culture in general.

Those responsible for the systematization of classical Arabic grammar from the first/seventh century onward have borne convincing witness to the poetical *and* oral origins of the *ᶜarabīya,* both through their attachment of primary importance to the evidential value of poetry for determining "correct" usage and also through their recognition that that usage in its living form was to be heard only in the unlettered milieu of the Bedouins—specifically, in the person and poetic performance of an accomplished Bedouin *rāwī* poet.

1. See Zwettler *BFOT* 207–8; chap. 1, § C, above. I have not considered Petráček's linguistic studies to which he refers in *VAL* 45 n. 47.

2. For a more detailed treatment of the Homeric *Kunstsprache* in this sense, see P. Chantraine in Mason *Intro* chap. 4 (esp. 105–15); L. R. Palmer in Wace/Stubbings *CH* chap. 4 (esp. 97–106); idem in *FYT* 19–21 and 35 nn. 15–24; M. Bowra in Wace/Stubbings *CH* 26–28; etc.

3. Cf., inter alia, Lord *ST* 43, 49, and passim; Palmer in *FYT* 21–24, 35–36 nn. 25–32; Bowra *HP* 388–98 (with references to other traditions); Nagler *TGV* 284–88; and esp. A. Hoekstra *Homeric Modifications of Formulaic Prototypes*, and Edwards *LHTC*. See also the important observations of M. B. Emeneau on the Toda song language in Emeneau *OPSI*, esp. 337; further developed on the linguistic level in Emeneau *SMOL*.

4. = Parry *SET* II = *MHV* 325–64.

5. Characteristically, Parry made a careful distinction between the terms *language, diction*, and *style*, which I have tried to adhere to in the following discussion. "All three," he writes, "have to do with the sum of words, word-forms, and word-groupings used by a man. As *language*, however, we look at them as used by a certain people, at a certain time, and in a certain place; as *diction*, as the material by which thought is expressed; and as *style*, as the form of thought" (*SET* II 1 = *MHV* 325). In view of Parry's distinction, then, Petráček's term *style* (*Stil*) might more aptly be exchanged for *diction*; see Petráček *VAL* 56–58, esp. 47–48.

6. For other theories of the origin of the Homeric language and Parry's critique of them, see *SET* 2–6 = *MHV* 326–29.

7. The eight traits are as follows:

"I.—The spoken dialect of the author of an oral poem is shown by his poetic language, which will tend to be the same as his spoken language wherever he has no metrical reason to use an older or foreign word or form or construction. . . .

"II.—On the other hand an oral poet, composing in a diction which follows his own language where it can, may be using phrases and passages which are neither his own work nor that of other poets of the same dialect, whether of his own or of an earlier time, but borrowings from the poetry of another dialect. . . .

"III.—A given word, form or group of words can be proved to be the original work of poets speaking a given dialect only when it can be shown that no other dialect which had had a part in the history of the poetry had, in either its spoken or its poetic language, the same word or form or group of words with the same metrical value. . . .

"IV.—Conversely, a word or form or group of words which is metrically false, or fails to make sense, must be the work of a dialect whose words and forms when used would make the verse correct, or give it meaning. . . .

"V (exception to I).—A foreign or older form may be kept in the poetic language even when the poet's own language has a form which could take its place, but such a keeping, apart from metrical reasons, will be due to the regular use of the form along with other words which are always used as a group and which the poet feels as such, or to the poetic character of the word, or to some other such special reason. . . .

"VI (exception to IV).—The working of a formulaic diction may itself be the cause of metrical faults.

"VII (exception to III).—A form which seems old or foreign may be a creation by analogy from forms which are really so. . . .

"VIII.—A word, form, or group of words which is old or foreign is not in itself proof that the verse or passage in which it is found is the work of an older or foreign singer. . . ."

8. See, e.g., Hoekstra *HMFP;* Hainsworth *FHF*; and others.

9. See, e.g., Hoekstra *HMFP* 18–20, 29–30 and passim; though with the reservations about the meaning of *recitation* expressed by Hainsworth *FHF* 1–2.

10. Cf. J. Blau's remark about "the thorny problem as to whether Classical Arabic emerged as the language of a particular tribe or was from the beginning a super-tribal tongue" (*ELB* 2).

11. Though already in use earlier, this term was seriously advanced by W. Marçais, as quoted by H. Fleisch *IELS* 99 (cf. Rabin *AWA* 17); adopted also by Blachère *HLA* 79–80 and *Intro* 164–65; used with reservations by Rabin *BCA* 24. The term was used rather more precisely, with reference to a common *spoken* form of Arabic and in *contrast* to the classical *ᶜarabīya*, by H. Fleischer in his *Kleinere Schriften* III (Leipzig: S. Hirzel, 1888): 384 (from an article first appearing in *ZDMG* 1 [1847]: 148–60). Detailing the introduction of Greco-Aramaic elements

into Arabic shortly after the expansion of Islam, Fleischer writers: "So bindete sich die [*koinē diálektos*] des Arabischen (Hajji Khalīfa IV 323), wahrend die durch Koran and Sunna geheiligten Formen der alten Beduinensprache, gleichsam der [*atthís*] des Arabischen, in den Städten nur noch unter den höher Gebildeten mehr künstlich als natürlich fortlebten, nach Gesetzen, denen sich keine Sprache des täglichen Verkehrs entziehen kann, auch aus diesen Kreisen immer mehr verschwanden und endlich nur noch in den Schulen und der Literatur gepflegt wurden." A more recent use of the term as denoting a common spoken language is to be found in Ferguson *AK* (but cf. also Blau *ELB* 14–17): and see esp. Cohen *KLD*.

12. Quoted by A. Spitaler in rev *Ar* 145b.

13. See references and summary of opinions in Rabin *AWA* 17–24. Cf. also, e.g., Nöldeke/Schwally *GQ* II 58–59; Fleisch *IELS* 97–99, 101; Blachère *HLA* chap. 2, esp. 79–82; Rabin *BCA*; idem, "ᶜArabiyya" *EI*² I 565a; Brockelmann *GAL Suppl* I 15–16 and n. 2; idem, in Spuler *Sem* 214—16. Besides Fück (for whose position see chap. 3, § C.8.a, below), others who hold that the *ᶜarabīya* was a spoken language or dialect include Nicholson *LHA* xxii-xxiii; Mukarram *QKA* 13–15 (accepts the traditional view: language of Qur'ān = dialect of Quray̌s = poetic *ᶜarabīya*); Chejne *ALBH* 52–58 ("Arabic, i.e., the Arabic of the Qur'ān and that of poetry, . . . would seem to have been [at Mecca] both the common language of the people and poetical koine" [*ALRH* 53]).

14. See discussions in Nöldeke/Schwally *GQ* II 58–59; Fleisch *IELS* 99–101; Blachère *Intro* 156–69; Rabin *AWA* 3–4, 19–24, and passim; idem *BCA* 24–29; Brockelmann in Spuler *Sem* 216–17; Bell/Watt *Intro* 82–85. The important opposing views are those of K. Vollers (*VSA*), and P. Kahle (*CG*², *AQ*, *ARK*).

15. The assumption, often perhaps unintentional, that *to write* and *to compose* are synonymous, and hence mutually interchangeable, enters the scholarship of many Western orientalists, even of those who might readily acknowledge the existence of a so-called oral tradition in other contexts. Cf., e.g., Vollers' term *Schriftsprache;* also the more sophisticated, but unnecessarily paradoxical, expression of H. Birkeland, *vorliterarische Schriftsprache,* in Birkeland *AP* 7; Goldziher's supposition that "the spread of script made possible the formation of a supertribal and uniform literary language" (*SHCAL* 3); Rabin's casual suggestion that the Qur'ān "was perhaps the first attempt to *write* Arabic prose" (*BCA* 24, my italics); esp. A. Guillaume's occasional tendency, in his translation of the *Sīra,* Guillaume *LM* (second page number refers to Wüstenfeld's Arabic edition), to render Arabic *qāla,* "he said, uttered," by English *he wrote:* e.g., *LM* 59/88, 120/169, 208/304, 350/527, 598/889, 719 n. 181/194. Cf. also Parry *SET* II 12 n. 1 = *MHV* 333 n. 2.

16. E.g., Jacob *AB* xx–xxii, 198–99; Fleisch *IELS* 101; Gibb *ALI*² 10–11; etc.

17. Spitaler rev *VSA* esp. 317–18; idem rev *Ar* 146 n. 17; idem in Levi Della Vida *LSPS* 125–26. Cf. Corriente *FY* 37 n. 27.

18. See, e.g., W. Caskel in von Grunebaum *SICH* 41; M. Höfner in Gabrieli *ASB* 53–59; Brockelmann in Spuler *Sem* 208–9; Petráček *VAL* 42–43.

19. See Lichtenstädter *NAQ* esp. 24–81; Bloch *Qas;* etc.

20. See Birkeland *AP* 14, 16; Fleisch *TPA* 191 n. 2, but cf. idem *AC*² 28 n. 1.

21. Details and terminology of Arabic rhyme-praxis can be found in Wright *AG* II 350–58.

22. Cf., besides the references cited by Birkeland and Fleisch on these differences, the important remarks of Ibn Jinnī *Xas* I 69–71, pointing out the special pausal phenomena at the ends of hemistichs (*wuqūf ᶜala l-ᶜarūḍ*) that deviate from pause both in rhyme-position and in "*kalām.*" This should be mentioned, he adds, but it never has been.

Although the grammarians seem to employ the word *kalām* in reference to *non-casual* "literary" prose utterances made in the *ᶜarabīya* by linguistically acceptable Arabs and in the formal diction of certain tribes, Fleisch regards their observations as having been just as applicable to prose spoken in normal conversation: " . . . the latter [being] source of the former; for pause has been noted in literary prose only because it existed in common usage" (*TPA* 173 n. 1; *AC*² 29).

23. The most complete treatment of Arabic pausal phenomena is that of Birkeland *AP*. Cf. Wright *AG* 368–73, also 373–90 passim; Kramers *AO* 3–13; Fleisch *TPA* 172–97; idem *AC*² 28–30; and references cited in Birkeland *AP* 5–6 and Fleisch *TPA* 172.

24. On *iqwā'* (sometimes called *ikfā'*), see, e.g., Ibn Kaysān *TQ* 55–57; Wright *AG* II 357A (also note by De Goeje, ibid. 357D); Nöldeke *BKPA* 37–38; Gaudefroy-Demombynes *ILPP* 77–80 n. 113; Blachère *DCHM* 137–40; etc.

25. See Birkeland *AP* 7; Kramers *AO* 4–5; Fleisch *AC*² 29.

26. On the phenomena called *išmām, rawm,* and *taḍᶜīf,* see Birkeland *AP* 7, 22–31; Fleisch *TPA* 173–75; on *taḍᶜīf* cf. also Wright *AG* II 369A. It may be asked whether the analysis of *taḍᶜīf* as a gemination or, as Birkeland and Fleisch suggest, a lengthening of the *rawīy* consonant really arrives at the truth of the matter. We know for a fact that early Arabic philologists, despite their otherwise brilliant understanding and description of phonetic principles, took little or no account of the phenomenon of *accent* (see, e.g., Fleisch *TPA* 169–71; idem *AC*² 26–28, 159, 242 n. 7). We can observe further that in some contemporary dialects (in my experience those of Cairo, Beirut, and Damascus, at least) classical and medieval poetry is ordinarily recited with noticeable emphasis on the penultimate syllable of both hemistichs of poems with *qāfiya muṭlaqa* (e.g., *qifā nabki min ḏikrā ḥabībin wa manzíli—MuIQ* 1; *hal ġādara š-šuᶜarā'u min mutaraddámi—Mu ᶜAn* 1; *daᶜā-ka l-hawā wa stajhalat-ka l-manāzílu—DNāb* 21:1). Since in the normal forms of most standard meters the penultimate syllable would be short, this accent is heard today in general contrast with the accentual patterns of similar words in context in many dialects. Now, if this accent had been present, and had been considered noteworthy, in some modes of poetical recitation at the time of the early grammarians, and if, moreover, it had been carried over into (or had existed previously in) recitation with *iskān* (thus making the final syllable in pause an accented one: e.g., *manzíl, mutaraddám, manāzíl*), then the grammarians could have been at a loss to depict such a condition in terms of their phonetic concepts and notation. Hence, they may have resorted to the fiction of *taḍᶜīf*—i.e., a pausal geminated consonant—on the assumption that such a theoretical lengthening of the syllable would sufficiently indicate the shift in accent (at least, according to our admittedly hypothetical notions of early accentuation) and with complete awareness that the consonant itself would not be pronounced with gemination in pause in any event (according to conventional pausal treatment of geminated consonants; cf. Wright *AG* II 373C; Birkeland *AP* 53; Fleisch *TPA* 175). That this phenomenon of *taḍᶜīf* was also alleged to occur in poems recited with *tarannum* could be due as much to a maintenance of the same "fiction" (if it was one) to explain the artificial accentuation of penultimate short syllables that we observe in modern recitation, as to an actual lengthening of the *rawīy*-consonant. Cf. a similar conclusion, expressed in somewhat different terms, by W. Fischer in Fischer *SVA* 51–52. (Unfortunately I have not been able to see the revelant study by Birkeland, *Stress Patterns in Arabic, Avh . . . det Norske Videnskaps-Akademi i Oslo, II. Hist.-Filos. Kl* [1954], No. 3.) See also note 90, below.

27. Or sometimes as an inflectional fault (*ᶜayb fi l-iᶜrāb*); cf. Ibn Qutayba in Nöldeke *BKPA* 40; Gaudefroy-Demombynes *ILPP* 31.

28. A good testimony to the oral-improvisational origin of many such features is to be found in Ibn Qutayba's remark about the apocopated form occurring in a line attributed to Imra'alqays *(DIQ* 55:24; *DIQ* (Ahl) 51:10): *fa l-yawma ašrab* (for *ašrabu*) *ġayra mustaḥqibin iṯman mina llāhi wa lā wāġili*. The line was so read also by Sībawayh (*Kitab* II 297). Ibn al-Anbārī (*Muf* I 737:6, cf. 480:9), Ibn as-Sikkīt (*IM* 245:7, 322:17; *TA* 225:6, 256:9), as-Sukkarī, and others (Ibrāhīm *DIQ* p. 412, to 16:8–10). Ibn Qutayba (*ILPP* 31–32) comments: "Were it not that the grammarians cite this verse in illustration of the apocopation of a syllabic vowel because of the [over-] accumulation of vowels [i.e., at that point of the metrical foot] and that many of *rāwīs* render it thus, I would suppose it to be: *fa l-yawma usqā* etc." (*law-lā anna n-naḥwīyīna yaḏkurūna hāḏa l-bayta wa yaḥtajjūna bi-hi fi taskīni l-mutaḥarriki li jtimāᶜi lḥarakāti wa kaṯīran mina r-ruwāti yarwūna-hu hākaḏā la-zanantu-hu . . .*). (Nöldeke *BKPA* 40 does not include this passage in his translation of Ibn Qutayba.) Ibn Jinnī (*Xas* I 73–74; II 340) explicitly ascribes this apocopation, as well as a number of similar cases, to the demands of the specific metrical context. Although *usqā* was indeed attested (*DIQ* 16:10; al-Baṭalyūsī *DIQ* p. 138:11; al-Mubarrad *Kāmil* I 244:10; as-Sīrāfī, in

Sībawayh Kitāb *Kitāb* II 298:12), its provenance seems to have lain practically exclusively with the Baṣrans, who would anyway have preferred it as sounder analogically (see esp. al-Baṭalyūsī *DIQ* p. 138:11 sch). Incidentally, it is ironic that scholars who adduce the presence of apocopated forms in post-classical poetry as evidence of an uninflectional spoken language would not admit the same circumstance as evidence for the classical period (see, e.g., Fück *Ar* 52).

29. This, of course, excludes the instances of *qāfiya muqayyada* ending in *CVCVC* (i.e., either *mutadārika* or *mutarākiba mujarrada*), which often involve forms of *CVCC* already epenthesized to *CVCVC* for metrical reasons.

30. For the range of semantic possibilities, including infinitives, substantives, broken plurals, etc., see Wright *AG* I 110CD, 112D, 113C–134C, 158C, 200A, 224C, 263D, 264D; Fleisch *TPA* 349–50, 478–79, 481; cf. also Ibn as-Sikkīt *IM* 3–94; Ibn Qutayba in Fleisch *TPA* 352, on the degree of interchangeability of these various forms with and without anaptyxis.

31. See Wright *AG* I 97C, II 384B; Flesich *TPA* 156–59.

32. Sources consulted were the following (see Bibliography for abbreviations): *Divans, Muf, Aṣm, Jam, SAH, DVCA, D*^{c}*Ab, D*^{c}*Ad, DAfwā, D*^{c}*Ām, D*^{c}*Amr, DA*^{c}*šā, DAws, DBišr, DHād, DHam, DHass, DHāt, DHut, DKa*^{c}*b, DLab, DMut, DQays, DQut, DSam, DSan, DSuh, DṬuf, D*^{c}*Ur, DXan, DXuf.* More than 950 *qaṣīdas* with nine lines or more were counted. The *rawīy* consonants in the 52 rhyme-words with final consonantal pairs are distributed as follows: *CVCr*$\bar{V}$: 17 (32.5%) / *CVCl*$\bar{V}$: 15 (29%) / *CVCm*$\bar{V}$: 6 (11.5%) / *CVCd*$\bar{V}$: 5 (9.5%) / *CVCb*$\bar{V}$: 4 (7.5%) / *CVCs*$\bar{V}$: 2 (4%) / *CVCz*$\bar{V}$: 1 (2%) / *CVC*$^{c}\bar{V}$: 1 (2%) / *CVCf*$\bar{V}$: 1 (2%). The poets to whom are ascribed the lines with *rawīys -d, -b, -s, -z,* ^{c}, and *-f* are: ^{c}Āmir b. Ṭufayl (*mux*) *D*^{c}*Ām* 3, *-d* / al-A^{c}šā Qays b. Maymūn (*jah*) *DA*^{c}*šā* 50, *-d* / Asmā' b. Xāriya (*mux*) *Aṣm* 11, *-b* / Bašāma b ^{c}Amr al-Ġadīr (*jah*) *Muf* 122, ^{c} / Dawsar b. Ḏuhayl al-Quray^{c}ī (unknown, prob. *jah*) *Asm* 50, *-b* / al-Hādira Qutba b. Aws (*jah*) *DHād* pp. 11–13, *-d* / al-Hāriṯ b. Hilliza (*jah*) *Muf* 25, *-s* / al-Hutay'a (*mux*) D*Huṭ* 85, *-f* / Abū Saxr al-Huḏalī (*isl*) *SAH* pp. 970–71, *-b* / ^{c}Uqba ba. Sābiq (unknown) *Aṣm* 9 *-b* / al-Xansā' (*mux*) *DXan* pp. 6–9, *-b;* 150–53, *-s;* 143–47, *-z* / Yazīd b. al-Xaḏḏāq (*jah*) *Muf* 78, *-d* (*n. b.: jah = jāhilī,* pre-Islamic; *mux = muxaḍram,* one who lived partly in pre-Islamic and partly in Islamic times; *isl* = post-Islamic).

33. As is obvious, such a count shows only the amount of attention, in terms of pages written, a particular final radical elicited. It actually shows neither the number of existent roots or words ending in that radical (a much more arduous calculation), nor certainly the number of available *CVCC*-forms. As a rough estimate, however, it may serve for the present purposes. The number of pages devoted to each letter are as follows: '-29 / *b*-110 / *t*-20 / *ṯ*-17 / *j*-38 / *ḥ*-44 / *x*-18 / *d*-80 / *ḏ*-12 / *r*-205 / *z*-33 / *s*-67 / *š*-35 / *ṣ*-29 / *ḍ*-27 / *ṭ*-36 / *ẓ*-8 / ^{c}-105 / *ġ*-14 / *f*-96 / *q*-86 / *k*-34 / *l*-152 / *m*-123 / *n*-85 / *h*-17 / *w* and *y*-110. These results correspond to a great extent with those arrived at for phoneme distribution in final root-radical position in J. H. Greenberg's more scientifically conducted study "The Patterning of Root Morphemes in Semitic," *Word* 6 (1950): 162–81. But like mine, Greenberg's calculations give no information as to the number of available *CVCC*-forms.

34. Fleisch *TPA* I gives a thorough and concise treatment of Arabic phonetics with a survey of the existing literature; see esp. *TPA* 51–62, 161–97 and Section III; cf. also Fischer *SVA*.

35. Except, perhaps, insofar as that greater availability is itself a function of the underlying phonetic structure of the Arabic language.

36. *Pace* Fleisch *TPA* 60. Cf. Pretzl *WK* 326–30; Rabin *AWA* 99 (for *r*). The exceptional properties of *r* and *l* in many languages were noted for Arabic quite early by the Muslim grammarians; see Fleisch *TPA* 60–61 and n. 2, 76, 227–28.

37. Later literary poets seem to have had much less difficulty finding enough rhyme-words with final consonants other than *-r, -l,* and *-m*: e.g., Ru'ba b. al-^{c}Ajjāj *DRu'* nos. 5–6 (139 ll.), *-b;* 29(63 ll.), *d;* 44 (63 ll.), *-k*/al-Mutanabbi *D mutan* pp. 166–72 (41 ll.), *-f* / Mihyār ad-Daylamī *DMih* I pp. 180–82 (49 ll.), *-j;* 199–202 (51 ll.), *-h;* II pp. 128–31 (45 ll.), *-s*/Ibn al-Mu^{c}tazz *DiMu* III no. 262 (31 ll), *-d;* no. 263 (27 ll.), *-t* / etc. This points, of course, to their employing the *tarannum*-forms sheerly as part of a *literary,* rather than *oral,* tradition.

38. See n. 32 above. The fact that al-Xansā', a female contemporary of Muḥammad, accounted for three of these poems is most striking. Could it be due to the often-noted circumstance that women in many traditional societies, because of their generally segregated status, spoke an idiom that preserved many archaic features when contrasted with the language in use among the men? (Cf. Blau *ELB* 14 n. 2.) Or might it be related to the relatively higher antiquity usually attributed to the elegy as a poetic form and to its special cultivation by poetesses?

39. Cf., in support of this view, Fischer *SVA* 51, who suggests that poems rhyming in *ī* (which, in fact, seem to predominate in the recorded tradition) indicate a similar lack of concern for inflectional niceties at verse-ends. The written tradition of the poetry shows us that not only were the short inflectional vowels *-i* treated as equivalent to the long-vowel morpheme *ī* for rhyme purposes, but also forms ending in consonants were included as equivalent too (cf. Wright *AG* II 385–86). Fischer believes that, rather than accept the conventional doctrine that all of these rhyme-words were pronounced with final *ī* in pause, one might better assume that their final consonants were pronounced with an essentially non-inflectional explosive vocalic. The fact that the early written tradition seldom indicated the long *ī*, even when it represented an independent morpheme or root element, is taken as confirmation.

40. Except that the long *ū* suffix is retained in the 2d pers. plural verb (*-tum*) and attached pronoun (*-kum*) when either is followed by another pronominal suffix: e.g., *ra'aytumū-ni, yurīkumū-hum* (see Wright *AG* I 102B).

41. Rabin *BCA* 30–31 questions whether this phenomenon actually constitutes an archaism or whether, because of older Semitic parallels, "it may . . . be preferable to follow for once the Arab philologists in treating this confusion as a poetic license." Or it may also have arisen and spread so widely, he suggests, owing "to different usages in this respect in the home-dialects of the poets." The fact that the choice of declension was metrically determined, however, is evidence for its formulaic nature, regardless of origin. Cf. Fleisch *AC*² 38–40; *TPA* 276–80.

42. Nöldeke *NBSS* 69 n. 4; Rabin *AWA* 9 (citing also Ibn al-Anbārī). For more detailed discussion of the *aḍdād* phenomenon in Arabic, see, e.g., Fleisch *TPA* 393–96, 528–29 ("pour p. 395") and references.

43. See, e.g., Ahlwardt *BAAG* 5; Brockelmann *GAL Suppl* I 16; Fleisch *IELS* 103 n. 2 (citing G. Kampffmeyer), 114; Rabin "ᶜArabiyya" *EI*² I 565a, 566a; Chejne *ALRH* 55; Wiet *ILA* 22–23. Cf. also the instances of dialectisms in the Huḏayl *Dīwān*—both those peculiar to Huḏayl and those of other tribes: *SAH* index 2 (p. 1656); Bräunlich *VLB* 203–4; Rabin *AWA* chap. 8 passim.

44. "The Qur'ān is *aᶜrabu wa aqwā fī l-ḥujja* than the poetry," according to al-Farrā' and the early Kūfan school of Qur'ānic recitation; see Beck *ASAK* 194–95; also Kopf *BIAP* 46–50. This principle must not, of course, be confused with the quasi-doctrine of the inimitability (*iᶜjāz*) of the Qur'ān, which was a somewhat later elaboration associated more with rhetoric and literary criticism than with grammar and of which the linguistic matter was only one aspect (cf. von Grunebaum "Iᶜḏjāz" *EI*² III 1018a–20b).

45. See again Beck *ASAK* 180–204 and passim; Rabin *AWA* 19–20 and passim; idem *BCA*.

46. Cf. Ibn Fāris *SFL* 52 (quoted also in as-Suyūṭī *Muz* I 210); Lane *Lex s. v. ᶜarabīya* (on authority of Qatāda b. Diᶜāma [d. 118/736]); also Rabin "ᶜArabiyya" *EI*² I 565a.

47. D. 224/838; Brockelmann *GAL* I 106–7; *Suppl* I 166–67.

48. See, most recently, Thilo *OAP*; discussion of earlier geographical studies: 15–20.

49. "Thus the *qaṣīda* is fundamentally a message in verse which is to be delivered, preceded by a traveling-song [*Reiselied*] serving as a pasttime for the messenger" (*Qas* 132; cf. Jacobi *SPAQ* 2, 6).

50. Cf. Lammens *BI* 13–16, 122–24, 128–30. For a concise treatment of what R. Pfeiffer calls "the unrealities in Homeric geography" (*HCS* 166), see H. Thomas and F. Stubbings in Wace/Stubbings *CH* 283–310 passim. On the question of the historicity and factual accuracy of oral heroic poetry in general and their relation to the manner of composition, see, e.g., Bowra *HP* chaps. 8 and 14, and passim.

51. For Barth's Law, see Bloch *VIP* 34–35; cf. also Fleisch *TPA* 137–38, idem *AC*² 241 n. 5.

52. See Ferguson *AK* 621, to be supplemented by Blau *ELB* 16–17 (esp. 17 n. 2, for the Bedouin dialects). It might be noted also that almost all the occurrences of the imperfect in the many passages given by Musil *MCRB* are transcribed with *i* or *e* (vs. *a*) in the preformatives, thus indicating a similar feature for the Rwala dialect.

53. See, e.g., Rabin *AWA* 20, 79. One wonders if the allegations of Huḏalī linguistic expertise might not have received a certain amount of ideological support from the frustrated partisans of Ibn Masᶜūd's recension of the Qur'ān. Their vocal and prolonged reaction to the imposition of the ᶜUṯmānic codex as the canonical text (see Blachère *Intro* 63–65, 73–75, 106–7) would naturally have led them to adopt the claim of the dialectal precedence of their eponymous hero's tribe, Huḏayl, as another arrow in their polemical quiver. On the role of Ibn Masᶜūd and his partisans and the "readings" attributed to him in the early history of the Qur'ānic text, see Beck *SGKK* IV; also idem *UKK*, 358 n. 2; idem *ASAK* 181–82.

54. It is important to remember that, contrary to Vollers's and Rabin's assertion, most of the variant "readings" adduced in *VSA* came from recognized and authoritative sources, and cannot hence lightly be called "non-canonical" or "*šawāḏḏ*"; cf. Nöldeke *NBSS* 1–2.

55. Rabin quite rightly points out that statements regarding the excellence of a tribe's language did not refer to the correctness of their dialect so much as to their expertise in handling the poetic *ᶜarabīya* (*AWA* 20). But he also warns against "Voller's mistake of assuming that Koran readers lightly imported features of their native dialects into their recitation" (ibid. 86). Thus, the readings with *i*-imperfect would have represented, if not the Prophet's pronunciation, the renderings that were for many the proper usage for high discourse. Cf. also Nöldeke *BSS* 11–12 and n. 1; *NBSS* 3.

56. Cf. Goldziher *BGSA* III 525.

57. See, e.g., Rabin *AWA* 12–13, 18; Pellat *MB* 125 and n. 2, 126–27; Fück *Ar* 30–31, 48, 57, 66, and passim; Blau *ELB* 8–10; Blachère *SIBB* and Blau *RBA*.

58. I have not seen Vollers's earlier articles in *Zeitschrift für Assyriologie* 10 (1894) (thus in Blachère *Intro* 159 n. 216; in *HLA* 78, however, Blachère cites 11 [1896]; Vollers himself refers to a study of his in *ZA* 12, and it is this one to which Nöldeke *BSS* 1 n. 1 refers; are these all separate studies or has there been some confusion of the references?).

59. But cf. Nöldeke *BSS* 5; also Corriente *FY* 27 n. 9, 39 n. 29. Although this etymology of the word may well correspond to the sense "to speak lucidly or properly or as an Arab (=Bedouin ?)"—that is, although it may indeed, as the verbal noun of *aᶜraba*, convey the conventional meaning of that verb as it was used in the Jāhilīya—it ignores two important points: (1) we have no basis for assuming that what was obviously in the second and third centuries A.H. a technical term, denoting correct usage of case and mood suffixes, would have implied the same thing during a period before philological sophistication took over; and (2) there is good reason for believing that precisely this technical sense of the word may have been a direct semantic borrowing from the Greek *hellēnismos*, in *its* technical sense of "to speak Greek according to the established analogical patterns"; cf. Steinthal *GSW* II 121, 361–62; Clark *RGRE* 84–86; Pfeiffer *HCS* 274. The second point has already been raised in this connection: Merx *HAG*, 143–44; idem in "Reflections . . ." 22–23; von Gruenbaum *AFAL* 337–38 = *KD* 147–48. However, the full range of its implications has yet to be explored. One could add that the semantic correspondence goes further yet; for the Greek terminological trichotomy, *hellēnismos-barbarismos-soloikismos* (cf. Steinthal *GSW* 361–62), where the second term and the third mean respectively phonetic or morphological errors and syntactical errors, finds its exact counterpart in Arabic with *iᶜrāb-iᶜjām* (or *ᶜujma*)-*laḥn*. Although Merx *HAG* 143–44 may be right to see in the Arabic term *salīqa*—or *salīqīya;* cf. Fück *Ar* 30, 91 n. 26—a transliteration from the Greek, nevertheless in technical usage it was *laḥn* that was most commonly opposed to *iᶜrāb;* cf. Fück *Ar* appendix.)

60. On the pervasiveness of the term *Schriftsprache* as misapplied to the language of traditional poetry, see, e.g., Parry *SET* II 12 n. 1 = *MHV* 333 n. 2, referring to O. Böckel; cf. n. 15 above.

61. Stating at one point (rev *VSA* 19) that "Muḥammad probably spoke and *wrote* the Ḥijāzī dialect of the *ᶜarabīya,*" Geyer appends after the word *schrieb* the following note, highly indicative of how deeply the very vocabulary of scholarship has been influenced by the belief that serious verbal creativity presupposed the ability or desire to write: "Durch diesen Ausdruck will ich natürlich keine Parteinahme in der Frage, ob Muḥammad wirklich lesen und schreiben konnte oder nicht . . . , markieren, sondern nur *seine literarische Betätigung* schlechtweg bezeichnen" (19 n. 1; my italics).

62. Cf. Bergsträsser/Pretzl *GK* 2–3; Beck *UKK* 362.

63. *Pace* Blau *ELB* 3 n. 1, 127 n. 1. Blau, in the course of arguing that the pre-Islamic dialects retained the inflectional endings, declares: "As to urban dialects, we regard the proofs of Nöldeke, *Neue Beiträge,* 1–5, as to the 'Classical' character of the language of Mecca as conclusive." Unless he is referring perchance to Nöldeke's earlier treatment in *BSS* 1–14, I cannot see how the remarks in *NBSS*, cogent as they may be on many points, can be accepted as "conclusive" of anything in regard to the *iᶜrāb.*

64. The attested forms *-en* and *-in* seem to be only phonologically conditioned allomorphs of *-an*; see Blau *ELB* 188, citing Cantineau; cf. also Matar *LB* 239.

65. One must, I think, be wary of adducing the many dialectal forms involving the phonemes *š-n* (e.g., *šayn, šinu, äšnak, ašen,* etc.) as instances of the word *šay'* with nunation; see Nöldeke *BSS* 2–3; Blau *ELB* Index II *s. v. shay';* cf. also Fischer *AA* 810–11. *Š-n* bears a close phonological resemblance to the word *ša'n,* whose semantic range by no means totally excludes that of *šay'*. In some cases, particularly where the idiomatic sense required is "how?", *ša'n* provides a more appropriate nuance than *šay'*: the expression *äšnak* "how are you?" from Mosul, which Nöldeke interprets as *ayšin* (<*ayyu šay'in*) + *-ka,* might more plausibly be analyzed as the interrogative *ayy* (= *ē* ?) + *ša'nuka.* Adding an attached pronoun to a contracted noun-form (*-šn-* <*ša'n*) would seem a more feasible linguistic process in Arabic than adding it to a *tanwīn*-suffix. This is not to say, of course, that *šay'* has not lain at the basis of such constructions; just that a dialectal fusion of *šay'* and *ša'n,* because of close phonological and at least overlapping semantic correspondences, may have taken place *in these particular instances,* and that this factor, rather than preserved nunation, might then account for the presence of *n.* The possibility, at any rate, should not be ignored.

66. Cf. the similar conclusions of Maṭar *LB* 233–48, discussing nunation and long final vowels in the Bedouin dialect of the northwestern Egyptian desert.

67. See, e.g., M. De Goeje in Wright *AG* I 72 n; Nöldeke *BSS* 11; Bergsträsser/Pretzl *GK* 42–51; Fleisch *IELS* 100 n. 2; Blachère *Intro* 151–52; Rabin *AWA* 130–31; etc.

68. In connection with the possible existence before Islam of a hieratic, written form of Arabic in conjunction with an incipient Arab "national" Christian church, centered at Najrān, see Shahīd *MN* 10, 40, 62, 96–98, 157–58, and esp. 242–50 (but cf., too, Köbert rev *MN,* esp. 466).

69. See, e.g., Wolf *SOM* 329–44; Smith *EA;* Chelhod *ISI* chaps. 3–4, App. I; R. Serjeant in Arberry *RME* II 4–16; I. Shahīd in *CHI* I 3–29; etc.

70. The *hamza* "is most likely the oldest" of the diacritical signs used in the Qur'ānic manuscripts: Abbott *RNAS* 39–40.

71. Particularly unconvincing is the *ḥadīṯ* that depicts the Prophet rebuking a man who addressed him as *nabī'u llāh* (i.e., instead of *nabīyu llāh*). Muḥammad's response, according to Rabin *AWA* 144–45, was *lā tanbir,* which Rabin translates, "Do not screech," but which might better be rendered "Do not raise your voice (i.e., with an expiratory stress)." In the first place, the use of *hamz* in *nabīy* was a peculiarly Ḥijāzī pseudo-correction and a feature neither of the *ᶜarabīya* nor of the other dialects (Rabin *AWA* 131–33). In the second place, the *ḥadīṯ* has been received by Ibn al-Aṯīr (*NGH* s. r. *n-b-r*) under two forms. In one Muḥammad is portrayed as saying, "We, O tribe of Qurayš, do not raise our voices" (*in-nā maᶜšara Qurayšin lā nanbiru*)—which is certainly a statement of dialectal fact, if the reference is to the *hamz.* The second is Rabin's quotation, *lā tanbir bi smī* ("don't raise your voice in pronouncing my name"); but given the isolated pseudo-correctness of *nabī'* (with *hamz*) to begin with, such a rebuke can

scarcely be interpreted as applying to *hamz* usage in general.

72. The example of orthographical representation of nunation, *kā'in* (or *ka'ayyin*), written with *nūn* (Bergsträsser / Pretzl *GK* 29) can be seen from its frequent occurrence in poetry to have been a frozen interrogative or exclamatory particle in which the *n* had ceased to hold any inflectional significance. Its diverse orthographical and morphological forms (cf. Wright *AG* I 276D, II 127B) probably reflect dialectal differences in pronunciation (often adopted for metrical needs), but also indicate a consensus as to its conventional nature (cf. Rabin *AWA* 137).

73. For occasional exceptions to pausal *ā*, see Nöldeke / Schwally *GQ* I 37 n. 2; Geyer rev *VSA* 53.

74. E.g., II:180/76; VII:177/6; XI:31/3; XXXIX:29/30. This does not, of course, take into account the special problems presented by words pronounced now with final *ā*, but written with *yā'* or *waw*, and related phenomena; see Bergsträsser/Pretzl *GK* 36–42.

75. Apart from the unanswerable psycho-linguistic questions of how someone dictating, presumably at this earliest point without benefit of a textual exemplar, would have maintained a sense of structure and continuity while delivering each word or small word-group one after another in isolated pausal form; and how, under such conditions, he would have come to observe always and only the contextual (i.e., syntactically conditioned) forms of undetermined accusatives, and certain other isolated evidences of inflection (e.g., *ābā'unā, ābā'inā,* etc.).

76. Cf. also Blau *ELB* 168–69, 210–12, on the retention of *-an* vs. *-un/-in;* idem *IMAD* 218 n. 36, 222–23. Further, esp., Fischer *SVA* 59 n. 84.

77. A further instance of this non-inflectional nunation can be seen in the pausal phenomena heard among the Banū Tamīn (and Qays), known as *tanwīn at-tarannum;* see De Goeje in Wright *AG* II 390C; Fleisch *TPA* 192–03. Birkeland *AP* 15 concluded from this final *-n* (sometimes occurring, however, contrary to normal grammatical usage; cf. Wright *AG* II 369C; Fleisch *TPA* 193) that poetical recitation in these dialects reflected a very early stage of the language when *tanwīn* was retained even in pause. But Rabin *AWA* 36–37 (and 41 n. 13) argues that the *tanwīn at-tarannum* had a purely phonological origin and represented simply an automatic nasalization of pausal vowels. Rabin's view is followed also by Fleisch *TPA* 193 n. 3.

78. E.g., the use of accusative forms with *mā or lā* (*mā/lā l-ḥijāzīya*) or with *illā* (cf. Wright *AG* II 337B).

79. It might be noted, also, that a terminal *ā,* with the syntactical meaning of a definite article, was retained in Western Aramaic dialects, especially Nabataean, upon whose script the Arabic writing system is thought to be based. In Syriac and the Babylonian dialects, this final *ā* became an integral part of the substantive so that it altogether lost the sense of the definite article. In either case, however, and particularly in that of Nabataean, there existed a solid precedent in orthographies that strongly influence Arabic orthography for graphic expression of final *ā,* as opposed to other vocalic terminations; see, e.g., Cantineau *CPA* 93, cf. 105. But cf. also J. Starcky, "Pétra et la Nabatène II, i, 2, g. Écriture nabatéenne et écriture arabe."

80. Needless to say, the approach and conclusions presented here depart considerably from those of Vollers *VSA* 163–75 in many important respects. In particular, I disagree substantially with his observations on the use of the accusative in the Qur'ān and the implications he draws therefrom (*VSA* 163–65). Geyer's refutation of Vollers on this point seems quite conclusive to me (rev *VSA* 52–55). Nevertheless, my own present judgment as to the presence of *iᶜrāb* in the Ḥijāzī and other Arab dialects generally concurs with Vollers's, though for quite different reasons and with this exception: the accusative desinence *-an* seems to have been retained to some extent in living speech, but greatly diminished in its inflectional significance and actually generalized for a number of non-synthetic purposes. Cf. Fischer *SVA* 54–60.

81. To be sure, Vollers *VSA* 169–70 held reservations as to whether the *iᶜrāb* was ever actually used in speech to the extent assumed by the later grammarians; but nonetheless, he did identify it with Bedouin linguistic usage; cf. chap. 3, § C.1.a, above.

82. For the sense of the term *non-casual* as it has been used here, see, e.g., the papers of C. F. Voeglin and E. Stankiewicz in Sebeok *SL* 57–68 and 69–81 respectively.

83. The MS of Rabin's *AWA* was sent to the publisher in 1947 (Rabin *BCA* 24 n. 6).

84. Rabin later implies that absence of *i^{c}rāb* would have been only one of several important features distinguishing the dialect of Qurayš from the Qur'ānic *^{c}arabīya* (*BCA* 26); but he bases his opinion, that that dialect "must have been more unlike the Classical than the present-day colloquials," upon the no longer tenable assumption that those colloquials "after all are derived from Classical Arabic or from a *Vulgärarabisch* closely related to it"; see Fleisch *IELS* 103 (with nn. 1–2); Bloch *VIP* 22–29; Blau *RBA* 43–45; idem *ELB* 10–11; Cohen *KLD* 108 and passim.

85. Blachère's examples of a special poetic idiom among the *oral poets* of the North African Berbers and the Tuaregs of the Sahara are much more cogent in this respect. Elsewhere Fleisch dwells upon these dubious parallels with European literary languages, stressing particularly that of the formation of Italian presumably on account of the literary preeminence of the Florentine Dante (Fleisch *ACAD* 27–31, 36–37, 50–51).

86. Parry (*SET* II 2 n. 3 = *MHV* 326 n. 3) has pointed out the underlying fallacy of this kind of comparison in the case of an oral poetic language.

87. Cf. Corriente *FY* 35–41 for corroboration of this point.

88. Fleisch *TPA* 281–82, 357 n. 2; idem *ACAD* 42–45; idem AC^2 30, 51 n. 1. Blau *IMAD* 224–26; idem *RBA* 46; idem, *PSSL* 56–58; and esp. idem *ELB* 3–4 (with 3 n. 1) and passim.

89. What ought to be mentioned in connection with al-Azharī's account is that he relates it in the course of the introduction to his great dictionary, *at-Taḏhīb fī l-luġa,* as evidence of his own firsthand expertise in Arabic, the authenticity of the rare and obscure expressions he has included, and the consequent superiority of his dictionary over all previous efforts. In other words, al-Azharī's claim of linguistic probity for his Bedouin captors actually serves to buttress his own claim to lexicographical preeminence. In such a context, one can at least question Fleisch's unqualified acceptance of the statement as conclusive proof for the presence of *i^{c}rāb* in Bedouin speech—particularly since (1) it was their value as sources of *lexical* information that was really to the point, and (2) the account fits well into the tradition of apocryphal and semi-apocryphal anecdotes about the inborn linguistic infallibility of the "natural" Bedouins. See references in Fück *Ar* 91 n. 26; cf. Haywood *AL* 53–56; Blau *RBA;* and below, n. 102, and chap. 3, § C. 11.a-c.

90. It should be noted, moreover, that most nouns of this pattern had equivalent, alternative forms that ended in *hā' at-ta'nīṯ* (or *tā' al-marbūṭa).* thus obviating the problem of pronouncing a final geminated consonant without a following vowel-suffix. In addition, one might ask why the pronunciation of forms like *fi^{c}all, fi^{c}ill, fu^{c}ull,* etc., without final inflectional vowels, should have caused pre-Islamic Bedouins any more difficulty than, say, modern colloquial speakers of Arabic have with a name like *Muḥibb* (>*moḥíb*) or a verb like *yuḥibb* (>*biyḥíb*). In other words, the final radical might be articulated with gemination when a final auxiliary vowel could be appended to it; otherwise, "gemination" would be indicated by somehow stressing or accenting the final syllable. Cf. the conjecture regarding the nature of *tad^{c}īf* advanced above, n. 26.

91. For Blau's analyses, see *IMAD; ELB* 4–8 and App. I; *PSSL* chap. 5. Cf. also Grohmann *ECAP* 103–7.

92. For a report that Muḥammad feared, too, that he had become a poet, see Guillaume *LM* 106, translating phrases from Ibn Isḥāq's *Sīra* found in aṭ-Ṭabarī's *History* I 1150, but omitted from Ibn Hišām's version.

93. Corriente specifies his terminology as follows: "For the purpose of this paper, 'Middle Arabic' is a generic designation often including later periods, while 'Old Arabic' comprehends both Early and Classical (= ^{c}Arabīya) Arabic" (*FY* 20 n. 1). That such a comprehensive use of "Old Arabic" raises some problems will become evident in the ensuing section (chap. 3, § C.10. a–d).

94. See n. 54 to this chapter; also Corriente *FY* 27–28 nn. 9–11, 37 n. 26, 44; idem FY_2 155–58 and references cited.

95. In FY_2 157, he calls it "an apparent linguistic scandal."

96. Corriente often refers to the *i^{c}rāb* suffixes simply as "morphs."

97. The method of commutation is described in *FY* 32.

98. The texts chosen for analysis are ennumerated in *FY* 35, and the results of the analyses are given at *FY* 36–38.

99. I.e., "external markers with independent [or semi-independent—M.Z.] word status, like articles, prepositions, conjunctions, etc." (*FY* 31). Examples of Arabic morph-words include: *MIN hunā, KAY yarḍā* (*FY* 31 n. 18).

100. This statement should be read in conjunction with the rather lengthy qualificative and elaborative notes that accompany it, especially as regards "the daily speech of many Bedouin tribesmen" (n. 8), "some urban dwellers" (n. 9), and other points (nn. 10–16). Cf., most importantly, *FY* 38–41; FY_2 157–58. For the sake of comparison, I quote here Corriente's most concise statement of his adherence "to the thesis of coexistence somewhere and sometime of both types of dialects within a single structural frame, where *I^{c}rāb* did not mean much (except for its rhetorical prestige and social value), and this because, no matter whether it was present or absent, its functional yield was almost zero, and it would not impede mutual understanding between, let us say, the tribes of Naǧd and the *^{c}ulūǧ* of Lower Mesopotamia" (FY_2 159).

101. See, further, Corriente's continuation, outlining the psycholinguistic problems that might be confronted "by speakers and writers who no longer have the ability to identify forms and functions (morphemes and logemes) instinctively . . . " (*FY* 32–33).

102. Cf. also FY_2 160–61, where Corriente replies to Blau's warning that "one should refrain from simply equating the linguistic structure of Middle Arabic with that of classical Arabic" (*PSC* 33). Corriente insists that his "proposal is to diminish the emphasis usually placed upon the synthetical characters of Semitic languages and not to deny the presence, even in the most analytical members of this family, of a considerable array of synthetic devices, such as markers of gender, number, aspect, etc." (FY_2 160). The general drift of the language surely may have tended to reduce the functionality of many of these synthetic traits "outside the field of the case and mood-systems," as Blau suggests (*PSC* 32–33), thus giving the impression of a cleavage between a basically synthetic classical Arabic and a basically analytic Middle and dialectal Arabic. But this still does not explain why, with *all* forms of post-classical Arabic, as with "all Semitic languages that lived long enough to complete the cycle," it is the case- and mood-markers that comprise "the two areas mainly affected by the reduction suggested" (Corriente FY_2 160); whereas, at the same time, several of the non-inflective synthetic devices of classical Arabic, which Blau cites as having been reduced to analytic expressions in Middle Arabic (e.g., fem. pl. of pronouns, verbs, and adjectives, superseded by masc. pl., and limitation of the dual, to mention only two; cf. Blau *PSC* 32–33), seem as a matter of fact still to be retained in certain rural and Bedouin dialects, much to the surprise of many urban Arabs and scholarly linguists (private communication from Prof. F. Cadora, who is preparing a study dealing with a substantial body of such retentions). Thus, I believe, one is led, with Corriente, to "consider the structural and typological evolution from Old to Middle Arabic as less significant, in agreement with the just slight decrease of the true rates of functional load observed between both forms of the Arabic language" (FY_2). Cf. below (in text of chap. 3).

103. Corriente here misreads Blau's argument, construing the "rich display" as evidence that Middle Arabic word order deviates from classical, where "a determinate object is often inserted in Old Arabic prose between verb and indeterminate subject" (Blau *PSC* 33, quoted in Corriente FY_2 161). In fact, the only "rich display of Middle Arabic examples" adduced in (e) applies to the difference between classical and Middle Arabic "treatment of direct objects preceding the verb" (*PSC* 33). The phraseology of Corriente's (unexpectedly perfunctory) reply to objection (e) makes it altogether uncertain that he has really caught the gist of the argument Blau advances there.

104. Corriente appears not to have noted this inconsistency.

105. Chomsky, *Aspects*, p. 127. Chomsky's short treatment of "the phenomenon of so-called 'free word-order'" is most cogent to this problem; for he indicates that (1) although "richly

inflected languages tolerate stylistic reordering much more extensively than languages that are poor in inflection, for obvious reasons, . . . [nevertheless] even richly inflected languages do not seem to tolerate reordering when it leads to ambiguity''; and (2) the ''reordering'' in question is a function of *style,* not *grammar*—''an interesting phenomenon . . . that has no apparent bearing, for the moment, on the theory of grammatical structure'' (ibid., pp. 126–27; cf. p. 221 n. 35).

106. The instances specified occur in the Qur'ānic passage chosen by Corriente for analysis (XII:1–30), whose functional yield he had determined at zero. It might be mentioned that a frequent instance of commutability, overlooked by both scholars, is to be found in noun phrases consisting of an undefined noun followed by one or more simple attributes: e.g., in the passage under discussion, *qur'ān- ᶜarabīy-, ᶜadūw- mubīn-, qawm- sālihīna, dam- kaḏib-, i.a.* (such noun phrases occur in *āyas* 2, 5, 6, 8, 9, 18bis, 19, 25, 30). Because in Arabic what we call adjectives can—and do—regularly do double duty as substantives (i.e., *jamīl* can denote both 'good-looking, handsome'' *and* ''a good-looking, handsome man''), noun phrases of this pattern may also occur as noun phrases of the genitive-construct type. So, without even commuting the *case-vowel* of the first member (though eliminating its *tanwīn*), one arrives at a very different, grammatically legitimate (but ordinarily contextually ill-suited) expression. Instead, then, of ''an Arabic recitation,'' ''an obvious enemy,'' ''a righteous tribe,'' ''false blood,'' we might have *qur'āna ᶜarabīyin* ''as an Arab's recitation,'' *ᶜadūwa mubīnin* ''the enemy of one who clarifies,'' *qawma ṣāliḥina* ''the tribe of (some) righteous men,'' *dami kaḏibin* ''(with) a liar's blood.'' Whether or not such a commutation is consistent with Corriente's approach cannot readily be ascertained from his article; but it obviously increases the functional yield of the case system (and incidentally, of the nunation) for this Qur'ānic passage.

107. Corriente uses this term in the sense discussed above, n. 11 to this chapter.

108. In several respects, Corriente's position here is reminiscent of Geyer's (discussed above, chap. 3, § C. 2), though Geyer rev *VSA* is nowhere cited.

109. Whose inflective morphs would have been only secondary, however, and whose structure would have been basically analytic, if Corriente is right in his conjecture relative to the inflective stage of all Semitic languages. But cf. n. 115 to this chapter.

110. That is to say, it was sensed, if not specifically as an archaism, certainly as a linguistic anomaly proper only to the utterances of poets and other skilled wordsmiths.

111. ''Functional'' and ''vital'' with such reservations as Corriente's findings may now impose. But cf. n. 115, below, and chap. 3, § C.10.d.

112. Corriente notes that ''Arabic literature, including oral pre-Islamic traditions, is rich in stories about plagiarism (*intiḥāl*), which is condemned, even though it was brazenly committed by many authors'' (*FY* 40 n. 31). This, of course, misses the point completely, as I hope to demonstrate in the following chapter. Cf. also his remark about Akkadian poetry in a similar vein (*FY* 42 n. 35).

113. The reports by the third/ninth and fourth/tenth-century philologists regarding the linguistic propensities of the Bedouins, which are only too frequently adduced as evidence that *iᶜrāb* had been retained in use in some Bedouin dialects of that time, cannot be accepted at face value. Corriente himself is aware of the dubious value of these reports (*FY* 26 n. 8), but he opts anyway for admitting them as proof of *iᶜrāb* used in living speech. See chap. 3, § C.11, below.

114. Never, that is, except perhaps for some hypothetical protohistorical juncture at the outset of the oral-poetic tradition when a poet's spoken language and his poetic diction might momentarily have been one.

115. One of the ramifications of this theory that the classical *ᶜarabīya* was an oral-poetical language would be that generalizations, based upon observing its structure, about earlier stages of Arabic could be made only with the greatest care. If the structure of all forms of Arabic spoken in the sixth and seventh centuries was basically analytic, as I think Corriente's studies make more certain than he himself seems willing to grant, then it would not be at all surprising, following Parry's methodology (see n. 7 above and chap. 3, §B.3.d), to find the structure of the oral-poetic diction analytic to a similar degree. Corriente's very low functional yield of the *iᶜrāb*-suffixes for

the Qur'ān and the slightly higher, but still rather unimpressive, figures for the poetic sample may reflect no more than the circumstance that these suffixes were retained in poetry because of the prosodic pressures of the formulaic tradition. There the exigencies of meter and especially rhyme might enhance their functionality in certain key positions, but otherwise the poet's natural way of speaking analytically would have prevailed. The case-endings were imported into the recited Qur'ān quite simply because the Qur'ān was revealed and rendered in the poetic *ᶜarabīya* (see chap. 3, §D, below), of which they were an inseparable constituent. But the pausal convention of the Qur'ān, particularly, to a very great extent reduced the need for their contrastive function and permitted the analytic structure of the spoken forms to show through even more. Thus, low or negligible functional yield of *iᶜrāb*-suffixes in recorded pre-literary verbal works, like classical verse and the Qur'ān, can really tell us little or nothing about how vital and functional those suffixes might have been in standard speech at the time when they were originally incorporated into the fabric of the oral-formulaic diction of pre-Islamic poetry; cf. Corriente *FY* 34 n. 22. As for subsequent adaptation and adoption of a standardized and systematized *ᶜarabīya* as a genuine *Schriftsprache,* which was to be studied and learned for purposes of *writing* poetry and prose (and even of *speaking,* in certain very conventionalized, erudite, and sophisticated milieus; cf. Corriente *FY* 29 n. 15, 32 n. 20), that constitutes a state of affairs that is altogether different from the one under consideration here and almost totally incommensurate with it.

116. The second alternative, however, may have sometimes obtained later, *after* the poetico-Qur'ānic *ᶜarabīya* had become literarized and standardized as the imperial language of Islamic administration and culture—again a quite unrelated phenomenon (cf. the previous note).

117. Diem's citations from the inscriptional texts are made in Aramaic script, which I have merely transliterated here, usually into consonantal form.

118. Diem notes as ''remarkable [*auffällig*]'' the writing *'lh* ''God'' with one *l* as against Arabic *'llh* with two (*FKA* 233 n. 39). If the proposed etymology of the name of God in classical Arabic (*Allāh* <*al-ilāh*) is correct, the Nabataean spelling may reflect a stage at which *Ilāh* alone was used as a proper name; hence *ᶜAbda'ilāhi, Wahba'ilāhi,* etc.

119. Only one name of this kind is to be found written with a final *-y/i,* along with the other two regular spellings, and this instance (*'bn'lqyny* <Ibn al-Qayni), Diem believes, is influenced by the orthography of theophoric names (*FKA* 233).

120. ''Emerged'' or ''arose'' (*hervorgehen*), however, may not adequately characterize the genesis of the poetic *ᶜarabīya* or its relationship with the spoken dialects at any period; see this chapter, passim.

121. Unfortunately, Blau shares with many other scholars a predisposition to view poetic composition only as a function of literacy. The *ruwāt*, he says, ''were experts in Classical Arabic poetry, as they continued to live among the same conditions as their ancestors and, therefore, were inclined to *write* in the same way'' (*RBA* 45, my italics). Not recognizing the basic difference in *kind* between the mode of existence of an oral verbal work and that of a written one may well turn out to have been among the more inhibiting factors in the progress of both linguistic and literary scholarship in Arabic studies. Cf. n. 15 to this chapter.

122. See also the brief critique of this opinion of Blau's by Cohen *ELA* 182–83.

123. Cf. the identical point made by Spitaler (rev *Ar* 145b–146a) and Wehr (rev *Ar* 183–84).

124. The other arguments advanced by Blau in the same note to support the view that the pre- and early Islamic dialects retained the *iᶜrāb* have been touched upon in the course of this chapter; cf. section C, passim.

125. Cf. also the example cited by Fück later (*Ar* 135), where *laḥn* occurs in conjunction with *ikfā'*. In this context, *ikfā'* is better understood as identical in meaning to *iqwā'*, with which at an early period it was used interchangeably (see Blachère *DCHM* 137–38): i.e., as variation of the rhyme-vowel rather than of the rhyme-consonant. Cf. also following note.

126. *wa l-iqwā'u huwa l-ikfā'u (mahmūzun). wa huwa an yaxtalifa iᶜrābu l-qawāfī, fa takūna* [text reads: *takūnu*] *qāfiyatun marfūᶜatan wa uxrā maxfūḍatan aw manṣūbatan. wa huwa fī šiᶜri*

l-aᶜrābi kat̠īrun; wa huwa fī man dūna l-fuhūli mina š-šuᶜarā' i akt̠aru, wa lā yajūzu li-muwalladīn li-anna-hum qad ᶜarifū ᶜayba-hu. wa l-badawīyu lā ya'bahu la-hu fa huwa aᶜd̠aru.

127. *Aᶜd̠aru* here is understood according to the interpretation of the word given by H. Wehr, *Der arabische Elativ* pp. 50:17–18 and 55:22–23, though its elative or comparative sense is not necessarily applicable in this instance (cf. M. M. Bravmann, *The Arabic Elative: A New Approach*, pp. 24–27).

128. Cf. al-Maydānī, *Majmaᶜ al-amt̠āl* I 113:30–114:4.

129. See Brockelmann *GAL Suppl* I 165; al-Qifṭī *IR* II 157–58 and references; also al-Marzubānī/al-Yaġmūrī *NQ* 47. Brockelmann cites as-Suyūṭī (*BW* II 74) for the information that Abu l-Xaṭṭāb al-Axfaš was the first to write interlinear scholia to poetry. It is entirely possible that as-Suyūṭī has confused this al-Axfaš with al-Axfaš al-Awsaṭ Abu l-Ḥasan Saᶜīd b. Masᶜada (d. 210/825 or 221/835). No source that I know prior to as-Suyūṭī mentions this innovation among Abu l-Xaṭṭāb's accomplishments. On the other hand, Abu l-Ḥasan al-Axfaš al-Awsaṭ is explicitly credited by at least two earlier biographers (both on the authority of T̠aᶜlab) with being the first to *dictote* the explanation of difficult expressions in a verse *beneath* the verse (*sic*: *awwalu man amlā ġarība kulli baytin mina š-šiᶜri taḥta-hu l-Axfašu* [*l-Awsaṭ*]; see az-Zubaydī *TNL* 76:8–9 and al-Qifṭī *IR* II39:1–2.

130. *qāla Abu l-Xaṭṭābi: inna ᶜāmmata ahli l-badwi laysat tafhamu mā yurīdu š-šāᶜiru wa lā yuḥsinūna t-tafsīra. wa innamā atā iqwā'u hād̠ā min qillati fahmillad̠īna rawaw-hu. wa innama ᶜana š-šāᶜiru "wa qad yuᶜdi l-ajrabu ṣ-ṣaḥīḥa mabrakan." fa lammā wajadū-hu muqaddaman wa mu'axxaran lam yuḥsinū talxīṣa-hu wa wajadū "mabārik-" lā yanṣarifu fa aẓlama l-maᶜnā ᶜalay-him.*

131. al-Marzubānī/al-Yaġmūrī *NQ* 47:9–10: *wa kānā lā yadaᶜu l-iᶜrāb.*

132. On the much-discussed subject of Muḥammad's relation to the poets and soothsayers, see, i.e., Nöldeke/Schwally *GQ* I 34–44; Goldziher *MI* I 52–53; Nicholson *LHA* 159–63; Watt *MMec* 127–92; Bell/Watt *Intro* 77–79, 153–54; Blachère *HLA* 188–97, 209–12, 230–33; Paret *MK* 21–23, 48–51; etc. See, esp., Blachère *PC*; Shahīd *CKE*.

133. Cf., in addition to sources mentioned in the preceding note, Goldziher *AAP* 1–105 passim, esp. 3–25 and 57–83; Macdonald *RALI*, esp. 24–36; Guillaume *PD*, chap. 6; Lecerf *DPC*, esp. 366–71; Meier *SAI*.

134. This translation, which departs somewhat from the usual renderings (cf. translations of Bell, Pickthall, Blachère, Arberry, Paret, et al.), draws upon the insights of I. Shahīd's exegesis of *Sūra* XXVI:224–27/8 (*CKE*). Translating the verb *ittabaᶜ* by "to attend" is quite within the semantic range of its contemporary and even Qur'ānic usage, and seems closer to the sense suggested by Shahīd (e.g., *CKE* 566, 569, 570–71). Shahīd has expressed the hope of devoting a future study to *āya* 226, which "needs and deserves a separate treatment" (*CKE* 568 n. 2), but I am not aware that such a study has been published to date.

135. The passage on poetry reads in the text: *mā huwa bi šāᶜirin; laqadᶜarafna š-šiᶜra kulla-hu—rajaza-hu wa hazaja-hu wa qarīḍa-hu wa maqbūḍa-hu wa mabsūṭa-hu—fa mā huwa bi š-šiᶜr*. Cf. Ibn Fāris *SFL* 38 (with variants); also Ibn al-At̠īr *NGH* IV 57:6–10. The passage is discussed by Ullmann *UR* 1–2; and esp. Blachère *DCHM* 133 and passim.

136. Cf. esp. Nöldeke *NBSS* 5–23 and von Grunebaum *MWO*. Both studies offer detailed and well-documented evidence of substantial Qur'ānic departures from the linguistic usage, stylistic conventions, and conceptual sphere proper to pre-Islamic poetry and to that of the earliest Islamic period as well.

137. On the inimitability and miraculous nature of the Qur'ān, the purely *Qur'ānic* foundation for which seems to have been in essence linguistic and stylistic (cf. Nöldeke *NBSS* 22–23; von Grunebaum *MWO* 29–30 and passim), see, e.g., Andrae *PM* 94–100 and passim; Blachère *Intro* 169–72; idem *HLA* 230–63; von Grunebaum "Iᶜd̠jāz" EI^2 III 1018a–1020b. We do not, unfortunately, know enough about either the form or the content of the "revelations" proclaimed by the so-called false prophets shortly before and after Muḥammad's death. They received a

rather bad press from later Muslim historians, but we do discover that their words, too, moved men's minds and hearts and that the doctrines preached by some of them closely resembled Muḥammad's, at least along general lines; cf. Nöldeke/Schwally *GQ* I 56–57 and references.

138. See, e.g., Geyer rev *VSA* 17–19 (with reservations expressed above); Blachère *Intro* 164–65; Rabin *BCA* 27–29; Spitaler rev *Ar* 146; Wehr rev *Ar* 184; Fleisch *ACAD* 39; etc. My colleague Frederic Cadora has reminded me that Muḥammad seems usually to have sought and gained the allegiance of tribal groups outside Mecca and Medina through dealings with their leaders or one of their leading factions; and since "total conversion"—as opposed to "formal adhesion" (manifested chiefly by the later Meccan adherents) and "enforced adherence" (most typical of the Bedouins)—was after all comparatively rare among the early Muslims (cf. Gibb *SCI* 5), one need not assume *universal* intelligibility of the poetic *ᶜarabīya* among Arabic-speaking peoples in order to understand why its use in formulating the Qur'ānic message would have enhanced that message's prestige, efficacy, and wide appeal.

139. See, e.g., Nöldeke/Schwally *GQ* I 117–64; Jeffery *QS* 3–88 passim; Watt *MMec* 123–33; Bell/Watt *Intro* 114–18, 121–66 passim; Paret *MK* 52–101 passim; etc.

140. According to Blachère's chronological enumeration, they cover the period from no. 57 (XX) to no. 92 (XIII). For other orderings, see Bell/Watt *Intro* 206–9.

141. Cf. Watt *MMed* 143–44; idem *IIS* 92; Chelhod *ISI* 52–53 and passim; J. Henninger in Gabrieli *ASB* 77–78; etc.

142. For more extensive discussions of the following points, see, e.g., D. H. Müller, "Arabia," in Pauly/Wisowa *RECA* II 344–59 (with appendix on "Arabia als römische Provinz," by Pietschmann, 359–62); Th. Nöldeke, "Arabia, Arabians" *EB* I 272b–275a; R. Aigrain, "Arabie" *DHGE* III 1158–1339, esp. 1158–1292 passim; Dussaud *PAS* passim; Poliak *AOS* 35–93; W. Caskel in von Grunebaum *SICH* 36–44; idem *BBGA* 5–11, 26–27; M. Höfner in Gabrieli *ASB* 53–68; J. Henninger in ibid. 71–87; Moscati *SAH* chap. 4; von Grunebaum *NAU*; H. von Wissman "Badw. (c) Bedouin Nomadism in Arabia" *EI*² I 880b–887a; etc.

143. See esp. Aigrain *DHGE* III 1163–66; and R. Devreese "Le Christianisme dans la province d'Arabie."

144. See examples cited by Nöldeke in *EB* 274b; Goldziher *MS* I 103 (with n. 2); Poliak *AOS* 37 n. 1; Asad *MSJ* 5–9. An interesting case where the opposition is even more frankly linguistic may be seen in *Muf* 91:21–23. The date of the poet, al-Xaṣafī al-Muḥāribī, is unknown, though the poem's style is decidedly archaic. In the three lines cited the poet first opposed *d̲ū bayān* "articulate" (lit., "possessor of articulateness, clarity") to *aᶜjam*, thus obviously equating *d̲ū bayān* with *ᶜarab*; and he follows this with praise of his tribe's orator (*xaṭīb*), whose eloquence stifles all competition. Cf. n. 151 below; also *DZuh* (ed. Dār) p. 364:8 (*d̲u . . . bayānī*).

145. The word *al-aᶜrāb* occurs ten times in the Qur'ān, all with a deprecatory tone and all in passages definitely dated to the Medinan period: IX:90/1, 97/8, 98/9, 99/100, 101/2, 120/1; XXXIII:20; XLVIII:11, 16; XLIX:14. Cf. Watt *MMed* 143.

146. Cf. M. J. Kister, "A Work of Ibn al-Kalbī on the Arab Peninsula."

147. See, e.g., Watt *MMed* 72–85; idem *MMed* 142–50; Serjeant in Arberry *RME* II 4–16; von Grunebaum *CI* 28; etc.

148. This is not at all to deny the possibility of a Christian liturgy in Arabic established at Najrān raised by Shahīd *MN* (see n. 68 to this chapter). This important question needs further investigation.

149. See chap. 1, n. 40, and chap. 2, n. 117, above. Add also Widengren *LPA* 11–34.

150. The case of ᶜAdīy b. Zayd and other pre-Islamic "scribal poets" (see Asad *MSJ* 113–18) requires special consideration. If they did actually *write* their poems, then formulaic analysis might indicate this fact. Unfortunately, the preliminary research necessary for such a "negative check" is wholly lacking to Arabists at this stage.

151. It is possible that the words *mubīn* "articulate, clear, distinguishing" and *bayān* "clear

exposition, articulateness,'' as applied in the Qur'ān to language and verbal expression, refer in a quasi-technical way to the poetic idiom itself. Most of the commentators propose ''language'' as the meaning of *al-bayān* in *Sūra* LV:4/3 (*^{c}allama-hu l-bayān*), whereby they intend, of course, the *^{c}arabīya par excellence*; although Blachère, in a note on this *āya* (*Le Coran* 567 n), prefers the sense ''l'Exposé,'' elsewhere (*Le Coran* 626 n. 19) he admits that the probable sense there would be ''langage clair.'' In *Sūra* LXXV:19 (*ṯumma inna ^{c}alay-nā bayāna-hu*) *bayāna-hu* is mentioned in conjunction with, and as an accompaniment to, *qur'ana-hu* ''its (i.e., revelation's) recitation.'' Usually interpreted as ''its explanation'' or ''its exposition'' or the like, the phrase *bayāna-hu* can better be understood as signifying ''its clear (*or* proper) articulation''—especially since it occurs in the context (LXXV:16–19) of an injunction not to rush the vocal utterance of the message, but rather to follow God's recitation (*qur'āna-hu*) (cf. Ibn al-Aṯīr *NGH* I 175:5: *alā inna t-tabayyuna mina llāhi ta^{c}ālā wa l-^{c}ajalatu mina ššayṭāni, fa tabayyanū*). In poetry, too, *bayān* sometimes is found in the sense of ''linguistic articulateness,'' as opposed even to ''inarticulateness'' or ''incomprehensibility''—or, more precisely *^{c}arab* vs. *^{c}ajam*; cf. n. 144 above. As for *mubīn*, Yāqūt, in his short and generally overlooked sketch of the linguistic history of the Arabian peninsula (*MB* III 634–36), quite explicitly uses *al-mubīn* as the proper name for the *sixth* language spoken in Arabia, the language first spoken by Ishmael and that of Ma^{c}add b. ^{c}Adnān, and the language that prevails among the Arabs ''today''—i.e., none other but the *^{c}arabīya* itself. Yāqūt may, of course, simply have appropriated the term out of its Qur'ānic context; but if so, then his use of it as an appellative for the inflective *^{c}arabīya* shows that he assumed, as I have, that such was the sense in which one had been meant to take it. Furthermore, if we recall that a main significance of the root *b-y-n* would be ''to part, separate'' and that *abāna* would mean ''to set apart'' or ''to separate sth. from sth.''—as well as ''to be *or* make clear, articulate''—then the use of *mubīn* (and *bayān* too) to designate an inflective and synthetic form of Arabic recognized by all Arabs would not be surprising, for it would have effectively denoted that distinguishing and differentiating property of the poetic and Qur'ānic *^{c}arabīya* which the dialects in general seem to have lost—namely, the *i^{c}rāb*.

152. For a detailed and perceptive discussion of the Arabic root *^{c}-l-m* ''knowing, knowledge,'' its etymological relationship to visual ''signs'' or ''marks,'' and its significance in pre-Islamic poetry and fundamental importance in Qur'ānic usage, see Rosenthal *KT* 5–32. The apparently close connection that the Qur'ān established between knowledge (*^{c}ilm*) and writing (*^{c}allama bi l-qalam*, etc.) gains added meaning when we contrast the occurrences of *^{c}-l-m* with those of *š-^{c}-r*, which in its verbal form was nearly synonymous with *^{c}alima*, but was equally—if not more—familiar as the noun *ši^{c}r* ''poetry'' (originally ''knowledge''; cf. Goldziher *AAP* 17–19; Rosenthal *KT* 12–13). The preeminent position of *^{c}ilm* in the Qur'ānic conceptual scheme needs no elaboration after Rosenthal's treatment. The position of *ši^{c}r* and the *šā^{c}ir*, on the other hand, is scarcely one of eminence at all, while the use of the verb *ša^{c}ara* (26 times) is confined almost entirely to negative predicates addressed to opponents and other more or less reprehensible parties (''you/they do not know''). From this the inference might be drawn that the *jinn*-inspired ''knowledge'' of the poets—their ''embellished speech'' (*zuxruf al-qawl*: VI:112), which was directly susceptible to the manipulations and interpolations that the *jinn* and demons tried to effect in the Qur'ānic message (i.e., the normal fluctuations of an oral poetic tradition; cf. XVI: 98/100–105/7; XXII:52/1–2)—was simply not to be classed in the same league with the divinely revealed, scripturally fixed ''knowledge'' preached by Muḥammad.

153. Cf. n. 151 above.

154. No. 67 (from ^{c}A'iša) is cited by Asad (*MSJ* 210:12) with *ta^{c}ḏub alsinatu-kum* ''your tongues will be sweet'' instead of *yu^{c}ribu alsinata-kum* ''it (sc., poetry) brings the *i^{c}rab* onto your tongues.''

155. Blau interprets these deviations from classical usage and pseudo-correct features as evidence of a *breakdown* of the case system (e.g., *ELB* 128) or a *disappearance* of case endings from the spoken dialects (e.g., *IMAD* 223). That such a breakdown and disappearance did occur at some period is undoubtedly true, but probably—if the arguments presented here are accepted—much earlier than Blau indicates. With regard to deviations as exhibited in early Christian Arabic, he expressly rejects the possibility, raised by Rabin (''^{c}Arabīya'' *EI*^{2} 564b),

that they might be a ''Classical Arabic not yet standardized by the grammarians'' (see Blau *PSSL* 64). Nevertheless, I do not see, given the arguments advanced in this study, how one can acknowledge the presence of such features in first/seventh-century texts and generalize their implications to the contemporary spoken (urban) dialects, while at the same time denying that they might have equal relevance to dialects spoken less than a century earlier. Rather than assuming a ''breakdown'' or a ''disappearance,'' could we not just as naturally assume a failure of the earliest scribes, accustomed perhaps to recording their language(s) as spoken, to assimilate the grammatical principles of the *ᶜarabīya*, just newly or still incompletely codified? As Blau points out, later authors managed to write correct classical Arabic, though they ''no doubt, used a literary language entirely different from their vernaculars''; and that was because ''by that time the Arab philologists had established the science of grammar, so that writers speaking various vernaculars could learn Classical Arabic and compose works in it'' (*PSSL* 58 n. 15). Would not the corollary also be valid: that before ''that time'' writers would have had an inadequate understanding of how to record the language of poetry, much less compose in it? (In the case of early Christian Arabic, there remains the as-yet unanswered question of the form of Arabic used for writing at Ḥīra and other Syrian or Mesopotamian centers of Arab culture, or even at Najrān. Had it been significantly different from the *ᶜarabīya*, that linguistic form, developed and used already among Christians, rather than the poetic *ᶜarabīya* adopted by the Muslims, may have been the real influence behind Christian scribal practices or linguistic habits. Cf. chap. 3, § D.4.a, above.) Cf. chap. 3, § C.10.a-d; also Corriente *FY* 40–41. See further Blau, ''Sind uns Reste arabischer Bibelübersetzungen . . . geblieben.''

156. The extent to which the poetry of such poets actually deviated from the standard of the more purely oral poets can be determined only by careful comparative formulaic analysis. Meanwhile, Brockelmann *GAL Suppl* I 87–88 raises some important considerations in the area of imagery, at least.

157. The question may be raised (though it must for now remain unanswered) whether the classicistic philologists, working mainly under the patronage of the ruling ᶜAbbāsid dynasty and its supporters, extended the range of the ''classical'' poets to the end of Umayyad rule on the basis of purely disinterested linguistic and literary critical criteria, or whether their approach might not have been inspired, at least in part, by the vigorous, pervasive, and sometimes unbelievably subtle propagandistic campaign waged on behalf of the ᶜAbbāsids to defame the memory of the overthrown house. Such an approach would have conformed well to the official view that the Umayyads had imposed an exclusivist Arab ''kingship'' upon the Muslim community and had perpetuated the customs and attitudes of the pagan *jāhilīya* under the banner of Islam, and true religion and true culture were inaugurated only with the advent of the ᶜAbbāsids. See, e.g., Mackenson *ABL* I 245–46, III 58–61, s. n. 157; Abbott *SALP* I 19–31. Admitting most of the Umayyad poets to the classical canon and alleging Umayyad interest and support for no other cultural activity but this poetry so closely associated with pre-Islamic pagandom, the philologists could well have chosen to gloss over a number of important differences between the productions of many of these poets and those of their earlier predecessors; cf., e.g., Fück *Ar* 19–28; Haddāra *ISA* passim.

158. Cf., as a noteworthy instance of post-classical improvisation, the case of al-Mutanabbī, reported in Ibn Jinnī *Xas* I 327:3–9. Here, this most Arab of poets, requested to describe a hunt, takes *pen and paper*, sits off in a corner, and turns out in short order fifty-six *rajaz* lines—no mean accomplishment, but altogether apart from oral tradition however understood. (The poem is found in *DMutan* pp. 201–6).

*

Chapter Four

Variation and Attribution in the Tradition of Classical Arabic Poetry

A. One of the most frequently noted characteristics of oral-traditional poetry almost wherever it has been found is the wide range of variation that a poem may exhibit from one rendition (i.e., version) to another. Lord, of course, has considered this feature in some depth (*ST* chap. 5, App. II, V, and passim). It has also been studied, for example, in the Old English and Old French traditions, among others.[1] The fluidity and multiformity of an oral poem constitute the hallmark of its tradition, stamping it as a reasonably authentic product of oral art. Traditional—that is, oral—poetry is, as R. Menéndez Pidal has said, "a poetry that lives through variants" (*CR* chap. 2). How ironic, therefore, that scholars of Arabic poetry have so often cast doubt upon the "authenticity" or "genuineness" of this or that verse, poem, or body of poems or, sometimes, of pre-Islamic poetry in general, because they have found it impossible to establish an "original version."

A.1 Some, however, have shown a greater understanding of the textual state of classical Arabic poetry and a greater sensitivity to the implications of the myriad variant readings and divergencies offered both in the medieval commentaries and philological and literary treatises and in the critical apparatuses to many modern editions. These writers would agree that, as much as the Spanish ballad or French *chanson de geste,* Arabic poetry was "a poetry that lives through variants." In the words of E. Bräunlich,

> Even those Arabists who have not been especially concerned with early Arabic poetry are aware that scarcely a single verse which is transmitted in several places is to be found with the same form in these various citations. (*FEAP* 825)

This fact Bräunlich sees as the result of

> the perhaps unparalleled wealth of the language in synonymous or nearly synonymous expressions, on the one hand, and the rigid schematically and analogically worked-out morphology of Arabic, on the other. . . . [Through these] it could easily happen that, despite the relatively inflexible accommodation of the metrical bond in Arabic versification, a large number of variants found their way into many verses, as long as the tradition was carried on exclusively by word of mouth. (ibid.; cf. Bräunlich *VLB* 211)

In this regard, R. Blachère also holds that "much equivocation and useless research would be avoided if one takes into account that, from the moment it appeared, an archaic work in verse is characterized, virtually and actually, by its multiform or unstable aspect" (*HLA* 86). From an investigation of traditions reported by the Arabic philologists and of methods employed by nineteenth- and twentieth-century Bedouins in verse composition, he insists that variation is inherent in a piece since its origin—variation in the details of the verses, their number, or their sequence (*HLA* 88–89). Like Bräunlich, Blachère seeks to explain these divergencies by falling back upon a postulated period of oral transmission that could have had "disastrous effects . . . for works going back to the end of the VIth century A.D." (*HLA* 179). Discussing the problem posed by "textualization" of these early poems—*la mise par écrit*—he asks the question: "Faced with the multiple forms taken by a poem, either from the outset . . ., or in the course of its oral passage, how did the Iraqi scholars [of the second-fourth/eighth-tenth centuries] proceed?"

> Not daring to choose, they confined themselves to juxtaposing the different recensions of a particular poem, without trying to fuse them together. Most often, besides, in the present state of our documentation, the existence of parallel recensions is known to us only through recourse to several sources. These divergencies in form bear upon the number of verses, a fact resulting, in many cases, from the work's having survived only in the anthologies. Very often, too, they touch the order of the verses: each of the latter, forming in effect a whole,[2] can be displaced in a passage, without the sense of the passage being thereby obscured. But what is especially striking is the number and breadth of the variants within each verse. The origin of these divergencies is impossible to trace. That many arise from lapses of memory in the course of oral transmission is not to be doubted. That a small number among them may be imputed to the imperfections of the writing system or to substitutions by synonymy is just as certain. Nevertheless, nothing grants us the right to say that these variants in detail are not early . . . and do not go back to the very inception of the work. In particular, such would be very plausible each time that the simplicity of form and substance could not have occasioned alteration during passage through the oral phase. (*HLA* 181–82)

Just how complex and wide-ranging were these variants to which Bräunlich, Blachère, and others allude? Does the evidence of the existing texts of early Arabic poems actually permit us to subscribe to the conclusions of a scholar such as Menéndez Pidal with regard to traditional works rendered orally from generation to generation over several centuries? Menéndez Pidal maintains that no such work

> assumes a fixed, sculptural form; it takes on rather a living form which is continually renewed throughout its constitutive elements. It is a work that *lives through variants and reworkings*. These innumerable variations are the very essence, the life of the poetry which is inscribed in the collective memory and which is perpetuated down through the generations. (*CR* 67–68)

Certainly, the statements of the Arabists quoted above would suggest that the case would be much the same for early Arabic poetry; but let us consider in greater detail the particular case of a single Arabic ode—an object of study too seldom given the attention it merits.

A.2.a Arabs and speakers of Arabic, whose literary history has been exceptionally rich in poets, have almost unanimously accorded the laurels of poetic preeminence to Imra'alqays, son of Ḥujr, the last king of Kinda.[3] The poems of this sixth-century artist, who has often been called the "Homer of the Arabs,"[4] were circulated during the Middle Ages in no fewer than seventeen individual recensions. These are known to us either directly, through still extant manuscripts and editions, or indirectly, through references in bio-bibliographical works, philological treatises, and the commentaries that accompany the recensions we do have. A reasonably authoritative and comprehensive study of the textual tradition of the *dīwān* of Imra'alqays has been undertaken by Nāṣiraddīn al-Asad (*MSJ* 485–526), who identified and discussed the recensions of sixteen scholars, and concluded that the recensions of two of them—al-Mufaḍḍal aḍ-Ḍabbī,[5] a Kūfan, and al-Aṣma^{c}ī,[6] a Baṣran—had served as "the two primary and original versions and principle sources" for the subsequent recensions. The seventeenth recension, that of one Abū Sahl Xorābandād b. Māxoršīd,[7] has been discussed by Muḥammad Abū Faḍl Ibrāhīm, who drew upon it in preparing his excellent edition of *Dīwān Imri'ilqays*. (*DIQ* Taṣdīr 16–17).

In addition, one *qaṣīda* in particular, the classic *Qifā nabki,* received special attention from literati, scholars, and textual critics alike. This poem, along with six (sometimes eight or nine) other Jāhilī odes, was included in a collection that enjoyed a long and complex textual tradition, apart from the *dīwān* itself, and that has been one of the fundamental cornerstones of Arab-Islamic culture to the present day.[8] Since the ode of IQ is set first in all known recensions of the *Mu^{c}allaqāt* (as the collection is frequently entitled) and in at least half of the known recensions of his *dīwān,*[9] and has made "an overwhelming impact . . . on the minds and imaginations of later composers, . . . it is no exaggeration to say that [it] is at once the most famous, the most admired and the most influential poem in the whole of Arabic literature" (Arberry *SO* 41). Its textual tradition, moreover, which has been characterized since the second/eighth century by a generally scrupulous concern to clarify obscurities, cite variants, and credit authorities, offers a wealth of evidence for determining something of the poem's nature and origin.

For the following study, I have adopted as a basic[10] text of the poem, for purposes of comparison and collation, that which appears in the recension of the "seven long pre-Islamic odes" (*al-qaṣā'id as-sab^{c} aṭ-ṭiwāl al-jāhilīyāt*) made by Abū Bakr Muḥammad b. al-Qāsim al-Anbārī.[11] In extensive introductions to each ode and in bulky interlinear scholia, Ibn al-Anbārī provides a prodigious amount of biographical, circumstantial, philological, and textual information, making his recension and commentary one of the great tours de force of medieval scholarship. Of recensions of IQ's ode prior to, or contemporary with, Ibn al-Anbārī's five have been preserved: those of Abū Sa^{c}īd ad-Darīr ("the blind"),[12] Abū Sa^{c}īd as-Sukkarī,[13] Abu l-Ḥasan aṭ-Ṭūsī,[14] Abū l-Ḥasan Ibn Kaysān,[15] and Abū Ja^{c}far an-Naḥḥās.[16] Besides these five, a sixth recension of the poem, though prepared and issued in the fifth/eleventh century by the Andalusian scholar Abu l-Ḥajjāj al-A^{c}lam aš-Šantamarī,[17] is accepted as being substantially that of al-Aṣma^{c}ī.[18] Although al-A^{c}lam or one of the intermediate links in the chain of transmission from al-Aṣma^{c}ī[19] may have been responsible for certain departures from al-Aṣma^{c}ī's original recension,[20] it is unquestionable that in al-A^{c}lam's version we have a tradition of the ode that is quite distinct from the one that came to predominate in the Arab-Islamic world and that can conveniently and, as Asad (*MSJ* 489, 506–14) has shown, justifiably be labeled the "Baṣran," as opposed to either the "Kūfan" or the so-called "mixed," tradition. Ibn al-Anbārī, on the other hand, offers the best and most accessible example of the "Kūfan" tradition, aṭ-Ṭūsī's and Abu Sa^{c}īd aḍ-Darīr's recensions being unavailable to me (except through citations in Ibrāhīm's appendix to *DIQ*; see nn. 12, 14 to this chapter), and as-Sukkarī's[21] having been edited without any of the important textual and philological scholia that that scholar usually composed.

The precise relation of Ibn Kaysān's recension to the two major traditions is not entirely clear, due to the lack of any edition of aṭ-Ṭūsī or Abū Sa^{c}īd. It seems basically to follow the Kūfan tradition, although it presents a few readings not known to Ibn al-Anbārī or any of his predecessors whose recensions we still have. I have chosen Ibn al-Anbārī's text, rather than Ibn Kaysān's, because (1) it is longer (82 as against 76 lines), including, in some identifiable form, all the verses of known earlier or contemporary recensions; (2) the supplementary textual information contained in its scholia is unequaled by any other medieval source; (3) it has served as the basis of at least two of the most important later recensions, az-Zawzanī's[22] and at-Tibrīzī's[23] in particular. An-Naḥḥās' version, on the other hand, must be considered to be on the whole derivative from Ibn al-Anbārī, whose student he had been and whose readings he follows in all but twelve verses,[24] and from Ibn Kaysān, whom he cites several times in his scholia and who seems to have been his source for at least half of those twelve divergences.[25]

Along with the texts already mentioned, I have also consulted, either directly (when possible) or indirectly, recensions and commentaries of the following scholars who, like an-Naḥḥās, az-Zawzanī, and at-Tibrīzī, have adopted a tradition predominantly Kūfan (i.e., based upon the recension of al-Mufaḍḍal; see above), but "mixed" with many elements of the Baṣran (i.e., based upon al-Aṣmaᶜī's recension): Abū Sahl Xorābandād̲ (?) b. Māxoršīd̲ (see above) and Abū Zayd al-Qurašī[26] in his anthology *Jamharat ašᶜār al-ᶜArab*. Further, I have also drawn upon the recension of the vizier Abū Bakr al-Baṭalyūsī,[27] who relied mainly upon the Baṣran tradition of al-Aṣmaᶜī, though sometimes preferring the readings of aṭ-Ṭūsī or others.[28] Finally, reference will be made occasionally to variants noted by S. Gandz in his translation of IQ's *muᶜallaqa* and accompanying commentary.[29]

A.2.b Thus, for the single ode of IQ we are provided with twelve recensions,[30] nine of them available in printed form and three cited by the editor of *DIQ* where they diverge from al-Aᶜlam's version.[31] These are not, it must be emphasized, simply diverging manuscript exemplars of the ode, derived from one or more "archetypes," such as classical scholars of Renaissance and modern times have often had to deal with. The text-critical techniques evolved by these later Western scholars[32] have been invaluable in establishing accurate editions of the published *recensions* of the ode; but the recensions themselves, in each case, constitute the finished products of a methodical and more or less proficient application of text-critical principles and techniques at least as sophisticated as (and, I am convinced, greatly influenced by) those that were in use among the Hellenistic and Byzantine editors of Homer and the Greek classics. Consequently, in a good copy or well-edited publication of one of these recensions (disregarding for the moment scribal or editorial lapses introduced *after* the recension's completion and, hence, *ascribable to its own textual transmission rather than to that of the poem as such*), we may expect to find the scholarly approach and considered judgment of a professional philologist and textual critic whose integrity and reliability cannot, as a rule, be seriously impugned. Certain tendencies in his approach and attitude, as well as the constitution and condition of his sources, contributed, of course, to the final state of a given scholar's recension; but we must recognize his text as a reasonably authentic and authoritative witness to a phase in the poem's tradition and as a work that would have had to meet his own professional standards and pass the exacting review of his colleagues (cf. Bräunlich *FEAP* 830; Blachère *HLA* 126).

When, therefore, we meet with such a striking range of variation as will be found in the several recensions of IQ's *mu^{c}allaqa* or other classical Arabic *qaṣīdas,* we are no longer entitled to proceed as if all these versions can ultimately be traced to a single (lost) archetype composed in a finished form by an individual poet at a particular moment in time. Blachère, as we have seen, and Bräunlich before him, have stressed the "multiformity" and "fluidity" of the tradition of classical Arabic poetry; but both view that circumstance as the deplorable outcome of the imperfections and imprecisions inherent in an oral mode of *transmission* (Bräunlich *FEAP* 825–26, 828–29; Blachère *HLA* 83–186 passim, esp. 86–91). Blachère, indeed, goes so far as to admit—even insist—that, in the early classical period of Arabic verse, "the author *composes orally* and his verses first become fixed only through direct transmission from speaker to listener. *It is, in part, to this fact* that one owes the divergencies of recension which the ineptitude of later copyists and the uncertainty of long oral passage (*cheminement*) have only made worse. Thus, a work destined to last, being scarcely born, was already exposed to a horde of dangers" (*HLA* 90; my italics). From the earlier discussion of oral tradition in the Parry-Lord sense, it can be gathered how close Blachère has come to the edge of articulating the theory, yet how far he is from taking the decisive plunge.

A.3 Returning now to an examination and collation of the various recensions of the *mu^{c}allaqa* of Imra'alqays, we should be able, particularly through the earliest ones, to reach some conclusions regarding the mode of existence through which this poem, a not untypical witness to the tradition, had passed. The first question to be considered is that of divergences in the number and sequence of verses among the various recensions, apart from internal variations within the verses themselves (for abbreviations used, see Bibliography, Section III). Here I have been able to compare only the published texts, since the citations of *W, X,* and *Y* in Ibrāhīm's critical apparatus to *DIQ* treat, in general, only verbal variants. This circumstance is regretable in that *W* and *X,* at least, are actually earlier, or certainly no later, than our earliest (unredacted)[33] text *S*. The results of this collation,[34] in terms of the 82-line numeration of *A,* fall into the following sequential relationships:[35]

D: 1–7, 9–19, 21, 20, 22–29, 8, 30–31, 41, 32–36, 38–39, 37, 40, 42–48, 53–55, 57, 56, 58–60, 62, 70, 64–69, 63, 61, 71–73, 75, 77, 79, 78, 80, 82, 74, 76 (*A* 49–52, 81 omitted; 77 lines total).

B: 1–7, 9–19, 21, 20, 22–29, 8, 30–48, 53–60, 62–70, 61, 71–73, 75, 77–80, 82, 74 (*A* 49–52, 76, 81 omitted; 76 lines total).

S: 1–2, 5–48, 53–82 (*A* 3–4, 49–52 omitted; 76 lines total).[36]

K: 1–2, 5–19, 21, 20, 22–47, 53–62, 48, 63–82 (*A* 2–3, 49–52 omitted; 76 lines total).

N: *1*–2, 5–19, 21, 20, 22–48, 53–56, 59, 58, 60, 57, 61–82 (*A* 3–4, 49–52 omitted; 76 lines total).[37]

J: 1–2, 2A, 3, 5, 5A–5B, 6–8, 4, 10, 9, 11, 11A, 12, 12A, 13–15, 15A–15B, 16–20, 20A, 21–38, 41, 39–40, 42–62, 64–69, 63, 70–75, 81, 76–79, 82, 80 (90 lines total).[38]

Z: 1–31, 41, 32–40, 42–47, 49–82 (*A* 48 omitted;[39] 81 lines total).

T: 1–19, 21, 20, 22–82 (82 lines total).

Assuming again that *D* comprises, in most particulars, the recension of al-Aṣmaᶜī and that it hence would have been actually prior to any of the other recensions considered here, one may well wonder at the obvious disparity between its sequence of verses and the verse-sequences of *S*, *K*, *N*, and *A*, not to mention *Z* and *T*. Even *B*, which is also founded mainly upon al-Aṣmaᶜī's recension and resembles *D* rather closely in its general delineations, seems to have adopted the sequence followed by *S* and *A* in certain 7- or 8-verse passages, where the sequence in *D* is quite at variance. What is apparent is that *A*'s verse-sequence has been derived either from *S* directly or from another (undoubtedly written) recension common to both.[40] *K* and *N*, on the other hand, while adhering closely to the verse-order of *S* and *A*, both introduce certain minor deviations perhaps arising from either a third recension,[41] their own editorial conjecture or emendation,[42] or the information of an oral informant (although, as the number of authoritatively constituted poetical texts increased from the late second/early ninth century on, reliance upon oral renderants—the *rāwīs* of an earlier era—dwindled to insignificance).[43] *J* presents a special problem: the verse-sequence of the first half (particularly *J* 14–46 = *A* 11–38), leaving out the additional verses, does not depart significantly from that of *A* except in the case of *J* 11 = *A* 4 and *J* 47 = *A* 41; and in the second half there is at some points an approximate correspondence to the sequence of *D*. But most of *J*'s divergences in verse-sequence cannot be traced to any known recension (the same is true of many of *J*'s variant readings within the verses); and they are, one suspects, quite possibly due to al-Qurašī's own initiative.[44] Of course that *Z* and *T* have adopted the verse-sequence of *S* and *A* is obvious, although *Z* follows *D* in the position of *Z* 32 = *D* 32 = *A* 41[45] and *T* 19–21 follows *D* 18–20 = *A* 19, 21, 20 (as do, in fact, *B*, *K*, and *N*).[46]

B. Six verses in *A* have been the subject of particular disagreement among the medieval text critics. *A* 3–4 are to be found in *X*, *Y*, *D*, *B*, *J*, *Z*, and *T*, whereas *W*, *S*, *K*, and *N*[47] do not include them. According to *A* 3 sch, *A* 3 (and undoubtedly *A* 4 as well) occurred in the recension of Abū ᶜUbayda.[48] Other sources (e.g., *K* p. 12:11–12, *T* 3 sch) claim that the two verses were "interpolated" (*yuzādu*), noting that, according to al-Aṣmaᶜī, the Bedouins add the verses in rendering the *qaṣīda* (*al-aᶜrābu tarwī-himā*). Abū Aḥmad al-ᶜAskarī[49] gives us the interesting note that Abū ᶜUbayda heard the single verse *A* 4 recited to him by one of his sources who attributed it to the Jāhilī poet Ibn Xiḏām.[50]

Verses *A* 49–52, also, have been included in *W*, *X*, *A*, *J*, *Z* and *T*, but omitted in *D*, *B*, *S*,[51] *Y*, *K*, and *N*.[52] *A* 52 sch remarks that "these four verses are admitted in the recensions of some tradents, although al-Aṣmaᶜī, Abū ᶜUbayda, and others allege (*zaᶜama*)[53] that they do not belong to (the *qaṣīda*)." *W* sch adds the comment (after *A* 51) that *A* 49–51 were also transmitted under the name of Ta'abbaṭa Šarrā (a famous pre-Islamic brigand-poet); *W* further cites a variant to *A* 51 that occurred when the lines were ascribed to the latter poet rather than to IQ[54] (Ibrāhīm *DIQ* p. 372, to *D* 48). *Z* 49 sch and *T* 48 sch both indicate that all four verses are sometimes given to Ta'abbaṭa Šarrā (cf. *N* p. 40 n. b). Al-ᶜAskarī, who could well be expected to have made an issue of such a question, cites *A* 50 in passing and ascribes it to IQ with no reservation whatsoever (*SMYT* 242:10).[55]

B.1 At root, however, lies one of the difficulties of classical Arabic poetry most distressing to medieval and modern scholars alike: the problem of correctly attributing the extant poetical texts. We should recall that, as conceived by most of these scholars, a poem would have had to have been the work of a particular poet composing at a particular time. Historical circumstances; confusions, accidents, and errors in the course of (oral or written) transmission; even deliberate fabrication or alteration of verses, however well-intentioned: all these could be admitted as factors affecting the state of the received texts. But the textual tradition of the poetry has, from the first, been based upon the implicit assumption or explicit predication of an "original version"; differing versions of a poem or of verses within a poem have been treated in general as "variants" from that original. Furthermore, as a corollary, verbal correspondences of greater or less extent that were found in different poems—by the same poet or by different poets—have been viewed as cases of interpolation, misattribution, plagiarism, commonplace usage, or mere coincidence. One need hardly dwell on the numerous instances where lines, passages, and even entire poems recur in identical or nearly identical form "under the name"[56] of more than one poet: commentaries on the old *dīwāns,* philological and literary-historical treatises of the medieval Arabic scholars, and critical apparatuses of many a modern edition—all bear witness to an abiding uncertainty and disagreement in matters of attribution.

The long-standing problem of *intiḥāl* in early Arabic poetry, too often interpreted as one of forgery or falsification of verses, ought actually to be understood as one of false, dubious, or mixed attribution: that is, verses judged to be by one poet were thought to have been wrongly claimed by, or ascribed to, another.[57] The vagaries of "propriété literaire" during the early period have been treated in some detail by Blachère (*HLA* 156–61), who suggests that a number of factors may have been involved: an over-zealous "insistence upon fixing the 'paternity' of a work"; the difficulties raised by several names for a single poet, by several variant forms for a single name, or by several poets bearing the same name or tribal designation;[58] the grouping of fragments, probably anonymous by that time, under the name of a poet known to have composed works of similar theme or content. He further observes that more willful confusions of authorship were not unknown and were often the outcome of academic, political, or tribal rivalries. ᶜAbadalḥamīd Maslūt (*NISJ* 66–67) specifies another factor, of equal importance in the matter of conscious misattribution: namely, the material advantages that accrued to a later *rāwī* who could flatter the poetical tastes or appeal to the partisan sentiments of a patron by producing effective verses of celebrated (and, where possible, kindred) authorship.

Yet consideration of factors inherent in an oral tradition of poetical composition has been left out almost entirely. Given the fact that oral poets share as formulas certain linguistic, stylistic, and thematic usages, and that their works are undertaken preeminently to re-create, if not to reproduce, a traditional standard, it should not be surprising to find similar and even identical passages in different poems ascribed to a single poet or in poems put under names of different poets. We must, at least, with Blachère (*HLA* 183–84), reject as artificial and rather arbitrary Ahlwardt's hypothesis concerning these verbal coincidences. "Such correspondences," Ahlwardt maintained, "in cases where they may not involve a proverbial expression or traditional phrase, are, it seems to me, simply to be set down to the *rāwī* or compiler, and such verses are to be ascribed neither to this (poet) or that one. It is a little different if such similar verses or half-verses are found in the works of the same poet: e.g., Imra'alqays [in *DIQ* (Ahl)] 4:39 = 48:55; 4:67 = 48:57; etc.

But here also I am firmly of the opinion that the whole verse always, and the half-verse generally, is wrongly placed'' (*BAAG* 30). This principle had also been enunciated somewhat earlier by Nöldeke, who observed: ''The situation many times recurs that one and the same verse, perhaps with small, hardly noticeable variants, is found in two different poems by one or separate poets; in this event we usually have to assume that it appears in *one* passage by mistake, or that the passages, through confusion on a transmitter's part, have come to resemble one another more closely than they did originally'' (*BKPA* viii).

Blachère's discussion of the same phenomenon shows considerably more sensitivity to the complexities involved. Nonetheless, here, as elsewhere he seems only to ''flirt'' with that ''fickle mistress,'' oral tradition (cf. Lord *ST* 9). To account for these reduplicated verses or half-verses, Blachère writes:

> Many hypotheses could be advanced among which it is risky to choose. Perhaps it is a question of a lapse in the oral transmission. Perhaps, too, one ought to consider a simple cliché reused by the same or by several poets. Perhaps, on the contrary, one should think of an infinitely more serious contingency, of the fusion of two fragments of identical meter and rhyme (if it is a matter of the same verse recurring in a like poem), or of two fragments collected in the same *dīwān* on account of the similarity of a cliché or a theme (*HLA* 184; cf. Bloch *VSA* 19).

B.2.a Since, as Blachère states, it is ''risky to choose'' among the hypotheses advanced to explain these verbal coincidences and poems of multiple authorship that seem so typical of early Arabic poetry (if not, indeed, intrinsic to it), perhaps one might reconsider the phenomenon itself in light of insights afforded by the oral-traditional theory of poetic composition. As regards the full-, half-, and even quarter-line repetitions, these represent, I no longer have any doubt, verbal formulas of the kind found in Homer, the Hebrew psalms, Romance ballads and *chansons de geste*, Anglo-Saxon epics, and other bodies of orally composed and rendered poetry. And thus, so far from being lapses of the *rāwī* or compiler who transmitted and attributed them, on the one hand, or from being ''spurious'' when they recur in the works of the same poet, on the other, these formulaic elements may be the surest proof that we are dealing, by and large, with an *authentic and conscientiously recorded* body of poems composed and rendered within an oral tradition as it has come to be understood.[59]

Yet within the context of an oral tradition of poetry, the very circumstance of uncertain attribution and multiple authorship finds a quite credible explanation. It is an explanation that is, in fact, more acceptable than the alleged ineptitude, lack of judgment, and unscrupulosity of the early philologists such as even the relatively moderate position of Blachère would presuppose. On the contrary, the known and deducible facts concerning the approach and techniques of those early textual scholars must command our respect and prevent us from making easy generalizations about their results. We find again in the work of Menéndez Pidal, if not a solution to the problem, at least a direction more worth following. "At the origin of all literatures," he projects, "before poetic creation becomes specialized, there is an *anonymous era* that includes all literary forms" (*CR* 65). A distinction must be made, he insists, between "individual poetry," which was modeled upon a set text, even if circulated orally (cf. Chaytor *FSP* chap. 6), and "traditional poetry," which was modeled upon successive sung performances.

> The traditional poem, in a perpetual state of metamorphosis, belongs to all who sing it, to all who hear it. If anonymity is essential to it, it is because each man who repeats it remakes it in some way, either causing it to undergo superficial retouching or altering its substance profoundly. Whether it be a question of the first composer of a song, of the one who reworks it in depth, or of the one who gives it a new episode—in every case the author who exercises his creative faculty on the whole poem is always anonymous; for he is dominated, in the very act of poetic creation, by a feeling common to all (the others) and he creates only to hand over his creation to the singers who repeat it and spread it abroad. (*CR* 64; cf. 500–502)

While this idea of an "anonymous era" can be accepted only with some reservation (see Zwettler *BFOT* 210 n. 41; § B.2.b, below) as a characterization of one external aspect of an oral-poetic tradition, just as seen through received texts, it serves a useful purpose.

B.2.b The Arabic poetic tradition professes to name for us an astonishing number of poets whose poems fill the pages of philological and literary treatises, bio-bibliographical and historical works, and numerous anthologies and florilegia. Whole volumes have been devoted to anecdotal biographies of scores of different poets, together with selections of their verses; and others have detailed the careers of individual poets, often in a distinctly novelistic fashion.[60] Besides these, Arabic sources inform us of the existence of more than 150 separate *dīwāns*, constituted during the Middle Ages (mostly before the fifth/eleventh century) and attributed to distinct classical poets,[61] apart from some 80 or so collections, each comprising poems by poets of a specific tribal affiliation.[62] To judge from such a state of affairs, we would hardly seem justified in speaking of an "anonymous era" of early Arabic poetry.

Approaching the Arabic "classicistic" tradition as an evolving, rather than stable, cultural phenomenon, however, one observes that this penchant for ascribing poems to individual poets and for individualizing and differentiating poets seems not to have been very characteristic of pre- and early Islamic times, nor even of the first stages of the written tradition itself. There are few, if any, acceptable poetical texts put under the names of poets living before the end of the fifth century A.D.; and yet, even in the earliest specimens of *qaṣīda* poetry, we find essentially the same form, externally and internally, as in poems of the time of Muḥammad and somewhat thereafter. Most scholars, rejecting the spontaneous-generation theory of early Arabic critics who sought to pinpoint the origins of the *qaṣīda* in a particular poet or tribe,[63] have little doubt that the near identity in style and content, linguistic and technical features, between the productions of the first known poets and those of later ones could not but have been "the outcome of a long education in construction of verse, . . . a long previous study and cultivation of the art of expression and the capacities of their language, a study of which no record now remains" (Lyall *AAP* xvi).[64] This period of Arabic poetry—mid-fifth century and before—can certainly, then, be spoken of as *anonymous*, even though there have been preserved no texts to prove it conclusively. If "anonymity" is sought, moreover, there is no reason why the very uncertainties of attribution and questions of authorship could not themselves be interpreted as *prima facie* evidence of a far greater element of anonymity prevailing in the pre-Islamic poetic tradition than what is suggested by the superimpositions of professional scholars and researchers of a later era. Let it be noted, first of all, that, apart from poems obviously fabricated for purposes of propaganda or entertainment, the works of disputed authorship were nearly always acknowledged to be authentic products of the Jāhilīya, and the dispute itself was confined to poets known to have lived before or during the earliest years of Islam.[65]

B.2.c The cultural level of Arabs before and at the time of Muḥammad varied widely and ranged from nomadic and pastoral to sedentary and agricultural or commercial; from a rigidly kinship-based tribal organization to one where traditional relationships were beginning to break down; from almost total illiteracy to a relatively high level of literacy (among certain segments of the population, at least); from near isolation from contact with other cultures to close communication, even coexistence or interpenetration, with civilizations of great antiquity, power, prestige, and cultural attainment.[66] Yet in all this diversity of milieu there can be found two important constants: a set of attitudes, values, aspirations, and conventions that was still fundamentally and inextricably linked to the social and cultural organization of the Bedouin tribe and a poetic tradition that—in language especially, as well as in style, form, and content—exhibited a remarkable homogeneity as regards conception, execution, and intent.[67] Furthermore, poetry was an essential element of that Arab tribal culture, "the public register of the Arab people: by its means genealogies are remembered and glorious deeds handed down to posterity" (Ibn Fāris,[68] in Lyall *AAP* xv; cf. Goldziher *MS* I 45 n). The poet himself, who would thus immortalize the tribal ancestors and confound the pretensions of other tribes, was respected, feared, and even venerated by his fellow tribesmen and by outsiders, as well: his appearance in a tribe was an occasion for their rejoicing; his poems were valued, it seems, for their effectiveness in defending the tribe's honor, enhancing its prestige, or shaming its adversaries, more than for their artistry *per se*.[69] The same principle operated, though perhaps in a less sociologically vital fashion and with a more active personal interest on the poets' part, at the Laxmid and Ġassānid courts, in the urban settlements of the Ḥijāz, and in the camps of eminent Arab chieftains (*sayyids*), where tribal customs and ideals still shaped attitudes and policies and where the ruler's authority derived, at least nominally, from his position as leader of a tribe.[70]

"The poets—as can be inferred from their name—are considered 'those who are knowledgable' (*shāʿir*),[71] first of all about the traditions of their tribe which are to be used in war" (Goldziher *MS* I 45 and nn.). They possessed a supernatural, magical knowledge and, because of their faculty, were held to be a kind of oracle of the tribe and, in the pre-Islamic period, were sometimes accorded the (frequently hereditary[72]) institutional dignity of *kāhin* "seer," "diviner," or "soothsayer" (Goldziher *AAP* 17–18).[73] Even in urban and court situations, poets, often *sayyids* themselves, continued to represent the interests of their tribes (though they might be relegated at times to the status of other "courtiers" or "clients") and to exert a marked influence by virtue of their charisma and the propagandistic and rhetorical (if no longer supernatural) power of their verse.

The significance attached to the function of the poet in pre-Islamic tribal society is well brought out by the traditional view of the Arabs that "a 'perfect' man (*kāmil*) must . . . be a poet, i.e., must know the glorious traditions of his tribe which he can use for the honour of his own people in war against opponents whose aim is to stress shameful facts of the past of his tribe" (Goldziher *MS* I 45 and nn.). It should be no surprise, then, that poets have played such a material role in the "historiological"[74] lore of the pre-Islamic Arabs, particularly when it is recalled that the poet himself, as the *porte-parole* of his clan, tribe, or even tribal confederation (Blachère *HLA* 339), would most often serve as tradent of that lore. Folk heroes of a sort and embodiments of a tribal ideal, the poets' own exploits and those in which they may have been involved (along with verses ascribed to them) form the subject matter and content of much of the *ayyām* literature and other quasi-historical narratives that have been preserved.

Poets, therefore, were known and commemorated as historical personages, and it would have been only through the most natural of processes that poems would come to be rendered and remembered as being theirs, as long as those poems retained some constant and recognizable aspects. To this extent, Menéndez Pidal's insistence on the anonymity of traditional poetry is inapplicable to the classical Arabic tradition (cf. Bloch *KWAV* 237–38, quoted in Zwettler *BFOT* 208–09). Indeed, perhaps his emphasis on "anonymity" is misplaced altogether, since the term appears to serve as little more than a euphemism for the "collectivity" of the *Volk* so vigorously affirmed by *Rezeptiontheoretiker* like Petráček (see Zwettler *BFOT* passim, esp. 210 n. 41). One must acknowledge and admit the reality of individual poetic personalities. Bowra, though granting "some truth" to the idea that anonymity is often an element in traditonal heroic poetry, cautions that

> this does not mean that heroic poetry is necessarily anonymous, or that bards are always too modest to claim their creations for themselves. In fact, they are often far from modest, but even if they were, their audiences would not allow them to remain unknown. . . . However anonymous their poems may be, the bards themselves are often well known, and that makes it unlikely that they disclaim any share in works of their own composition. (*HP* 404 and chap. 9; cf. Lord *ST* 101–02)

In other words, that a work is anonymous or that it is attributed—that is, whether it "belongs" to the people or to a poet—is an index not that it is intrinsically a traditional or an individual poem, *Volks-* or *Kunstgedichte*. Rather what is indicated by the circumstance of anonymity or attribution is simply the importance that a community attaches to the *social and cultural role of its poets*. It is evident that in that regard the pre-Islamic Arabs and the medieval Franks and Spaniards differed considerably (see Zwettler *BFOT* 204).

B.3.a Yet, as I have suggested above, precise attribution was not so necessary a consideration to those who dealt in poetry during the first century and a half after Muḥammad (Petráček, I believe, overestimates its prevalence; cf. *QAAL* 404). That it was not deemed too essential can be gathered from the casualness and even utter disregard that was typical of the treatment given poetry during the Umayyad period by singers and compilers of lyrics, who were among the first we know to have prepared and utilized poetical texts.[75] It becomes even more evident when we consider that the earliest monuments of Arabic philology—such as al-Xalīl's[76] *Kitāb al-ᶜayn,* Sībawayh's[77] *Kitāb,* Abū ᶜAmr aš-Šaybānī's[78] *Kitāb al-jīm*, and others—which based the bulk of their investigations and conclusions upon the evidential support of poetical citations, left the majority of their cited lines unattributed. Yet scholars only a few decades later would feel called upon to identify more precisely the authors of those lines or else would cite the lines in their own works with the "correct" attributions.[79]

W. Diem quite reasonably suggests that this urge to assign designated poets to the poetical citations (which themselves were so essential to all phases of Arabic philological activity) may well have been linked to a similar movement in the sphere of Islamic religious sciences—Ḥadīṯ, in particular.

> Anonymous citations could be justified, of course, only as long as 1) a close familiarity with the poetry could be presumed and 2) no strict criteria were as yet applied (in determining) the classical status [*Klassizität*] of a poet. At first, in the course of setting up a canon of "classics," which is paralleled in other literatures and the motives for which have still not finally been made clear, and further, under the influence of the Ḥadīṯ, with its *ᶜilm ar-rijāl* (whose methods were carried over into philology), it became important to name the poet in order to have a guarantee of his classical status and, thence, a conclusive piece of evidence [*Beweiskraft*]. (Diem *KG* 61–62; cf. Wild *KA* 45–46)

Thus, as H. Fleisch had earlier realized, the questions of authenticity and the problems of correctly identifying the poetical citations were raised by the third-century philologists "not so much in order to determine the author . . . as to be sure of having to deal with a poetry that had come out of the Bedouin milieu, an authentic product of the desert *ᶜarabīya*, and not a forgery of a *rāwī* who was more or less an urbanite and not very scrupulous" (*OEP* 139).

One finds corroboration for this view in other works of the third/sixth century and later, where attitudes and approaches that had become proper to the collection and criticism of Ḥadīṯ were adapted, perhaps simply as a matter of course, to literary and philological studies. In particular, "Arabic lexicography, soon after its inception, gradually developed into a traditionary discipline to which the principles of the sciences of Ḥadīth came to be applied" (Kopf *RIAP* 38; cf. Fleisch *OEP* 139). Literary history, too, as it first appeared, was composed in a form closely associated with Ḥadīṯ science[80]—the *ṭabaqāt* division.[81] In fact, the opening chapter of the earliest such work that we possess—Muḥammad b. Sallām al-Jumaḥī's[82] *Ṭabaqāt fuḥūl aš-šuᶜarā'*[83]—reads almost as a manifesto of a new order of methodical, scrupulous, and highly critical scholars, versed in standards for the authenticity and canoncity of traditions, whose aims were (1) to set up the heretofore undisciplined study of poetry along the same "scientific" lines as the Ḥadīṯ; (2) to determine which poetical texts were acceptable, from the point of view of linguistic and stylistic purity, and could be correctly ascribed to known and reputable poets; and (3) to establish their own authority as the proper—indeed, the only—interpreters of the poetry and judges of its authenticity and excellence (see Ibn Sallām *TFS* 5–42). Such is the importance of Ibn Sallām's introductory section as a document of early Islamic intellectual history that it would merit a special study in itself. Here I wish only to refer to his complaint of a mass of inferior, dubious, and uncritically gathered poetry, which "some have transmitted from text to text, neither receiving it from the Bedouins, nor submitting it (for approval) to the scholars" (*TFS* 6). Although Ibn Sallām dwelt chiefly upon such obviously spurious examples as lines attributed to quasi-mythical eponymous heroes, ᶜĀd, ᶜAdnān, and others, it is quite clear that he was alluding to the existence of a considerable body of *written* poems, compiled before his time, whose transimission, attribution, and present textual state did not at all meet the standards of the new literary critics and scholars. That such a body of poems did indeed exist has been further confirmed by the invaluable researchers of Nāṣiraddīn al-Asad (*MSJ* 134–84, 588–91; cf. Sezgin *GAS* II 14–33, 33–46 passim).

Given this state of affairs, there can hardly be any question that precise attribution of poems in the earlier stages of the Arabic tradition mattered little, if at all, either to the poets' contemporaries or to the first Muslim generations. Undoubtedly certain unique lines, passages, images, or themes may have come to be associated with particular figures, perhaps even with their originators. Moreover, if a poem, for some reason, became written down under specific, definable circumstances, there is no reason why its attribution, if it were to have been mentioned in the record, could not have been preserved more or less intact. But on the whole, the poetic tradition that was known to pre- and early Islamic Arabs and that was carried down to the early Muslim compilers and philologists cannot be said to have recognized "authorial rights" or "propriété littéraire" significantly more than any other "folk" tradition. Thus, it seems quite unnecessary for Petráček to have postulated a "special" kind of folk-poetry because of a presumed lack of anonymity in the classical Arabic tradition, and to have sought support for his view through recourse to shaky folkloristic principles and questionable ethnological interpretations of Bedouin society (e.g., QAAL 404-5; cf. Zwettler *BFOT*). Yet, failure of the renderants and auditors of a traditional poem to include specific information regarding its "authorship" (if such a term is even appropriate here) is not the same as "anonymity" in Menéndez Pidal's sense of the word nor in the sense implied by others who would substitute "anonymous" poets for poets whose names are lost or are only loosely associated with poems that the tradition has preserved.

B.3.b Where Bedouin tribal society did contribute to the question of attributions, however, was in providing later, more literate and systematic generations with a "historiological" tradition replete with the names of poets whose deeds and poems had been part of the glory of their tribes. But in those *ayyām* accounts, as they may be read now, the poetry is most often only loosely connected with the narrative and, in many cases, probably even prior to it; and thus, a poem cannot of itself be accounted a stable or intrinsic element of any but a very few such narratives (see Caskel *AA* 59–75). That such poems were actually composed by the poets to whom they were ascribed in the narrative or for the occasion alleged is open to serious doubt. But that they may often represent a parallel tradition, independent or semi-independent of the prose narrative, but just as ancient (if not more so), is quite probable (*AA* 66). The precise relationship between verse and prose in the *ayyām* and similar accounts usually varies from case to case and must be determined accordingly. Nevertheless, it seems necessary to admit that the relationship itself was largely a function of the *rāwī* from whom the account was received and of his grasp on the parallel verse and prose traditions, combined with his own creative or adaptive powers (*AA* 75).

At any rate, when, in the middle second/eighth century and for various reasons, scholars began to apply to the collection and study of poetry criteria and techniques similar, in systematic rigor and concern for the identity and integrity of sources, to those evolved for the science of Ḥadīṯ, they were not without materials to work with. At their disposal they would have had, on the one hand, a mass of relatively "uncritical" poetical texts, often of anonymous or indefinite attribution,[84] and on the other, a quasi-historical narrative tradition rich in the names and recounted deeds of poets. It would have been easy and, under the circumstances, quite understandable for them to have effected a connection between the two, much in the manner suggested by Blachère (see § B.1 above). Whether such considerations as he has mentioned gave rise to the later disputes over attribution or whether, as seems more likely, it was rather a question of formulaic correspondences inherent in an oral tradition, we are simply no longer justified in treating the occurrence of identical expressions, lines, or passages in poems ascribed to different (or the same) poets as evidence of the "corruption" of the tradition. Nor ought we to take too seriously the problems of attribution and even, except in the most blatantly tendentious or propagandistic instances (see, e.g., Asad *MSJ* 465–66), of "authenticity." They are problems that evidently did not overly concern those who were actively involved in the living tradition of early Arabic poetry—poets, *rāwīs*, or audience. Neither did they seem to be of great importance to the earliest compilers and connoisseurs of poetry, whose competence to judge what conformed to that tradition we have no reason to doubt. And even when more rigid criteria came to be applied, scholars tended, as in the case of the disputed verses of IQ mentioned above, to include lines that they considered of questionable attribution or authenticity (though they might express their doubts) rather than to omit them without any comment.[85]

C. After considering the implications for our understanding of classical Arabic poetry of variations in the number and sequence of verses in the poetical texts, a third and even more important kind of variation must be brought to attention. Much more striking than divergent line-order and multiple attribution of an early Arabic poem, as Blachère has indicated (see § A.2.b, above), is the range of literal variation within its lines. Nowhere is the scrupulosity and thoroughness of the medieval philologists and editors more evident than in their conscientiously seeking out, acknowledging, and recording alternative renderings for a major portion of those lines. As a result, we are doubly fortunate in Arabic, in that we often have not only two or more recensions of many poems (apart from simple manuscript texts—see § A.2.b, above) but also a mass of additional variants presented in the scholia to the poems or in various supplementary philological and literary-historical sources where poetry held a paramount position. And nowhere does the inherent instability or, better, fluidity of the early Arabic poem—its essential multiformity—emerge with greater clarity than through consideration of the body of those *lectiones variae* that the textual tradition has preserved.

C.1 Naturally, a good number of variants must be ascribed to lapses in the course of textual transmission, many of which perhaps originated quite early before the script became stabilized and the dotted letters fully differentiated.[86] Such textual imperfections are not dissimilar, granting the differences in writing systems, from the scribal and clerical errors that plagued the transmission of Greek and Latin literary texts and that have been analyzed and studied by several Classical scholars.[87] Of this species of "corruption" the medieval Arabic philologists were fully cognizant. Entire monographs were written that discuss in detail the subject of *taḥrīf* and *taṣḥīf*—i.e., aurally and visually induced discrepancies in the poetical texts.[88]

Nevertheless, these *lapsus calami*, ordinarily identifiable as such, do not constitute a major source of variation—especially when compared with the many verses where divergencies of a more substantive nature coexisted side by side and were accepted as more or less equally valid. To blame such fluctuations on failures of memory during oral *transmission*, as is usually done, is convenient and may indeed be justified when it is a matter of simple alternation by synonymy. But too often the variations give indication of differing conceptions of the poem at hand—or at least of the particular passage—and of differing approaches to solving immediate and specific compositional problems. In other words, I would choose to read most of the non-scribal variants preserved by the textual tradition of classical Arabic poetry as documentary evidence—however circumstantial—of the origins of that poetry in a tradition of oral composition and rendition.

C.2 Once more, it might usefully be recalled that the comparative brevity and more rigid prosodic conditions of the Arabic *qaṣīda* could well have led to straight memorization and retention of its verbal lineaments more readily than would have been the case had it been longer or more prosodically flexible (cf. chap. 1, § B.2, above). Moreover, one might reasonably argue that the non-narrative character of the poetry, and the consequent absence of any preoccupation with maintaining a story line as such, occasioned closer attention to the verbal form of the poetic utterance. Thus, the precise wording of a passage may have acquired a greater value and the preservation of many of its features intact from rendition to rendition may have been of somewhat greater concern than with a longer narrative poem. There are not, therefore, many Arabic *qaṣīdas* like the *Chanson de Roland* where, for instance, three of the earliest manuscript versions have not a single identical verse among them (Menéndez Pidal *CR* 60–63).

On the contrary, there are accounts of poetic performances in which the poet, interrupted by his hearers with approbation or criticism of particularly trenchant or felicitous verses, would be required to repeat such verses more than once.[89] Many poets, too, had well-known sobriquets (*laqabs*) derived from memorable lines that they had uttered on some occasion.[90] Further, most of the considerable number of gnomic verses that can be found in the works of the classical poets display, besides their aphoristic content, a patently mnemo-technical formulation.[91] And that such verses frequently did endure in the popular memory can be gathered from several anthologies of familiar or proverbial verses mentioned in Ibn Nadīm's *Fihrist*.[92] All these considerations may lead one to suppose that verbatim reproduction—of certain verses or passages at least—could have been an operative factor in the Arabic poetical tradition to a somewhat greater degree than in the Greek, Romance, Germanic, Yugoslav, or other epic narrative traditions with which most study has so far been concerned (cf. § D, below).

Furthermore, the important study by Jan Vansina on oral tradition among the Kuba of the Congo and tribes of Rwanda and Burundi reveals that the "distortions" that happen to a "testimony"—including a poetic "testimony"—during the course of oral transmission and that show up as "variants" in recorded texts are by no means a constant or necessary feature of such a tradition, either as regards the frequency of their occurrence or the extent of their deviation from a "received" version. Within a given society, factors of control over the transmission may exist, such as formal instruction; social, political, material, or religious sanctions and rewards; mnemonic devices of various sorts; or, quite significantly, the formal and internal structure of the testimony itself. The "purpose [of these factors] is to preserve the tradition as faithfully as possible and transmit it from one generation to the next" (Vansina *OT* 31; cf. 31–43, 54–65; also Finnegan *OLA* 88–90, 106–7). Vansina and Lord would approach a recorded oral poem with differing (though not necessarily conflicting) objectives in mind: Vansina to evaluate it as a source of historical information and Lord to understand and interpret it as verbal art. However, since oral poetry is by its very nature an intensely social (not to say communal) phenomenon, it would be well for us to realize that oral composition and rendition do not always of themselves entail a necessary or predictable measure of variation (or, as Vansina rather unfortunately puts it, "distortion"; cf. Zwettler *BFOT* 211 n. 43). So we are justified, I believe, in dealing with classical Arabic verse, if we recall the structural factors that might have contributed to its being more easily preserved verbatim. Considering also the importance and esteem attached to poets and poetry in Arabian tribal society, as well as the indispensable function that a poem served as a tribal chronicle, register, encomium, manifesto, and even weapon, we should keep in mind Vansina's useful dictum: "As a general rule it may be said that the more a tradition is associated with a vested interest, and the more this interest is a concern of the public as a whole and is functionally important, the more exacting will be the control over its recital, and the better the guarantee against distortion through failure of memory" (*OT* 42; cf. Chadwicks *GL* III 867–69).

C.3.a The sample of classical Arabic poetry chosen here, Imra'alqays' ode, which runs to 82 lines in its longest version and 76 in its shortest, includes a total of 49 lines that vary in a significant non-scribal way.[93] Necessarily, in some instances, the judgment as to what constitutes "non-scribal" variation has been a rather subjective one, since alterations may be effected in a transmitted text through means other than just errors or ineptitudes of the copyist. Actual "emendations" or "interpolations" by editors or scribes—whether intentional or inadvertent—may also occur, not to mention occasional grammatical normalizations proposed (or imposed) by some of the philologist-redactors themselves (cf. chap. 3, n. 28). Al-Aṣma^{c}ī seems to have been the source for a number of the latter type of variant, perhaps because of his intimate association with the Baṣran school of grammarians, who came to be identified—and not altogether without reason—as proponents of an "analogistic" view of language, as opposed to a Kūfan "anomalistic" view.[94]

The first verse of the ode exemplifies al-Aṣma^{c}ī's—and the normalists'—approach. There, instead of *bayna d-Daxūli fa Ḥawmalī*, the generally accepted version, *D* reads *bayna d-Daxūli wa Ḥawmali*. The scholia to *A* 1, *K* 1, *N* 1, and *B* 1 all indicate that al-Aṣma^{c}ī had adopted this reading with *wa* in correction of the received, and allegedly solecistic, *fa*. Treating IQ's "ungrammatical" usage in this verse "as a schoolmaster" would (*G* p. 12–13), al-Aṣma^{c}ī apparently raised no objection to it when it was continued into the second verse (*fa Tūḍiḥa fa l-Miqrāti*), nor did it occasion any comment when it occurred in other odes by IQ and many different poets (at least no comment has been recorded). S. Gandz, in his commentary on this feature (*G* pp. 12–14), gives ample evidence to prove that the conjunction *fa* linking place-names after *bayna* and the like was regularly employed by classical poets in their enumeration and description of the traces of abandoned encampments (*aṭlāl*) that they visited, as well as in their mention of sites overshadowed and drenched by a passing rain cloud.[95]

Elsewhere this normalizing tendency is even more apparent, and has been observed and criticized by many of the early Arabic textual critics as well. Most sources agree with *A*'s version of the first hemistich of *A* 16—even though it met "with reproach on the part of all authorities on the Arabic language" (al-Baqillānī *TCD* 68): *fa miṯli-ki ḥublā qad ṭaraqtu wa murḍi^{c}in*, "Many's the pregnant woman like you, aye, and the nursing mother I've night-visited" (Arberry *SO* 62). Al-A^{c}lam's recension (*D* 15), though, reads *fa miṯla-ki . . . wa murḍi^{c}an*, with the accusative rather than the genitive. This would have been a more analogistically "correct" choice, particularly preferred among those grammarians who objected to what they considered an anomalous use of *fa* as a substitute for the *wāw rubba*. However, as had early been pointed out by several authorities (e.g., *A* 16 sch, *N* 14 sch, *T* 16 sch), the verse had simply never been rendered that way by any authority of stature.[96]

C.3.b On looking through the body of observed variants to *A* (Appendix B), one finds many lines that are especially illustrative of the kind of non-scribal variation I am here concerned with: e.g., 6, 8, 16, 17, 24, 30, 46, 47, 48, 61, 62, 69, 71, 72, 75, 76, 78, 79. These and other verses, where variation cannot properly be set down just to confusions in script or pronunciation or even to similarities in meaning, would seem to represent instances of alternative rendering, rather than of variant reading—as it were, recorded moments of independent creation during oral rendition of a traditional, and traditionally prized, poem.

The first hemistich of *A* 8, for example, occurs in *A* and most other sources with the form: *iḏā qāmatā taḍawwa^{c}a l-misku min-humā*. "When both arise the scent of musk is wafted from them." In *D, B,* and *Y*, however, as well as *A* 8 sch, the hemistich is read: *iḏa ltafatat naḥwī taḍawwa*ᶜ*a rīḥu-hā*, "When she turns toward me, her fragrance is wafted (through the air)." Although the thematic content, syntactic structure, and key verb are the same in both versions, the semantic and imagistic intent are obviously quite different. And, most important, this difference is closely tied up with the different positioning of the verse in each of the two sets of versions. For the first phrasing occurs within the first ten verses of the recensions that include it (*A* 8, *S* 6, *D* 6, *N* 6, *Z* 8, *T* 8, *J* 10), but the second is found only much later in *D* and *B* as line 29. Without raising the question of the "proper" position of the verse (a question that is both irrelevant and unanswerable in the context of an oral tradition), one may easily ascertain that the use of the dual in the first version would have been conditioned by the mention of two women, Umm al-Ḫuwayriṯ and Umm ar-Rabāb, in the immediately preceding line. The version in *D* and *B* (cited also in *A* 8 sch), on the other hand, with the feminine singular, occurs as part of the poet's encounter with a particular woman. The biformity of the hemistich, then, indicates (1) that its essential features were rendered very much intact as remembered (*not* memorized) components of a familiar poem; and (2) that its realized verbal formulation depended upon where in the course of his rendition the particular renderant called it to mind. The two hemistich variants actually make up what Parry defines as a *formulaic system*: i.e., "a group of phrases which have the same metrical value and which are enough alike in thought and words to leave no doubt that the poet who used them knew them not only as single formulas, but also as formulas of a certain type" (*SET* I 85 = *MHV* 275; cf. chap. 2, § A, above). Other variations, such as some of those attested for lines *A* 6, 10, 21, 28, 62, 71, 72, and elsewhere, may be similarly accounted for (see Appendix B). Likewise, also, the factor of verse position seems to have been involved in the less substantive variation of *A* 48 (*ka-anna ṯṮurayyā*) with *K*56 (*ka-anna nujūman*) (see Appendix C, n.f).

C.3.c Another case of variation, entailing a more serious disparity than the previous one, is connected with lines *A* 29–30 (corresponding to *S* 26–27; *K* 26–27; *N* 26–27; *J* 37–38; *Z* 29–30; *T* 29–30; *D* 28, 30; *B* 28, 30). A glance at the several recorded versions of these two verses (Appendix B) indicates that here we have a difficulty of greater complexity than a slight modification of semantic or syntactic form to fit a different context. The question as viewed by the medieval philologists reduces itself simply to whether or not the sentence begun in *A* 29 is completed in the following verse, or whether it is completed at all. *A* 29 reads: *fa lammā ajaznā sāḥata l-ḥayyi wa ntaḥā bi-nā* *baṭnu xabtin ḏī qifāfin ᶜaqanqalī*, "After we crossed the tribe's enclosure and a spacious, dune-twined vale veered us down."[97] The variations recorded for this verse are relatively minor. But its understanding from version to version of the ode has depended almost wholly on what comes afterward—and that *has* varied significantly. If the following line reads as in *A* 30—*madadtu bi ġuṣnay dawmatin*, "I spread out (her) two fronded (tresses)"[98] or as in several other sources (see Appendix B) *haṣartu bi fawday ra'si-hā*, "I twisted her side-tresses to me" (Arberry *SO* 63)[99]—then no problem exists: the first verse is to be understood as the protasis of a temporal-conditional sentence and the second as its apodosis. This was the judgment of Abū ᶜUbayda, who transmitted the version *haṣartu* . . . and thus explained it.[100]

B, D, K, and *N,* however, transmit a version of the first hemistich of the second verse that not only substantially differs from the version of *A* and Abū ᶜUbayda, but has also led to a complete reinterpretation of the syntax of the preceding verse as well. All four of these sources adopt the following reading, undoubtedly on the ultimate authority of al-Aṣmaᶜi's unnamed informant (*D* 30, *B* 30, *K* 28, *N* 28): *iḏā qultu hātī nawwilī-nī tamāyalat ᶜalay-ya*, "When I said, 'Here! Let me have it!,' then she swayed above me." Most of the scholiasts, even those who had adopted Abū ᶜUbayda's reading, have discussed al-Aṣmaᶜi's in some detail, if only because of its greater heuristic interest. For al-Aṣmaᶜī's *riwāya* changes the syntax of the second verse from two coordinated sentences (*haṣartu* . . . *fa tamāyalat*) into a single, self-contained temporal-conditional sentence (*iḏā qultu* . . . *tamāyalat*). This leaves the *lammā* clauses in the preceding verse without any apodosis, thus constituting for most authorities an incomplete and grammatically unacceptable utterance.

That *D* and *B* both introduce another verse (*D* and *B* 29) between the two verses under consideration (*D* and *B* 28, 30) merely complicates and only slightly modifies the problem. The verse, already discussed above (§ C.3.b) in a related context, is syntactically identical with the second of the two lines (*iḏa ltafatat* . . . *tadawwaᶜa* / *iḏā qultu* . . . *tamāyalat*) and the arguments set forth in interpretation of the latter would serve equally for the former, as will be seen. Other scholiasts, however, utterly ignored *D* and *B* 29 in this position, having considered it—if at all—only insofar as it represented a variation of *A* 8. Even *K* and *N*, who adopted al-Aṣmaᶜī's version (*iḏā qultu hātī nawwilī-nī*) seem to have thought *D* 29 extraneous in that position, preferring instead both the placement and the reading of *A* 8. Thus, their comments, too, are based on the consecutive order *K* and *N* 27–28.

As already mentioned, the reading *haṣartu bi fawday ra'si-hā* . . . (or any of its parallel versions) occasions no difficulty in understanding the previous verse, for the *lammā* condition finds its apodosis in the immediately following verse. But if the following verse is read with an initial *idā*—i.e., as a second temporal-conditional sentence—the *lammā* clause is left unresolved. The earlier grammarians and scholiasts adopted in general, then, two possible interpretations of this seeming anomaly. According to the first interpretation, usually identified with the Kūfans (see Ibn al-Anbārī *IMX* 189–92, § 64), the *lammā* verse was to be read as a complete sentence, *intahā* introducing the apodosis and the *wāw* serving but as a pleonastic particle (*zā'ida muqhama*) that preceded the apodosis or main-clause after *lammā*.[101] Most of the Baṣrans, on the other hand, insisted that the *wāw*, in this case and in the others usually cited, simply served as a correlative conjunction (*ᶜāṭifa*) joining *intahā* with *ajaznā*, while the apodosis or main clause of *lammā* was left unexpressed (*maḥdūf*) as being implied or understood (*muqaddar*). The sense implied by the omission, then, would be something like: "After we crossed the tribes's enclosure and a spacious, dune-twined vale veered us down, (we were alone and at ease—*xalawnā wa naᶜimnā*)." Only at-Tibrīzi, so far as I know, offers the suggestion that the apodosis to *lammā* might be introduced with *tamāyalat*. The clause *idā qultu hātī nawwilī-nī* would be considered a second adverbial clause subordinate to the main clause.[102] In this event, the interpretation would be: "After . . . down, when I said, 'Here! Let me have it!' *then* she swayed. . . ."[103]

The existence of such disparate, even irreconcilable, alternatives for many verses of a *qaṣīda*—alternatives quite unaccountable to scribal error—is adequately explained only as a function of the mode of composition and rendition through which the *qaṣīda* came to be, and to be recorded. To reduce such variations in our received poetical texts merely to fluctuations or failures *of memory* would be to ignore the fact that the state of those texts corresponds very closely to that of texts that are known, or can be assumed, to be records of oral-traditional renditions. Furthermore, it may be observed that, as with poems in many other oral traditions, the number and range of substantive variations increase significantly within the later sections of most well-documented Arabic *qaṣīdas*. In Lord's words, "The endings of songs are less stable, more open to variation, than their beginnings" (*ST* 119).

D.1 The reason that some portions of classical *qaṣīdas* appear more stable than others may be suggested by a passage found in Ibn Rašīq's *ᶜUmda*, in a chapter on "fragmentary and full-length poems" (*al-qiṭaᶜ wa ṭ-ṭiwāl*). Ibn Rašīq writes:

> We were told by Sheikh Abū ᶜAbdallāh ᶜAbdalᶜazīz b. Abī Sahl[104]—God most exalted rest his soul!—that Abūᶜ Amr b. al-ᶜAlā' was asked if the [early] Arabs

used to compose at great length [*hal kānat al-ᶜArab tuṭīl*]. He replied, "Yes, so as to be heard" [*li yusmaᶜa min-hā*]. "And would they be brief?" "Yes, so as to be memorized" [*li yuḥfaẓa ᶜan-hā*]. Al-Xalīl b. Aḥmad has said that discourse [*kalām*] is diffuse and lengthy in order to be understood, and that it is concise and condensed in order to be remembered. (*Umda* I 186)

These remarks may well refer to an essential feature of the compositional technique that was characteristically employed in the production of classical Arabic *qaṣīda* poetry. In other words, the pre- or early Islamic poet, working without the stabilizing influence of script, would perhaps have known a *qaṣīda* as a concise core of verse passages with a constant rhyme and meter that were learned more or less independently of one another, but in a generally fixed sequence that identified that *qaṣīda*. We may even speak of these core passages as having been "memorized" if we admit that such "memorization" would never have precluded the continual reshaping, polishing, and adjustment of sound and sense that typically occur in any tradition of live oral performance and rendition, not to mention composition. Before an audience, then, or perhaps sometimes before a scribe, the poet would rely upon his store of analogous formulas and his grasp of the practically self-generating language of poetry to enable him to produce the many harmonious verses necessary to weave together and adequately flesh out the relatively discontinuous verse passages of the core. Core verses, of course, would have been less subject to substantive variation (though by no means immune to it), whereas those produced during performance "so as to be heard" could have been far more free to fluctuate (cf. Parry *MHV* 457).

D.2 Such a view of Arabic poetical composition is borne out most convincingly, I believe, by a closer examination of the formulaic table and chart given in chapter 2, § A.4.a, above. A glance at the table, for example, indicates that the highest percentage of verbal formularity for the entire *muᶜallaqa* is to be found in its opening verses (ll. 1–15: 56.4 percent).[105] This we might have suspected on purely theoretical grounds: it would be during the initial, "warm-up" phase of oral rendition that a poet might be inclined to rely most heavily upon the traditional and well-remembered elements of his art, both because of their greater familiarity to him and his audience and because they could give him a chance to temporize in anticipation of an imminent need to extemporize—a chance to acclimatize his faculties to the non-vernacular linguistic and structural patterns on the basis of which later verses could be generated.

What we might not have suspected, however, is that this state of affairs carries over to the opening verses of each of the other two major passages, II and III, of *MuIQ*. Section II.A (ll. 53–63) is 52.6 percent verbally formulaic as against 35.7 percent for Section II.B; and the first half of Section III (ll. 71–76)[106] exhibits 46.4 percent verbal formularity *versus* the second half (ll. 77–82) with 35.1 percent. Thus, we have the over-all result that the opening verses of thematically differentiable passages in *MuIQ* are 53.2 percent verbally formulaic, whereas the rest of the verses average only 29.6 percent—a difference of over twenty percentage points. Analogous figures may be obtained for the levels of combined verbal and syntactic formularity, though the difference between the two levels is not as striking.

This result points definitely to the operation of a certain principle of composition—in this *qaṣīda*, at any rate—according to which a poet-renderant would move from one major thematic unit to another, rendering in each, first, those verses built out of elements most closely and habitually associated with the particular *qaṣīda*-entity—namely, verbal formulaic material—and, thereafter, verses of a more distinctly "improvised" nature. Here, though, the graphs reveal that in the latter sections of each passage verses of above-average formularity still occur, thus raising the likelihood that such verses provided the poet with the respite and/or impetus needed to produce verses of a perhaps less "traditional," more "individual" cast (see § D.3.c below). Consider, for instance, lines 16–52 from Passage I, the extended *nasīb* of *MuIQ*. By any standards, the *nasīb* in this *qaṣīda*—52 verses in *A*[107] —runs extraordinarily beyond the average 7–10-line *nasīb* of the traditional classical *qaṣīda*. Among the *qaṣīda*s studied by Jacobi, only one (also by Imra'alqays: *DIQ* 2 = *DIQ* [Ahl] 52) has a *nasīb* even approaching in length that of *MuIQ* (37 verses; see *SPAQ* 12–13). The rather non-traditional character of this portion of *MuIQ* on the level of thematic development finds its counterpart on the level of oral formularity; for we observe that, as a continuous section, these verses have the lowest density of verbal formulaic material (27.6 percent) to be met with anywhere else in the poem. Yet, within this low-density section one can note verses (e.g., 30, 32–33, 37, 40, 48) of above-average formularity. This circumstance strongly hints at the utility of such verses in enabling the poet-renderant to sustain such an uncommon performance. On the other hand, however, even within the high-density introductory sections of passages, there are verses of low or relatively lower formularity (e.g., 2, 7, 57, 62, 75).

The compositional technique thus suggested is one in which formulaic reiteration would alternate with what might be called, for want of a better expression, "free improvisation" (so long as we make it clear that "free" is used here in a very relative sense: structural or syntactic formulaic elements contribute more or less continuously to the underlying formulaic texture of the *qaṣīda* as a whole). But in rendition, it seems, verses of above-average verbal formularity were deployed chiefly at the outset of passage developments and intermittently later on in the passages, perhaps (as suggested above) to provide a certain measure of fixed and familiar underpinning for those less stable, more-individualized stretches of comparatively spontaneous improvisation.[108] Such would appear to have been their manner of functioning in the *nasīb* of *MulQ*. There, after an initial amplitude, verbal formulas as verse constituents decrease to an extreme low (ll. 16–22: 17.3 percent), resurging somewhat between lines 30–48 (see graph A)[109]—though never attaining the high levels found in passage-opening verses—and ultimately falling to another low just before Passage II begins.

D.3.a M. Bateson's monograph *Structural Continuity in Poetry: A Linguistic Study of Five Pre-Islamic Odes* (*SCP*) corroborates the view of oral-formulaic composition proposed in the preceding section, although Bateson herself rejects the applicability of such a view to Arabic poetry. In this original and often insightful contribution to our understanding of classical Arabic poetry, Bateson first defines the structure of the poems that she is dealing with (the *mu*ᶜ*allaqāt* of Imra'alqays, Ṭarafa, Zuhayr, Labīd, and ᶜAntara) in terms of a division into recognizable thematic passages (*SCP* chap. 3). Then, parallel to the thematic divisions, she analyzes the linguistic form of the poems on the basis of their phonological,[110] morphological, and syntactic patterning (chaps. 4–6). Her analyses indicate a truly surprising degree of correlation between the thematic structure of an ode and its linguistic patterning (chap. 7). As she says, "There is a correlation between the sound and the sense: between what a poem *is*—the internal, linguistic relationships—and what a poem *means*—the external, semantic relationships" (*SCP* 15).

Bateson further proposes that "the types of regularity observed in passages of these five poems may be variously used as evidence of technique of composition" (*SCP* 122). "It is reasonable to conclude," she maintains, "that all passages marked [by these types of regularity] . . . represent unified and carefully reworked or 'tuned' compositions, which had to be memorized for use in public recitation" (*SCP* 123). This conclusion, however, is not so reasonable as we might be led to believe, for it is founded on the essentially subjective—and ultimately unprovable—judgment that a high degree of stylistic regularity and verbal patterning (Bateson's "fine tuning") is incompatible with oral improvisation. Analyses of orally improvised and rendered poems by Lord (*ST* 54–58), Emeneau (*SMOL*), Sebeok (in Sebeok *SL* 221–35), and others—not to mention the obvious complexity and regularity of linguistic patterning in the Germanic skaldic poems and other genres known to thrive on extemporaneity (see Finnegan in Horton/Finnegan *MT* 127–28 and references)—would, in fact, signify the contrary.

D.3.b Bateson explicitly raises the issue of applicability of the Parry-Lord theory to classical Arabic poetry, but she maintains that "this theory may be rejected for Arabic on the basis of both internal and external evidence" (*SCP* 34). Her judgment is totally unsubstantiated and untenable. The "evidence" submitted consists of five points (*SCP* 34–35), each of which indicates an unfortunately oversimplified and limited conception of what an oral-formulaic tradition would entail and a rather serious misreading of, or disregard for, what students and theorists of oral tradition have written.

Her first point (*a*) alludes to the fact that "Arabic tradition includes two different roles for the joint role played by the 'singer of tales'" (*SCP* 34)—as if Lord or, earlier, Parry or any other oral-traditionist had ever claimed that only one unique *modus operandi* (e.g., that of the Yugoslav *guslars*), to the exclusion of all others, must be expected to obtain among practioners of any and every kind of oral verse. But, of course, such a claim has never been advanced. Although these scholars have frequently stressed that oral poetry is composed *in*—not just *for*—performance, that the dual activities of composition and delivery are, within an oral tradition, generally a single one (which I have called "rendition"; see Zwettler *BFOT* 199 n. 5), to the best of my knowledge they have nowhere denied the possibility that differences among various traditions could exist. Thus, traditions may and can be found in which poets who are recognized primarily as composers might coexist and cooperate with poets who act primarily as reciters or performers,[111] or in which a poet who *purports* to recite the poems of another might be viewed and even designated differently from one who *purports* to render his own verses,[112] or in which a poet in the earlier, formative, "apprentice" stage of his career might confine his public poetic performances to works that he and his audience would ascribe to poets other than him.[113] Bateson admits, "It is true that, especially in early times, the rāwī was an apprentice poet" (ibid.; cf. chap. 2, § D, above). But, she adds, "there was also pressure for poets to maintain their roles as rāwīs, since this was considered a different kind of skill" (ibid.). The operative distinction as Bateson sees it was made between "the poet, /šā^{c}ir/, [who] composes poetry and is identified as the creator, the one with the special powers" and the "rāwī, 'transmitter, reciter,' [who] memorizes the poetry composed by the poet and recites it publicly" (ibid.). Even were such to have been the actual state of affairs among the early Arabs, the operation of an oral-formulaic tradition would be thereby in no way inhibited. The same formulaic elements that are discernible in the "composition'' of a *qaṣīda* would have been no less in force in its subsequent ''rendition''—to the extent that the two activities would validly and in reality have been separated. In the classical Arabic tradition, one might perhaps at most be able to distinguish something similar to what Homeric scholars and Menéndez Pidal have called a ''period of the *aoidos*'' and a later ''period of the rhapsode'' (see, e.g., Menéndez Pidal *CR* 69).

I do not see why Bateson supposes (*b*) that a slow, deliberate, perfectionist approach to poetic composition (such as that said to have been followed by Zuhayr) should be beyond the range of oral-formulaic poets. The identity of ''composition'' and ''performance,'' which Parry and Lord do stress, is taken far too literally in *SCP*. Nowhere is it implied that oral composition precludes a certain measure of preparation and planning; and, such being the case, there is every reason to expect this ''pre-performance'' phase to vary in duration and intensity from poet to poet and from tradition to tradition.[114] Further, it should be superfluous to point out that simply by rendering and re-rendering a particular poem—especially one as short as the *qaṣīda*—the poet-renderant would naturally bring it to a level of perfection higher than might be attained in a first-time rendition of a newly experienced poem (cf. Lord *ST* 151–53). Bateson's single supporting instance—Zuhayr's *ḥawlīyāt* ''annuals'' (i.e., *qaṣīda*s that supposedly took a year to compose)—is scarcely the only, or the most typical, example of ''the process of composition [that] is discussed in the Arabic tradition'' (*SCP* 34).[115]

The reference to ''field studies of the Bedouin tribes,'' and to a Bedouin poet's involving his fellow tribesmen in the compositional process, again has no bearing on the applicability of the oral-formulaic theory;[116] nor, as I have argued earlier (chap. 1, § B.2 above), has the circumstance of the shorter length of the *qaṣīda* (Bateson's *c* and *d*).

Bateson argues as a final point (*e*) that,

> in contrast to Greek and Yugoslavian epics, within the *qaṣīda* there was a high premium on originality of phrasing, a dislike of repetition, and only a few lists of the type that Lord finds characteristic.[117] Arabic poetry, while not stressing originality of content or imagery, does stress form for form's sake [?] and verbal complexity and concision, which Lord believes to develop only when writing is introduced. (*SCP* 35)

In light of the foregoing chapters and of a closer reading both of classical Arabic poetry and Arabic literary scholarship and of oral-formulaic studies, such a proposition is misleading and wrong. Not only does it imply that Parry's and Lord's work have no relevance outside the areas of Homeric and South Slavic epic, apply retroactively to pre- and early Islamic poetry criteria established and prescribed only many generations afterwards, and deny formal artistry, verbal complexity, and concision to oral poetry—all positions quite without foundation. It also, on what appear to be sheerly subjective and impressionistic grounds, dismisses the possibility of oral-formulaic composition and rendition practically out of hand. Nevertheless, as subsequent analyses—Monroe's (*OCPP*) and the present study—indicate, formularity is not just *present* in many classical *qaṣīda*s, it *prevails*—at least in those that have been examined so far.[118]

Yet, Lord's *Singer of Tales*[119] brings out many elements essential to oral style and tradition that are also essential to *qaṣida* style and the classical Arabic tradition—too many to be altogether disregarded and glossed over. So, Bateson posits an "intermediate position" for classical Arabic poetry (*SCP* 35), apparently somewhere between "mere improvisation" and wholly literary composition (though that is not clear). But this course merely introduces an unnecessary and unwarranted complication; and the Parry-Lord theory, in its bearing upon the tradition of classical Arabic poetry, is in no danger of rejection on the basis of Bateson's five points. To be always kept in mind, though, is the qualification voiced earlier (p. 34): that it be "*judiciously adapted and applied to the particular circumstances of pre- and early Islamic Arab culture and Arabic poetry.*"

Why Bateson should have wished so earnestly to reject the theory, when there is such persuasive *prima facie* evidence (her own included) for accepting it, is a question that might be asked. The answer, I think, can be inferred from the following statement, made with respect to Arabic poetry's so-called "intermediate position": "We must expect to find remnants of all the important elements of an oral style, slowly evolving into *a more complex one*, in this particular form [i.e., the *qaṣīda*]" (*SCP* 35, my italics). If there is any evolution to be observed, it is in our growing realization, through Parry's work and the successive, wide-ranging offshoots therefrom, of just how imposingly complex and diversified oral styles—and oral traditions—can be.[120] It is disappointing, therefore, that a perceptive and innovative scholar like Bateson could read even Lord's *Singer of Tales* (if no other work on oral poetry) and still make such an unreflective statement as that quoted above.

D.3.c This having been said, if Bateson's findings are considered within the context of a more complete and flexible view of oral-formulaic poetry than that which she has rejected, then they must be found a valuable resource both for arriving at a sense of the formula and formulaic in the Arabic tradition and for a fuller and richer understanding of the *qaṣīda* itself than we have enjoyed before.

Bateson gives the following description of early Arabic poetic composition:

> The accurate picture of the composition of pre-Islamic poetry is probably a combination of improvisation and careful tuning. The professional poet would have composed his poems a passage at a time, dwelling on a series of lines dealing with one theme until he was satisfied that they formed a unit and then either pushing them to the back of his mind or entrusting them to a rāwī. When called upon to recite, the poet might recite whole odes in which the passages had been carefully united to form a totality, or he might improvise long stretches at the interstices of the original, to suit a mood or an audience. When faced with a particular occasion, a very large portion of the poem might be improvised, but he would still draw upon his repertory of nasībs and travel themes to meet the more formal requirements of the qaṣīda. (*SCP* 123)

Were one to play down the forced and, to my mind, unjustifiable opposition between "improvisation" and "careful tuning," recognizing that in the act of rendition the two would have been in effect indistinguishable (regardless of how the poet may have prepared himself for rendition), then it is clear that Bateson's picture does not differ substantially from that of oral poetic production as portrayed for many other traditions. Indeed, her comparison of this mode of poetic composition to "the procedure of many modern jazz musicians" (*SCP* 123–24) is one that has already been applied by scholars to forms of oral formulaic poetry.[121] Finally, if my analysis of the *muᶜallaqa* of Imra'alqays is correct, the passages judged by Bateson to be most highly patterned in language also appear to exhibit the highest ratio of discernible formulas and formulaic usages (see Appendix A and chart of formular distribution).

Still, both traditional ideas concerning poetic composition and rendition as transmitted by Ibn Rašīq and the demonstrable structural facts as revealed through Bateson's research (as well as formulaic analysis itself), support the conclusion that some portions of a classical *qaṣīda* would tend to exhibit a greater degree of verbal regularity and patterning than others. That such passages, in Imra'alqays' *muᶜallaqa* at least, do seem to employ a significant proportion of formulas *identifiable as such* (i.e., phrases and constructions that recur elsewhere in the works of the poet or of his coevals) offers some ground for conjecture. Rather than distinguishing between "improvisation" and "careful tuning," perhaps we might consider the possibility of "individual" and "traditional" aspects in the rendition of a given poem.[122] What Bateson would call the "finely tuned" passages of a *qaṣīda* would often actually embody a greater percentage of formulaic elements. To that extent, such passages would represent what was more malleable in the practice and experience of the poet, what was more deeply impressed in his—and his audiences'—poetic sensibility, what had traditionally worked best: namely, relatively interchangeable verbal and thematic configurations familiar to both the poet and his audience through recollecting and re-creating past poetic renditions—renditions of the poet himself and those of poets he has heard. Such elements would constitute the "traditional" aspect of a poem or, more precisely, of a poetic rendition—the *remembered*, because previously experienced and executed, core of a past and presumably successful performance. Around and within this remembered[123] core of verses and parts of verses the "individual" renderant might weave any number of phrases, verses, or even subsidiary passages conditioned by circumstances attendant upon his rendition and generated out of remembrance of, or analogy to, already known configurations.[124] These "individual" elements might vary considerably from rendition to rendition in their quantity, order of occurrence, and verbal form; but many of them too might gradually and accretively come to be identified with a particular *qaṣīda* attributed to a particular poet.

For it should be emphasized that the range of variation discernible in early Arabic poems was not so great as to invalidate totally every attribution to a poet of the pre-Islamic period. The rigid specifications of rhyme and meter, the relative brevity of the poetic genres, and the conservativeness inherent in any oral tradition (especially in its diction and style) would have guaranteed a substantial measure of continuity and stability from one rendition to another. But continuity and stability were important only to the extent that they mattered to the audiences and to the poets themselves. And the presence of an equally substantial measure of variation in the renditions of given poems which have been preserved shows us that verbatim repetition of a poet's words was by no means an indispensable requisite for "authentically" experiencing a poet's work.

E. And with this understanding of variation and attribution in oral poetry, as with the understanding or oral tradition itself, our notions of "authorship" and "authenticity," as applied to classical Arabic poetry, will have to be substantially or completely revised. In few, if any, cases could the text of a given poem, even as it existed in the early ᶜAbbāsid period of philological hyperactivity, purport to be the record of the *ipsissima verba* of the poet to whom it was attributed. For the main body of early Arabic poetry, the texts we have—which are essentially the texts constituted by the great medieval philologists—were founded upon renditions recorded seldom earlier than the first/seventh century, and often a good deal later. If, as is held here, these poems were composed without the aid of writing and rendered for some time thereafter without the aid of textual exemplar—even poems said to have been produced after premeditation and long labor (such as Zuhayr's *ḥawlīyāt*)—

then they too would have *flourished* (not merely *survived*) in the fluid and multiform state that obtains wherever oral poetry is still a living tradition.

> The multiplicity of variants and attributions and of formulaic phrases and elements attested for the great majority of classical Arabic poems may undermine our confidence in ever establishing an "author's original version"—as indeed they should! But they ought to convince us that we do have a voluminous record of a genuine and on-going oral poetical tradition (even if in its latest stages), such as no other nation can match in breadth of content *and* scrupulosity of collection and documentation. (Zwettler *BFOT* 212)

Thus, although we may not possess the verbatim record of Imra'alqays' *mu^{c}allaqa* as uttered by the poet himself on a specific occasion, we do possess something perhaps even more valuable: a verse-by-verse delineation of a fine and majestic living poem in all its protean states of oral existence—a carefully developed multiple exposure, as it were, of a fluctuating poetic organism that still kept its own unique identity so as to be recognized by all who knew and heard it.[125]

E.1.a The fact that the main body of classical Arabic poetry was taken down during the early Islamic period has a further implication. In almost every case that we can imagine, the renderants of this poetry—usually Bedouin *rāwī*-poets—were men or women who had become for the most part at least nominally Muslim. In this light, then, we must reconsider the alleged "inconsistencies," "anachronisms," and "Islamic emendations" that do crop up in our received texts and have so frequently been adduced as proof of the "corruption" of the tradition. Such phenomena as the introduction of post-Islamic expressions or other neologisms into archaic poems, elimination of pagan theophoric names or substitution of the name *Allāh*, allusions to Qur'ānic passages or Islamic concepts or rituals, and so on, can all legitimately be seen as a natural result of the circumstance that versions of those poems were derived from oral renditions performed by Muslim renderants conditioned now to the sensibilities of Muslim audiences. In the same way, Lord has noted how new formulas, containing quite modern words or ideas, can be generated during the course of performance and incorporated into poems of ancient vintage (*ST* 43–44). Further, a singer singing the "same" song before audiences of differing religious or political persuasions might automatically vary the outcome of battles or suppress certain themes and phrases in order to accommodate their tastes and feelings (*ST* 19, 49, 118). In the case of the Old English tradition, usages of the *Beowulf* poet indicate the likelihood that among the oral poets "the pagan myths had given place to or had been reinterpreted in terms of the Judaeo-Christian myth" (Lord *ST* 200).

So too in the skaldic tradition a transition from pagan to Christian kennings has been observed subsequent to the Christianization of Norway and Iceland without entailing any noticeable change in the art itself (Hollander *Skalds* 21–22). It is altogether possible that a similar development took place among the Arab poets of the later seventh century, however superficial may have been their conversion to Islam at that time (cf. Monroe *OCPP* 39–40).

Yet these reflections of a post-*jāhilī* outlook are relatively rare and are really quite accidental, in general, to the spirit and substance of the poems in which they occur. The faithfulness of the seventh- to tenth-century Bedouin *rāwī*-poets to the tradition of their pre-Islamic forebears remained for the most part unquestioned. In all essential features—form, themes, imagery, style, language, and point of view—the recorded renditions that we call pre-Islamic poetry were, and still can be, accepted and recognized as equivalent to what those earlier poets had first uttered. Among the unlettered Bedouins, despite their formal adherence to Islam, the art and technique of oral verse composition and rendition persisted alive and intact. The continuity and integrity of the tradition of the poetry was assured because its traditional oral-formulaic mode of existence continued unchanged.

E.I.b When Abū ᶜUbayda, for instance, went to listen to the poetry of Mutammim b. Nuwayra as rendered by a Bedouin grandson of his who was trading in Baṣra, he found that,

> after his [grand]father's poetry had been exhausted, [the grandson] began to add to the poems and to make them up for our sake. And (it struck us that) what was uttered was apart from what Mutammim had uttered and (that) [his grandson] was imitating what he had uttered, mentioning places that Mutammim had mentioned and battles in which he had participated. When that kept on without interruption, we knew that he was fabricating. (Ibn Sallām *TFS* 40; cf. Asad *MSJ* 236, 347, 467)[126]

Abū ᶜUbayda was brought up in an educational and cultural tradition that, for all its insistence upon oral transmission and verification and its pretense of preferring the spoken to the written word, was overwhelmingly dominated by, and oriented toward, books and writing. This was true, even though it may well have been assumed that the verbal work represented by a text was just as stable and unvarying as that textual representation—perhaps even more so, given eventualities of clerical deficiencies and material decay. The Qur'ān, of course, following its textualization and the growth of a body of techniques and activities devoted to its accurate *verbatim transmission and rendition,* was a crucial factor underlying this assumption. But the assumption itself of the immutability of the uttered and recorded word, which so conditioned Abū ᶜUbayda's response to Mutammim's grandson's "fabricated" renditions, belongs to a Near Eastern scribally dominated tradition of education and culture far more ancient than Islam, of which Islam came to be only the most recent bearer. Abū ᶜUbayda, then, was intellectually (and perhaps religiously) committed to the notion of original versions and a fixed corpus of poems by an identifiable poet. Any deviations from those versions (as established, naturally, upon the authority of reputable and trustworthy sources) had to be viewed as evidence for the corruption of the poems' tradition, and any additions to that corpus constituted misattributions, at best, and interpolations or forgeries, at worst.

That Abū ᶜUbayda and his fellow scholars, philologists, and textual critics were, as a rule, proceeding with integrity and in good faith is no longer open to serious doubt. But that their Bedouin *rāwī* informants and renderants, especially those from whom were derived the earliest first/seventh- and second/eighth-century records of classical poetry, were often careless in their renditions and attributions, sometimes overly inventive, and occasionally downright unscrupulous has been more or less taken for granted. But can it be taken for granted any longer? I do not think so. Bowra writes, speaking of alleged inconsistencies, contradictions, and interpolations in the Homeric epics:

> We must in principle beware of accusing lines of being interpolations just because they do not suit our theories. We must instead try to understand the methods of oral composition and ask if the inconsistencies can be explained by them. Evidence from such methods in the modern world shows that the oral performance of poetry presupposes conditions quite different from those presupposed by writing and that a listening audience must be treated by means uniquely appropriate to it. An examination of such poems suggests that many of the alleged Homeric inconsistencies are inherent in the oral manner and more suitably explained by it than by theories of additions and alterations. (In Wace/Stubbings *CH* 46)

Thus, we have to distinguish carefully between the Arab poets of the pre- and early Islamic period, whose works—even the finest ones and those much labored over—were almost always the product of a formation in oral-formulaic techniques of composition and rendition, and between the poets of a subsequent literary age, who were educated to read and write and who usually learned poetry through immersion in *dīwāns,* anthologies, literary histories, and rhetorical textbooks. But we have to distinguish, too, between the often unnamed *rāwīs*—for the most part Bedouins—who kept those early works alive through skillful rendition before appreciative and demanding audiences, and between those first/seventh- to third/ninth-century memorizers, compilers, textual critics, and philologists who usurped the name *rāwī*. Despite the encroachments of literacy throughout the Islamic world, the real *rāwīs* managed to maintain, in the desert and within poetically gifted tribes and families, a tradition of oral poetry that, Ibn Sallam tells us, was exceedingly difficult for the literary scholars (*ahl al-^{c}ilm*) to tell from the real thing—difficult in a way that the additions and alterations of compiler-*rāwīs* and contemporary poets were not (*TFS* 40).

Of course, the Bedouin product was difficult to tell from the classical poetry that those scholars upheld as the real thing precisely because it was all of a piece with that earlier poetry. The Bedouin *rāwī*-poets of the late first/seventh century to perhaps the end of the fourth/tenth century (when the interest of the literate world in classical Arabic poetry for its own sake seems to have practically died out and with it attention to the Bedouin poetical tradition—see Fück *Ar* chaps. 9–10) uttered poems that, in form, style, themes, diction, and—notably—use of the "poetico-Qur'ānic-*koinē*" (Cohen *KLD* 105 and passim; *ELA* 183) were so similar to poems known or thought to be genuinely old as to be indistinguishable from them and even, at times, identical with them. This inherent conservatism of oral tradition is what should reassure us when cries of inauthenticity, plagiarism, and forgery are raised; for with all the disputations about genuineness and attribution, "the works of disputed authorship were nearly always acknowledged to be authentic products of the Jāhilīya, and the dispute itself was confined to poets known to have lived before or during the earliest years of Islam" (see p. 200 above). If there are more or less substantive variations in a given ode put under the name of a certain poet or in the corpus of odes ascribed to a certain poet, this too should reassure us that we are dealing with "an *authentic and conscientiously recorded* body of poems composed and rendered within an oral tradition as it has come to be understood" (see p. 198 above).

Lord makes the following remarks concerning the epic song and the singer's attitude toward his rendition of it—remarks that the textual and circumstantial evidence of early Arabic poetry allows us to apply *mutatis mutandis* to the *rāwī*-poet and his rendition of his own or another's *qaṣīda:*

> We may say that any song is a grouping of themes which are essential to the telling of the tale plus such descriptive or ornamental themes as the singer chooses either habitually or at the moment of performance to use as decoration for the story. We can, therefore, expect that a song as sung by a given singer may vary in respect of minor or ornamental themes, themes of details, but that it will not vary in respect of the essential themes of the story. In fact, singers boast that they sing a song word for word as they heard it; they mean, essential theme for essential theme. They say that they always sing it in the same way and never change anything either by addition or subtraction; they are really talking about

essential themes, because to them the story consists of those themes. (In Wace/ Stubbings *CH* 191)

E.2 Stability of the essential thematic structure, variation of many thematic and verbal details, recurrence of longer or shorter line-building phrases and constructions from poem to poem or poet to poet, conservatism and lack of self-conscious originality, small regard for literary proprietorship, preservation of non-vernacular, archaic, and often anomalous linguistic features—these are some of the salient characteristics that mark a number of poetic traditions known to have been carried on for years—even centuries— without the use of writing either in composition or transmission. They are characteristics also of the classical Arabic poetic tradition. It is time, then, that we stop for a moment in our incessant quest for that scholarly will-o'-the-wisp, the original version; for such a concept has little meaning where oral poetry is concerned. It is time, further, that we stop to look at, read, and seek to appreciate and understand something of the really quite considerable body of poems that we do have—that, following the example of critics like Alfred Bloch, Mary Bateson, Renate Jacobi, James Monroe, and Kemal Abu-Deeb, we start thinking of these works as *poems* rather than texts, dealing with them as *poems,* and above all responding to them as *poems*. Recognizing the principle of *orality* as intrinsic to classical Arabic poetry does not, of itself, solve all the problems which that poetry presents, since a fundamental problem raised by that very principle still remains unsolved. As Nagler has stated, "No coherent aesthetic theory has as yet emerged which would equip us to understand or appreciate the special nature of oral poetry as poetry" (*TGV* 273). Given the quantity and variety of early poems just in published form alone and the demonstrable integrity and continuity of their textual tradition from first recording, it is possible for us—even incumbent upon us—as scholars, Arabists, and lovers of poetry to participate with students of other literatures in trying to frame such a "coherent aesthetic theory", or at least in finding out if such a theory could be validly framed at all.

1. See, e.g., Menéndez Pidal *CR* chap. 2; A. Gyger (*née* Jones), "The Old English *Soul and Body* as an Example of Oral Transmission"; et al. Cf. also Lord *ST* App. 1 and 2.

2. For the significance of the avoidance of enjambement in early Arabic poetry, see chap. 2, §B, above.

3. For detailed bio-bibliographical information, see Brockelmann *GAL* 124, *Suppl* 148–50; Blachère *HLA* 261–63; Arberry *SO* 31–49; Sezgin *GAS* II 122–26. Al-Bāqillānī (d. 403/1013), in his demonstration of the rhetorical superiority of the Qur'ān over IQ's *muᶜallaqa,* voiced some of the commonly held opinions regarding the excellence of IQ's poetry (the *muᶜallaqa,* in particular)—opinions that he then set out to refute; von Grunebaum *TCD* 59–60; cf. ibid., n. 10.

4. Medieval Arabic scholars, such as al-Bīrūnī (d. ca. 440/1048), who were aware of Homer's position in Hellenistic culture, sometimes referred to him as the "Imra'alqays of the Greeks"; see Kraemer *AH* 285 n. 3.

5. D. ca. 170/786; see Brockelmann *GAL* I 116, *Suppl* I 179; Qifṭī *IR* III 278–305 and references; Lyall *Muf* II xi-xiv.

6. D. ca. 216/831; see Brockelmann *GAL* I 104–5, *Suppl* I 163–5; Qifṭī *IR* 197–205 and references; Arberry *SO* 43–48 and passim.

7. He is otherwise unknown. Sezgin *GAS* II 124 gives his name in the form "Ḫarābundāḏ b. Māḫuršīḏ," apparently following the vocalization of the ms (see *DIQ* plate 5).

8. For historical, circumstantial, and textual details about this famous collection of poems, now known as the *Mu^{c}allaqāt,* see Brockelmann *GAL* I 17–18, *Suppl* I 34–36; Blachère *HLA* 143–48 (with references cited in both); Arberry *SO,* esp. "Prologue": and more recently, ^{c}Alī *TSJ* esp. 536–44; M. Kister "The Seven Odes . . . "; Sezgin *GAS* II 46–53.

9. See Ibrāhīm *DIQ* p. 367.

10. "Basic," but without any implication of "original."

11. D. 328/940; Brockelmann *GAL* I 119, *Suppl* I 182–83; Qifṭī *IR* III 201–8. Ed. by ^{c}Abdassalām Muḥammad Hārūn, Ibn al-Anbārī *SQS* 3–112. See also Sezgin *GAS* II 50.

12. Flourished in Xurāsān under ^{c}Abdallāh b. Ṭāhir and his son Ṭāhir (213–48/828–62); Qifṭī *IR* I 41 and references (esp. Yāqūt *IA* I 118–23). His recension of the Seven Odes, perhaps the earliest extant, is still unpublished, but is cited for variants to IQ's ode by Ibrāhīm (*DIQ* pp. 367–76 passim). See also Sezgin *GAS* II 50.

13. 212–75/827–88; Brockelmann *GAL* I 108, *Suppl* I 168 (but that he was a student of al-Aṣma^{c}ī [d. ca. 216/831], as Brockelmann states, is hardly possible, if the given dates are remotely close to correct; cf. ^{c}Abdalḥalīm an-Najjār in his Arabic translation of Brockelmann, *Ta'rīx al-adab al-^{c}arabī* II 163 n); Qifṭī *IR* I 291–93 and references. The MS recension of as-Sukkarī was discussed by Ahlwardt (who used it as the basis of his edition of IQ's *dīwān*) in *Divans* vi–vii, xxi; largely corrected and supplanted by Asad *MSJ* 494–500; Ibrāhīm *DIQ* (Taṣdīr) 13–14. The *mu^{c}allaqa* appears as no. 48 in Ahlwardt's edition, but minus any of the critical apparatus as-Sukkarī customarily provided in his scholia. See also Sezgin *GAS* II 124.

14. Contemporary with as-Sukkarī; Flügel *GSA* 156–57; Qifṭī *IR* II 285 and references; Arberry *SO* 127–29. The recension of aṭ-Ṭūsī (not yet published) has been discussed in detail by Asad *MSJ* 501–2; Ibrāhīm *DIQ* (Taṣdīr) pp. 11–13. It is also cited for variants in *DIQ* pp. 367–76 passim. See also Sezgin *GAS* II 124.

15. D. 299/911 or 320/932; Brockelmann *GAL* I 110, *Suppl* I 170 (where the earlier date is judged more probable); Qifṭī *IR* III 57–59 (cites an assertion by az-Zubaydī that the date 299 is wrong; but this assertion does not appear in the edition of Zubaydī *TNL,* in the section devoted to Ibn Kaysān, p. 170–71); Arberry *SO* 200. IQ's ode in the recension and with the commentary of Ibn Kaysān was published by F. L. Bernstein in *ZA* 29 (1914): 1–77. See also Sezgin *GAS* II 50.

16. D. ca. 337/949; Brockelmann *GAL* I 132, *Suppl* I 201; Qifṭī *IR* I 101–4 and references. E. Frenkel published an-Naḥḥās' commentary and recension in 1876. See also Sezgin *GAS* II 50.

17. 410–76/1019–83; Brockelmann *GAL* I 309, *Suppl* I 542; A. R. Nykl, *Hispano-Arabic Poetry,* pp. 167–68. See also Sezgin *GAS* II 109.

18. Al-A^{c}lam's "reissue" of al-Aṣma^{c}ī's recension was first published by the Baron de Slane in 1837. I have used the more recent edition of M. A.-F. Ibrāhīm, who describes the MS originals in *DIQ* (Taṣdīr) pp. 9–11; cf. de Slane, Introduction; Ahlwardt *Divans* iii-v, xvii-xviii; esp. Asad *MSJ* 503–10. IQ's ode in the first poem in the Aṣma^{c}ī/A^{c}lam recension.

19. For the *isnād* of al-A^{c}lam's *riwāya* of the dīwān, see Ibn Zayr *Index* 389, cited in *DIQ* (Taṣdīr) pp. 9–10 and Asad *MSJ* 505.

20. These departures may be observed from citations, in commentaries composed by other scholars, of variants attributed to al-Aṣma^{c}ī's "*riwāya*" (recension, in this case) that are not

found in al-A^{c}lam's version. For example (abbreviations used hereafter are clarified in the Bibliography, section III): (1) *DIQ*(Baṭ) 3:6–7 and *G* p. 28 note that al-Asma^{c}ī would render *A*14 (= *D*13) *ya mra'a llāhi* instead of *ya mra'a l-Qaysi* because he hated to pronounce the name of the pagan idol, Qays; but *D*13 reads *Qays* (this is admittedly an exceptional, if not apocryphal, instance); (2) *A*72 sch indicates that al-Aṣma^{c}ī reads *ka-anna sanā-hu,* but *D*68 has *yuḍī^{c}u sanā-hū;* (3) *A*74 sch cites from al-Aṣma^{c}ī a variant reading for the whole line, including at the end *^{c}ala n-Nibāji waṮaytalī,* but *D*76 reads *^{c}ala s-Sitāri fa Yaḏbulī* (cf. n. 85 below); (4) *A*80 sch, *N*74 sch, and *T*80 sch cite as variant from al-Aṣma^{c}ī *ka sar^{c}i l-Yamānī,* but *D*74 reads *nuzūla l-Yamānī;* 5) *A*47 sch notes that the line (i.e., *A*47) is not in al-Aṣma^{c}ī's recension (*lam yarwi hāḏa l-bayta l-Aṣma^{c}īyu*), but that Ya^{c}qūb (Ibn as-Sikkīt) and others include it; nevertheless it appears as *D*47 on al-A^{c}lam's authority. It should be noted, though, that in cases 2 and 4, in particular, the variants attributed to al-Aṣma^{c}ī may have derived from his own critical apparatus or scholia, rather than from the text of his recension.

21. That as-Sukkarī's recension derives chiefly from Kūfan sources, rather than Baṣran (as Ahlwardt *Divans* vi had alleged), has been shown by Asad *MSJ* 494–96 and is evident, in the case of the *mu^{c}allaqa,* from a line-by-line comparison, as will be seen.

22. D. 486/1093; Brockelmann *GAL* I 288, *Suppl* I 505; Qifṭī *IR* I 320–21 and references. Az-Zawzanī's recension and commentary have enjoyed great popularity since the later Middle Ages and exist in many MSS. It has been reprinted several times. See also Sezgin *GAS* II 51.

23. D. 502/1109; Brockelmann *GAL* I 279, *Suppl* I 492; Arberry considers at-Tibrīzī "perhaps the greatest of all commentators on old Arabic poetry" (*SO* 24): but, in my opinion, Ibn al-Anbārī is far superior. At-Tibrīzī's recension with scholia was published by Sir Charles Lyall in 1894 and by M. M.-D. ^{c}Abdalḥāmid in 1964. I have used the former text. See also Sezgin *GAS* II 51.

24. *A*10, 11, 30, 32, (37), 42, (53), (55), (60), (69), 72, (74) = *N*8, 9, 28, 30, (35), 40, (47), (49), (53), (63), 66, (68). Parentheses indicate an insignificant variation in vocalization or orthography, or an interchange of the conjunctions *wa* and *fa*.

25. *A*30, 32, (37), (53), (55), (60) = *N*28, 30, (35), (47), (49), (53) = *K*28, 30, (35), (46), (48), (53).

26. Otherwise unknown. On the problems surrounding the authorship and date of this famous and valuable collection, see Th. Nöldeke, "Einige Bemerkungen über das Werk Ǧamharat aš^{c}ār al-^{c}Arab"; Brockelmann *GAL Suppl* I 38–39 and references; Blachère *HLA* 142–43; esp. Asad *MSJ* 484–88 (who places the author in the fourth/tenth century). I have used the Būlāq edition of 1308/1890 (91), admittedly, as Blachère *HLS* 147 comments, a "totally insufficient" one. See also Sezgin *GAS* II 56–57.

27. D. 494/1101 (or acc. to *GAL Suppl* 521/1127); Brockelmann *GAL* I 309, *Suppl* I 543; Qifṭī *IR* II 384 and references. See also Sezgin *GAS* II 109–10.

28. See Asad *MSJ* 502–3; Ibrāhīm *DIQ* (Taṣdīr) pp. 14–15. I have used the 1347/1928 Cairo edition.

29. "Die Mu^{c}allaqa des Imrulqais," *SBAW* 170:iv (1913). Gandz employed Ahlwardt's edition of as-Sukkarī's text as his basis.

30. I have not considered the recension of Ibn an-Naḥḥās (different from an-Naḥḥās; see Ibrāhīm *DIQ* [Taṣdīr] 15–16), which is referred to by Ibrāhīm in his notes for some variant readings and which is unavailable to me. The recension, according to Ibrāhīm, is rather late and does not seem to add anything significant to our knowledge of the poem or to have been very popular in the Arab-Islamic world (cf. Sezgin *GAS* II 125). Nor have I seen the MS version, referred to by Abu-Deeb, which "differs substantially [from Ibn al-Anbārī's] and has thirty more lines" (*TSA* II 68 n. 5).

31. For abbreviations used, please see Bibliography, section III.

32. See, e.g., P. Maas, *Textual Criticism;* L. Bieler, "The Grammarians Craft"; Dain *MSS* (and Bibliography); Reynolds/Wilson *SS* (and Bibliography).

33. On possible redaction or revision of al-Aṣmaᶜī's version, see above and n. 20 to this chapter.

34. Cf. Ahlwardt *Divans* (critical apparatus) 109, where a similar comparison was undertaken between *S* and five other available versions.

35. For a clearer indication of the line-by-line correspondence among the recensions as collated with *A*, see Appendix C below.

36. But cf. App. C, n. e.

37. But cf. App. C, nn. b and g.

38. The eight additional verses (= *J*3, 6, 7, 15, 17, 21, 22, 28) are, so far as is known, unique to *J*, whose origin and sources are still quite obscure and would require a special and careful study to ascertain. Cf. n. 26 to this chapter; also n. 44 below.

39. But cf. App. C, n. d.

40. Perhaps *W*, *X*, or, as Asad (*MSJ* 486–87, 489–93) holds, the version of al-Mufaḍḍal aḍ-Ḍabbī.

41. On this possibility in *K*'s case, see App. C, n. f.

42. For a discussion of the procedure followed by some medieval redactors in such instances, see chap. 4, § C.3.a., below.

43. See, e.g., Bräunlich *FEAP* 825; Blachère *HLA* 120–21; Asad *MSJ* 175–76, 189–90, 251, 282–83. On the extent to which oral Bedouin informants were employed and trusted by the second/eighth- and third/ninth-century philologists, see Blachère *SIIB*; Blau *RBA;* Fück *Ar* 44–47, 106, 131, chap. 9. Cf. the disparaging judgment pronounced by Abu l-Xaṭṭāb al-Axfaš al-Akbar (d. 177/793) against the average Bedouin as an oral transmitter and interpreter of poetry (chap. 3, § C.11.b, above). Nevertheless, oral sources continued to be consulted, to a limited degree, until the early fourth/tenth century at least: Ibn Durayd (d. 321/934) adduced a variant to *A*17 of *MuIQ* (*bi ṯinyin wa taḥtī ṯinyu-hā*), saying that he had sometimes *heard* the line so rendered by the *rāwīs* (*rubba-mā samiᶜtu-hu mina r-ruwāt*—in Ibrāhīm *DIQ* p. 369 [to *D*16], from Ibn an-Naḥḥās).

44. Consider the effect that his ᶜAlid learnings have had on his version of the traditional account of Kaᶜb b. Zuhayr's composition of the "Burda" poem and conversion to Islam (*Jam* 13–14). There ᶜAlī b. Abī Ṭālib, who is not mentioned in any other known version, is given a prominent role as protector of Kaᶜb. Moreover, at one point in the verses that Kaᶜb is alleged to have uttered in praise of the Anṣār, the phrase, "They did indeed strike (the clan of) ᶜAlī on the 'day' of Badr" (*ḍarabū ᶜAlīyan yawma Badrin ḍarbatan*—Ibn Hišām *Sīra* 893:9; *DKbZ* 2:19 reads: *ṣadamū . . . ṣadmatan*), is read instead "They indeed leapt upon us the 'day' of Badr" (*ṣālū ᶜalay-nā yawma Badrin ṣawlatan*—*Jam* 14:10). The slight but, in the context, certainly tendentious alteration of *ᶜAlīyan* (name of a clan, not an individual; see *DKbZ* 2:19 sch.) to *ᶜalay-nā*, with the accompanying change of verb, does not instill unreserved confidence in al-Qurašī's scholarly integrity or his editorial technique. Cf. Nöldeke *FM* I 13, 18.

45. On *Z*'s omission of *A*48 see App. C, n. d.

46. For the relationship of this divergence (18–20 = *A*19, 21, 20) to the formulaic composition of the ode, see chap. 4, § C.3.b, below.

47. But cf. App. C, nn. a–b.

48. D. ca. 210/825; Brockelmann *GAL* I 103–4, *Suppl* I 162; Qifṭī *IR* III 276–87 and references. Asad *MSJ* 487–88 discusses Abu ᶜUbayda's recension on the basis of allusions to it in other sources.

49. Not Abū ᶜAlī, as in the Arabic translation of Brockelmann *TAA* II 250–51. D. 382/933; Brockelmann *GAL* I 126, *Suppl* I 193; Qifṭī *IR* I 310–12 and references.

50. ᶜAskarī *SMYT* 212:16–213:2 (On 212:17 read, instead of "al-Waṯīq," "Abu l-Waṯīq," a Bedouin informant of Abū ᶜUbayda, cited also in *Naq;* see III index, *s. n.*). Cf. Āmidī *MM* 155. Ibn Sallām *TFS* 69:4 cites the line and ascribes it to IQ without reservation.

51. But cf. App. C, n. e.

52. But cf. App. C, nn. b and g.

53. Cf., concerning the conventional usage of this word, Guillaume *LM* 3 n. 2: "The phrase employed [*fī mā za*^{c}*amū*] indicates that the writer doubts the statement. There is a saying in Arabic: 'There is a euphemism for everything and the polite way of saying "It's a lie" is "they allege" (*za*^{c}*amū*).'"

54. The variant consists of substituting the phrase *inna Ṯābitan* (the actual name of Ta'abbaṭa Šarrā) for *inna ša'na-nā*, quite possibly as the result of a scribal lapse.

55. See also Appendix A, especially line 50, note a, indicating that thematically and verbally these lines are quite compatible with what is known of IQ's formulaic repertoire.

56. The phrase is used frequently by Blachère *HLA* passim.

57. See, e.g., Maslūt *NISJ* 51–62; Asad *MSJ* 465–78; Gaudefroy-Demombynes *ILPP* 49 n. 34bis. Cf. chap. 3, n. 112.

58. With regard to the last circumstance, Blachère points out the tendency to put an anonymous work under the name of the most renowned poet bearing that designation (*HLA* 158). Notable, too, is the fact that the Ibn Xiḏām, mentioned above as the alleged author of *A*4, was also called Imra'alqays according to some authorities; see ^{c}Askarī *SMYT* 210–13 for various forms of the name.

59. This question is discussed in greater detail above, chapter 2. Cf. Monroe *OCPP* passim, esp. 37–38; Zwettler *BFOT* 211–12.

60. See Blachère *HLA* 132–41; Trabulsi *CPA* 34–57; Rosenthal *HMH* 105, 423–25. Cf., esp. on the latter genre, Blachère, "Problème de la transfiguration du poète tribal en héros de roman 'courtois' chez las 'logographes' arabes du IIIe/IXe siècle."

61. See Blachère *HLA* 153–54, 248–330 and 465–539 passim; Trabulsi *CPA* 16–18; Asad *MSJ* 481–85.

62. See I. Goldziher, "Some Notes on the Dīwāns of the Arabic Tribes"; Trabulsi *CPA* 30–33; Asad *MSJ* 543–61; Sezgin *GAS* II 36–46.

63. See, e.g., Ibn Sallām *TFS* 23–34. Cf. Nöldeke *BKPA* i–iii; Ahlwardt *PPA* 9–10; Brockelmann *GAL Suppl* I 17 and n. 2; Gibb *ALI* 13–14; Blachère *HLA* 375–76; etc.

64. Cf. Nallino *LAOU* 36–37; Gibb *ALI* 14–15; von Grunebaum *GSAP* 122 = *KD* 18. Von Grunebaum *CFD* finds evidence, however, showing that important developments in internal techniques of versification and description took place during the sixth century and can be associated with certain "schools" of poets (but cf. Blachère *HLA* 363 n. 1; Jacobi *SPAQ* 205 n. 1). See esp. Petráček *QAAL* and *VAL*.

65. See esp. the important arguments of Asad *MSJ* 465–78.

66. Sources for the study of the social and cultural conditions of the pre-Islamic Arabs are too numerous to cite in detail. Mention is made here only of bibliographical references in Sauvaget/Cahen *IHME* chap. 14; Blachère *HLA* 3–82 passim; and elsewhere.

67. W. Caskel *BBGA* 10–11; von Grunebaum *NAUI* 12–15, 18–19; Watt *MMec* 16–20; Goitein *SIHI* 67, 39; Blachère *HLA* 18–23, 79–82; etc.; also chap. 3 above; and esp. Jacobi *SPAQ*.

68. D. 395/1005 or a little before; Brockelmann *GAL* I 130, *Suppl* I 197–98; Qifṭī *IR* I 92–95 and references.

69. Goldziher *MI* I 40–50; idem *AAP* 26–41 (stresses the magical or supernatural powers imputed to *hijā'*-poetry); Lyall *AAP* xvi–xvii; Blachère *HLA* 338–42; von Grunebaum *GSAP* 123 = *KD* 18–19. Note also the view of Abū ^{c}Amr b. al-^{c}Alā' on the reasons for the precedence held by poets over orators during the Jāhilīya, in Jāḥiẓ *BT* I 241:11–16.

70. Cf. Chaytor's discussion of patronage and poets for early Romance literature (*FSP* 129–33). Taking into account differences between feudal and tribal societies, we can find his observa-

tions relevant to the "court poets" of the classical Arabic tradition. The relationship between the Old Germanic skald and his prince was also similar to that between the Arab poet and his patron, and the analogies between the skaldic tradition itself ("largely odic, encomiastic, frequently satiric, sometimes lyric" [Hollander *Skalds* 19]) and the Arabic seem remarkably close on many points; cf. *Skalds* 6, 18–22. This apparent resemblance between the two traditions was noted by A. Heusler (cited in *Skalds* 20 n. 27) and suggested by A. Bloch *Qas* 107 n. 8. Bloch *KWAV* nn. 14, 22 considerably elaborates his suggestion and concludes (p. 238): "der grosse Parallel-fall [zur altarabische Verskunst] ist die norwegisch—isländische Skaldenkunst" (cf. Jacobi *SPAQ* 209 n. 9). See also, for more details about Arabic "court" or urban poetry, Nallino *LAOU* 50–57; Goldziher *SHCAL* 17–20; Blachère *HLA* 293–329, 343–52; for the Umayyad period, see esp. Lammens *CO;* A. Renon, "Les trois poètes Omeyyades."

71. See, on the sense of the root *š-ᶜ-r*, chap. 3, n. 152, above.

72. Cf. the "dynasties" of poets, chap. 2, n. 110.

73. On the "institution" of the *kāhin* in pre-Islamic Arabia, see Goldziher *AAP* 17–18, 21–22, 25 n (in part following Wellhausen *RAH* 130–140), 107–8; D. MacDonald *RALI* 24–25, 29–37; Blachère *HLA* 190–95; A. Fischer, "Kāhin" *EI*¹ II 624–26 (denies hereditary character of office); T. Fahd, "Kāhin" *EI*² IV 420–22.

74. The word may avoid some of the pitfalls and preconceptions involved in the notion of historio*graphy*.

75. See Blachère *HLA* 596–97; Asad *QGAJ* 217–24; Sezgin *GAS* I 368–82. By 125/742, at least, there existed a body of lyrics and related material sufficient to enable Yūnus the Scribe, a singer of Persian origin and a government functionary at the court of al-Walīd II, to compile and edit the first known "Book of Songs" (Farmer *HAM* 75, 83–84; Mackenson *ABL* iii 42; cf. also *Ag* [ed Dār], Intro. 37–38). *Aġānī* offers a vast number of instances exemplifying the problems of attribution later scholars uncovered in these selections; see, e.g., (ed. Dār) I 345–46, 417; II 63, 80, 216–17, 375–76, 378, 392–93; III 8, 114, 366; IV 213, 299; V 117, 193; VI 5–6, 100–101, 139–41, 158–59, 163, 170, 172, 208, 226, 308–9, 333; VIII 279–80; VIII 121, 235 (cf. 383), 267, 323; etc. Cf. Blachère *HLA* 138, 682–83.

76. D. 175/791 or before; Brockelmann *GAL* I 100, *Suppl* I 159–60; Qifṭī *IR* I 341–47 and references.

77. D. between 177/893 and 194/809; Brockelmann *GAL* I 101–2, *Suppl* I 160; Qifṭī *IR* II 346–60 and references.

78. D. 206/821; Brockelmann *GAL* I 116, *Suppl* I 179 (cf. correction by Najjār in Brockelmann *TAA* II 202 n): Qifṭī *IR* I 221–29 and references.

79. Wild *KA* 45; Asad *MSJ* 592–98; Diem *KG* 60–63. In the case of Sībawayh, particularly, it is probable that most, if not all, of the nominal attributions that appear in the printed texts were interpolated by a later scholar (Abū ᶜUmar al-Jarmī—d. 225/839—is suggested) or scholars; see Brockelmann *GAL* I 101 n. 1, citing Baġdādī *XA* I 178; and esp. Asad *MSJ* 593–97.

80. See Rosenthall *HMH* 93–94 for details; also Sezgin *GAS* II 92–97.

81. See Blachère *HLA* 139–140; Trabulsi *CPA* 34–39. As applied to *ḥadīṯ*, it is probably true that, as Rosenthal states, the *ṭabaqāt* division was genuinely Islamic," and that, in its sense of "layers" or "people belonging to one layer or class in the chronological succession of generations," it "was the natural consequence of the concept of 'Men around Muḥammad', the 'Followers', etc., which in conjunction with the *isnād* criticism of the science of traditions, developed in the early second century of the hijrah" (*HMH* 93–94). Yet when, in the literary field, it implied the application of critical criteria or the exercise of a value judgment, as it so obviously did in Ibn Sallām's work (see below), one is tempted to seek some connection (no doubt impossible to prove) between the *ṭabaqāt aš-šuᶜarā'* ("classes" of poets) and the Latin *classici* (writers of the first class). Equally interesting and maybe easier to accept is the use of Arabic *ixtiyārāt* or *muxtārāt* ("selections" or "selected pieces") in practically the same semi-technical sense as the Greek equivalent *enkrithentes,* the poets and authors (or their works) "chosen" by

the Alexandrian grammarians and registered in a selective list. It was these authors and works to which the Romans applied the term *classici* and which we call "classical" (see Pfeiffer *HCS* 203–8). Likewise, it was the *ixtiyārāt* of the great philologists—al-Mufaḍḍal, al-Aṣmaʿī, and others—and the *ṭabaqāt* of Ibn Sallām and his colleagues that formed the substance of the "classics" of the Arabic tradition.

82. D. 231/845; Brockelmann *GAL Suppl* I 165; Qifṭī *IR* III 143–45 and references.

83. I have used the fine edition of Maḥmūd Muḥammad Šākir (Cairo, 1371/1952).

84. Not to mention, of course, what they could get from such oral poets, tradents, or reciters who still remained—a different situation altogether; see n. 43 above.

85. In this, too, they were operating upon a principle almost identical with that followed by Aristarchos and other Hellenistic textual critics in indicating lines in Homer and elsewhere that they thought questionable or spurious, but that they continued to retain in their texts (see Sandys *HCS* I 132–36; Reynolds/Wilson *SS* 11–13; Pfeiffer *HCS* 229–31). The Greek critics employed a symbol (the *obelos*) to mark such lines in the text as "interpolations" (the practice was called *athetesis*). They reserved explanation and justification of their *atheteses* for separate commentaries (*hypomnēmata*). The Arabic critics, however, who generally provided their editions of poems with accompanying scholia, would as a rule state their objections to a line or lines, rather than signal them with a symbol. The instance cited by C. Rabin *AWA* 69, of Abū ʿUbayda's indicating a doubtful word in a poem by means of dots has been adduced by von Grunebaum as evidence of "the taking over [by the Arabs] of the Alexandrine *athetesis*" (in *CMH* IV:i 672 n. 2). But, considering Abū ʿUbayda's Jewish origins, such a practice may as easily have been influenced by the Rabbinic and Massoretic system of dotting ambiguous or doubtful words in the Torah; this was a technique no doubt ultimately traceable to the Alexandrians (see Liebermann *HJP* 38–46), but not of itself indicative of "the infiltration of Hellenism and its prestige." One would like more examples of such usages for similar purposes before going so far as to claim a direct borrowing. Even without such examples, though, one must recognize the existence of a communion of interest and approach among both groups of scholars—Greek and Arabic.

86. See, e.g., Krenkow *UWP* 266–67; Asad *MSJ* 175–78.

87. See the short bibliography (no. 1) in Maas *TC* 55; also Dain *MSS* 40–55; Reynolds/Wilson *SS* 150–62.

88. Two of these works have been edited and published: Abū Aḥmad al-ʿAskarī, *Šarḥ mā yaqaʿu fī-hī t-taṣḥīf wa t-taḥrīf* (= *SMYT*); Ḥamza b. al-Ḥasan al-Iṣfahānī (d. 360/970), *at-Tanbīhḥīfʿalā ḥudūṯ at-taṣḥīf* (= *THT*). Cf. also al-Marzubānī *Muw* passim; as-Suyūṭī *Muz* II 353–94.

89. E.g., Ibn Hišām *Sīra* 243–44; Ibn ʿAbdrabbih *IF* V 275–82; Arberry *SO* 214; etc.

90. See, e.g., Muḥammad b. Ḥabīb *Kitāb alqāb aš-šuʿarā'* (in Hārūn *NM* II 299–328) passim; Ibn Rašīq *Umda* I 46–48; also Barbier de Meynard, "Surnoms et sobriquets dans la littérature arabe." Both Ibn al-Kalbī (d. 204/819) and al-Madā'inī (d. 234/849) composed monographs on poets who were named after verses they had uttered: *Fih* 97:16, 104:2; see Sezgin *GAS* II 98–101 for further examples.

91. See, e.g., A. Bloch, "Zur altarabischen Spruchdichtung."

92. E.g., books of *abyāt sā'ira* (*Fih* 48:17–18, 49:8, 78:28) or, by al-Madā'inī, books about those who uttered gnomic verses on specific occasions—in their illness, while stopping at a grave, on learning of someone's death, etc. Cf. also the works of Ibn Fāris and al-Mubarrad in Hārūn *NM* I 137–73; further, Sezgin *GAS* II 98–101.

93. See Appendix B, "Table of Variations . . . ," lines 3, 6–8, 10–12, 16, 17, 21, 22, 24, 27–30, 32, 34, 35, 37, 41, 42, 44–48, 53, 56–59, 61, 62, 64, 66, 68, 69, 71–80, 82.

94. On the question of the "analogistic-anomalistic" controversy in early Arabic linguistic studies, and its frequently oversimplified identification with a Baṣra-Kūfa rivalry, see especially G. Weil *GSBK:* Fleisch *TPA* chap. 2; Ḍayf *MN* passim.

95. One can perhaps give al-Aṣma^{c}ī more credit for consistency than might appear—in this poem at least. *A*74 of the ode describes the progress or extent of a rain-cloud and reads in *A* and elsewhere (including *D*) *^{c}ala s-Sitāri fa Yaḏbulī*. *A*74 sch, *T*74 sch, and *N*68 sch, however, cite as a variant *^{c}ala n-Nibāji wa Ṯaytalī* (*N* reads *wa Yaṯṯalī*—a simple transposition of dots). Moreover, *A*74 sch specifically cites this variant on al-Aṣma^{c}ī's authority. Cf. App. B. n. 37.

96. "Had it [the line] been rendered . . . [with the accusative], it would have been unobjectionable, as *miṯl* would be in the accusative as the direct object of *ṭaraqtu*, and *murḍi^{c}an* would be joined to it (by coordinate conjunction). However, we know of no one who has rendered (or read) it in the accusative (. . . *illā anna-nā lā na^{c}lamu aḥadan rawā-hu naṣban*)" (*N* p 15:3–5). There had been an early variant adduced by Sībawayh (*Kitāb* I 293; cf. *N*14 sch, *T*16 sch)—*wa miṯliki bikran qad ṭaraqtu wa ṯayyiban*—which may have prompted the normalized version just considered, if only through adaptation of the *textus receptus* to the sanctioned use of the accusative in the Master's *Book* (cf. Gandz's commentary, *G* p. 30).

97. Cf. Arberry *SO* 63 (apparently following *Z*); Gandz *G*27, p. 49.

98. A unique reading adopted by *A*, attested only as a variant in *T*30 sch.

99. Cf. also analogous versions cited in *A*30 sch, *Z*30 sch, and von Grunebaum *TCD* 78–79.

100. See *N*27–28 sch, *B*28 sch. *K*27 sch also indicates Abū ^{c}Ubayda as source both of the reading and of the rationale for it (but at *K* p. 30:1, read *haṣartu l-jawābu* instead of *haṣarti l-jawāba*). Cf. however, *A*29 sch. (p. 56), where Abū ^{c}Ubayda is mentioned as holding a quite different opinion; also n. 101 below.

101. Reckendorf *AS* 483 discusses under § 253 "Partikeln des Hauptsatzes," section 6, the possibility of *waw* as such a pleonastic particle. He cites the examples usually adduced (see n. 100 above) and comments with regard to the verse in question: "Mit Unrecht wird auch Imr. Mu^{c}all. 29 [ed. Arnold ?] hierhergezogen . . . ; der Haupts[atz] beginnt erst Vs. 30." It would appear, however, that Reckendorf had not considered the alternative version of 30 that we are dealing with here, for this is precisely the reason why 29 would have been adduced in the first place.

102. *wa man rawā "iḏā qultu hātī nawwilī-nī" fa . . . yakūnu "iḏā" ẓarfa "tamāyalat" wa huwa* [i.e., *"tamāyalat"*] *al-jawābu.*

103. At-Tibrīzī's suggestion, though syntactically quite feasible, is not entirely consistent with the practice of the classical poets as regards enjambement; cf. chap. 2, § B, above.

104. D. 406/1015–16. See al-Qifṭī *IR* II 178 and reference.

105. As against 27.6% verbal formularity for the rest of Passage I and 52.6% for the next highest distinct segment of the poem (II.A—11. 53–63).

106. Passage III did not seem legitimately susceptible of thematic subdivision: hence the arbitrary halving.

107. But cf. App. C for varying lengths of the *nasīb* in other recensions.

108. Cf. Jacobi's remarks about the less traditional, more individual quality of *MuIQ* 23–30 = *S* 21–28 (*SPAQ* 48–49).

109. One might, with a somewhat different interpretation of the thematic structure of the ode, opt to treat 11. 44–48 (I.C.l), the long, lonely night scene, as introducing a separate passage, distinct from the *nasīb* (cf. chap. 2, n. 33 above). In that case, the *relatively* higher proportion of verbal formularity for those lines (35%) would perhaps follow from their passage-opening function. But since there is considerable disparity between 35%, on the one hand, and, on the other, the percentages of verbal formularity for the well-established passage-openings (56.4, 52.6, and 46.4 respectively for I, II, and III), such an approach would seem neither satisfactory nor called for.

110. However, Bateson's phonological analysis has been subjected to a thorough and exhaustive critique by E. Wagner ("War die kontinuerliche Vokalfrequenzabweichung ein Stilmittel der arabischen Dichter?"). Wagner points out a number of shortcomings in the approach and questions the validity of her conclusions regarding vowel-patterning in *qaṣīda* style. Cf. also G. Windfuhr's review of Bateson *SCP* and Jacobi *SPAQ*.

111. Cf. such a situation in the case of some African oral-poetic traditions, discussed in Finnegan *OLA* 105–7 and passim.

112. The distinction between the two activities may, however, be little more than nominal, as instances reported about many an early Arab *rawī* tend to confirm; cf. chap. 4, § E.1.b, below.

113. Besides the phase of *rāwī*-"apprenticeship" discussed above (chap. 2, § D), consider also the several other cases of "provision for specialist education in the composition and delivery of oral literature" mentioned by Finnegan (in Horton/Finnegan *MT* 123). How complex and varied some oral traditions might be, both as to their practice and their practioners, is related with much detail in Finnegan *OLA* chap. 4 and passim.

114. See Lord *ST* 26; and esp. Finnegan in Horton/Finnegan *MT* 127–31.

115. See Ibn Rašīq *Umda* I 189–96; and especially the many anecdotes concerning spontaneous or improvised composition and rendition (*irtijāl* and *badīha*) by classical poets in al-Azdī, *Badā'iᶜ al-badā'ih*, passim.

116. What Bateson alludes to here is the custom recorded for some Bedouin poets of composing "short passages for his friends to memorize, allowing him to move on, while at the same time he solicits opinions about his work" (*SCP* 34). She implies that, since "eventually the poem is preserved in the memories of several different individuals," such a situation is somehow contrary to the expectations of oral-traditional theory. But the very passages she cites in support of this view (Blachère *HLA* 88–89 and Musil *MCRB* 283–84 [Bateson cites only 283]) emphasize that this procedure results, not in increased stability of the poem, but in acceleration and intensification of the process by which the "original poem" becomes varied and transformed in a manner entirely consistent with oral tradition as Parry and Lord describe it.

117. Bateson refers here to Lord *ST* 106, where the "lists" in question are of the "extended catalogue" type that, Lord says, are "typical of *epic, especially of dictated oral epic*" (my italics). In her use of sources, Bateson seems at times to be guilty of "stacking the deck" in her favor and against Parry and Lord and the oral-formulaic theory in general.

118. What "Lord believes to develop only when writing is introduced" has also been rather misrepresented and oversimplified by Bateson; cf. Lord *ST* 220–21 (Bateson's citation).

119. Lord's *ST* appears to be the *only* source on oral-formulaic theory employed in Bateson's work. Her allusion (*SCP* 39 n. 22) to Parry *SET* I is *apud* Lord *ST* 4.

120. One of the more recent contributions to oral-formulaic studies that rigorously investigates the concept of the "oral formula" and goes well beyond it is M. Nagler's *Spontaneity and Tradition: A Study in the Oral Art of Homer*. Because of the current state of literary and oral-traditional scholarship in our field, I have not attempted to incorporate the important and sophisticated results of his investigations into the present study, though I have learned much from them and owe much to them. I hope in the future to be better prepared to utilize his work and the approach it embodies in studying classical Arabic poetry.

121. E.g., E. Havelock for Greek oral composition and rendition and R. Stevick for Anglo-Saxon; see studies cited in Nagler *TGV* 284 n. 26 (cf. chap. 1, § A.6, above).

122. Not to be confused with Menéndez Pidal's idea of "traditional" and "individual" *poetry*; cf. Zwettler *BFOT* 209–10.

123. "Remembered" more accurately characterizes the situation than "memorized," as suggested in § D.1, above. Cf. Lord's remark that "oral composition . . . is a technique of remembering rather than of memorization" (cited p. 26, above).

124. The most sensitive and complete discussion of the nature of oral composition and the interaction of traditional and individual elements in producing a given oral poem remains Nagler *TGV* and now his more recent book (see n. 120, above).

125. A possible application of the findings of this study might be to seek to determine, on the basis of formulaic analysis, the authenticity or correctness of attribution of certain poems or portions of poems. As Monroe suggests, "If a dubious poem shares few formulas in common with those most used by the poet to whom it is attributed, it can be accepted as a likely assumption

that it was not composed by him. If its formulaic content turns out to be low, it can further be assumed that it was forged by a literate poet in Islamic times'' (*OCPP* 42). In principle, I agree; but it may be that the matter of a *qaṣīda's integrity*—something that we are only beginning to understand—is of far greater importance than its authenticity or attribution. For example, the extremely low density of verbal formulas in *MuIQ* 49–52 (I.C.2), the short passage of dubious attribution discussed above (chap. 4, § B), could be exploited and construed so as to give solace to those who, like Bateson and others (see above), would want to exclude the lines from the *qaṣīda* as inauthentic. But neither do these lines, with a verbal formulaic density of 22.3%, comprise the least formulaic subdivision of the poem (cf. I.B.2, 11. 16–22, with 17.3% verbal formularity); nor do they in any way represent a jarring dissonance at variance with the thematic structure at that point (cf. Abu-Deeb *TSA* II 25–28 and passim). That these verses may ultimately have derived from the formulaic repertoire of a poet other than Imra'alqays is entirely possible, but it is also quite irrelevant: for it is clear that they had come to form an integral part of the poem as it was rendered, received, and experienced within the living oral tradition—however much the philologists may have railed against their ''authenticity.''

126. *fa lammā nafida ši*^{c}*ru abī-hi ja*^{c}*ala yazīdu fi l-aš*^{c}*āri wa yaḍa*^{c}*u-hā la-nā wa iḏā kalāmun dūna kalāmi Mutammimin wa iḏā huwa yaḥtaḏī* ^{c}*alā kalāmi-hi fa yaḏkuru l-mawāḍi*^{c}*a llatī ḏakara-hā Mutammimun wa l-waqā'i*^{c}*a llatī šahida-hā fa lammā aṭāla ḏālika* ^{c}*alimnā anna-hu yafta*^{c}*ilu-hu*.

*

Appendix A

Formulaic Analysis of the *Muᶜallaqa* of Imra'alqays

The approach and results of the following analysis have been discussed above, in chapter 2, § A. Items underlined may be assumed to occur in other poems both in the same metrical position and in lines of the same *ṭawīl* meter, unless otherwise indicated. Indication of differing position will be made, taking the usual fourteen-syllable hemistich as base, by noting the hemistich (*a* or *b*) and the position of the last syllable of the item in question. Thus, *b*6 would indicate that the item occurs in the second hemistich with its last syllable falling in the sixth syllable-slot of that hemistich.

A question-mark (?) after a citation indicates that the poet may be thought too late in the tradition to provide acceptable evidence of orality (many examples given in *G* have been left out for this reason).

The text used in the analysis, of course, is the recension of Ibn al-Anbārī mentioned above, which is here referred to as *MuIQ* rather than *A*. Abbreviations of sources consulted will be found in the Bibliography, section II.

ANALYSIS

1. *qifā nabki min ḏikrā ḥabibin wa manzilī*

```
______________________________ ------a
          ________ ----------b _______g
          ---_____________h
```

bi siqṭi l-liwā bayna d-Daxūli fa Ḥawmalī

```
___________________ -----------------c
.......... ______d.......... ________________e
               ______ -----------------f
```

a. *DIQ* 9:1 = *DIQ* (Ahl) 65:1.
b. $D^{c}An$ 7:3 / $DA^{c}s\bar{a}$ 77:1.
c. *DBišr* 21:1 / *DḤāt* p. 45:1 (w. *bi siqf*).
d. *Aṣm* 63:1 / $D^{c}Ur$ p. 28:3 / *SAH* p. 945:2.
e. *Muf* 121:2 / Cf. *DḤass* 13:1 (m. *kāmil*).
f. *MuIQ* 74 / *DIQ* 88:1 = *DIQ* (Ahl) 63:1 / $D^{c}Al$ 1:2 / *Aṣm* 42:1
g. In rhyme position: *MuIQ* 76.
h. *DḤass* 21:2 (*a*6; w. *li*).

It has frequently been noted that the classical poets represent themselves as being accompanied by *two* companions whom they address in the grammatical *dual* (here: *qifā;* elsewhere: *xalīlay-ya, abliġā,* etc.; cf. *G* 10–11; Blachère *HLA* 366; Bloch *Qas* 128; etc.). Whether use of the dual can be considered formulaic on the verbal level is not certain, but that it is so on the thematic level is beyond question. Although this usage has been variously interpreted (e.g., as addressed to the poet's fictive traveling companions or to his inspiring demons, or as an intensive form of the imperative singular), one may see it as analogous to its apparently formulaic occurrence in the Homeric epics and, possibly, in biblical and other ancient Near Eastern contexts as well. There the depiction of a character or a figure attended by two persons (or sometimes spirits or demons) seems to have served to exalt the one so attended—or at least, to highlight his rank or importance.[1]

There can be little doubt that the (grammatically anomalous) use of *fa,* rather than *wa,* to join together place names in the *nasīb* is a formulaic element deeply rooted in the poetic tradition (see pp. 114, 209, above; cf. *G* pp. 12–14; Nöldeke *GCA* 59; Reckendorf *SVA* 457–58; idem *AS* 319–20; Blachère/Gaudefroy-Demombynes *GAC* 475). One can find repeated examples of this usage in *qaṣīda* after *qaṣīda* (see citations in previous references). Gandz (*G* 13), moreover, has noted the very important fact that the same usage shows up often in poetic descriptions of rainstorms, linking together the places over which a rain cloud extends or upon which it showers. That these two themes—the naming of places deserted by a beloved and the naming of places affected by a rainstorm—are so closely associated on the formulaic level suggests that the themes of the absent beloved and the returning rains might themselves have been related at one time, perhaps even on a cultic level. The subject of the imagery that appears in the classical *qaṣīdas* and its function both within the poems and within the culture deserves further study.[2]

2. *fa Tuḍiḥa fa l-Miqrāti lam ya*^{c}*fu rasmu-hā*

a b

li-mā nasajat-hā min janūbin wa šam'alī

a. See above, comment to line 1.

b. *DNāb* 17:2 / (cf. *DIQ* 16:2 = *DIQ*(Ahl) 51:2—m. *sarī*^{c}).

The theme of the obliterated traces of a former encampment (with the verb ^{c}*afā* in some form) recurs frequently enough to be considered formulaic in itself; cf. *DIQ* 9:1b = *DIQ* (Ahl) 65:1b: *wa rasmin* ^{c}*afat āyātu-hū*.

For the sequence of toponyms as formulaic, see above, comment to line 1.

3. *tarā ba*^{c}*ara l-ar'āmi fī* ^{c}*araṣati-hā*

a b c

e

wa qī^{c}*āni-hā ka-anna-hū ḥabbu fulfulī*

d

a. In this position, a frequently recurring formula in either the 2d or 1st person: *DIQ* 3:41 = *DIQ*(Ahl) 4:49 (cf. *D*^{c}*Al* 1:35) / p. 344:1 = 4:51 / 4:27b = 20:30b / 4:46 = 20:20 / etc.

b. *DIQ* 8:14 = *DIQ* (Ahl) 63:14 / *DZuh* 16:3 / *DAws* 30:5 / *DNāb* 20:12b.

c. *DBišr* 40:3 / *DTam* 7:2 / *DḤass* 135:8 (m. *kāmil*).

d. Cf. *MuIQ* 81 (*mufalfalī*).

e. *DḤass* 2:13 (w. *fī-hā*).

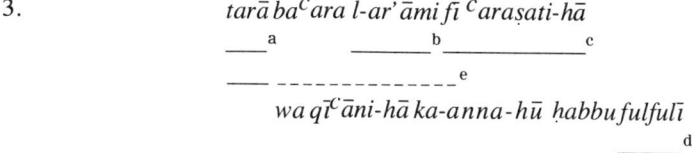

4. *ka-annī ġadāta l-bayni yawma taḥammalū*

a

b c d

f

ladā samurāti l-ḥayyi nāqifu ḥanẓalī

e

a. *DA^{c}šā* 15:54 (*wa naḥnu ġadāta l-^{c}Ayni yawma Quṭaymatin*).
b. On *ka-anna* as introductory element to syntactic formulas, see von Grunebaum *CFD* 33n. 5; Jacobi *SPAQ* 124–26.[3]
c. *DṬar* 9:9 / *DŠamm* 2:16 (w. *al-bayhi*).
d. *DIQ* 4:3 (cf. p. 390:7) = *DIQ*(Ahl) 20:3 / *DLab* 35:39, 40 / (cf. *DTam* 3:4 and *DQays* 8:3b)/*DIQ* p. 443:12/*DMuz* p. 79:2.
e. In rhyme position: *MuIQ* 62 / *DQays* 8:2 / *DḤass* 13:14 (*li naqfi l-ḥanẓalī;* m. *kāmil*).
f. *DḤass* 27:10.

Note, in connection with (e), that *ḥanẓal* stands at the end of the line as the predicate (or part of the predicate) of a subject introduced at the beginning of the line by *ka-anna* in the three *ṭawīl* cases cited. This formulaic correspondence, particularly between the two sections of *MuIQ*, suggests important aspects of an over-all structural and thematic unity within the *qaṣīda* that have yet to be explored; cf. line 1 comment.

5. *wuqūfan bi-hā ṣaḥbī ^{c}alay-ya maṭīya-hum*

b c

yaqūlūna lā tahlik asan wa tajammalī

a

d e

a. *DṬar* 9:2.
b. *J* 6 / *DIQ* 78:1b / *DZuh* 16:4 / *DBišr* 4:3 / *DA^{c}šā* 9:14, 10:18 / *DNāb* 21:2 / *Aṣm* 42:5 / *D^{c}Ab* 17:3.
c. *MuIQ* 11 / *DIQ* 9:16 = *DIQ*(Ahl) 65:16v / *Muf* 30:16 / *DNāb* 18:3.
d. *DA^{c}šā* 9:13 / *DḤāt* p. 50:7 /*DṬuf* 3:36/ (cf. for syntactic correspondences, *DIQ* 30:33 = *DIQ*(Ahl) 40:33 / 35:4 [w. variants] = 41:4 [w. variants]).
e. See line 14, note e, below.

6. *wa inna šifā'ī ^{c}abratun muharāqatun*

——— ....[a]

fa hal ^{c}inda rasmin dārisin min mu^{c}awwalī

———[b] ———[c] - - - - - -[d]

a. *MuIQ* 6v (see Appendix B) / *DNāb* 17:7.

b. Frequently introduces a rhetorical question in this position; e.g., *DIQ* 2:1b, 2, 3 = *DIQ*(Ahl) 52:1b, 2, 3 / *DNāb* 17:21 / *DLab* 28:1, 8:25 / etc.

c. *DŠamm* 5:1.

d. See line 12, note f, below.

7. *ka da'bi-ka min Ummi l-Ḥuwayriṯi qabla-hā*

———[a]

wa jārati-hā Ummi r-Rabābi bi Ma'salī

..... ———[b]

a. In this position: *Muf* 96:2 / *DNāb* 6:11 / *DṮar* 9:3 / *DLab* 8:36, 25:5 / *DṬuf* 9:3 / *DḤum bā'*:7 / *DBišr* 3:2.

b. *Muf* 20:7 / *D^{c}Ur* p. 63:3.

8. *iḏā qāmatā taḍawwa^{c}a l-misku min-humā*

——————————→

...... ———[b] ——————[c]

nasīma ṣ-ṣabā jā'at bi rayya l-qaranfulī

——————..........[a]

——- - - - - -[d]

a. *DIQ* 14:7 = *DIQ*(Ahl) 17:7.

b. See *MuIQ* p. 16:12.

c. Cf. *Aṣm* 70:5 (*taḍawwa^{c}a min-hal-misku*—*a*8).

d. *MuIQ* 30.

9. *fa fāḍat dumū^{c}u l-^{c}ayni min-nī ṣabābatan*

- - - - - ———[a] ———[b]

^{c}ala n-naḥri ḥattā balla dam^{c}iya miḥmalī

———[c] - - - - - - ———[d]

a. *DIQ* 9:4 = *DIQ*(Ahl) 65:4 / (cf. analogous formulas with m. *kāmil* cited in *G* p. 20; these examples also relate to d) / *SAH* p. 1162:6b, 1180:9b / *DŠamm* 17:5 (w. *fādat*).

b. *MuIQ* 40 / *Muf* 15:20 / *D^{c}Ab*(Naṣ) 37:5 = *D^{c}Ab* 17:5v / *SAH* p. 1025:6.

c. *DNāb* 17:7 / *DḤum wāw*:23; *jim-yā'*:15 / see below.

d. See *G* p. 20 / cf. *DLab* 35:86 (*wa qad balla n-najī^{c}u l-maḥāmilā*).

The preposition ^{c}*alā* (also *ilā* and *ladā*) stands more frequently at the beginning of a hemistich than anywhere else in lines of classical poetry. The combination ^{c}*alā* (*ilā, ladā*) + *CVCCV* (or $C\bar{V}CV$) occurring in that position can definitely be accounted formulaic. See, e.g., *MuIQ* 26, 28, 56a, *DIQ* 2:51 = *DIQ*(Ahl) 52:54, 3:22a-b = 4:25v, 3:37 = 4:46, 3:49 = 4:59, 4:37v = 20:46, 4:38 = 20:48, 6:6 = 10:6, etc.

10. *alā rubba yawmin la-ka min-hunna ṣāliḥin*

———————————————————— a

——————————— b

——————— - - - - - - c

wa lā sīyamā yawmin bi dārati Juljulī

a. Cf. *MuIQ* 10v (Appendix B): *alā rubba yawmin ṣaliḥin* . . . = *DIQ* 4:52 = *DIQ*(Ahl) 20:53.

b. *DIQ* 2:10 = *DIQ*(Ahl) 52:9v, 13:7 = 30:7, 79:4 / *DṬar* 10:7.

c. *MuIQ* 43 / *DṬar* 10:5b / cf. *DIQ* 9:7 = *DIQ*(Ahl) 65:7 (*fa yā rubba makrūbin*).

11. *wa yawma ^{c}aqartu li l-^{c}aḏārā maṭīyatī*

——————— - - - - - - a ——————— b ——————— c

fa yā ^{c}ajabā li raḥli-ha l-mutaḥammilī

——————————— d - - - - - - - - - - - - e

a. *MuIQ* 13 / *DLab* 29:9, 10.

b. In that position: *DḤum alif*:17.

c. See line 5, note c, above.

d. Cf. esp. *MuIQ* 11v (*min raḥli-hā*): *J* 15 / *DṬar* 16:1 / *SAH* p. 799:1 / citations in *G* pp. 23–24 / *DIQ* 60:3.

e. Attributives of the pattern *mutafa^{cc}i/a$l\bar{V}$* are often found in this line-end position: *J* 15 / *MuIQ* 26, 34, 39, 55, 73 / cf. Bloch *KWAV* p. 216 n. 13.

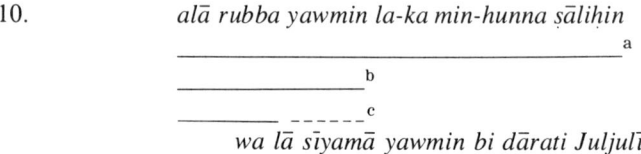

12. *fa ẓalla l-^{c}aḏārā yartamīna bi laḥmi-hā*

_______ ---------------------------- a

------ _____________________ -------- b

_______ c _________ d

wa šaḥmin ka huddābi d-dimaqsi l-mufattalī

_____________________ -------- e

-------- f

_________ g

a. *DIQ* 30:33 = *DIQ*(Ahl) 40:33 / *DṬar* 4:92, 16:3 / *D^{c}Al* 1:41 / *DḤāt* p. 52:7 / *DḤum jīm-yā'* :26 / *DNāb* app. 24:5 / *DLab* 36:42 / see p. 52, above.

b. *D^{c}Ab* 10:3.

c. In that position: *DIQ* 2:33 = *DIQ*(Ahl) 52:34 (cf. *D^{c}Ab* 10:3), 3:35b = 4:44b (cf. *MuIQ* 64) / *DṬar* 9:7 / *DZuh* 15:3 / *DḤum alif:* 17b, 41b.

d. In that position: *DIQ* 2:44 = *DIQ*(Ahl) 52:49.

e. *Muf* 106:10 / *DA^{c}šā* 30:12, 77:23 / *DḤum alif:*55 / citations in *G* pp. 25–26 / cf. *DIQ* 73:11 (. . . *banānun ka hudbi d-dimaqsi nfatal*—m. *mutaqārib*).

f. Attributives of the pattern *mufa^{cc}a/ilV̄* are often found in this line-end position; e.g., *MuIQ* 15, 6, 22, 25, 28, 33, 36, 41, 49, 50, 57, etc.

g. In rhyme position: *MuIQ* 72 (cf. line 72, note c, below).

13. *wa yawma daxaltu l-xidra xidra ^{c}Unayzatin*

_________ ------ a ---------- __________ b

---- __________ c

fa qālat la-ka l-waylātu inna-ka murjilī

_______ ------------ _______ ------ d

------- ___________ e

_______ f

a. See line 11, note a, above.

b. Cf. *DIQ* 81:2 = *DIQ*(Ahl) 2:2 (*fa marra ^{c}ala l-xabtayni xabtay ^{c}Unayzatin*) / *DNāb* 1:6.

c. *DIQ* 31:3 = *DIQ*(Ahl) 34:3 / *Muf* 36:17, 83:3.

d. *DIQ* 2:21 = *DIQ*(Ahl) 52:21.

e. *Aṣm* 10:8a = *D^{c}Ur* p. 68:2a / *DA^{c}šā* 66:1a.

f. *fa/wa qālat* and its metrical equivalents in this position (i.e., with *qultu*, *qulnā, qālū,* etc.), together with its imperfect alternatives (*taqūlu, aqūlu, naqūlu* etc.), occur at the beginnings of lines in classical Arabic poetry with a frequency that must be acknowledged as formulaic; e.g., *MuIQ* 14, 15, 27, 45, 51.

14. *taqūlu wa qad māla l-ġabīṭu bi-nā ma^{c}an*

______ - - - - a ______ b ______ c

______ d ______ f

^{c}aqarta ba^{c}īrī ya mra'alqaysi fa nzilī

- - - - - - e

a. *MuIQ* 26v / *DIQ* 51:12 = *DIQ*(Ahl) 36:11 / *DṬar* 4:89 / *Muf* 30:8, 67:23 / *N* p. 7:11 (al-Muṯaqqib al-^{c}Abdī) / *DḤāt* p. 80:5 (*fa qultu wa qad ṭāla*).
b. In that position: *MuIQ* 80 / *DLab* 36:28b.
c. *D^{c}An* 26:4.
d. See line 13, note f, above.
e. Final imperative or jussive: *MuIQ* 5, 19, 20, 21, 46v, 52, 69.
f. In that position: *MuIQ* 54.

15. *fa qultu la-hā sīrī wa arxī zimāma-hū*

______ - - - a - - - - ______ b

______ c ____ - - - - - - - - - d

______ e

wa lā tub^{c}idīnī min janā-ki l-mu^{c}allilī

______ f

a. DIQ 30:26 = *DIQ*(Ahl) 40:26 / *DZuh* 15:22 / *D^{c}Al* 1:10 / *DQays* 18:2 / *DḤum alif*:42 / *D^{c}Amr* 3:2 / *D^{c}An* 26:10 / *Aṣm* 15:6 / *Muf* 106:3b = *D^{c}Ām* 11:3b / *DBišr* 22:4 / etc.
b. *DḤum alif*:55 / *Muf* 47:11.
c. *MuIQ* 45 / *DIQ* 4:35 = *DIQ*(Ahl) 20:44 / *Muf* 67:30 / *DḤāt* p. 47:2 / *DNāb* 15:8, 23:16 / *D^{c}An* 26:9
d. Cf. *MuIQ* 44 (*arxā sudūla-hū*).
e. See line 13, note f, above.
f. See line 12, note f, above.

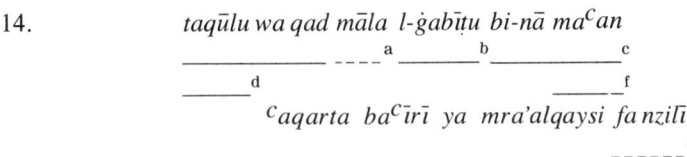

16. *fa miṯli-ki ḥublā qad ṭaraqtu wa murḍi^{c}in*

——— a

fa alhaytu-hā ^{c}an ḏī tamā'ima muḥwilī

a. *DIQ* 2:14 = *DIQ*(Ahl) 52:14 / *DA^{c}šā* 10:5.

The theme of this line recurs in very similar terms in *DIQ* 2:14 = *DIQ*(Ahl) 52:14 and *DIQ* 51:7 = *DIQ*(Ahl) 36.6.

17. *iḏā-mā bakā min xalfi-ha nsarafat la-hū*

——— a

bi šiqqin wa taḥtī šiqqu-hā lam yuḥawwalī

——— - - - - - - - - - b

a. In that position: *MuIQ* 25, 40b, 57.

b. *MuIQ* 18, 51, 66 / *DIQ* 3:3, 50 = *DIQ*(Ahl) 4:3, 61 / etc.

18. *wa yawman ^{c}ala ẓahri l-kaṯībi ta^{c}aḏḏarat*

——— - - - - a

^{c}alay-ya wa ālat ḥalfatan lam taḥallalī

——— b ——— - - - - - - - - c

a. *DIQ* p. 389:12–13 (cf. 3:34) = *DIQ* (Ahl) 4:68–69.

b. In that position: *MuIQ* 24, 30, 44.

c. See line 17, note b, above.

19. *a Fāṭima mahlan ba^{c}ḍa hāḏa t-tadallulī*

——— a

wa in kunti qad azma^{c}ti surmī fa ajmilī

——— - - - - - - - - - - - - b

——— - - - - - - c ——— - - - - - - - d

a. *Muf* 56:15, 18.

b. *MuIQ* 46v (see Appendix B) / cf. *D^{c}An* 21:13 (*in kunti azma^{c}ti l-firāqa;* m. *kāmil*).

c. *MuIQ* 21v / *DNāb* 21:21 / *DBišr 4:5*.

d. See line 14, note e, above.

20. *a ġarra-ki minnī anna ḥubba-ki qātilī*

____________________ [a]

wa anna-ki mahmā ta'muri l-qalba yaf^{c}alī

- - - - - - [b]

a. See *G* p. 34 (*Kuṯayyir*) (?).

b. See line 14, note e, above.

21. *wa in taku qad sā' at-ki minnī xalīqatun*

______________- - - - [a]

fa sullī ṯiyābī min ṯiyābi-ki tansulī

- - - - - - [b]

a. See line 19, note c, above (cf. *MuIQ* 21v in Appendix B).

b. See line 14, note e, above.

22. *wa mā ḏarafat ^{c}aynā-ki illā li taḍribī*
bi sahmay-ki fī a^{c}šāri qalbin muqattalī

- - - - - - - - [a]

a. See line 12, note f, above.

23. *wa bayḍati xidrin lā yurāmu xibā' u-hā*

- [a]

- - - - - - - - - ____________ [c]

tamatta^{c}tu min lahwin bi-hā ġayra mu^{c}jalī

_____ - - - - - - - [b]

a. Cf. *MuIQ* 49 / *DIQ* 9:8, 9 = *DIQ*(Ahl) 65:8, 9 / *DNāb* 8:2b, 20:16 / *DṬar* 4:87 / *DA^{c}šā* 77:27.

b. *MuIQ* 43, 70 / *DIQ* 2:16, 17 = *DIQ*(Ahl) 52:15, 16; 3:33 = 4:41 / etc.

c. *DMuz* p. 68:5, 7.

24. *tajāwaztu aḥrāsan ilay-hā wa ma^{c}šaran*
^{c}alay-ya ḥirāṣan law yusirrūna maqtalī

________ [a]

a. See line 18, note b, above.

25. *iḏā-ma ṯ-Ṯurayyā fi s-samā'i ta^{c}arraḍat*

______________________________ a

______ b   __________ c

ta^{c}arruḍa aṯnā'i l-wišāḥi l-mufaṣṣalī

- - - - - - - - d

a. See citations in *G* pp. 42–43 (two lines, one with *ka-anna-hā* in place of *ta^{c}arraḍat*)(?).

b. See line 17, note a, above.

c. In that position: *DIQ* 69:27 / *SAH* p. 75:13.

d. See line 12, note f, above.

26. *fa ji'tu wa qad naḍat li nawmin ṯiyāba-hā*

— - - - ——— - - - - a

lada s-sitri illā libsata l-mutafaḍḍilī

—— - - - - b   - - - - - - - - - - c

a. See line 14, note a, above (cf. *MuIQ* 26v in Appendix B).

b. See line 9, comment, above.

c. See line 11, note e, above.

27. *fa qālat yamīna llāhi mā la-ka ḥīlatun*

________________ a ______________ b

________ c

wa mā-in arā ^{c}an-ka l-ġawāyata tanjalī

a. *DIQ* 2:22 = *DIQ*(Ahl) 52:22 (cf. 2:21 = 52:21: *fa qālat sabā-ka llāhu*) / *DNāb* 15:17.

b. Citation in *G* 45 (Kuṯayyir)(?).

c. Cf. *MuIQ* 42 below.

28. *fa qumtu bi-hā amšī tajurru warā'a-nā*

____________.... a

^{c}alā iṯri-nā aḏyāla mirṭin murahḥalī

________ ......b______ - - - - - - - - - - - - - - - c

- - - - - - - - - d

a. *DIQ* 30:22 = *DIQ*(Ahl) 40:22 / *DḤāt* p. 52:2 / *DḤass* 154:8.

b. *DIQ* 30:6a = *DIQ*(Ahl) 40:6a / *DNāb* 18:5a / *SAH* 1037:12.

c. *DṬar* 4:43.

d. See line 12, note f, above.

Cf. *DIQ* 30:15bv = *DIQ* 40:15bv = al-Jawharī *Siḥ* 1563b:10: *tu*^{c}*affī bi ḏayli l-mirṭi iḏ ji'tu mawdiqī*. Cf. also *MuIQ* 28v (in Appendix B).

29. *fa lammā ajaznā sāḥata l-ḥayyi wa ntaḥā*

b

bi-nā baṭnu xabtin ḏī qifāfin ^{c}*aqanqalī*

a

a. In that position: *MulQ* 62v = *Z* 61. Followed by *bi-nā/hī/hā* (*b*2): *D*^{C}*Ab* 15:15v / *DTam* 32:34 / *DŠamm* 8:50; 17:16 / etc.

b. *DIQ* 2:24 = *DIQ*(Ahl) 52:23 / *DḤass* 318:1.

30. *madadtu bi ġuṣnay dawmatin fa tamāyalat*

a b

^{c}*alay-ya haḍīma l-kašḥi rayya l-muxalxalī*

e d

a. *DIQ* 2:24 = *DIQ*(Ahl) 52:23 (cf. *MuIQ* 30v with *haṣartu*).

b. In that position: *DIQ* 4:17 = *DIQ* (Ahl) 20:18 / *SAH* p. 1040:4.

c. See line 18, note b, above.

d. See line 8, note d, above.

Cf. *DṬar* 16:2b (. . . *wa anna la-hū kašḥan iḏā qāma ahḍamā*); also *DBišr* 38:3 (*mahḍūmati l-kašḥayni rayya l-mi*^{c}*ṣami*).

31. *muhafhafatun bayḍā'u ġayru mufāḍatin*

a

b

tarā'ibu-hā maṣqūlatun ka s-sajanjalī

a. *DIQ* 2:16 = *DIQ* (Ahl) 52:15.

b. In that position: *DIQ* 3:13 = *DIQ*(Ahl) 4:7 / *DA*^{c}*šā* 40:11.

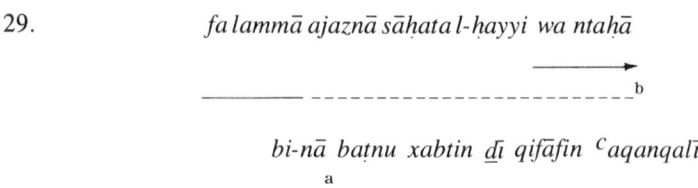

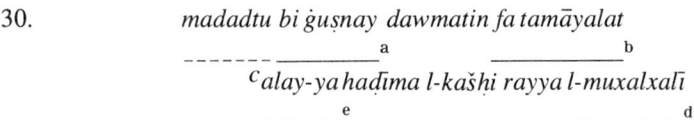

32. *taṣuddu wa tubdī ^{c}an asīlin wa tattaqī*

- - - - - - - ______________ - - - - -[a] __________[b]

bi nāẓiratin min waḥši Wajrata mutfilī

______________[c]

a. *DBišr* 16:10
b. *DIQ* 3:45 = *DIQ*(Ahl) 4:55 (*wa muttaqin*) / *DZuh* 3:11, 16:35 / *DṬar* 4:15 / *Muf* 42:19.
c. *DNāb* 5:10, App. 26:30 (both m. *basīṭ*).

33. *wa jīdin ka jīdi r-rīmi laysa bi fāḥišin*

________________________ - - - - - -[a]

______________[b] __________ - - - - - -[c]

__ - - - - __ - - - - - - - -[d]

iḏā hiya naṣṣat-hū wa lā bi mu^{c}aṭṭalī

__________[a]

- - - - - - - -[e]

a. *DIQ* 2:7b = *DIQ*(Ahl) 52:7b (w. *bi mi^{c}ṭālī*).
b. *DQays* 6:3.
c. *MuIQ* 61 / *DIQ* 2:27, 29, 31 = *DIQ*(Ahl) 52:28, 30, 32; 3:16, 55 = 4:20, 39 / etc.[4]
d. *MuIQ* 44, 50 / *DIQ* 9:13 = *DIQ*(Ahl) 65:13; *DIQ* 79:14, 100:8 / cf. *DIQ* 6:8b = *DIQ* (Ahl) 10:8b; *DNāb* 17:4 / *SAH* pp. 83:8b, 10; 1036:7 / *DŠamm* 2:19 / etc. (see pp. 57–58, above).
e. See line 12, note f, above.

Cf. *DA^{c}šā* 77:11 (. . . *wa jīdu-hā / ka jīdi ġazālin ġayra an lam yu^{c}aṭṭalī;* also *D^{c}Al* 4:3 (*wa jīdi ġazālin*).

34. *wa far^{c}in yazīnu l-matna aswada fāḥimin*

__ - - - - - - - - - - - - - - - - - -[a]

aṯītin ka qinwi n-naxlati l-muta^{c}aṯkilī

- - - - - - - - -[b]

a. *DIQ* 30:14 = *DIQ* (Ahl) 40:14; *ṬDIQ* 60:8; 79:12 / *DNāb* 1:1b, 3 / *DṬar* 4:99 / cf. *MuIQ* 55 and *DNāb* 1:22 / etc. (see p. 52, above).
b. See line 11, note e, above.

Cf. *DIQ* 3:30 = *DIQ*(Ahl) 4:35 = *D^{c}Al* 1:17 (*^{c}aṯākīlu/a qinwin*) and *DIQ* 4:6 = *DIQ*(Ahl) 20:9v (. . . *aṯītin furū^{c}u-hū / wa ^{c}ālayna qinwānan*).

35. *ġadā'iru-hū mustašzarātun ila l-ᶜulā*

a

c

taḏillu l-ᶜiqāṣu fī muṯannan wa mursalī

b b

a. *DNāb* 6:17 / cf. *DṬuf* 6:5; also *DMuz* p. 59:14–17.

b. Cf., esp., *MuIQ* 35v (*taḏillu l-madārā*): *DṬuf* 6:5a–b (*taḏillu l-madārā fī ḏafā'iri-ha l-ᶜulā / iḏā ursilat aw hākaḏā ġayra mursalī*), 14a–b (*taẓallu madāray-hā . . . ġayra mursalī*).[5]

c. See p. 58, above.

36. *wa kašḥin laṭīfin ka l-jadīli muxaḍḍarin*

c

wa sāqin ka unbūbi s-saqīyi l-muḏallalī

b c

a. *DIQ* 60:19 / *DṬar* 4:19 / *DZuh* 3:3 / etc.

b. *MuIQ* 59 / *DIQ* 3:27 = *DᶜAl* 1:16 / *DIQ* 6:13 = *DIQ* (Ahl) 10:13 / *DNāb* 1:22b / *DṬar* 4:32 / *DᶜAl* 1:4 / etc.

c. See line 12, note f, above.

37. *wa yuḍḥī fatītu l-miski fawqa firāši-hā*

a

na'ūmu ḍ-ḍuḥā lam tantaṭiq ᶜan tafaḍḍulī

b

c

a. *MuIQ* 75 / *DNāb* 8:15b / *DTam* 4:23.

b. *DṬuf* 6:8.

c. *LŠan* 9a.

Cf. corresponsional citations in *G* pp. 63–64.

38. *wa taᶜṭū bi raxṣin ġayri šaṯnin ka-anna-hū*

a

asārīᶜu Ẓabyin aw masāwīki Isḥilī

b

a. See line 4, note b, above.
b. *DIQ* App. 40:2 = *DIQ*(Ahl) App. 26:6 (*fa stākat bi a^{c}wādi Isḥilī*).

39. *tuḍī'u ẓ-ẓalāma bi l-^{c}išā'i ka-anna-hā*
[a] [b]
[c]
manāratu mumsā rāhibin mutabattilī
[d]

a. *DIQ* 79:8b.
b. See line 4, note b, above.
c. *MuIQ* 72 (!) / *DḤāt* p. 80:1 / *DIQ* 2:11 = *DIQ* (Ahl) 52:10, 5:1b = 35:1b.
d. See line 11, note e, above.

For important thematic corresponsions, see *MuIQ* 72 / *DIQ* 2:11, 19 = *DIQ* (Ahl) 52:10, 20 / *G* pp. 66–67. It is not, I think, accidental that the two themes—that of the absent beloved and that of the on-going rainstorm—are so closely linked together in IQ's ode, both through the recurrence of identical verbal formulas (note c and line 1 comment, above) and similar imagery (i.e., the monk's lamp). This circumstance gives some support to the conjecture advanced in note 2 to this Appendix.

40. *ilā miṯli-hā yarnu l-ḥalīmu ṣabābatan*
[a] [b]
iḏā-ma sbakarrat bayna dir^{c}in wa mijwalī
[c] [d]

a. *DṬar* 4:39 / cf. *Muf* 55:14 (w. *^{c}alā miṯli-hī*).
b. See line 9, note b, above.
c. See line 17, note a, above.
d. *MuIQ* 67a / *DIQ* 2:48a = *DIQ*(Ahl) 52:53a, 3:52 = 4:64 (= *D^{c}Al* 1:43) (cf. 30:34 = 40:34), 9:8 = 65:8, 35:3a = 41:3a / *DNāb* 1:15, 20:18 / *D^{c}An* app. 18:3 / *DṬar* 4:48 / *D^{c}Ab* 9:4 / etc. (cf. *G* p. 68; Reckendorf *SVA* 455; idem *AS* 195, 242–43; also, pp. 52–54, above).

41. *ka bikri l-muqānāti l-bayāḍi bi ṣufratin*
ġaḏā-hā namīru l-mā'i ġayra muḥallalī
[a]

a. See line 12, note f, above.

42. *tasallat ^{c}amāyātu r-rijāli ^{c}ani ṣ-ṣibā*

__________a

----------b

wa laysa fu'ādī ^{c}an hawā-ki bi munsalī

_____ ---------c

a. *DIQ* 63:2 / *DŠamm* 11:10 (read: *ṣibā*).
b. See line 35, note c, above.
c. See line 33, note c, above.
Cf. *MuIQ* 27v (w. *al-^{c}amāya*); also *DZuh* 14:4 (. . . *salūwa fu'ādin ġayra ḥubbi-ka mā yaslū*).

43. *alā rubba xaṣmin fī-ki alwā radadtu-hū*

_________ ------a __________c

--- ______________b

naṣīḥin ^{c}alā ta^{c}dāli-hī ġayri mu'talī

_____ ------d

a. See line 10, note c, above
b. *Muf* 113:5.
c. *DNāb* 17:7 / *DḤass* 13:23 (m. *kāmil*) / *DLab* 2:21 / *DŠamm* 2:14.
d. See line 23, note b, above.

44. *wa laylin ka mawji l-baḥri arxā sudūla-hū*

___ -------------------a_____ ---------b

^{c}alay-ya bi anwā^{c}i l-humūmi li yabtalī

________c

a. See line 33, note d, above.
b. See line 15, note d, above.
c. See line 18, note b, above.
Cf. *G* pp. 70–71.

45. *fa qultu la-hū lammā tamaṭṭā bi ṣulbi-hī*

_____________a

_____________________ ------b

wa ardafa a^{c}jāzan wa nā'a bi kalkalī

a. See line 15, note c, above.
b. *MuIQ* 51 / *DṬuf* 6:27 / *DMuz* p. 51:17 / etc.

46. *alā ayyuha l-laylu ṭ-ṭawīlu ala njalī*

———————————— a

———— b ———— c

bi ṣubḥin wa ma l-iṣbāḥu fī-ka bi amṯalī

———————— - - - - - d

- - - - - - - - e

a. *G* p. 72 = *DṬir* 1:1 (?).
b. *DṬar* 4:54.
c. *DaZub* 11:18.
d. *G* p. 72 = *DṬir* 1:1 (?).
e. Cf. line 33, note c, above (and note 4 to this Appendix).

47. *fa yā la-ka min laylin ka-anna nujūma-hū*

———————— - - - - - a ———— - - - - - - - - - b

bi kulli muġāri l-fatli šuddat bi Yaḏbulī

———— c

a. *DIQ* 13:12v (p. 406) = *DIQ*(Ahl) 30:12v / *DṬar* 13:3 / *DTam* 18:9.
b. See line 4, note b, above.
c. In rhyme position: *MuIQ* 74.

48. *ka-anna ṯ-Ṯurayyā ^{c}ulliqat fī maṣāmi-hā*

———————————— - - - - - - - - - a

———— b

bi amrāsi kattānin ilā summi jandalī

——— c ——— d

a. *K* p. 76:17–18 = al-Mubarrad *Kāmil* I 22 n. 2 = al-Marzubānī *MS* 199:10 (Ibn ^{c}Anqā' al-Fazārī).
b. See line 4, note b, above.
c. Cf. *DBišr* 40:25 (. . . *bi jandali ṣ-ṣummi*—*b*11).
d. In rhyme position: *MuIQ* 77.

49. *wa qirbati aqwāmin ja^{c}altu ^{c}iṣāma-hā*

—— - a

^{c}alā kāhilin min-nī ḏalūlin muraḥḥalī

- - - - - - - - - b

a. See line 23, note a, above.
b. See line 12, note f, above.

50. *wa wādin ka jawfi l-^{c}ayri qafrin qaṭa^{c}tu-hū*

— ----- ——————[a]

— ----------------- ——————[b]

— -----——-----------[c]

bi-hi ḏ-ḏi'bu ya^{c}wī ka l-xalī^{c}i l-mu^{c}ayyalī

-------------[d]

a. *DIQ* 9:13 = *DIQ*(Ahl) 65:13 = *MuIQ* 50v (w. *wa xarqin*).
b. *DLab* 12:4 / *LŠan* 65 (w. *wa xarqin*).
c. See line 33, note d, above.
d. See line 12, note f, above.
Cf. *DA^{c}šā* 11:8, 33:25 (*wa xarqin maxūfin qad qaṭa^{c}tu bi jasratin*).

51. *fa qultu la-hū lammā ^{c}awā inna ša'na-nā*

—————— ----[a]

——————[b]

qalīlu l-ġinā in kunta lammā tamawwalī

—— ---------[c]

a. See line 45, note b, above.
b. See line 15, note c, above.
c. See line 17, note b, above.

52. *kilā-nā iḏā-mā nāla šay'an afāta-hū*

wa man yaḥtariṯ ḥarṯī wa ḥarṯa-ka yuhzalī

--- —— ----------------------------[a]

a. For analogues to the apothegmatic syntax of this hemistich, cf. esp. *DZuh* 16:21, 50–59 / etc.

53. *wa qad aġtadī wa ṭ-ṭayru fī wukunāti-hā*

——————————→

——————————→

——————————[c]

——————[d]

bi munjaridin qaydi l-awābidi haykalī

______________________________ a

______________ b

a. *DIQ* 3:20a + 21a = *DIQ*(Ahl) app. 2:1a + 2a / *D*^{c}*Al* 1:19a + 20a.
b. *DIQ* 5:14 = *DIQ*(Ahl) 35:15.
c. *DIQ* 2:42 = *DIQ*(Ahl) 52:47.
d. *DIQ* 3:20v (p. 384:5) = *DIQ*(Ahl) 4:23; 29:20 = 19:19 (m. *mutaqārib*); 30:17 = 40:17 (w. *haykalin*); 34:3 = 39:3 / *D*^{c}*Ab* 8:7, 9, / etc.
Cf. also *G* pp. 75–77.

54. *mikarrin mifarrin muqbilin mudbirin ma*^{c}*an*

____ a

\- - - - - - - - - - - - - - ___________________________ b

______ c

ka julmūdi ṣaxrin ḥaṭṭa-hu s-saylu min ^{c}*alī*

________ d

a. *DIQ* 8:11 = *DIQ*(Ahl) 63:11v.
b. *DIQ* 8:11v (p. 399:12) = *DIQ*(Ahl) 63:11.
c. In that position: *MuIQ* 14.
d. *SAH* p. 535:3 / *DḤass* 89:1 (*min* ^{c}*alū*).

55. *kumaytin yazillu l-libdu* ^{c}*an ḥāli matni-hī*

___________________________ - - - - - - - - - - - ►

\- - - - - - - ______ - - - - - - ___ - - - - - - - - - - - b

________ c ____________ d

ka-mā zallati ṣ-ṣafwā'u bi l-mutanazzili

___________ a - - - - - - - - - - e

a. *A* p. 84:10 = *DAws* 30:19v.
b. *D*^{c}*Al* 10:2 / *DBišr* 16:2 / *DIQ* p. 394:3 = *DIQ*(Ahl) 20:60 / cf. *MuIQ* 58.
c. Very frequently in this position (cf. *G* p. 79): *MuIQ* 61v (from *G* p. 85) / *DIQ* 2:44b = *DIQ*(Ahl) 52:49b / *DṬar* 4:57b / *D*^{c}*Al* 1:22 / etc.
d. *DIQ* 30:24 = *DIQ*(Ahl) 40:24.
e. See line 11, note e, above.

56. *^{c}ala d̲-d̲abli jayyāšun ka-anna htizāma-hū*

—— - - - - - - ——————————[a]

id̲ā jāša fī-hi ḥamyu-hū ġalyu mirjalī

a. *MulQ* 56v (w. *^{c}ala ḍ-ḍumri*) = *DIQ* 3:22 = *DIQ*(Ahl) 4:25v.

57. *misaḥḥin id̲ā-ma s-sābiḥātu ^{c}ala l-wanā*

————[a] - - - - - - - - - -[b]

at̲arna l-ġubāra bi l-kadīdi l-murakkalī

- - - - - - - - -[c]

a. In that position: *DIQ* 8:8b = *DIQ*(Ahl) 63:8b / *Aṣm* 9:9 (m. *hazaj*).
b. See line 35, note c, above.
c. See line 12, note f, above.

58. *yazillu l-ġulāmu l-xiffu ^{c}an ṣahawāti-hī*

——— - - - - - - - - - - - - —— - - - - - - - - - -[a]

————————[b]

wa yulwī bi at̲wābi l-^{c}anīfi l-mut̲aqqalī

—————— ....[c] - - - - - - - - -[d]

a. *DNāb* 8:15 / *DTam* 6:12 / cf. *MuIQ* 55.
b. *DIQ* 30:36 (*a*13) = *DIQ* (Ahl) 40:36.
c. *DZuh* 3:10 / *DA^{c}šā* 77:23 (w. other meters: 13:26, 18:56, etc.).
d. See line 12, note f, above.

59. *darīrin ka xud̲rūfi l-walīdi amarra-hū*

——————————[a]

tatābu^{c}u kaffay-hi bi xayṭin muwaṣṣalī

- - - - - - - - -[b]

a. *DIQ* 3:40b = *DIQ* (Ahl) 4:48b (w. *yamurru—b*3) / *DAws* 29:3v = Ibn al-Kalbī *AX* 78:1 / *DṬuf* 1:18b.
b. See line 12, note f, above.
Cf. *G* p. 83.

60. *la-hū iṭilā ẓabyin wa sāqā na*^{c}*āmatin*

wa irxā'u sirḥānin wa taqrību tatfulī

a. *DIQ* 3:24 = *DIQ*(Ahl) 4:27.
b. *DIQ* 5:15 = *DIQ*(Ahl) 35:16.
c. *DIQ* 60:14.

On the formulation of descriptions through the use of an introductory *la-hu* phrase, see von Grunebaum *CFD* 331–32; Jacobi *SPAQ* 175.

61. *ḍalī*^{c}*in iḏa stadbarta-hū sadda farja-hū*

bi ḍāfin fuwayqa l-arḍi laysa bi a^{c}*zalī*

a. *DIQ* 3:55v (see p. 389:14) = *DIQ* (Ahl) 4:39; 60:13.
b. *DḤam alif*:21 (cf. *alif*:60: *fa lamma sama stadbarna-hū*).
c. *DAws* 32:6a.
d. See line 33, note c, above.

Cf., in connection with *MuIQ* 61v (*kumaytin iḏā* . . .), line 55, note c, above.

62. *ka-anna sarāta-hu lada l-bayti qā'iman*

madāku ^{c}*arūsin aw ṣalāyatu ḥanẓalī*

a. *DIQ* 31:15 = *DIQ*(Ahl) 34:15; 3:22 = 4:25v / *DMut* 14:4 (*a*14) / cf. *G* p. 87.
b. See line 4, note b, above.
c. See line 4, note e and comment, above.

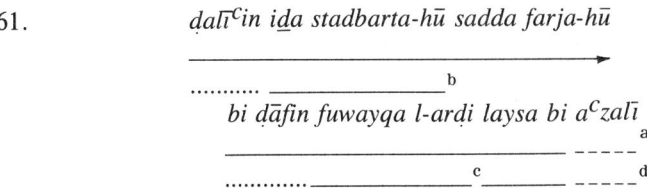

63. *ka-anna dimā'a l-hādiyāti bi naḥri-hī*

b c

d

^{c}uṣāratu ḥinnā'in bi šaybin murajjalī

a

e f

a. *DIQ* 3:54 = *DIQ*(Ahl) 4:67; 30:37 = 40:37.
b. See line 4, note b, above.
c. *DLab* 35:29b.
d. In that position: *MuIQ* 66 / *DŠamm* 16:16b.
e. *DIQ* 63:5.
f. See line 12, note f, above.

64. *fa ^{c}anna la-nā sirbun ka-anna ni^{c}āja-hū*

a

^{c}adārā Dawārin fī mulā'in mudayyalī

b

c

d

a. *DḤuṭ* 54:3 (*a*6) / cf. *DḤam bā'*:13; *DŠamm* 2:30 / *DLab* 35:41 (*a*6).
b. *LŠan* 67.
c. *DIQ* 3:35 = *DIQ*(Ahl) 4:44 = *D^{c}Al* 1:32 (w. *ka mašyi l-^{c}adāra* . . .) / *DIQ* p. 386:13 = *DIQ* (Ahl) 4:43 / cf. *J* 3 (. . . *kasā-ha ṣ-ṣabā saḥqa l-mulā'i l-mudayyalī*).
d. See line 12, note f, above.

65. *fa adbarna ka l-jaz^{c}i l-mufaṣṣali bayna-hū*

bi jīdi mu^{c}ammin fī l-^{c}ašīrati muxwalī

a

a. *DIQ* 30:27 = *DIQ*(Ahl) 40:27.

66. *fa alḥaqa-hū bi l-hādiyāti wa dūna-hū*

a

jawāḥiru-hā fī ṣarratin lam tazayyalī

b

a. See line 63, note d, above.
b. See line 17, note b, above.

67. *fa ^{c}ādā ^{c}idā'an bayna ṯawrin wa na^{c}jatin*

——————————————— a

——— - - - - - - - - - - - - - - - b

dirākan wa lam yunḍaḥ bi mā'in fa yuġsalī

- - - - - - ——————————— - - - - - - c

a. *DIQ* 2:48 = *DIQ* (Ahl) 52:53v; 3:43 = 4:53v / *D^{c}Al* 1:39.
b. See line 40, note d, above.
c. *DIQ* 30:29 = *DIQ* (Ahl) 40:29.

68. *fa ẓalla ṭuhātu l-laḥmi min bayni munḍijin*

———— a.

ṣafīfa šiwā'in aw qadīrin mu^{c}ajjalī

- - - - - - - - b

a. On forms of *ẓalla* as a line-opening formula, see line 12 and note a, above.
b. See line 12, note f, above.

Cf. also *DIQ* 30:33 = *DIQ* (Ahl) 40:33 (*wa ẓalla ṣiḥābī yaštawūna bi na^{c}matin / yaṣuffūna ġāran bi l-lakīki l-muwaššaqī*) and *DṬar* 9:5a (*tabītu imā'u l-ḥayyi taṭhā qudūra-nā*).

69. *wa ruḥnā yakādu ṭ-ṭarfu yaqṣuru dūna-hū*

———— a - - - - - - - - - - - - - ►

matā-mā taraqqa l-^{c}aynu fī-hi tasahhalī

.... - - - - - - - ———— b - - - - - - - - c

a. *DIQ* 30:34, 35 = *DIQ* (Ahl) 40:34, 35 / *D^{c}Al* 1:43.
b. *DIQ* 30:35 = *DIQ* (Ahl) 40:35 (*wa ruḥnā bi ka bni l-mā'i yajnabu wasṭa-nā / taṣawwabu fī-hi l-^{c}aynu ṭawran wa tartaqī*).
c. See line 14, note 3, above.

Cf., in connection with *MuIQ* 69v = *DIQ* 1:64 (*wa ruḥnā wa rāḥa ṭ-ṭirfu yanfuḍu ra'sa-hū*), the following formulaic corresponsions: *DIQ* 3:53 = *DIQ* (Ahl) 4:65v / *A* p. 98:10 = *Aṣm* 15:26 / *Muf* 47:16 / cf. *DIQ* (Ahl) 4:65 and *DTam* 32:33 and *D^{c}Al* 1:44 (w. *yanġuḍu ra'sa-hū*); also *DIQ* 30:19 = *DIQ* (Ahl) 40:19 (w. *yarfa^{c}u ra'sa-hū*).

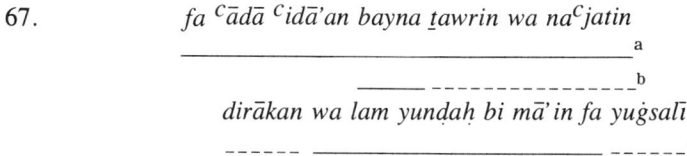

70. *fa bāta ^{c}alay-hi sarju-hū wa lijāmu-hū*

________________ - - - - - - - - - - - - - - - - - -[a]

________________[b]

wa bāta bi ^{c}aynī qā'iman ġayra mursalī

______ - - - - - -[c]

a. *Muf* 28:7.
b. *DIQ* 12:6 = *DIQ*(Ahl) 31:6 / *DA^{c}šā* 33:52b.
c. See line 23, note b, above.

71. *a ṣāḥi tarā barqan urī-ka wamīḍa-hū*

____[a]

____________________[b]

.... ____________________________[c]

ka lam^{c}i l-yadayni fī ḥabīyin mukallalī

- - - - - - - -[d]

a. *DṬuf* 7:13.
b. *DIQ* 28:1 = *DIQ*(Ahl) 22:1 (w. *MuIQ* 71v: *a Ḥāri*; m. *wāfir*); 54:12 (m. *mutaqārib*).
c. W. *MuIQ* 71v (*a^{c}in-nī ^{c}alā barqin . . .*): *DIQ* 5:1 = *DIQ*(Ahl) 35:1 / Yāqūt *MB* III 549:4 (as-Samharī al-Laṣṣ).
d. See line 12, note f, above.
Cf. for similar thematic treatments *G* pp. 96–98.

72. *yuḍī'u sanā-hu aw maṣābīḥu rāhibin*

________________[a]

_______ - - - - - - -[b]

amāla s-salīṭa bi ḏ-ḏubāli l-mufattalī

____[c]

_____________[d]

- - - - - - - -[e]

a. *DIQ* 54:13 (m. *mutaqārib*); 58:1b = *DIQ*(Ahl) 43:1b / *DṬuf* 7:13b / *DA^{c}šā* 28:24b / *SAH* p. 129:19.
b. See line 39, note c, above.
c. *DAws* 35:9 / cf. citations in *G* p. 99.
d. *MuIQ* 12.
e. See line 12, note f, above.

Cf. line 39, comment; also *G* pp. 98–99.

73. *qa^{c}adtu la-hū wa ṣuḥbatī bayna Ḍārijin*

wa bayna l-^{c}Uḏayfi bu^{c}da-mā muta'ammalī

a. *DIQ* 5:4 = *DIQ*(Ahl) 35:4.
b. *DMuz* p. 24:20.
c. *Muf* 12:36.
d. See line 11, note e, above.

On the construction *bayna . . . wa bayna*, see Reckendorf *SVA* 239, *AS* 242; cf., e.g., *DḤass* 84:1–2.

74. *^{c}alā Qaṭanan bi š-šaymi aymanu ṣawbi-hī*

wa aysaru-hū ^{c}ala s-Sitāri fa Yaḏbuli

a. W. *MuIQ* 74v (*^{c}alā Qaṭanin*—*^{c}alā* as preposition rather than verb): *DMuz* 49:10b.
b. *DṬuf* 7:14.
c. See line 1, note f and comment, above.
d. In rhyme position: *MuIQ* 47.

Cf., as verbal formulas in connection with *MuIQ* 74v (. . . *^{c}ala n-Nibāji wa Ṯaytalī*), Yāqūt *MB* I 942:14 (Rabī^{c}a b. Ẓarīf al-^{c}Anbarī), IV 736:5a (Muḥriz aḍ-Ḍabbī).

75. *fa adḥā yasuḥḥu l-mā'u ḥawla Kutayfatin*

yakubbu ^{c}ala l-aḏqāni dawḥa l-kanahbulī

a. W. *MuIQ* 75v (*^{c}an/min kulli fīqatin*—a14): *DIQ* 5:7 (cf. p. 395:8–9) = *DIQ*(Ahl) 35:8 / cf. citation in *G* p. 101:23.
b. *G* p. 101:31–32.

76. *wa marra ᶜala l-Qanāni min nafayāni-hī*
fa anzala min-hu l-ᶜuṣma min kulli manzilī
_______________a
_______b

a. Also w. *MuIQ* 76v (*fī kulli manzilī*): *DNāb* 20:22a / *DZuh* 16:13a / *DṬuf* 1:70a / *Muf* 114:9a / *DAᶜšā* 33:34a.
b. In rhyme position: *MuIQ* 1a.

Cf., in connection with *MuIQ* 76v = *DIQ* 1:77 (*wa alqā bi Busyānin maᶜal-layli barka-hū*), *MuIQ* 80. Cf. also *G* pp. 102–3.

77. *wa Taymā'a lam yatruk bi-hā jiḏᶜa naxlatin*
___________a
wa lā ujuman illā mašīdan bi jandalī
_______b

a. *DŠamm* 5:2b / Yāqūt *MB* I 908:6b.
b. In rhyme position: *MuIQ* 48.

78. *ka-anna Ṯabīran fī ᶜarānīni wabli-hī*
_______a
kabīru unāsin fī bijādin muzammalī
_________ - - - - - - - - - -b
- - - - - - - - - -c

a. See line 4, note b, above.
b. *DṬar* (Sel) app. 11:2.
c. See line 12, note f, above.

79. *ka-anna ḏurā ra'si l-Mujaymiri ġudwatan*
_______a _________b
mina s-sayli wa l-ġuṯṯā'i fulkatu miġzalī

a. See line 12, note f, above.
b. In that position: *DIQ* 2:46v = *DIQ*(Ahl) 52:51 / *DṬar* 4:3 = *DAᶜšā* 10:27; 30:2; 72:2 / etc.

80. *wa alqā bi ṣaḥrā'i l-Ġabīṭi ba^{c}ā^{c}a-hū*

a

b c

d

nuzūla l-yamānı ḏi l-^{c}iyābi l-muḥammalī

e

a. Citation in *G* p. 107:22–23, 25 (Ibn Muqbil?) / *DTam* 4:25.
b. *MuIQ* 76v= *DIQ* 1:77 / *DŠamm* 8:44 / cf. Nöldeke *FM* I 67.
c. See line 14, note b, above.
d. *DLab* 21:11 (w. *al-Ġabīṭi*); 35:66 / *DŠamm* 5:31.
e. See line 12, note f, above.

Cf. *G* pp. 107–8, on the anomalous concord of rhyme attributives in lines 12, 29 (?), 64, 72, and 80. This phenomenon, in essence a form of *iqwā*, was noted by Reckendorf (*AS* 59 and n. 2). It obviously results from the rhyme position of the attributive in question and cannot be treated as a distinct syntactic possibility; cf. p. 103, above. (In this verse the anomaly disappears is *muḥammal* is construed as an attribute of *yamānī* rather than of ^{c}*iyāb*.)

81. *ka-anna makākīya l-jiwā'i ġudayyatan*

a b

ṣubiḥna sulāfan min raḥīqin mufalfalī

c

d

e

a. See line 4, note b, above.
b. In that position: *MuIQ* 82v = *DIQ* 1:75 / *DIQ* 12:8 = *DIQ*(Ahl) 31:8 / *Muf* 83:4 / *DA^{c}šā* 55:22 / *DBišr* 21:15 / etc.
c. *DLab* 2:12.
d. In connection with *MuIQ* 81v (. . . *raḥīqin musalsalī*): *SAH* p. 1069:7 (m. *kāmil: mina r-raḥīqi s-salsalī*) / *DḤass* 13:13 (m. *kāmil: bi r-raḥīqi s-salsalī*).
e. Cf. *MuIQ* 3 (*fulfulī*).

82. *ka-anna s-sibā^{c}a fī-hi ġarqā ^{c}ašīyatan*

a b

bi arjā'i-hi l-quṣwā anābīšu ^{c}unṣalī

a. See line 4, note b, above.
b. In that position: *DIQ* 3:52 = *DIQ*(Ahl) 2:64; 25:2 = 16:2; 31:23 = 24:33 / *Muf* 85:3; 119:14 = D^cAl 2:18 / etc.

1. I owe this insight to discussions with Professor Michael Nagler and to observations included in his doctoral dissertation *FMHE*. In the Near Eastern tradition, one might draw important parallels from information in a study like that of A. L. Oppenheim, "The Eyes of the Lord," *JAOS* 88 (1968): 173–80 (esp. 179–80).

2. Cf., e.g., the possible cultic interrelationships suggested by the inconography of "The Rain-goddess as Represented in Early Mesopotamia," article by E. Van Buren, in *Analecta biblica* 12 (1959): 343–55.

3. The syntactical ramifications of the *ka-anna* formula require, for the sake of completeness, a separate analysis that cannot be undertaken here.

4. The negative formula (*laysa* or *mā* + *bī* + substantive or attributive) is quite common in classical poetry. It often includes a comparative adjective + *min* (von Grunebaum *CFD* 331), frequently involving enjambement (Bloch *KWAV* 221 n. 15, example f). I have not seen the study by I. Krachkovsky, "Formula otritstate nogo sraveniya v drevrearabskoe poezii," *Zapiski Instituta vostokovedeniya akademii nauk SSSR* 7 (1939): 176–84 (ref. in Pearson *IIsl* §23399).

5. Gandz (*G* p. 62) holds the variant *al-madārā/ī* to be "certainly false," both because it "improves the meter" and because it is not the *lectio difficilior*. However, its presence in the formulaic repertoire of Ṭufayl al-Ganawī, a predecessor and earlier master of the "school" to which IQ belonged (Krenkow *DṬuf* p. xvi), makes its "genuineness" (if we wish to use that term) quite likely. On the fallacy of the principle of *lectio difficilior*, see, e.g., E. Hirsch, Jr., *Validity in Interpretation*, p. 189 n. 13.

*

Appendix B

Table of Variations to Ibn Al-Anbāri's Recension of the *Mu*ᶜ*allaqa* of Imra'alqays

The following table has been prepared on the basis of the sources outlined in the study above (chap. 4, § A.2.a). The abbreviations employed here are explained in the Bibliography, section III, with the addition of some that will be noted when they occur. Where the scholiast has named the source of his variant, I have included this information; otherwise, variants are cited anonymously in the scholia. The abbreviations used by Gandz (= *G*) are clarified on pp. 6–10 of his study.

1. *wa Ḥawmalī*: *D*1 / *K*1v (Aṣmaᶜi) / *B*1v (Aṣm) / *A*1v (Aṣm) / *N*1v (Aṣm); *wa manzilī* (w. *yā'* finally): *G*1 (Sīb).
2. *nasajat-hu:* *A*2v / *T*2v; *fī l-miqrāti* (w. *fī*): *G*2 (Bāqir).
3. Omitted: *S* / K^1 / N^1 / *W*; *qulquli:* *B*3v; *ba*ᶜ*ara ṣ-ṣīrāni:* *J*4.
4. Omitted: *S* / K^1 / N^1 / *W*: *takammašū:* *B*4v.
5. *taḥammali:* *J*5 / *G*3 (from several sources).
6. ᶜ*abratun in safaḥtu-hā:* *A*6v / *D*6 / *B*6 / *N*4v (from ms).
7. *ka dīni-ka:* *A*7v (Abū ᶜUbayda) / *D*7 / *B*7v / *N*5v / *K*5v / *T*7v (a. ᶜUb) / *Y*; *wa jārāti-hā:* *G*5 (Bāqir).
8. *id̲a ltafatat naḥwī tad̲awwa*ᶜ*a rīḥu-hā:* *A*8v / *D*29 / *B*29 / *Y; bi rayya s-safarjali:* *J*10v.

9. *wa fāḍat: Y*.
10. *sāliḥin la-ka min-humā: S*8 / *N*8 / *T*10v / *Ag*11[2]; *ṣāliḥin la-ka min-humū: B*9v / *T*10v / N8v; *kāna min-hunna ṣāliḥin: Z* 10v; *lī mina l-bīḍi ṣāliḥin: J*12; *yawman: X* / *B*9v; *lā siyamā: B*9v / *N*8v (Axfaš).
11. *wa-yawmin: N*9; *min raḥli-hā: D*10 / *B*10 / *K*9 / *N*9 / *N*9v / *J*14 / *Z*11v / *X* / *Y* / *Ag*12; *fa yā* ᶜ*ajaban: D*10 / *B*10 / *K*9 / *Z*11 / *Z*11v / *X* / *Y; fa yā* ᶜ*ajabī: S*9; *fa wā* ᶜ*ajabī: Ag*12; *min kūri-hā: Z*11.
12. *yaẓallu: D*11.
13. *yawma* ᶜ*Unayzatin: A*13v (b. Ḥabīb) / *B*12v / *K*11v / *T*13v / *G*11 (see *G* p. 27).
14. *ya mra'a llāhi: B* p. 3:6–7 (Aṣm) / *G*12 (see *G* p. 28).
15. *al-mu*ᶜ*allali: B*14v / *K*13v / *N*13v (*K*) / *Z*15v / *T*15v (*K*) / *W; wa lā tub*ᶜ*idī-nā: Ag*15 / *G*13 (several) / *wa lā tamna*ᶜ*ī-nā: G*13 (Šarīšī).
16. *fa miṯla-ki . . . wa murḍi*ᶜ*an: D*15[3] / *B*15v / *Z*16v; *muġyali: D*15 / *A*16v (Aṣm, a. ᶜUb) / *B*15 / *N*14v / *Z*16v / *T*16v / *J*23v / *Y; fa miṯli-ki bikran: A*16v; *wa miṯli-ki bikran . . . wa ṯayyiban: N*14v (Sībawayh) / *T*16v (Sīb).
17. *(i) nḥarafat la-hu: A*17v (a. ᶜUb) / *D*16 / *B*16: *wa šiqqun* ᶜ*inda-nā lam: A*17v (a. ᶜUb) / *D*16 / *B*16v / *K*16v; *min ḥubbi-hā: A*17v / *B*16v / *T*17v; *wa naḥwī šiqqu-hā: K*15v; *bi ṯinyin wa taḥtī ṯinyu-hā: D* p. 369:10–11 (to *D*16; b. Naḥḥās).
18. *wa yawmin: A*18v; *tuḥallali: G*16 (Bāqir); *ḥilfatan: G*16 (IA).
19. *a Fāṭima abqī: A*19v (a. ᶜAmr aš-Šaybanī); *hajrī: A*19v; *qatlī: A*19v (a. ᶜUb) / *N*17v (a. ᶜUb) / *Z*19v (a. ᶜUb); *ṣarmī: D*18 / *B*18 / *K*17v / *Z*19 / *T*19 / *W* / *X* / *Y*.[4]
20. (No recorded variants.)
21. *wa in kunti: A*21v / *D*19 / *B*19 / *K*18 / *W* / *X* / *Y* / *Ag* 4; *fa in taku: S*19 / *J*29; *tansili: A*21v[5]; *tansali* (w. *yā'*): *Z*21v.
22. *li taqdaḥī: D*21[6] / *B*21v[7]; *li taršuqī: G*20 (*Muḥīṭ*).
23. *ġayri: Z*23v; *ma yurāmu: N*21[8]; *wa bayḍati xuldin . . .* ᶜ*an lahwin: G*21 (*Ḫiz*).
24. *taxaṭṭaytu abwāban: A*24v / *K*22v / *T*24v; *ahwālan ilay-hā: K*22; *wa ahwāla ma*ᶜ*šarin: D*23 / *D*23v / *B*23 / *Y; taxaṭṭaytu ahwālan ilay-hā: W;* ᶜ*alay-ya ḥirāṣin: D*23 / *Y;* ᶜ*alay-ya ḥirāsan (ḥirāsin): G*22 (*Ag*, *Ḫiz* et al.); *yuširrūna: A*24v / *S*22 / *D*23[9] / *B*23v / *N*22v / *K*22v / *Z*24v / *T*24 / *Y*.
25. (No recorded variants.)
26. *wa qad alqat: A*26v[10]; *naḍḍat* (?): *N*24 / *T*26 / *Z*26; *taqūlu wa qad: G*24 (Mufaḍḍal).

27. *yamīnu llāhi:* *B*26v / *K*25v / *N*25v / *T*27v; *al-^{c}amāyata:* *A*27v (Aṣm) / *D*26 / *B*26 / *N*25v (Aṣm) / *T*27v / *Z*27v.

28. *xarajtu bi-hā:* *A*28v / *D*27 / *B*27 / *J*36 / *Z*28; *namšī:* *K*26v; *tamšī:* *D*27 / *B*27; *^{c}alā aṯaray-nā ḏayla mirṭin:* *D*27 / *B*27[11] / *K*26v˙/ *J*36 / *Z*28 / *Y;* *^{c}alā aṯaray-nā nīra mirṭin:* *A*28v / *B*27v / *K*26 / *T*28v / *Z*28v; *^{c}alā aṯri-hā:* *S*26[12]; *aḏyāla nīrin:* *A*28v (a. ^{c}Amr, probably aš-Šaybani); *murajjali:* *S*26.[13]

29. *wa ntaḥat:* *J*37; *bi-nā ṯinyu ramlin:* *A*29v; *baṭnu ḥiqfin:* *B*28 / *N*27v; *ḥiqfin ḏī rukāmin:* *A*29v / *D*28 / *T*29v; *baṭnu janbin:* *G*27 (Ṭab); *ḏī ḥiqāfin:* *Z*29.

30. *iḏā qultu hātī nawwilī-nī:* *A*30v / *D*30 / *B*30 / *K*28 / *N*28 / *Z*30v / *W* / *X;* *haṣartu bi fawday ra'si-hā:* *A*30v (a. ^{c}Ub)[14] / *S*28 / *K*28v / *N*28v / *B*30v (a. ^{c}Ub)[15] / *J*38 / *Z*30 / *T*30v / *Y;* *bi fawday ra'si-hā:* *A*30v; *haṣartu bi ġuṣnay dawḥatin:* *Bāq*28[16]; *haṣartu:* *Z*30v.

31. *bi s-sajanjalī:* *A*31v (a. ^{c}Ub) / *B*31v (a. ^{c}Ub) / *N*29v (a. ^{c}Ub) / *J*39v / *T*31v (a. ^{c}Ub).

32. *^{c}an šatītin:* *A*32v / *B*32v / *K*30 / *N*30 / *T*32v / *W*.

33. *ar-ri'mi:* *D*34 / *S*31 / *K*31 / *N*31 / *T*33 / *Z*34; *naḍḍat-hu:* *G*31 (*Ḫiz*).

34. *yuġašši l-matna:* *D*35 / *B*34; *aṯītin:* *B*34 (probably a typographical error).

35. *taḍillu l-maḍārā:* *A*35v / *D*36 / *B*35 / *K*33v[17] / *N*33v / *J*43 / *T*35v; *yaḍillu:* *A*35v (Aḥmad b. ^{c}Ubayd[18]) / *K*33v (Bundār[19]) / *N*33v (*K*, Bundār); *mustašzirātun:* *A*35v / *B*35v / *K*33v (b. al-A^{c}rābī) / *N*33v (b. A^{c}r) / *T*35v (b. A^{c}r) / *Z*36v / *Y*v; *ġadā'iru-hā:* *Z*36.

36. (No recorded variants.)

37. *wa tuḍḥī;* *D*40 / *B*37 (a. Ja^{c}far?[20]) / *S*35 / *Z*38 / *W;* *na'ūma ḍ-ḍuḥā:* *B*37v / *K*35 / *N*35 / *T*37; *fa tuḍḥī:* *X*.

38. *asārī^{c}u ramlin:* *G*36 (Ḥalabī).

39. *bi l-^{c}ašīyi:*[21]

40. *dir^{c}in wa mijwabī:* *G*38 (*LA*, *Tāğ*).

41. [22]*ka bikrin muqānāti(-u) l-bayāḍi:* *A*41v (Sijistānī[23]) / *D*32 / *B*41; *ka bikri l-muqānāti bayāḍa(-u):* *K*39 / *N*39 / *T*41 (*K*) / *Z*32v; *muḥallilī:* *A*41v / *K*39v / *N*39v (*K*); *ġayru(-i):* *D*32v / *Z*32; *ġayru l-muḥallali:* *Z*32.

42. *wa laysa ṣibā-ya:* *D*42 / *B*42; *^{c}an ṣibā-hu:* *A*42v / *K*40v / *N*40v / *T*42v; *hawā-hā:* *D*42 / *B*42 / *A*42v / *S*40 / *N*40 / *J*50; *hawā-hu:* *K*40 / *T*42.

43. *bi naṣḥin ^{c}alā . . . ġayri mu'milī:* *G*41 (Bāqir); *bi naṣḥin ^{c}ala t-ta^{c}ḏālatin ġayri mu'malī:* *G*41 (Bāqir).

44. *murxin sudūla-hu:* *K*42 / *T*44 / *Z*44.

45. *bi jawzi-hi*[24]: *A*45v (Aṣm) / *D*45 / *B*45 / *K*43v / *N*43v (Aṣm) / *J*53 / *T*45v (Aṣm).
46. *wa in kunta qad azma^{c}ta d̲ālika fa f^{c}al(i): A*46v (b. Ḥabīb) / *K*44v / *N*44v (b. Ḥabib); *min-ka: K*44v / *N*44v / *J*54 / *T*46v / *Z*46.
47. *bi amrāsi kattānan ilā ṣummi jandali*[25]: *A47v* / *Z*47.
48. Omitted: *Z; ka-anna nujūman: A*48v / *K*56[26] / *T*48v / *Y*[26]; *fī masābi-hā: J*56 (typographical error ?); ^{c}*alā summi: B*48 / *G*46v (*LA*, *Tāǧ*); *fī niẓāmi-hā bi amri bni Nu^{c}māna ilā ṣummi Ṣandali* (?): *G*46 (Cheikho, Ḥalabī).
49. Omitted: *D* / *B* / *S* / *K* / *N* / *Y*.[27]
50. Omitted: *D* / *B* / *S* / *K* / *N* / *Y; wa xarqin: A*50v.
51. Omitted: *D* / *B* / *S* / *K* / *N* / *Y; ṭawīlu l-ġinā: A*51v / T51v / *Z*50v; *inna T̲ābitan: W*.[28]
52. Omitted: *D* / *B* / *S* / *K* / *N* / *Y*.
53. *fī wukarāti-hā: A*52v / *B*49 / *K*46 / *N*47 / *T*53v / *W*.
54. *mikarrin mumirrin: K*47v.[29]
55. *yuzillu l-libda: K*48 / *N*49 / *J*63; ^{c}*an ḥād̲i matni-hī: A*55v / *J*63v / *T*55v; *bi l-mutana^{cc}ili: J*63v.
56. ^{c}*ala l-^{c}aqbi jayyāšin(-un* ?): *A*56v (Aṣm, a. ^{c}Ub) / *D*53 / *B*52 / *K*49v (?) / *N*50v / *J*64 / *T*56v; ^{c}*ala ḍ-ḍumri: A*56v / *T*56v; ^{c}*ala d-da'li: A*56v (b. A^{c}r).
57. *ġubāran: D*52 / *B*53 / *S*51 / *N*54v[30] / *J*65 / *X; bi l-kat̲ībi s-samaw'ali: A*57v (a. ^{c}Ub); *bi l-kadīdi s-samawwali: T*57v / *D* p. 373:2 (b. Naḥḥās from a. ^{c}Ub); *al-muraḥḥali: Z*56v.
58. *yuzillu l-ġulāma l-xiffa: A*58v / *S*52 / *K*51v[31] / *N*52v / *J*66 / *T*58v / *Z*57v / *W* / *Y; yuṭīru l-ġulāma l-xiffa: A*58v (Aṣm) / *D*54 / *B*54 / *N*52v (Aṣm) / *T*52v (Aṣm) / *Z*57v / *X; al-xaff: A*58v (a. ^{c}Ub) / *D* p. 373:6 (b.Naḥḥas from a. ^{c}Ub).
59. *taqallubu kaffay-hi: A*59v / *D*55 / *B*55 / *T*59v; *yuqallibu: G*53 (several).
60. *ayṭalā ẓabyin: A*60v / *D*56 / *B*56 / *S*54 / *K*53 / *N*53 / *J*68 / *T*60 / *Z*59 / *W* / *X* / *Y; tanfuli: S*54; *tunfali: A*60v / *B*56v; *wa ġāratu sirḥānin wa taqrību tuffali: G*54 (*LA*, *Tāǧ*).
61. *wa anta id̲ā: D*66 / *B*66; *kumaytin id̲ā: G*55 (*Ḥiz*).
62. *ka-anna ^{c}ala l-kitfayni min-hu id̲a ntaḥā: A*62v / *D*57 / *B*57 / *T*62v / *Y; ka-anna ^{c}ala l-matnayni min-hu id̲a ntaḥā: N*56v / *Z*61 / *X; wa ka-anna*[32]: *N*56v (*K?*) / *W; ṣarāyata(-u) ḥanẓali: A*62v (Aṣm) / *D*57 / *B*57v / *N*56v (Aṣm) / *T*62v (Aṣm); *ṣirāya: A*62v (a. ^{c}Ub) / *B*57v (a. ^{c}Ub) / *T*62v (a. ^{c}Ub); *ṣarāba: G*56 (*LA*, *Tāǧ*).[33]

63. *wa ka-anna: N*37v (*K* ?) / *W*.

64. *fī l-mulāʾi l-muḏayyali: D*59 / *B*59 / *Y*.

65. *ka l-jiz^{c}i: A*65v (a. ^{c}Ub) / *N*59v (a. ^{c}Ub) / *T*65v (a. ^{c}Ub).

66. *fa alḥaqa-nā: A*66v / *D*61 / *B*61 / *S*60 / *J*73 / *Z*65.

67. *lam yandaḥ: J*74 / *Z*66; *lam yandiḥ: S*61.

68. *wa ẓalla: D*63 / *B*63 / *W; taẓallu: G*62 (*Muḥīṭ*); *ṭuhātu l-qawmi: J*75; *našīla qadīrin aw šiwāʾin mu^{c}ajjali: G*62 (b. Durayd).

69. *wa rāḥa ṭ-ṭirfu yanfuḍu raʾsa-hu: A*69v / *D*64 / *B*64 / *K*63v / *N*63v (Aṣm, a.^{c}Ub) / *J*76 /*T*69v (Aṣm, a. ^{c}Ub) / *Y; fa ruḥnā: N*63 (a. ^{c}Amr aš-Šaybānī); *tasaffali* (?): *Z*68.

70. Omitted: *Y; wa bāta ^{c}alay-hi: D*58 / *B*65; *ġayra muġfali: J*78v; *ġayra muhmali: G*64 (Ahl r).

71. *a Ḥāri tarā: A*71v / *D*67 / *N*65v (a. Ḥātim) / *T*71v; *a^{c}in-nī ^{c}alā barqin: A*71v / *B*67v / *K*65 / *T*71v; *mukallili: B*68v (a. ^{c}Ub) / *Z*60v.

72. *ka-anna sanā-hu fī maṣābīḥi rāhibin ahāna: A*72v (Aṣm) / *B*68v / *N*66v; *aw maṣābīḥi rāhibin: A*72v / *N*66v / *T*72v; *aw maṣābīḥa rāhibin: B*68v / *N*66v (Axfaš); *ahāna s-salīṭa: D*68 / *B*68 / *N*66 / *J*80 / *T*72[34]; *fī ḏ-ḏubāli: D*68 / *B*68.

73. *qa^{c}adtu wa aṣḥābī la-hū: J*81; *bayna Ḥāmirin wa bayna Ikāmin: D*69 / *B*69[35]; *bayna Ḥāmizin* (?) *wa bayna Ikāmin: A*73v; *bayna Ḥāmizin* (?) *wa bayna Lukāmin: A*73v; *ba^{c}da-mā: A*73v / *B*69v (Riyāšī[36]) / *N*67v (Riyāšī) / *T*73v (Riyāšī).

74. *^{c}alā Qaṭanin: A*74v (Aṣm) / *D*76 / *N*68v (Aṣm) / *T*74v (Aṣm) / *Z*73; *^{c}ala n-Nibāji wa Ṯaytali: Z*74v (Aṣm)[37] / *T*74v; *a^{c}la s-Sitāri: X; wa Yaḏbuli: N*68; *^{c}ala n-Nibāji wa Yaṯtali: N*68v.

75. *^{c}an kulli fīqatin yakubbu: A*75v (Aṣm) / *D*70 / *B*70 / *N*69v / *T*75v / *Z*74v; *min kulli tal^{c}atin: A*75v (a. ^{c}Ub) / *N*69v (a. ^{c}Ub) / *T*75v (a. ^{c}Ub); *min kulli fīqatin: N*69v / *T*75v; *fī kulli tal^{c}atin: Y* (a. ^{c}Ub) / *D* p. 375:11–12 (b. Naḥḥās from a. ^{c}Ub); *wa aḍḥā: D* p. 375:11 (b. Naḥḥās) / *G*69 (several); *fawqa Kutayfatin: G*69 (several); *bayna Kutayfatin: G*69 (several); *fa aḍḥā sabīḥa l-māʾi fī kulli biq^{c}atin: G*69 (Rāġib); *mukibbun: G*69 (Bāqir); *yasīḥu l-māʾu: J*83; *al-kanahbali:*[38].

76. Omitted: *B; alqā bi Busyānin ma^{c}a l-layli barka-hu: A*76v (Aṣm) / *D*77 / *N*70v (Aṣm); *al-^{c}ufra fī kulli manzili: A*76v / *N*70v (w. *min* ?); *munzali: K*70 / *N*70v / *T*76 / *Z*75; *mawʾili: J*85.

77. *wa lā uṭuman: A*77v (Aṣm ?) / *D*71 / *B*71 / *S*71 / *J*86 / *T*77v / *Z*76 / *X; wa lā ujuman uṭman* (?): *K*71;[39] *wa lā aṣiman: G*71 (Bāqir).

78. *wa ka-anna:* *N*72v (*K*) / *T*78v (*K*) / *G*72v (several); *ka-anna Abānan fī afānīni wadqi-hi:* *A*78v (Aṣm) *D*73 / *B*72 / *N*72v (Aṣm)[40] / *T*78v (Aṣm); *^{c}arānīni wadqi-hi:* *G*72 / (*LA*); *ka-anna Abānan fī afānīni nabti-hi:* *G*72 (Šantamarī zu Sīb); *fī bijādin muzammalu:* *N*72v.

79. *wa ka-anna:* *N*73v (*K*) / *G*63 (*K*); *wa ka-anna bi-hi ra'su:* *W*; *ka-anna ṭamīyata l-Mujaymiri:* *A*79v (Aṣm) *D*72 / *B*73 / *T*79v (Aṣm); *ka-anna ṭumayyata l-Mujaymiri:* *K*73v (?) / *N*73v (Aṣm); *ka-anna qulay^{c}ata l-Mujaymiri:* *A*79v (b. Ḥabīb) / *K*73 / *N*73v / *T*79v; *wa l-aġṯā'i:* *A*79v (Farrā'[41]) / *B*73 / *N*73v / *J*88 / *T*79v (Farrā') / *W* / *Y*; *ka-anna ṭulay^{c}ata l-Mujaymiri:* *N*73v; *mina s-sayli wa l-itrā^{c}i:* *J*88v; *ra'si l-Muḥammari* (?): *G*73 (Bāqir).

80. *fa alqā:* *W*; *ka ṣar^{c}i l-Yamānī ḏī l-^{c}iyābi l-muxawwali:* *A*80v (Aṣm)/*N*74v (Aṣm); *ka ṣaw^{c}i l-Yamānī ḏī l-qibābi l-muḥawwili:* *A*80v (MS, see *SQS* p. 104 n. 4); *al-muxawwali:* *D*74; *al-muḥawwili:* *B*74 / *K*74v / *T*80v (Aṣm); *ka ṣaw^{c}i l-Yamānī:* *A*80v / *T*80v; *ḏī l-^{c}ibābi l-muṯaqqali:* *G*74 (*Tāǧ*).

81. Omitted: *D* / *B*; *wa ka-anna:* *N*75v (*K*) / *W*; *ṣubiḥna raḥīqan min sulāfin:* *K*75; *ṣabaḥna:* *Z*80; *ṣabaḥna . . . raḥīqin musalsali:* *G*75 (Jaq); *našāwā tasāqaw bi r-raḥīqi l-mufalfali:* *J*84v; *našāwā tasāqaw bi r-riyāḥi l-mufalfali:* *G*75 (*LA*, Tāǧ).

82. *wa ka-anna:* *N*76v (*K*) / *W*; *ka-anna sibā^{c}an:* *D*75 / *B*75 / *N*76v (a. Ḥātim) / *J*89 / *W* / *G*76 (b. Duraid); *ġudayyatan:* *A*82v / *D*75 / *B*75 / *K*76 / *N*76v / *J*89 / *T*82v; *^{c}unṣuli:* *D*75 / *S*76 / *K*76 / *N*76 / *T*82 / *X* / *Y*.

1. But see App. C, nn. a–b.

2. See *Ag* VIII 59 = *Ag*(Dār) IX 69–70: fifteen lines from the *mu^{c}allaqa* cited in the following sequence (based on *A* = *MuIQ's* line enumeration): *A*1–2, 19, 21, 20, 22, 42, 23–24, 10–11, 54, 15.

3. Thus in *D*. But cf. *SQS* p. 40:3 and *T*16 sch; also chap. 4, § C.3.a, above, and chap. 4, n. 96.

4. Without specific reference to the vocalization of *ṣ-r-m*, either by means of diacritics or scholiast's note, it is difficult to know which reading (*ṣarm* or *ṣurm*) was adopted in a particular recension. Since both are synonymous, however, the question is academic.

5. See the discussion of this line in al-^{c}Askarī *SMYT* 220.

6. See *SQS* p. 48:12, citing an explanatory note of al-Aṣma^{c}ī where *li taqdiḥī* occurs, though not as a variant reading.

7. The text of *B*21 sch was *li taqraḥī* "to wound," a quite plausible reading, but probably a scribal or typographical error for *li taqdaḥī*.

8. *N* p. 29 n. c observes that the Berlin *MS* reads *lā*, the predominant version, and gives no justification for having preferred *mā*.

9. Opinion seems to have been divided as to the reading transmitted by al-Aṣma^{c}ī. In *Ag* VIII 61:5–6 = *Ag*(Dār) IX 73:13–14, it is noted that al-Aṣma^{c}ī's version was *yusirrūna*, which

others read *yuširrūna* with the dotted *šīn* (a view that conflicts with *D*). Al-ᶜAskarī *SMYT* 221:5, on the other hand, maintains that *yuširrūna* is al-Asmaᶜī's recension. *wa llāhu aᶜlam*!

10. Perhaps an intrusive gloss; see *SQS* p. 51:20 where *alqat* is used to explain *naḍat*.

11. Text of *B*27 has *zayl*, an obvious misreading for *ḏayl*.

12. See *G* p. 47.

13. See *G* p. 48.

14. See discussion in *SQS* p. 55:11–12.

15. See discussion in *B* p. 27:4–6 (i.e., *B* 28 sch).

16. I.e., al-Bāqillānī in von Grunebaum *TCD* p. 78–79.

17. *K* 33 sch treats *madrā*, but does not cite *al-madārā* explicitly as a variant. Cf. *G* p. 62, who considers *al-madārā* to be an intrusive gloss, though unjustifiably, as I believe; see App. A (to line 35) and n. 5.

18. Abū ᶜAṣīda Aḥmad b. ᶜUbayd b. Nāṣiḥ (also Abū Jaᶜfar), d. 273/886–87; Qifṭī *IR* I 84–86 and references; see also Sezgin *GAS* II 82.

19. Bundār al-Iṣfahānī, fl. 2d half of third/ninth century; Qifṭī *IR* I 256 and references. He was an acknowledged teacher of Ibn Kaysān and Ibn al-Anbārī. See also Sezgin *GAS* II 89.

20. Perhaps al-Naḥḥās (but not in *N*) or Ibn Nāṣiḥ (see n. 18 above).

21. *G* 37 (p. 66) indicates that this reading occurs in *J*, and *DIQ* p. 371:11 that it occurs in *Z*. The editions of *J* and *Z* that I have used, however, read *bi l-ᶜišā'i* as in *A* and elsewhere.

22. For an interesting discussion of this grammatically problematical verse, with special reference to Abū Saᶜīd aḍ-Ḍarīr, see Yāqūt *IA* I 123.

23. Abū Ḥātim as-Sijistānī, d. 250/864 or 255/869: Brockelmann *GAL* I 107, *Suppl* I 167; Qifṭī *IR* II 28–64 and references.

24. *G* p. 71 suggests that *jawz* may be an intrusive gloss for *ṣulb*.

25. Cf. chap. 4, n. 20 and App. C, n. d. *DIQ* p. 372:1 notes, from Ibn an-Naḥḥās, that Ibn Ḥabīb did not at all recognize this verse (as authentic).

26. See App. C, n. f.

27. See App. C, nn. b, e, and g.

28. See p. 196 and chap. 4, n. 55.

29. Cf. al-ᶜAskarī *SMYT* 83:5, where the same variant is cited on the authority of Abū ᶜUbayda.

30. *N* 54 sch notes that the reading of *al-ġubār* (with the definite article) is more frequent.

31. *K* 51 sch says, of the reading *yaẓillu*, that it occurs more frequently than *yuẓillu*—a statement not quite borne out by our existing sources.

32. Ibrāhīm, in his critical apparatus to *DIQ*, indicates that *W* transmits verses *A* 62, 63, 78, 79, 82 (= *D* 57, 65, 73, 72, 75—*A* 81 ommitted) with the conjunction *wa* before *ka-anna*, resulting in the prosodic fault known as *xazm* (the addition of an extra syllable at the beginning of a verse). According to *N* 72 sch (*N* p. 60:10–13) and *T* 78 sch (*T* p. 28:15–16), Ibn Kaysān's recension also included the *wa* at the beginning of all verses whose first word was *ka-anna* (cf. *G* p. 105, where the name appears incorrectly as Ibn Kaizām; also Ibn Rašīq *Umda* I 143). This reading does not appear, though, in the published text of *K*, although Bernstein mentions the comments of both *N* and *T* and adds that in only one *MS* did he find any basis for their statement and only as regards the last few verses, where a *waw* appeared before *ka-anna*, but had been inked out in red (*N* p. 77—to S. 59:5).

33. Cf. al-ᶜAskarī *SMYT* 223–24 (esp. 224:1).

34. *T* 72 sch (*T* p. 27:2) notes also that the alternative reading *amāla s-salīṭa* (= *A* 72 et al.) makes no sense (*lā maᶜnā li riwāyat man rawā "amāla s-salīṭa"*). A similar opinion, apparently quoted from al-Aṣmaᶜī, is expressed in *A* 72 sch (= *A* p. 101:11), although *amāla* is accepted in the text of the poem.

35. Thus also in Yāqūt *MB* I 341:18, II 188:8.

36. Abu l-Faḍl al-ᶜAbbās b. Faraj ar-Riyāši, d. 257/870; Brockelmann *GAL* I 108, *Suppl* I 168; Qifṭī *IR* II 367–73 and references.

37. The use of the conjunction *wa* here is consistent with al-Aṣmaᶜī's handling of the first verse, where he also rejects *fa* for *wa*. *D*, however, reads *fa Yaḏbuli*—perhaps due to al-Aᶜlam's emendation; cf. p. 209, above and chap. 4, nn. 20 and 95.

38. Al-ᶜAskarī *SMYT* 219–20 notes that "most people" render the last word in the verse *al-kanahbal* (with *fatḥa*), but that al-Aṣmaᶜi reads *al-kanahbul* (with *ḍamma*). Since *al-kanahbal* is indicated in none of the recensions available to me or in any of the scholia, one might speculate that the *riwāya* of *akṯar an-nās* refers to a version popular among the common people—possibly some sort of vulgate rendition or text.

39. There seems to have been some ambiguity in the MS of *K* such that the letters that Bernstein prints as *uṭman* ('*-ṭ-m-*')—on the basis, no doubt, of other variants of the line—might be interpreted also as *illā*, the generally accepted reading (see *N* p. 59 n.5, where the MS reading is transcribed '*-l-m-*').

40. With *waqd-hi*, an evident instance of scribal or typographical transposition of letters.

41. Abū Zakarīyā' Yazīd b. Ziyād al-Farrā', d. 207/822: see Brockelmann *GAL* I 116, *Suppl* I 178–79.

*

Bibliography

I. Abbreviations of Journals, Encyclopedias, etc.

AbhDMG Die deutsche morgenländisch Gesellschaft. *Abhandlungen.*

AO *Archiv Orientální.*

BO *Bibliotheca orientalis.*

BSOAS University of London. School of Oriental and African Studies. *Bulletin.*

BZ *Byzantinische Zeitschrift.*

DHGE *Dictionnaire d'histoire et de géographie ecclésiastiques.* Ed. A. Baudrillart et al. 17 vols. Paris: Letouzey & Ané, 1912–71.

EI[1] *Encyclopaedia of Islam.* Ed. "a number of leading orientalists." 4 vols. and Suppl. Leiden: Brill; London: Luzac, 1913–38.

EI[2] *Encyclopaedia of Islam.* New ed. Ed. "a number of leading orientalists." 4 vols. to date. Leiden: Brill; London: Luzac, 1960–.

EB *Encyclopaedia biblica.* Ed. T. K. Cheyne and J. S. Black. 4 vols. London: A. & O. Black, 1899–1907.

HSCP *Harvard Studies in Classical Philology.*

JAF *Journal of American Folklore.*

JAOS *Journal of the American Oriental Society.*

JNES *Journal of Near Eastern Studies.*

JQR *Jewish Quarterly Review.*

A	*D*	*B*	*S*	*K*	*N*	*J*	*Z*	*T*
12	11	11	10	10	10	16	12	12
						17		
13	12	12	11	11	11	18	13	13
14	13	13	12	12	12	19	14	14
15	14	14	13	13	13	20	15	15
						21		
						22		
16	15	15	14	14	14	23	16	16
17	16	16	15	15	15	24	17	17
18	17	17	16	16	16	25	18	18
19	18	18	17	17	17	26	19	19
20	20	20	18	19	19	27	20	21
						28		
21	19	19	19	18	18	29	21	20
22	21	21	20	20	20	30	22	22
23	22	22	21	21	21	31	23	23
24	23	23	22	22	22	32	24	24
25	24	24	23	23	23	33	25	25
26	25	25	24	24	24	34	26	26
27	26	26	25	25	25	35	27	27
28	27	27	26	26	26	36	28	28
29	28	28	27	27	27	37	29	29
30	30	30	28	28	28	38	30	30
31	31	31	29	29	29	39	31	31
32	33	32	30	30	30	40	33	32
33	34	33	31	31	31	41	34	33
34	35	34	32	32	32	42	35	34
35	36	35	33	33	33	43	36	35
36	37	36	34	34	34	44	37	36
37	40	37	35	35	35	45	38	37
38	38	38	36	36	36	46	39	38
39	39	39	37	37	37	48	40	39
40	41	40	38	38	38	49	41	40
41	32	41	39	39	39	47	32	41
42	42	42	40	40	40	50	42	42
43	43	43	41	41	41	51	43	43
44	44	44	42	42	42	52	44	44
45	45	45	43	43	43	53	45	45
46	46	46	44	44	44	54	46	46

A	*D*	*B*	*S*	*K*	*N*	*J*	*Z*	*T*
47	47	47	45	45	45	55	47[d]	47
48	48	48	46[e]	56[f]	46[g]	56		48
49[h]						57	48	49
50						58	49	50
51						59	50	51
52						60	51	52
53	49	49	47	46	47	61	52	53
54	50	50	48	47	48	62	53	54
55	51	51	49	48	49	63	54	55
56	53	52	50	49	50	64	55	56
57	52	53	51	50	54	65	56	57
58	54	54	52	51	52	66	57	58
59	55	55	53	52	51	67	58	59
50	56	56	54	53	53	68	59	60
61	66	66	55	54	55	69	60	61
62	57[i]	57	56	55	56	70	61	62
63	65	58	57	57	57	77	62	63
64	59	59	58	58	58	71	63	64
65	60	60	59	59	59	72	64	65
66	61	61	60	60	60	73	65	66
67	62	62	61	61	61	74	66	67
68	63	63	62	62	62	75	67	68
69	64[j]	64	63	63	63[k]	76	68	69
70	58	65	64	64	64	78	69	70
71	67	67	65	65	65	79	70	71
72	68	68	66	66	66	80	71	72
73	69	69	67	67	67	81	72	73
74	76	76	68	68	68	82	73	74
75	70	70	69	69	69	83	74	75
76	77		70	70	70	85	75	76
77	71	71	71	71	71	86	76	77
78	73	72	72	72	72	87	77	78
79	72	73	73	73	73	88	78	79
80	74	74	74	74	74	90	79	80
81			75	75	75	84	80	81
82	75	75	76	76	76	89	81	82

a. Bernstein (*K* p. 11 n. 5) adds, from the Berlins MS, *A*3–4 with scholia, but omits them from his enumeration.

b. Frenkel (*N* p. 5 n. i) notes that *A*3–4 follow in the MS after the phrase *wa yurwā ba*^{c}*da hāḏā*. He does not, however, include them in his edition. Likewise with *A*49–52 below; see note g.

c. Of these two verses (*A*3–4) Ibn al-Anbārī informs us (*A* p. 23:12) that Abū ^{c}Ubayda includes them in his recension, but for al-Aṣma^{c}ī they are falsely attributed (*manḥūl*) and not to be admitted (as IQ's: *lā yu*^{c}*rafu*); al-Aṣma^{c}ī adds: "Bedouin (informants: *al-a*^{c}*rāb*) include them in their rendition of (the *qaṣīda*)." Cf. *K* p. 12:11–12; *T* p. 3:23–24.

d. *Z*47 conflates *A*47a with *A*48b, making a single verse of the two, a reading cited in *A*47 sch as a variant (but cf. *B*48 sch) and earlier in Ibn Sallām *TFS* 71:4 and n.2.

e. Ahlwardt's edition of *S*, *DIQ* (Ahl) 48, omits *A*49–52 in this place with the comment that as-Sukkarī "notes that the verses are spurious" (*Divans* 101, app. crit. to IQ Appendix 26:7–10 = *A*49–52); Ibrāhīm, however, in *DIQ* p. 372, considers that *S* includes the verses. Although I have not seen the passage in the MS of *S*, I suspect the discrepancy has resulted from Ahlwardt's often unnecessarily strict interpretation of the term *manḥūl* as "spurious" rather than "of dubious or false attribution"; cf. chap. 4, §B.

f. The rather anomalous positioning of this verse in *K* seems to have been paralleled in *Y*, where it is found (Ibrāhīm *DIQ* p. 374 [to *D*57]) at the same point in IQ's description of his horse and with the same variant (*ka-anna nujūman* instead of *ka-anna ṯ-Ṯurayyā*), which does not occur in the text of any other known version. *A*48 sch acknowledges the existence of both the positioning and the variant by offering two interpretations of the verse, the first of which was the one advanced by "those in whose recensions it occurs later, after the description of the horse (*fa hāḏā tafsīru man yarwī-hi* [*sc.*, *al-bayta*] *mu'axxaran ba*^{c}*da ṣifati l-faras*)."

g. See note b; cf. Ahlwardt *Divans* (app. crit.) 109, where *A*3–4 and 49–52 are considered part of *N*'s text (y = *N*).

h. On the question of the attribution of *A*49–52, see chap. 4, §B.

i. See note f.

j. Ibrāhīm *DIQ* p. 374 (to *D*64) notes the presence in *Y*, after this verse, of two additional verses that do not occur elsewhere (but see note k).

k. Frenkel notes (*N* p. 53 n. 1) that the Leyden MS of *N* "hat hier von spätrer Hand zwei fremde Verse am Rande." These are undoubtedly the two verses alluded to above, note j, from *Y* itself or, perhaps, from an independent source.

*

Appendix C

Table of Variations in Verse-Order for Recensions of the *Mu*^{c}*allaqa* of Imra'alqays

The following table indicates the line-by-line correspondence among eight published recensions of the *mu*^{c}*allaqa* as compared with *A* (abbreviations are clarified in the Bibliography, part III).

A	*D*	*B*	*S*	*K*	*N*	*J*	*Z*	*T*
1	1	1	1	1	1	1	1	1
2	2	2	2	2[a]	2[b]	2	2	2
						3		
3[c]	3	3				4	3	3
4	4	4				11	4	4
5	5	5	3	3	3	5	5	5
						6		
						7		
6	6	6	4	4	4	8	6	6
7	7	7	5	5	5	9	7	7
8	29	29	6	6	6	10	8	8
9	8	8	7	7	7	13	9	9
10	9	9	8	8	8	12	10	10
11	10	10	9	9	9	14	11	11
						15		

JRAS *Journal of the Royal Asiatic Society.*

REI *Revue des études islamiques.*

RSO *Rivista degli studi orientali.*

SBWA Akademie der Wissenschaften zu Wien. Phil.-hist. Klasse. *Sitzungberichte.*

SI *Studia islamica.*

TAPA The American Philological Association. *Transactions and Proceedings.*

UCOIP University of Chicago. Oriental Institute. *Publications.*

URCSS Università di Roma. Instituto di Studi del vicino Oriente. Centro de Studi Semitici. *Studi semitici.*

WZKM *Wiener Zeitschrift für die Kunde des Morgenlandes.*

ZA *Zeitschrift für Assyriologie.*

ZDMG Die deutsche morgenländische Gesellschaft. *Zeitschrift.*

II. Poetry and Poetical Collections

Ahlwardt W. Ahlwardt, ed. *The Divans of the Six Ancient Arabic Poets. Divans* London: Trübner, 1870.

Asm Abū Sa^{c}īd ^{c}Abdalmalik b. Qurayb al-Aṣma^{c}ī. *Al-Aṣma^{c}īyāt.* Ed. Ahmad M. Šākir and ^{c}Abdassalām Hārūn. 2d ed. = *Dīwān al-^{c} Arab* 2. Cairo: Dār al-ma^{c}ārif, 1964.

D^{c}Ab *Dīwān ^{c}Abīd b. al-Abraṣ,* in *The Dīwāns of ^{c}Abīd Ibn al-Abraṣ, of Asad, and ^{c}Āmir Ibn aṭ-Ṭufail, of ^{c}Āmir Ibn Ṣa^{c} ṣa^{c} ah.* Ed. and trans. Ch. Lyall. = *E. J. W. Gibb Memorial Series,* vol. 21. Leiden: Brill; London: Luzac, 1913.

D^{c}Ab(Naṣ) *Dīwān ^{c}Abīd b. al-Abraṣ.* Ed. Ḥusayn Naṣṣār. Cairo: Muṣṭafā al-Ḥalabī, 1377/1957.

D^{c}Ad *Dīwān ^{c}Adīy b. Zayd al-^{c}Ibādī.* Ed. M. Jabbār al-Mu^{c}aybid. = *Silsilat kutub at-turāṯ* 2. Baghdad: Wizārat aṯ-ṯiqāfa wa l-iršād/Dār al-Jumhurīya li n-našr waṭ-ṭab^{c}, 1965.

DAfwa *Dīwān al-Afwah al-Awdī.* Ed. ^{c}Abdal^{c}azīz al-Maymanī. In *TA* 1–24.

D^{c}Al *Dīwān šī^{c}r ^{c}Alqama at-Tamīmī.* In Ahlwardt *Divans* 103–14; Appendix 194–95.

D^{c}Ām *Dīwān ^{c}Āmir b. aṭ-Ṭufayl.* In *The Dīwāns . . .* (see *D^{c}Ab,* above).

D^{c}Amr *The Poems of ^{c}Amr Son of Qamī'ah . . .* Ed. and trans. Ch. Lyall. Cambridge: Cambridge University Press, 1919.

D^{c}An *Dīwān šī^{c}r ^{c}Antara al-^{c}Absī.* In Ahlwardt *Divans* 33–52; Appendix 178–83.

DA^{c}šā *Dīwān al-A^{c}šā al-kabīr Maymūn b. Qays.* Ed. M. M. Ḥusayn. Cairo: Maktabat al-ādāb, (1950?).

DAws *Dīwān Aws b. Ḥajar.* Ed. M. Yūsuf Najam. Beirut: Dār Ṣādir/Dār Beirut, 1380/1960.

DaZub *Šī^{c}r Abī Zubayd aṭ-Ṭā'ī.* Ed. Nūrī Ḥammūdī al-Qaysī. Baghdad: Maṭba^{c}at al-ma^{c}ārif, 1967.

DBišr *Dīwān Bišr b. Abī Xāzim al-Asadī*. Ed. ᶜIzzat Ḥasan. Damascus: Wizārat aṯ-Ṯiqāfa wa l-iršād al-qawmī, 1379/1960.

DḤād *Al-Hādirae diwānus cum al-Yezīdii scholiis*. Ed. G. H. Engelmann. Leiden: Brill, 1858.

DḤass *Dīwān of Ḥassān ibn Thābit*. Ed. W. ᶜArafat. = *E. J. W. Gibb Memorial, New Series*, vol. 25, 1–2. London: Luzac, 1971.

DḤāt *Dīwān Ḥātim aṭ-Ṭa'ī*. Ed. Karam al-Bustani (?). Beirut: Dār Ṣādir/Dar Bayrūt, 1383/1963.

DHum *Dīwān Ḥumayd b. Ṯawr al-Hilālī*. . . . Ed. ᶜAbdalᶜazīz al-Maymanī. Cairo: Dār al-kutub al-miṣrīya, 1371/1951.

DḤuṭ *Dīwān al-Ḥuṭay'a bi šarḥ Ibn as-Sikkīt wa s-Sukkarī wa s-Sijistānī*. Ed. Nuᶜmān Amīn Ṭāhā. Cairo: Muṣṭafa al-Ḥalabī, 1378/1958.

DIQ *Dīwān Imri' ilqays*. Ed. M. Abu l-Faḍl Ibrāhīm. 2d ed. = *Ḏaxā'ir al-ᶜArab* 24. Cairo: Dār al-maᶜārif, 1964.

DIQ(Ahl) *Dīwān šiᶜr Imri' ilqays*. Ed. W. Ahlwardt, from recension of as-Sukkari. In Ahlwardt *Divans* 115–62; Appendix 196–207.

DIQ(Baṭ) Abū Bakr ᶜĀṣim b. Ayyūb al-Baṭalyūsī. *Šarḥ dīwān . . . Imri' ilqays b. Ḥujr al-Kindī*. Cairo: Maṭbaᶜat Hindīya, 1347/1928.

DiMu *Der Diwan des Abdallāh ibn al-Muᶜtazz*, Parts III-IV. Ed. B. Lewin. = *Bibliotheca islamica*, Vols. 17c–17d. Istanbul: Maṭbaᶜat al-maᶜārif, 1945–50.

DKaᶜb *DKbZ*.

DKbZ Abū Saᶜīd al-Ḥasan b. al-Ḥusayn as-Sukkarī. *Šarḥ dīwān Kaᶜb b. Zuhayr*. Cairo: Dār al-kutub al-miṣrīya, 1369/1950.

DKbZ (Kowalski) *Le Dīwān de Kaᶜb ibn Zuhair*. Ed. T. Kowalski. = *Mémories de la Commission orientaliste*, No. 38. Krakow: Polska Akademia Umiejetności, 1950.

DLab *Šarḥ dīwān Labīd b. Rabīᶜa al-ᶜĀmirī*. Ed. Iḥsān ᶜAbbās. = *at-Turāṯ al-ᶜarabi* 8. Kuwait: Wizārat al-iršād wa l-anbā', 1962.

DMih *Dīwān Mihyār ad-Daylamī*. 4 vols. Cairo: Dār al-kutub al-miṣrīya, 1344–50/1925–31.

DMut *Die Gedichte des Mutalammis*. Ed. and trans. K. Vollers. Leipzig: J. C. Hinrichs, 1903.

DMutan *Mutanabbii carmina cum commentario Wāḥidii*. Ed. Fr. Dieterici. Baghdad: al-Muṯannā, n.d. (Photo-offset reprint of 1861 edition.)

DMuz *Dīwān al-Muzarrad b. Ḍirār al-Ġaṭafānī*. Ed. Xalīl Ibrāhīm al-ᶜAṭīya. Baghdad: Maṭbaᶜat Asᶜad, 1962.

DNāb *Dīwān šiᶜr an-Nābiġa aḏ-Ḏubyānī*. In Ahlwardt *Divans* 2–32; Appendix 164—76.

DQays *Dīwān Qays b. al-Xaṭīm*. . . . Ed. Nāṣir ad-Dīn al-Asad. =*Kunūz aš-šiᶜr* 2. Cairo: Dār al-ᶜurūba, 1381/1962.

DQuṭ *Der Dīwān des ᶜUmeir ibn Schujeim al-Quṭāmī*. Ed. J. Barth. Leiden: Brill, 1902.

DRu' — *Der Dīwān des Reğezdichters Rūba Ben al-Ağğāğ*. Ed. W. Ahlwardt. = *Sammlungen alterarabischer Dichter,* Bd. III. Berlin: Reuther & Reichard, 1903.

DSam — *Dīwān as-Samaw'al*. In *Dīwānā ^{c}Urwa b. al-Ward wa s-Samaw'al*. Ed. Karam al-Bustānī (?). Beirut: Dār Ṣadir/Dār Bayrūt, 1384/1964. Pp 67–92.

DŠamm — *Dīwān aš-Šammāx b. Ḍirār al-Ġaṭafānī*. Ed. Ṣalāḥ ad-Dīn al-Hādī. *Ḏaxā'ir al-^{c}Arab* 42. Cairo: Dār al-ma^{c}ārif, 1968.

DŠan — *Dīwan aš-Šanfarā*. In *TA* 30–42.

DSuḥ — *Dīwān Suḥaym ^{c}abd Bani l-Ḥasḥās*. Ed. ^{c}Abdal^{c}azīz al-Maymanī. Cairo: Dār al-Kutub al-miṣrīya, 1369/1950.

DTam — *Dīwān* [*Tamīm b. Ubayy*] *Ibn Muqbil*. Ed. ^{c}Izzat Ḥasan. = *Maṭbū^{c}at Mudīrīyat iḥyā' at-turāṯ al-qadīm* 5. Damascus: Wizārat aṯ-ṯiqāfa wa l-iršād al-qawmī, 1381/1962.

DṬar — *Dīwān ši^{c}r Ṭarafa al-Bakrī*. In Ahlwardt *Divans* 53–74; Appendix 183–88.

DṬar(Sel) — *Dīwān de Ṭarafa ibn al-^{c}Abd al-Bakrī. . . .* Ed. M. Seligsohn. Paris: E. Boulion, 1901.

DṬir — *Dīwān aṭ-Ṭirimmāḥ*. In *The Poems . . .* (see *DṬuf,* below).

DṬuf — *Diwan Ṭufayl al-Ġanawi*. In *The Poems of Ṭufail Ibn ^{c}Auf al-Ghanawī and aṭ-Ṭirimmāḥ Ibn Ḥakīm aṭ-Ṭā'yī(sic)*. Ed. and trans. F. Krenkow. = *E. J. W. Gibb Memorial Series,* vol. 25. London: Luzac, 1927.

DUbaR — *Der Diwan des ^{c}Umar ibn abi Rebī^{c}a*. Ed. P. Schwarz. 3 vols. and Heft IV: *Umars Leben, Dichtung, Sprache, und Metrik*. Leipzig: Th. Weicher, 1901–9.

D^{c}Ur — *Dīwān ^{c}Urwa b. al-Ward. . . .* Ed. ^{c}Abdalmu^{c}īn al-Mulawwiḥi. Damascus: Wizārat aṯ-ṯiqāfa wa l-iršād al-qawmī, 1966 (?).

DVCA — *Delectus veterum carminum arabicorum*. Ed. Th. Nöldeke. Berlin: Reuther, 1890.

DXan — *Anīs al-julasā' fī šarḥ dīwān al-Xansā'*. Ed. L. Cheikho. Beirut: Imprimerie catholique, 1896.

DXuf — *Ši^{c}r Xufāf b. Nubda as-Sulamī*. Ed. Nūrī Ḥammūdī al-Qaysī. Baghdad: Maṭba^{c}at al-ma^{c}ārif, 1967.

DZuh — *Dīwān ši^{c}r Zuhayr b. Abī Sulmā al-Muzanī*. In Ahlwardt *Divans* 75—102; Appendix 188–94.

DZuh(Dar) — *Šarḥ dīwān Zuhayr b. Abī Sulmā. . . .* Cairo: Dār al-kutub al-miṣrīya, 1363/1944.

Ibn al-Anbārī *SQS* — Abū Bakr M. b. al-Qāsim al-Anbārī. *Šarḥ al-qaṣā'id as-sab^c aṭ-ṭiwāl al-jāhilīyāt*. Ed. ^{c}Abdassalām M. Hārūn. = *Ḏaxā'ir al-^{c}Arab* 35. Cairo: Dār al-ma^{c}ārif, 1963.

Ibrāhīm *DIQ* — = *DIQ*.

Jam — Abū Zayd M. b. Abil-Xaṭṭāb al-Qurašī. *Kitāb Jamharat aš^{c}ār al-^{c}Arab*. Ed. Sa^{c}īd Anṭūn ^{c}Ammūn. Būlāq: al-Amīrīya al-kubrā, 1308.

LŠan aš-Šanfarā. *Lāmīyat al-^{c}Arab.* In a poetical miscellany. Istanbul: Maṭba^{c}at al-Jawā'ib, 1300. Pp. 4–7

Muf *The Mufaḍḍalīyāt: An Anthology of Ancient Arabian Odes Compiled by al-Mufaḍḍal Son of Muḥammad According to the Recension and with the Commentary of . . . Ibn . . . al-Anbārī.* Ed. Ch. Lyall. Vol. 1: *Arabic Text.* Oxford: Oxford University Press, 1921. Vol. 2: *Translation and notes.* Oxford: Oxford Univesity Press, 1918. Vol. 3: *Indexes to the Arabic Text.* Comp. A. A. Bevan. = *E. J. W. Gibb Memorial Series,* New Series, vol. 3. Leiden: Brill; London: Luzac, 1924.

MuIQ *Mu^{c}allaqa* of Imra'alqays. In Ibn al-Anbārī *SQS* 3–112. (=*A;* see Section III, below.)

SAH Abū Sa^{c}īd al-Ḥasan b. al-Ḥusayn as-Sukkarī et al. *Kitāb šarḥ aš^{c}ār al-Huḏalīyīn.* Ed. ^{c}Abdassattār Aḥmad Farāj and Maḥmūd M. Shākir. 3 vols. = *Kunūz aš-ši^{c}r* 3. Cairo: Dār al-^{c}urūba, 1384/1965.

SQS Ibn al-Anbārī *SQS*

TA *Aṭ-Tarā'if al-adabīya.* Ed. ^{c}Abdal^{c}azīz al-Maymanī. Cairo: Lajnat at-ta'līf wa t-tarjama wa n-našr, 1937.

at-Tibrīzī
TAAP Abū Zakarīyā Yaḥyā b. ^{c}Alī at-Tibrīzī. *A Commentary on Ten Ancient Arabic Poems. . . .* Ed. Ch. Lyall. Ridgewood, N.J.: Gregg Press, 1965. (Photo-offset reprint of 1894 edition.)

az-Zawzanī
SMS Abū ^{c}Abdallāh al-Ḥusayn b. Aḥmad az-Zawzanī. *Šarḥ al-mu^{c}allaqāt as-sab^{c}.* Cairo: Maktabat al-Qāhira, 1381/1961.

III. *Recensions of IQ's Mu^{c}allaqa and Related Material*

A *MuIQ* (see section II above).

B al-Baṭalyūsī's recension of IQ's *mu^{c}allaqa,* in *DIQ*(Baṭ) 16–45 (see Section II above).

D al-A^{c}lam/al-Aṣma^{c}ī's recension of IQ's *mu^{c}allaqa* (see chap. 4, § A.2.a, and nn. 17–20, above), in *DIQ* pp. 8-26 (see Section II above).

G S. Gandz (trans. and comment). *Die Mu^{c}allaqa des Imruulqais* = *SBWA* 170:4 (1913).

J al-Qurašī's recension of IQ's *mu^{c}allaqa,* in *Jam* 39–47 (see Section II above).

K F. L. Bernstein, ed. "Des Ibn Kaisān Kommentar zur Mu^{c}allaḳa des Imru'ul-ḳais," *ZA* 29 (1914): 1–77.

N E. Frenkel, ed. *An-Naḥḥas Commentar zur Mu^{c}allaqa des Imruulqais.* Halle: M. Niemeyer, 1876.

S as-Sukkari's recension of IQ's *mu^{c}allaqa* = *DIQ*(Ahl) No. 48 (see Section II above).

T at-Tibrīzī's recension of IQ's *mu^{c}allaqa,* in at-Tibrīzī *TAAP* 1–29 (see Section II above).

W aṭ-Ṭūsī's recension of IQ's *mu^{c}allaqa* (see chap. 4, n. 14, above), as cited in *DIQ* pp. 367–76 (see Section II above).

X Abu Sa^{c}īd aḍ-Ḍarīr's recension of IQ's *mu^{c} allaqa* (see chap. 4, n. 12), as cited in *DIQ* pp. 367–76 (see Section II above).

Y Abū Sahl's recension of IQ's *mu^{c}allaqa* (see chap. 4, § A.2.a,above), as cited in *DIQ* 367–76 (see Section II above).

Z az-Zawzanī's recension of IQ's *mu^{c}allaqa,* in az-Zawzanī *SMS* 2–47 (see Section II above).

(Note also the following abbreviations: sch = scholium; v= variant reading cited in scholium or critical apparatus. Thus, e.g., *N* 17 sch indicates an-Naḥḥās's scholium to line 17 of his recension of IQ's *mu^{c}allaqa,* and *N* 17v indicates a variant reading cited in the scholium to that line.)

IV. General Bibliography

Abbott *RNAS* = N. Abbott. *The Rise of the North Arabic Script and Its Kur'ānic Development.* = *UCOIP* 50. Chicago: University of Chicago Press, 1939.

——— *SALP* I = *Studies in Arabic Literary Papyri.* I. *Historical Texts.* = *UCOIP* 75. Chicago: University of Chicago Press, 1957.

——— *SALP* II = *Studies in Arabic Literary Papyri.* II. *Qur'ānic Commentary and Tradition.* = *UCOIP* 76. Chicago: University of Chicago Press, 1967.

Abu-Deeb, K. "Towards a Structural Analysis of Pre-Islamic Poetry (I): The Key Poem." *International Journal of Middle East Studies* 6 (1975): 148–84.

——— *TSA* II = "Towards a Structural Analysis of Pre-Islamic Poetry (II): The Eros Vision." *Edebiyât* 1 (1976): 3–69.

Abū Zayd *KNL* = Abū Zayd Sa^{c}īd b. Aws al-Anṣārī. *Kitāb an-Nawādir fī l-luġa.* Ed. Sa^{c}īd al-Xūri aš-Sartūni. Beirut: Imprimerie catholique, 1894.

Ag = Abu l-Faraj ^{c}Alī b. al-Ḥusayn al-Iṣbahānī. *Kitāb al-Aġānī. 20 vols. Beirut:* S. Y. al-Xalīl & Dār al-fikr, 1970. (Photo-offset reprint of 1285 H. Būlāq edition.)

Ag XXI=*The Twenty-First Volume of the Kitab al-Aghānī.* Ed. R. Brünnow. Leiden: Brill, 1888.

Ag(Dār) = *Ag.* 16 vols., completed. Cairo: Wizārat aṯ-ṯiqāfa wa l-iršād al-qawmī, 1963. (Photo-offset reprint of 1923–48 edition.)

Ahlwardt *BAAG* = A. Ahlwardt. *Bemerkungen über die Aechtheit der alten arabischen Gedichte.* Griefswald: Bamberg, 1872.

——— *UPPA* = *Ueber Poesie and Poetik der Araber.* Gotha: F. A. Perthes, 1856.

Aigrain, R. "Arabie." In *DHGE* 3:1158–1339.

^{c}Ali *TSJ* = Jawād ^{c}Alī. "Tadwīn aš-ši^{c}r al-jāhilī." *Majallat al-Majma^c al-^{c}ilmī al-^{c}irāqī* 4 (1375/1956): 520–63.

Altekar, A. S. *Education in Ancient India.* 5th ed. Varanasi: N. Kishore, 1957.

al-Āmidī *MM* = al-Ḥasan b. Bišr al-Āmidī. *Al-Mu'talif wa l-muxtalif.* Ed. ^{c}Abdassattār Aḥmad Farāj. Cairo: ^{c}Īsā al-Ḥalabī, 1961.

Amin *FI* = Aḥmad Amīn. *Fajr al-Islām.* 10th ed. Cairo: Marktabat an-nahḍa al-miṣrīya, 1965.

Andrae *PM* = Tor Andrae. *Die Person Muhammeds in Lehre und Glauben seiner Gemeinde.* = *Archives d'études orientales* 16. Stockholm: P. A. Norstedt, 1918.

Arberry *RME* = *Religion in the Middle East.* Ed. A. J. Arberry. 2 vols. Cambridge: Cambridge University Press, 1969.

——— *SO* = *The Seven Odes: The First Chapter in Arabic Literature.* London: Allen & Unwin; New York: Macmillan, 1957.

Aristotle *Poetics* = Aristotle. *De Poetica.* Trans. I. Bywater. In *The Works of Aristotle Translated into English.* Vol. XI. Oxford: Oxford University Press, 1971. (Reprint of 1946 edition.)

——— *Rhetoric* = *Rhetorica.* Trans W. Rhys Roberts. In *The Works of Aristotle Translated into English.* Vol. XI. Oxford: Oxford University Press, 1971. (Reprint of 1946 edition.)

Asad *MSJ* = Nāṣiraddīn al-Asad. *Maṣādir aš-ši^{c}r al-jāhilī.* Cairo: Dār al-ma^{c}ārif, 1962.

——— *QGAJ* = *Al-Qiyān wa l-ġinā' fi l-^{c}aṣr al-jāhilī.* Beirut: Dār Ṣādir/Dār Bayrūt, 1379/1960.

al-^{c}Askarī *SMYT* = Abū Aḥmad al-Ḥasan b. ^{c}Abdallāh al-^{c}Askarī. *Šarḥ mā yaqa^{c}u fī-hi t-taṣḥīf wa t-taḥrīf.* Ed. ^{c}Abdal^{c}aziz Aḥmad. Cairo: Muṣṭafā al-Ḥalabī, 1383/1963.

Al-Azdi, ^{c}Ali b. Ẓāfir. *Badā'i^{c} al-badā'ih.* Ed. M. Abu l-Faḍl Ibrāhīm. Cairo: Maktabat al-anglu l-miṣrīya, 1970.

al-Baġdādi *XA* = ^{c}Abdalqādir b. ^{c}Amr al-Baġdādī. *Xizānat al-adab wa lubb lubāb lisān al-^{c}Arab.* 4 vols. Būlāq: al-Amīrīya al-kubrā, 1299 H.

al-Bāqillānī *TCD* = von Grunebaum *TCD.*

Barbier de Meynard, A. C. "Surnoms et sobriquets dans la littérature arabe." *Journal asiatique* (ser. 10) 9 (1907): 173–244, 365–428; 10 (1907): 55–118, 193–273.

Bateson *SCP* = M. C. Bateson. *Structural Continuity in Poetry: A Linguistic Study in Five Preislamic Arabic Odes.* Paris and The Hague: Mouton, 1970.

Baugh, A. "Improvisation in the Middle English Romance." *Proc. American Philos. Soc.* 103 (1959): 418–54.

——— *MER* = "The Middle English Romance: Some Questions of Creation, Presentation, and Preservation." *Speculum* 42 (1967): 1–31.

Beck *ASAK* = E. Beck. "^{c}Arabiyya, Sunna und ^{c}Āmma in der Koranlesung des zweiten Jahrhunderts." *Orientalia* n.s. 15 (1946): 180–224.

——— *SGKK* = "Studien zur Geschichte der kūfischen Koranlesung in den ersten zwei Jahrhunderten. I–IV." *Orientalia* n.s. 17 (1948): 326–55; 19 (1950): 328–50; 20 (1951): 316–28; 22 (1953): 59–78.

——— *UKK* = "Der ^{c}uṯmānische Kodex in der Koranlesung des zweiten Jahrhunderts." *Orientalia* n.s. 14 (1945): 355–73.

Bell/Watt *Intro* = W. M. Watt. [*R.*] *Bell's Introduction to the Qur'ān.* = *Islamic Surveys* 8. Edinburgh: Edinburgh University Press, 1970.

Benson *LC* = L. Benson. "The Literary Character of Anglo-Saxon Formulaic Poetry." *PMLA* 81 (1966): 334–41.

Bergsträsser/Pretzl *GK* = G. Bergsträsser and O. Pretzl. *Die Geschichte des Korantexts.* = Th. Nöldeke. *Geschichte des Qorāns,* 3. Teil. Hildesheim and New York: Olms, 1970. (Photo-offset reprint of 1938 edition.)

Bieler, L. "The Grammarian's Craft." *Folia* 2 (1947): 94–105; 3 (1948): 23–30, 47–58.

Birkeland *AP* = H. Birkeland. *Altarabische Pausalformen.* = *Skr. utgitt av det Norske Videnskaps-akademi i Oslo.* II. *Hist.-filos. Klasse.* 1940. No. 4.

Blachère, R. "Influences héréditaires et problèmes posés par la recension de la poésie archaïque." In G. Makdisi, ed. *Arabic and Islamic Studies in Honor of Hamilton A. R. Gibb.* Cambridge, Mass.: Dept. of Near Eastern Languages and Literatures, Harvard University, 1965. Pp. 141–46.

———. "Problème de la transfiguration du poète tribal en héros de roman 'courtois' chez les 'logographes' arabes du IIIe/IXe siècle." *Arabica* 8 (1961): 131—36.

Blachère *DCHM* = "Deuxième contribution à l'historie de la métrique arabe: notes sur la terminologie primitive." *Arabica* 6 (1959): 132–51.

——— *HLA* = *Histoire de la littérature arabe des origines à la fin du XVe siècle de J.-C.*, 3 vols. (with continuous pagination). Paris: Adrien-Maisonneuve, 1952–66.

——— *Intro* = *Introduction au Coran.* 2d ed. Paris: Maisonneuve-Besson & Chantermerle, 1959.

——— *PC* = "La Poésie dans la conscience de la première génération musulmane." *Annales islamologiques* 4 (1963): 93—103.

——— *SIIB* = "Les Savants iraqiens et leurs informateurs bédouins aux IIe–IVe siècles de l'Hégire." In *Mélanges offerts à William Marçais par l'Institut d'études islamiques de l'Université de Paris.* Paris: G.-F. Maisonneuve, 1950. Pp. 37–48.

Blachère/Gaudefroy-Demombynes *GAC* = R. Blachère and M. Gaudefroy-Demombynes. *Grammaire de l'Arabe classique (morphologie et syntaxe).* 3d ed. Paris: Maisonneuve & Larose, 1952.

Blau, J. "Sind uns Reste arabischer Bibelübersetzungen aus vorislamischer Zeit erhalten geblieben?" *Le Muséon* 86 (1973): 67–72.

Blau *ELB* = J. Blau. *The Emergence and Linguistic Background of Judaeo-Arabic.* = *Scripta judaica* V. Oxford: Oxford University Press, 1965.

——— *IMAD* = "The Importance of Middle Arabic Dialects for the History of Arabic." In U. Heyd, ed. *Studies in Islamic History and Civilization.* = *Scripta Hierosolymitana* IX. Jerusalem: Magnes-Hebrew University, 1961. Pp. 206–28.

——— *PSC* = "On the Problem of the Synthetic Character of Classical Arabic as against Judaeo-Arabic (Middle Arabic)." *JQR* 63 (1972–73): 29–38.

——— *PSSL* = *On Pseudo-corrections in Some Semitic Languages.* Jerusalem: Israel Academy of Sciences and Humanities, 1970.

——— *RBA* = "The Role of the Bedouins as Arbiters in Linguistic Questions and the *Mas'ala Zunburiyya.*" *Journal of Semitic Studies* 8 (1963): 42–51.

Bloch, Alfred. "Zur altarabische Spruchdichtung." In F. Meier, ed. *West-östliche Abhandlungen: Rudolf Tschudi zum* 70. *Geburtstag. . . .* Wiesbaden: Harrassowitz, 1954. Pp. 181–224.

Bloch *ADZ* = "Die altarabische Dichtung als Zeugnis für das Geistesleben der vorislamischen Araber." *Anthropos* 37–40 (1942–45): 186–204.

——— *KWAV* = "Der künstlerische Wert der altarabischen Verskunst." *Acta orientalia* 21 (1950–53): 207–38.

——— *Qas* = "Qaṣīda." *Asiatische Studien* 2 (1948): 106–32.

——— *VSA* = *Vers und Sprache im Altarabischen: Metrische und syntaktische Untersuchungen.* = *Acta Tropica,* Supplementum 5. Basel: Verlag für Recht and Gesellschaft, 1946.

Bloch *VIP* = Ariel Bloch. "The Vowels of the Imperfect Preformatives in the Old Dialects of Arabic." *ZDMG* 117 (1967): 22–29.

Bogatyrev/Jakobson *FBFS* = P. Bogatyrev and R. Jakobson. "Die Folklore als eine besondere Form des Schaffens." In *Donum natalicium Schrijnen.* Nijmegen and Utrecht: N. v. Dekker & van de Vegt, 1929. Pp. 900–913.

Bowra *HP* = C. M. Bowra. *Heroic Poetry.* London: Macmillan, 1964. (Reprint of 1952 edition.)

Bräunlich *FEAP* = E. Bräunlich. "Zur Frage der Echtheit der altarabischen Poesie." *Orientalistische Literaturzeitung* 29 (1926): 825–33.

——— *VLB* = "Versuch einer literargeschichtlichen Betrachtungsweise altarabischer Poesien." *Der Islam* 24 (1937): 201–69.

Bräunlich/Fischer *SI* = *Schawāhid-Indices.* E. Bräunlich and A. Fischer, comps. and eds. Leipzig: Harrassowitz, 1934–45.

Bravmann, M. M. *The Arabic Elative: A New Approach.* = *Studies in Semitic Languages and Linguistics II.* Leiden: Brill, 1968.

———. "Heroic Motives in Early Arabic Literature." *Der Islam* 33 (1958): 256–79; 35 (1960): 1–26; 36 (1961): 4–36.

Brockelmann *GAL* = C. Brockelmann. *Geschichte der arabischen Literatur.* 2 vols. 2. Auflage. Leiden: Brill, 1943–44. (Cited according to pagination of 1. Auflage, noted in margins.)

——— *GAL Suppl* = *Geschichte der arabischen Literature. Supplementbände.* 3 vols. Leiden: Brill, 1937–42.

——— *TAA* = *Ta'rīx al-adab al-ᶜarabī.* Trans. ᶜAbdalḥalīm an-Najjār. 3 vols. Cairo: Dār al-maᶜārīf, 1959–62.

Browne *LHP* = E. G. Browne. *A Literary History of Persia.* 4 vols. Cambridge: Cambridge University Press, 1956–59. (Reprint of 1902–24 reissue).

Campbell *OPS* = J. Campbell. "Oral Poetry in *The Seafarer.*" *Speculum* 35 (1960): 87–96.

Cantineau *CPA* = J. Cantineau. *Cours de phonétique arabe.* In *Études de linguistique arabe: Memorial Jean Cantineau.* Paris: Librairie C. Klincksieck, 1960. Pp. 1–125. (Reprint of 1941 edition.)

Caskel *AA* = W. Caskel. "Aijām al-ᶜArab. Studien zur altarabischen Epik." *Islamica* 4 = 3:5 (1931): 1–99.

——— *BBGA* = *Die Bedeutung der Beduinen in der Geschichte der Araber.* = *Arbeitsgemeinschaft für Forschung des Landes Nordrhein-Westfalen (Geisteswissenschaften)* 8. Cologne/Opalden: Westdeutscher Verlag, 1953.

——— *GN* = *Ǧamharat an-nasab, das genealogische Werk des Hišām ibn Muḥammad al-Kalbī.* 2 vols. Leiden: Brill, 1966.

CDC = *Classicisme et déclin culturel dans l'histoire de l'Islam. Actes du symposium international d'histoire de la civilisation musulmane (Bordeaux 25–29 juin 1956).* Ed. R. Brunschwig and G. E. von Grunebaum. Paris: Maisonneuve, 1957.

CH = Wace/Stubbings *CH*.

Chadwicks *GL* = H. and N. Chadwick. *The Growth of Literature*. 3 vols. Cambridge: Cambridge University Press, 1932—40.

Chaytor *FSP* = H. J. Chaytor. *From Script to Print: An Introduction to Medieval Vernacular Literature*. New York: October House, 1967.

Chejne *ALRH* = A. Chejne. *The Arabic Language: Its Role in History*. Minneapolis: University of Minnesota Press, 1969.

Chelhod *ISI* = J. Chelhod. *Introduction à la sociologie de l'Islam: de l'animisme à l'universalisme*. = *Islam d'hier et d'aujourd'hui* 12. Paris: Maisonneuve, 1958.

CHI = *The Cambridge History of Islam*. Ed. P. M. Holt et al. 2 vols. Cambridge: Cambridge University Press, 1970.

Chomsky, Noam. *Aspects of the Theory of Syntax*. Cambridge, Mass.: M.I.T. Press, 1965.

Christenson, R. "Myth, Metaphor, and Simile." In Seboek *MS* 64–80.

Clark *RGRE* = D. L. Clark. *Rhetoric in Greco-Roman Education*. New York: Columbia University Press, 1957.

CMH = *The Cambridge Medieval History*. Vol IV: *The Byzantine Empire*. Part I: *Byzantium and Its Neighbors*. Ed. J. M. Hussey. Cambridge: Cambridge University Press, 1966.

Cohen, *ELA* = D. Cohen. "Les Etudes linguistiques arabes à propos de quelques ouvrages récentes." *RES* 39 (1971): 169–83.

——— *KLD* = "*Koinè*, langues communes et dialectes arabes." In D. Cohen, *Etudes de linguistique sémitique et arabe*. = *Janua linguarum . . . series practica* 81. The Hague and Paris: Mouton, 1970.

Corriente *FY* = F. Corriente. "On the Functional Yield of Some Synthetic Devices in Arabic and Semitic Morphology." *JQR* 62 (1971–72): 20–50.

——— FY_2 = "Again on the Functional Yield of Some Synthetic Devices in Arabic and Semitic Morphology." *JQR* 64 (1973): 154–63.

Croce, B. *Aesthetic*. Rev. ed. Trans. D. Ainslie. New York: Noonday, 1960. (Reimpression of 1922 edition.)

Crosby, R. "Chaucer and the Custom of Oral Delivery." *Speculum* 13 (1938): 413–32.

Crosby *OD* = "Oral Delivery in the Middle Ages." *Speculum* 11 (1936): 88–110.

Culley *OFL* = R. Culley. *Oral Formulaic Language in the Biblical Psalms*. Toronto: University of Toronto Press, 1967.

Curschmann *OPML* = M. Curschmann. "Oral Poetry in Mediaeval English, French, and German Literature: Some Notes on Recent Research." *Speculum* 42 (1967): 36–52.

Dain *MSS* = A. Dain. *Les Manuscrits*. New ed. Paris: "Les Belles-lettres," 1964.

Ḍayf, Šawqī. *At-Taṭwwur wa t-tajdīd fa š-ši ᶜir al-umawī,* 2d ed. Cairo: Dār al-maᶜarif, 1959.

Ḍayf *MN* = Šawqī Ḍayf, *Al-Madāris an-naḥwīya*. Cairo: Dār al-maᶜarif, 1968.

Dégh *FS* = L. Dégh. *Folktales and Society: Story-telling in a Hungarian Peasant Community*. Trans. Emily M. Schossberger. Bloomington: Indiana University Press, 1969.

Devreese, R. "Le Christianisme dans la province d'Arabie." *Vivre et penser* 2 = *Revue biblique* 51 (1942): 110–46.

DHS = *The Dream and Human Societies*. Ed. G. E. von Grunebaum and R. Caillois. Berkeley and Los Angeles: University of California Press, 1966.

Diem *KG* = W. Diem. *Das Kitāb al-ǧīm des Abū ᶜAmr aš-Šaibānī: ein Beitrag zur arabischen Lexicographie* (Inaugural-Dissertation). Munich: Ludwig-Maximilians Universität, 1968.

——— *FKA* = "Die nabatäischen Inschriften und die Frage der Kasusflexion im Altarabischen." *ZDMG* 123 (1973): 227–37.

Dorson, R. "Oral Styles of American Folk Narrators." In Seboek *SL* 27–51.

Duggan, J. "Formulas in the *Couronnement de Louis*." *Romania* 87 (1966): 313–44.

——— *SR* = *The Song of Roland: Formulaic Style and Poetic Craft*. Berkeley and Los Angeles: University of California Press, 1973.

Dundes *SF* = *The Study of Folklore*. Ed. A. Dundes. Englewood Cliffs, N.J.: Prentice-Hall, 1965. (Studies by Bascom, Utley, et al.).

Dussaud *PAS* = R. Dussaud. *La Pénétration des Arabes en Syrie avant l'Islam*. = Institut français d'archéologie de Beyrouth. *Bibliothèque archéologique et historique* LIX. Paris: P. Geuthner, 1955.

Edwards *LHTC* = G. P. Edwards. *The Language of Hesiod in Its Traditional Context*. = *Publications of the Philological Society* 22. Oxford: Blackwell, 1971.

Eliade, M. *The Sacred and the Profane: The Nature of Religion*. Trans. W. R. Trask. New York: Harper, 1961.

Emeneau *OPSI* = M. B. Emeneau. "Oral Poets of South India—The Todas." In D. Hymes, ed. *Language in Culture and Society: A Reader in Linguistics and Anthropology*. New York: Harper & Row, 1964. Pp. 330–40. (Article first appeared in *JAF* 71 [1958]: 312–24.)

——— *SMOL* = "Style and Meaning in an Oral Literature." *Language* 42 (1966): 323–45.

Fabre-d'Olivet, A. *Le Vers Dorés de Pythagore*. . . . New ed. Paris: L. Bodin, 18--.

Farmer *HAM* = H. G. Farmer. *A History of Arabian Music to the XIIIth Century*. London: Luzac, 1967. (Reprint of 1929 edition.)

Ferguson *AK* = Ch. Ferguson. "The Arabic Koine." *Language* 35 (1959): 616–30.

Fih = Abu l-Faraj M. b. Isḥāq an-Nadīm. *Kitāb al-Fihrist*. Ed. G. Flügel, J. Roediger, and A. Müller. 2 vols. Beirut: Khayat's, 1964. (Photo-offset reprint of 1871–72 edition.)

Finnegan *OLA* = R. Finnegan. *Oral Literature in Africa*. Oxford: Clarendon Press, 1970.

al-Fīrūzābādī Majdaddīn M. b. Yaᶜqūb. *Al-Qāmūs al-muḥīṭ*. 4 vols. Cairo: Muṣṭafa al-Ḥalabī, 1952. (Photo-offset reprint of 1330–32 edition.)

Fischer *AA* = A. Fischer. "Arab. [*ayš*]." *ZDMG* 59 (1905): 807–18.

Fischer *SVA* = W. Fischer. "Silbenstruktur and Vokalismus im Arabischen." *ZDMG* 117 (1967): 30–77.

Fleisch *AC* = H. Fleisch. *L'Arabe classique: esquisse d'une structure linguistique*. New ed. = *Recherches publiées sous la direction de l'Institut de lettres orientales de Beyrouth*, series 2: *Langue et littérature arabes* 5. Beirut: Dār al-Machreq, 1968.

——— *ACAD* = "Arabe classique et arabe dialectal." *Travaux et jours* 12 (1964): 23–62.

——— *ALP* = "L'Aspect lexical de la phrase arabe classique." *Studia biblica et orientalia* III = *Analecta biblica* 12 (1949): 78–94.

——— *IELS* = *Introduction à l'étude des langues sémitiques: éléments de bibliographie*. = *Initiation á l'Islam* 4. Paris: Adrien-Maisonneuve, 1947.

——— *TPA* = *Traité de philologie arabe*. Vol. I: *Préliminaires, phonétique, morphologie nominale*. = *Recherches publiées sous la direction de l'Institut de lettres orientales de Beyrouth* 16. Beirut: Imprimerie catholique, 1961.

Flügel *GSA* = G. Flügel. *Die grammatischen Schulen der Araber*, 1. Abt. = *AbhDMG* 2:4 (1862). Neudeln, Lichtenstein: Kraus, 1966. (Photo-offset reprint of 1862 edition.)

Friedman *FIT* = A. B. Friedman. "The Formulaic Improvisation Theory of Ballad Tradition—a Counter-Statement." *JAF* 74 (1961): 113–15.

Fück *Ar* = J. Fück. *ᶜArabīya: Recherches sur l'histoire de la langue et du style arabe*. Trans. Cl. Denizeau. Paris: Librairie M. Didier, 1955. (Cited according to the pagination of 1950 German edition, noted in margins.)

FYT = *Fifty Years (and Twelve) of Classical Scholarship*. New York: Barnes & Noble 1968. (Studies by E. R. Dodds and L. R. Palmer).

Gabrieli, F. "Elementi epici nell'antica poesia araba." In *La poesia epica e la sua formazione*. = *Problemi attuali di scienza e di cultura* (Accademia Nazionale de Lincei), Anno CCCLXVII (1970), Quaderno n. 139, 751–58.

Gabrieli *ASB* = F. Gabrieli, ed. *L'antica società beduina*. = *URCSS* 2 (1959). (Studies by M. Höfner, J. Henninger, and F. Gabrieli.)

——— *LT* = "Literary Tendencies." In G. E. von Grunebaum, ed. *Unity and Variety in Muslim Civilization*. Chicago: University of Chicago Press, 1955. Pp. 87–106.

Gaudefroy-Demombynes *ILPP* = Ibn Qutayba. *Introduction au Livre de la poésie et des poètes*. Intro., trans. and ed. M. Gaudefroy-Demombynes. Paris: "Les Belles-Lettres," 1947.

Geyer rev *VSA* = R. Geyer. Review of Vollers *VSA*. *Göttingische gelehrte Anzeigen* 171 (1909): 10–56.

Gibb *ALI* = H. A. R. Gibb. *Arabic Literature: An Introduction*. 2d ed. Oxford: Oxford University Press, 1963.

——— *APAP* = "Arab Poet and Arabic Philologist." *BSOAS* 12 (1948): 574–78.

——— *SCI* = *Studies on the Civilization of Islam*. Ed. S. J. Shaw and W. R. Polk. Boston: Beacon Press, 1962.

Goldziher, I. "Der Dīwān des Ǵarwal b. Aus al-Ḥuṭej'a. A. Einleitung." *ZDMG 46* (1892): 1—53.

———. "Some Notes on the Dīwāns of the Arabic Tribes." *JRAS* 1897:, 325–34.

Goldhizer *AAP* = *Abhandlungen zur arabischen Philologie*. 1. Theil. Leiden: Brill, 1896.

——— *BGSA* = "Beiträge zur Geschichte der Sprachgelehrsamkeit bei den Arabern. I-III." *SBWA* 67 (1867): 207–51; 72 (1872): 587–631; 73 (1873): 511–52.

——— *EM* = "Education (Muslim)." In. J. Hastings, ed. *Encyclopaedia of Religion and Ethics* 5:198a–207b. New York: Scribner's, 1920.

——— *MS* = *Muhammedanische Studien*. In 2 parts. Hildesheim: Olms, 1961. (Photo-offset reprint of 1888–90 edition.) For *MS* I, I have used the translation of S. M. Stern and C. R. Berber. *Muslim Studies*. London: Allen & Unwin, 1967. (Cited according to pagination of original German edition, noted in margins.)

——— *SHCAL* = *A Short History of Classical Arabic Literature*. Trans. and ed. J. Desomogyi. Hildesheim: Olms, 1966.

Grohmann *ECAP* = A. Grohmann. *Einführung und Chrestomathie zur arabischen Papyruskunde* I. = *Monographie Archivu orientálního* 13:1. Prague: Státní Pedagogické Nakladatelstvi, 1954.

Grunebaum, G. E. von. "I^{c}d̲jāz." *EI*^{2} 3:1018a–1020b.

von Grunebaum *AFAL* = "The Aesthetic Foundation of Arabic Literature." *Comparative Literature* 4 (1952): 323–40.

——— *CFD* = "Zur Chronologie der früharabischen Dichtung." *Orientalia* n.s. 8 (1939): 328—45.

——— *CI* = *Classical Islam: A History, 600–1258*. Trans. K. Watson. Chicago: Aldine, 1970.

——— *CPAT* = "The Concept of Plagiarism in Arabic Theory." *JNES* 3 (1944): 234–53.

——— *GSAP* = "Growth and Structure of Arabic Poetry." In N. A. Faris, ed. *The Arab Heritage*. Princeton, N.J.: Princeton University Press, 1944. Pp. 121–36.

——— *KD* = *Kritik und Dichtkunst: Studien zur arabischen Literaturgeschichte*. Wiesbaden: Harrassowitz, 1955. (Consists mostly of German versions of articles originally published in English.)

——— *MWO* = "Von Muḥammads Wirkung und Originalität." *WZKM* 44 (1937): 29–50.

——— *NAU* = "The Nature of Arab Unity before Islam." *Arabica* 10 (1963): 5–23.

——— *SICH* = *Studies in Islamic Cultural History*. = *The American Anthropologist*. 56:2:2, Memoir no. 76, April 1954.

——— *TCD* = *A Tenth-century Document of Arabic Literary Theory and Criticism: The Sections on Poetry of al-Bāqillānī's I^{c}jāz al-Qur'ān*. Chicago: University of Chicago Press, 1950.

GTAML I = H. Hunger et al. *Geschichte der Textuberlieferung der antiken und mittelalterlichen Literatur*. I. *Antikes und mittelalterliches Buch- und Schriftwesen: Überlieferungsgeschichte der antiken Literatur*. Zurich: Atlantis, 1961.

Guillaume, A. *Prophecy and Divination among the Hebrews and Other Semites*. = *The Bampton Lectures, 1938*. London: Hodder & Stoughton, 1938.

Guillaume *LM* = *The Life of Muhammad: A Translation of Ibn Isḥaq's Sīrat Rasūl Allāh*. Trans. A. Guillaume. Lahore, Karachi, and Dacca: Oxford University Press, Pakistan Branch, 1957. (Reprint of 1955 edition.)

Gyger (née Jones), A. "The Old English *Soul and Body* as an Example of Oral Transmission." *Medium Aevum* 38 (1969): 239–44.

Haddara ISA = M. Muṣṭafa Haddāra. *Ittijāhāt aš-šiʿr al-ʿarabī fi l-qarn at̲-t̲āni l-hijrī*. = *Maktabat ad-dirāsāt al-adabīya* 29. Cairo: Dār al-maʿārif, 1963.

Hainsworth *FHF* = J. B. Hainsworth. *The Flexibility of the Homeric Formula*. Oxford: Oxford University Press, 1968.

Hall *CCT* = F. W. Hall. *A Companion to Classical Texts*. Oxford: Oxford University Press, 1913.

Harriott, R. *Poetry and Criticism before Plato*. London: Methuen, 1969.

Hārūn *NM* = *Nawādir al-maxṭūṭāt*. Ed. ᶜAbdassalām M. Hārūn. 2 vols. Cairo: Lajnat at-ta'līf wa t-tarjama wa n-našr, 1370–74/1951–55.

Havelock, E. *Preface to Plato*. Cambridge, Mass.: Harvard University Press, 1963.

Haywood *AL* = J. Haywood. *Arabic Lexicography*. 2d ed. Leiden: Brill, 1965.

Hell *AC* = J. Hell. *The Arab Civilization*. Trans. S. Khuda Bakhsh. Lahore: Sh. M. Ashraf, 1943.

Hirsch, E. D. *Validity in Interpretation*. New Haven, Conn.: Yale University Press, 1967.

Hoekstra *HMFP* = A. Hoekstra. *Homeric Modifications of Formulaic Prototypes: Studies in the Development of Greek Epic Diction*. = *Verhandelingen der knkl. Nederlandse Akad. van Wetenschappen, Afd. Letterkunde*, N. R. 71:i. Amsterdam, 1965.

Hollander *Skalds* = L. Hollander. *The Skalds*. Ann Arbor: University of Michigan Press, 1968.

Holoka *HOS* = J. Holoka. "Homeric Originality: A Survey." *Classical World* 66 (1973): 257–93.

Horton/Finnegan *MT* = *Modes of Thought: Essays on Thinking in Western and Non-western Societies*. Ed. R. Horton and R. Finnegan. London: Faber & Faber, 1973.

Ibn ᶜAbdrabbih *IF* = Abū ᶜUmar Aḥmad b. M. b. ᶜAbdrabbih al-Andalusī. *Kitāb al-ᶜIqd al-farīd*. Ed. Aḥmad Amīn et al. 7 vols. Cairo: Lajnat at-ta'līf wa t-tarjama wa n-našr; 1948–49.

Ibn al-Anbārī *IMX* = Abu l-Barakāt Ibn al-Anbārī. *Kitāb al-inṣāf fī masā'il al-xilāf bayna n-naḥwīyīn al-baṣrīyīn wa l-kūfīyīn*. Ed. G. Weil. Leiden: Brill, 1913.

——— = Ibid. Ed. M. Muhyiddīn ᶜAbdalḥamīd. 2 vols. Cairo: at-Tijārīya al-kubrā, 1380/1961.

Ibn al-Aṯīr *NGH* = Majdaddīn Abu s-Saᶜādāt al-Mubārak b. M. al-Jazarī Ibn al-Aṯīr. *An-Nihāya fī ġarīb al-ḥadīṯ*, 5 vols. Cairo: ᶜIsā al-Halabī, 1963–65.

Ibn Fāris *SFL* = Abu l-Ḥusayn Aḥmad b. Fāris. *Aṣ-Ṣāḥibī fī fiqh al-luġa wa sunan al-ᶜArab fī kalāmi-hā*. Ed. Moustafa el-Chouémi. = *Bibliotheca philologica arabica* I. Beirut: A. Badran, 1964.

Ibn Habīb, Muḥammad, Abū Jaᶜfar. *Kitāb alqāb aš-šuᶜarā'*. In Hārūn *NM* 2:299–328.

Ibn Hišām *Sīra* = Abū Muḥammad ᶜAbdalmalik b. Hišām. *Kitāb sīrat Rasūl Allāh: Das Leben Muhammed's nach Muhammed Ibn Ishak*. Ed. F. Wüstenfeld. 2 vols. Frankfurt: Minerva, 1961. (Photo-offset reprint of 1858–60 edition.)

Ibn Jinni *Xas* = Abu l-Fatḥ ᶜUṯmān b. Jinnī. *Al-Xaṣā'iṣ*. Ed. M. ᶜAlī an-Najjār. 3 vols. Cairo: Dār al-kutub al-miṣrīya, 1952–56.

Ibn al-Kalbī *AX* = Hišām b. Muḥammad al-Kalbī. *Ansāb al-xayl fī l-jāhilīya wa l-Islām wa axbāru-hā*. Ed. Aḥmad Zakī. Cairo: Dār al-kutub al-miṣrīya, 1946.

Ibn Kaysān *TQ* = Abu l-Ḥasan M. b. Aḥmad b. Kaysān. *Kitāb Talqīb al-qawāfī wa talqīb ḥarakāti-hā*. Ed. W. Wright. In W. Wright, ed. *Opuscula Arabica*. Leiden: Brill, 1859.

Ibn Manẓūr = LA.

Ibn Qutayba *SS* = Abū M. ^{c}Abdallāh b. Muslim b. Qutayba. *Aš-Ši^{c}r wa š-šu^{c}arā'*. Beirut: Dār aṯ-ṯiqāfa, 1964 (Edition based on 1902 De Goeje edition, with additional notes by Yūsuf Najm & Iḥsān ^{c}Abbās).

Ibn Rašīq *Umda* = Abū ^{c}Alī al-Ḥasan b. Rašīq al-Qayrawānī. *Al-^{c}Umda fī maḥāsin aš-ši^{c}r wa ādābi-hi wa naqdi-h*. Ed. M. Muḥyiddīn ^{c}Abdalḥamīd. 2d ed. 2 vols. Cairo: at-Tijārīya al-kubrā, 1963–64.

Ibn Sallām *TFS* = Abū ^{c}Abdallāh M. b. Sallām al-Jumaḥī. *Ṭabaqāt fuḥūl aš-šu^{c}arā'*. Ed. Maḥmūd M. Šākir. = *Ḏaxā'ir al-^{c}Arab* 7. Cairo: Dār al-ma^{c}ārif, 1952.

Ibn as-Sikkīt *IM* = Abū Yūsuf Ya^{c}qūb b. as-Sikkīt. *Iṣlāḥ al-manṭiq*. 2d ed. Ed. Aḥmad M. Šākir and ^{c}Abdassalām M. Hārūn. = *Ḏaxā'ir al-^{c}Arab* 3. Cairo: Dār al-ma^{c}ārif, 1970.

——— *TA* = *Kitāb Tahḏīb al-alfāẓ*. With commentary by at-Tibrīzī. Ed. L. Cheikho. Beirut: Imprimerie Catholique, 1896–98.

Ibn Xaldūn *Muq* = Abū Zayd ^{c}Abdarraḥmān b. M. b. Xaldūn. *Al-Muqaddima*. Ed. ^{c}Alī ^{c}Abdalwāḥid Wāfī. Vol. 1: 2d ed.; vols. 2–4: 1st ed. Cairo: Lajnat al-bayān al-^{c}arabī, 1384/1965 (vol 1); 1378–82/1958–62 (vols. 2–4). Usually referred to is the translation of F. Rosenthal. *The Muqaddimah: An Introduction to History*. New York: Pantheon, 1958.

Ibn Xayr *Index* = Abū Bakr M. b. Xayr al-Išbīlī. *Fahrasat mā rawā-hu ^{c}an šuyūxi-h. . . .* Ed. F. Codera and J. Ribera Tarrago. Baghdad: al-Muṯannā, 1963. (Reissue of 1893 edition.)

Irigoin, J. Review of *GTAML*. In *BZ* 55 (1962): 317.

al-Iṣfahānī *THT* = Ḥamza b. al-Ḥasan al-Iṣfahānī. *At-Tanbīh ^{c}alā ḥudūṯ at-taṣḥīf*. Ed. M. Ḥasan Āl Yāsīn. Baghdad: Nahḍa, 1387/1967.

Jacob *AB* = G. Jacob. *Altarabisches Beduinenleben*. Hildesheim: Olms, 1967. (Photo-offset reprint of 1897 edition.)

Jacobi *SPAQ* = R. Jacobi. *Studien zur Poetik der altarabischen Qaṣide*. = Akad. der Wissenschaften und der Literatur. *Veröffentlichungen der orientalischen Kommission* 24. Wiesbaden: Franz Steiner, 1971.

al-Jāḥiẓ, Abū ^{c}Uṯmān ^{c}Amr b. Baḥr. *Risāla fī madḥ al-kutub*. Ed. A. Rufai. Berlin (dissertation): 1935.

al-Jaḥīẓ *BT* = *Al-Bayān wa t-tabyīn*. 2d ed. Ed. ^{c}Abdassalām M. Hārūn. 4 vols. Cairo: al-Xānjī, 1960–61.

——— *KH* = *Kitāb al-Ḥayawān*. Ed. ^{c}Abdassalām M. Hārūn. 7 vols. Cairo: Muṣṭafā al-Ḥalabī, 1938(?)–45.

al-Jawharī *Sih* = Abū Naṣr Ismā^{c}īl b. Ḥammād al-Jawharī. *Aṣ-Ṣiḥāḥ—tāj al-luġa wa ṣiḥāḥ al-^{c}arabīya*. Ed. Aḥmad ^{c}Abdalġafūr ^{c}Aṭṭār. 6 vols. Cairo: Maṭābi^{c} Dār al-kitāb al-^{c}arabīy, 1377/1957.

Jebb, R. C. *Homer: An Introduction to the Iliad and the Odyssey*. 7th ed. Boston and New York: Ginn & Co., 189–.

Jeffery *QS* = A. Jeffery. *The Qur'ān as Scripture*. New York: R. F. Moore, 1952.

Jones *CMOT* = J. H. Jones. "Commonplace and Memorization in the Oral Tradition of the English and Scottish Popular Ballads." *JAF* 74 (1961): 97–112.

Kahle *ARK* = P. Kahle. "The Arabic Readers of the Koran." *JNES* 8 (1949): 65–71.

——— *CG^2* = *The Cairo Geniza*. 2d ed. Oxford: Blackwell, 1959.

——— *QA* "The Qur'ān and the ^{c}Arabīya." In S. Löwinger and J. Somogyi (eds). *Ignace Goldziher Memorial Volume I*. Budapest: 1948. Pp. 163–82.

Kister, M. "The Seven Odes: Some Notes on the Compilation of the *Mu^{c}allaqāt*." *RSO* 44 (1969): 27–36.

———. "A Work of Ibn al-Kalbī on the Arab Peninsula." *BSOAS* 33 (1970): 590–91.

Knox, B. M. W. "Silent Reading in Antiquity." *Greek, Roman, and Byzantine Studies* 9 (1968): 421–35.

Köbert, R. Review of Shahīd *MN*. *Orientalia* n.s. 42 (1973): 462–66.

Kopf *RIAP* = L. Kopf. "Religious Influences on Medieval Arabic Philology." *SI* 5 (1956): 33–59.

Kosegarten *PH* = *The Poems of the Huzailis*. Vol. I. Ed. J. Kosegarten. London: Oriental Translation Fund/Greifswald, 1854.

Kraemer, J. "Arabische Homerverse." *ZDMG* 106 (1956): 259–316.

Kramers *AO* = J. J. Kramers. *Analecta Orientalia*. Vol. 2. Leiden: Brill 1956.

Krenkow, F. "Ḳaṣīda." In *EI^1* 2:796.

——— . "Shā^{c}ir." In *EI^1* 4:285–86.

Krenkow *UWP* = "Use of Writing for the Preservation of Ancient Arabic Poetry." In T. W. Arnold and R. Nicholson (eds.). *A Volume of Oriental Studies Presented to Edward G. Browne. . . .* Cambridge: Cambridge University Press, 1922. Pp. 261–68.

LA = M. b. Mukarram Ibn Manẓūr al-Miṣrī. *Lisān al-^{c}Arab*, 20 vols. Būlāq: al-Amīrīya, 1300–1308 H.

Lammens, H. "La Corporation des 'Rāwia'." In H. Lammens. *Etudes sur le siècle des Omayyades*. Beirut: Imprimerie catholique, 1930. Pp. 263–64.

Lammens *BI* = H. Lammens. *Le Berceau de l'Islam*. Vol. I: *Le climat–les Bédouins*. Rome: Pontifical Biblical Institute, 1914.

——— *CO* = "Le Chantre des Omiades." *Journal asiatique* ser. 9:4 (1894): 94–176, 193–241, 381–459.

Lane *Lex* = E. W. Lane. *Arabic-English Lexicon*, Book I (1 vol. in 8 pts.). New York: F. Ungar, 1955–56. (Photo-offset reprint of 1863–93 edition.)

Lecerf *DFC* = J. Lecerf. "The Dream in Popular Culture: Arabic and Islamic." In *DHS* 365–79.

Leeuw, G. van der. *Sacred and Profane Beauty: The Holy in Art*. Trans. D. E. Green. New York: Holt, Rinehart & Winston, 1963.

Leipoldt/Morenz *HS* = J. Leipoldt and S. Morenz. *Heilige Schriften: Betrachtungen zur Religionsgeschichte der antiken Mittelmeerwelt*. Leipzig: Harrassowitz, 1953.

Lesky *HGL* = A. Lesky. *A History of Greek Literature*. Trans. J. Willis and C. de Heer. New York: T. Y. Crowell, 1966.

Levi Della Vida *LSPF* = G. Levi Della Vida. *Linguistica semitica: Presente e futuro.* = *URCSS* 4 (1961).

Lévi-Strauss, Cl. "The Structural Study of Myth." In Sebeok *MS* 81–106.

Lichtenstädter *NAQ* = I. Lichtenstädter. "Das *Nasīb* der altarabischen *Qaṣīde.*" *Islamica* 5 (1932): 17–96.

Lieberman *HJP* = S. Lieberman. *Hellenism in Jewish Palestine.* = *Texts and Studies of the Jewish Theological Seminary of America* 18. New York: Jewish Theological Seminary of America, 5722/1962.

Lord *HOP* = A. Lord. "Homer as Oral Poet." *HSCP* 77 (1968): 1–46.

——— *HPH* = "Homer, Parry, and Huso." *American Journal of Archaeology* 52 (1942): 34–44.

——— *ST* = *The Singer of Tales.* New York: Atheneum, 1965.

Lyall *AAP* = Ch. J. Lyall. *Translations of Ancient Arabian Poetry.* London: Williams & Norgate, 1930.

Maas, P. *Textual Criticism.* Trans. B. Flower. Oxford: Oxford University Press, 1958.

Macdonald *RALI* = D. B. Macdonald. *The Religious Attitude and Life in Islam.* Chicago: University of Chicago Press, 1909.

Mackenson *ABL* = R. Mackenson. "Arabic Books and Libraries in the Umaiyad Period." In three parts and "Supplementary Notes" (= s. n.).*American Journal of Semitic Languages and Literatures* 52 (1935–36): 245–53; 53 (1936–37): 239–50; 54 (1937): 41–61; 56 (1939): 149–57 ("Supplementary Notes").

Magoun *BSC* = F. P. Magoun. "Bede's Story of Caedman: The Case History of an Anglo-Saxon Oral Singer." *Speculum* 30 (1955): 49—63.

Margoliouth *OAP* = D. Margoliouth. "The Origins of Arabic Poetry." *JRAS* (1925): 417–49.

Marrou *HEA* = H. I. Marrou. *A History of Education in Antiquity.* Trans. G. Lamb. New York: New American Library, 1964 (Reprint of 1954 edition.)

al-Marzubānī *MS* = Abū ^{c}Ubaydallāh M. b. ^{c}Imrān al-Marzubānī. *Mu^{c}jam aš-šu^{c}arā'.* Ed. ^{c}Abdassattār Aḥmad Farrāj. Cairo: ^{c}Īsa al-Ḥalabī, 1379/1960.

———*Muw* = *Al-Muwaššaḥ—ma'āxiḏ al-^{c}ulamā' ^{c}ala š-šu^{c}arā' fī^{c}iddat anwā^{c} min ṣinā^{c}at aš-ši^{c}r.* Cairo: Nahḍa, 1965.

———/al-Yaġmūrī *NQ* = *Die belehrten Biographien des Abū ^{c}Ubaidallāh al-Marzubānī in der Rezension des Ḥāfiẓ al-Yaġmūrī.* Ed. R. Sellheim. (= *Kitāb Nūr al-Qabas al-muxtaṣar min al-Muqtabas*). Part I: *Text.* = *Bibliotheca islamica* 23a. Wiesbaden: F. Steiner, 1964.

Maslūt *NI* = ^{c}Abdalḥamīd al-Maslūt. *Naẓarīyat al-inithāl fī š-ši^{c}r al-jāhilī.* Cairo: Dār al-qalam, n.d.

Maṭar *LB* = ^{c}Abdal^{c}azīz Maṭar. *Lahjat al-badw fī iqlīm Sāhil Marbūt: dirāsa luġawīya.* Cairo: al-kitāb al-^{c}arabī, 1967.

al-Maydānī, Abu l-Faḍl Aḥmad b. M. *Majma^{c} al-amṯāl.* 2 vols. Cairo: al-Xayrīya, 1310 H.

Mazon *Intro* = P. Mazon et al. *Introduction a l'Iliade.* Paris: "Les Belles-Lettres," 1942.

Meier *SAI* = F. Meier. "Some Aspects of Inspiration by Demons in Islam." In *DHS* 421–29.

Menéndez Pidal *CR* = R. Menéndez Pidal. *La Chanson de Roland et la tradition épique des Francs.* 2d ed. Trans. I.-M. Cluzel. Paris: A. & J. Picard, 1960.

Merx. A. "Reflections historiques sur l'origine de la grammair arabe." *Bulletin de l'Institut egyptien,* 3ᵉ sér. 2 (1891): 13–26.

Merx *HAG* = A. Merx. *Historia artis grammatica apud Syros.* = *Abh. für die Kunde des Morgenlandes* 9:2 (1889). Neudeln, Lichtenstein: Kraus Reprint, 1966 (Photo-offset reprint of 1889 edition.)

Monroe *OCPP* = J. Monroe. "Oral Composition in Pre-Islamic Poetry." *Journal of Arabic Literature* 3 (1972): 1–53.

Moscati *SAH* = S. Moscati. *The Semites in Ancient History.* Cardiff: University of Wales Press, 1959.

al-Mubarrad *Kāmil* = Abu l-ᶜAbbās M. b. Yazīd al-Mubarrad. *Al-Kāmil.* Ed. M. Abu l-Faḍl Ibrāhīm and as-Sayyid Saḥḥātah. Cairo: Nahḍa, 1956.

Mukarram *QKA* = ᶜAbdalᶜāl Sālim Mukarram. *Al-Qur'ān al-karīm wa aṯaru-h fi d-dirāsāt an-naḥwīya.* Cairo: Dār al-maᶜārif, 1968.

Müller, D. H. "Arabia." In Pauly/Wisowa *RECA* II 344–59. (With appendix by Pietschmann on "Arabia als römische Provinz," 359–62.)

Musil *MCRB* = A. Musil *The Manners and Customs of the Rwala Bedouins.* = *American Geographical Society Oriental Explorations and Studies* No. 6. New York: American Geographical Society, 1928.

Nagler, M. *Spontaneity and Tradition: A Study in the Oral Art of Homer.* Berkeley and Los Angeles: University of California Press, 1974.

——— *FMHE* = *Formula and Motif in Homeric Epics: Prolegomena to an Aesthetics of Oral Poetry.* Ph.D. dissertation, University of California, 1955 (Microfilm Order No. 66-8347).

——— *TGV* = "Towards a Generative View of the Oral Formula." *TAPA* 98 (1967): 269–311.

Nallino *LAOU* = C.-A. Nallino. *La Littérature arabe des origines à l'époque de la dynastie umayyade.* Trans. Ch. Pellat. = *Islam d'hier et d'aujourd'hui* 6. Paris: Maisonneuve, 1950.

Naq = *The Nakā'iḍ of Jarīr and al-Farazdaḳ* Ed. A. A. Bevan. 3 vols. Leiden: Brill, 1905–12.

Nicholson *LHA* = R. A. Nicholson. *A Literary History of the Arabs.* Cambridge: Cambridge University Press, 1956.

Nöldeke, Th. "Arabia, Arabians." In *EB* 1:272b–275a.

———. "Einige Bemerkungen über das Werk Ǧamharat ăsᶜār al-ᶜArab." *ZDMG* 49 (1895): 290–93.

Nöldeke. *BKPA* = *Beiträge zur Kenntnis der Poesie der alten Araber.* Hildesheim: Olms, 1967. (Photo-offset reprint of 1864 edition.)

———*BSS* = *Beiträge zur semitischen Sprachwissenschaft.* Strassburg: Trübner, 1904.

——— *FM* = "Fünf Moᶜallaqāt übersetzt und erklärt." In three parts. *SBWA* 140:vii (1899); 142:v (1900); 144:i (1901).

——— *GCA* = *Zur Grammatik des classischen Arabisch*. (Im Anhang: die handschriftlichen Ergänzungen in dem Hand exemplar . . . Nöldekes bearbeitet und mit Zusätzen versehen von Anton Spitaler). Darmstadt: Wissenschaftliche Buchgesellschaft, 1963. (Photo-offset reprint of 1897 edition.)

——— *NBSS* = *Neue Beiträge zur semitischen Sprachwissenschaft*. Strassburg: Trübner, 1910.

———/ Schwally *GQ* = Th. Nöldeke. *Geschichte des Qorāns*. Rev. ed. Fr. Schwally et al. In two parts. Hildesheim and New York: Olms, 1970. (Photo-offset reprint of 1909–19 edition.) Cf. Bergsträsser/Pretzl *GK*.

Notopoulos, J. A. "Mnemosyne in Oral Literature." *TAPA* 69 (1938): 465–93.

Nykl, A. R. *Hispano-Arabic Poetry and Its Relations with the Old Provençal Troubadours*. Baltimore: n.p. [printed by J. H. Furst Co.], 1946.

Oppenheim, A. L. "The Eyes of the Lord." *JAOS* 88 (1968): 173–80.

O'Neil, W. A. "Another Look at Oral Poetry in *The Seafarer*." *Speculum* 35 (1960): 596–600.

Paret *MK* = R. Paret. *Mohammed und der Koran*. 2d ed. = *Urban-Bücher* 32. Stuttgard: W. Kohlhammer, 1957.

Parry EHV = M. Parry. "The Distinctive Character of Enjambement in Homeric Verse." *TAPA* 50 (1929): 200–220. = *MHV* 251–65.

——— *MHV* = *The Making of Homeric Verse: The Collected Papers of Milman Parry*. Ed. A. Parry. Oxford: Clarendon Press, 1971.

——— *SET* I = "Studies in the Epic Technique of Oral Verse-Making. I. Homer and Homeric Style." *HSCP* 41 (1930): 73–147. = *MHV* 266–324.

——— *SET* II = "Studies in the Epic Technique of Oral Verse-Making. II. The Homeric Language as the Language of an Oral Poetry." *HSCP* 42 (1932): 1–50. = *MHV* 325–64.

Pauly/Wisowa *RECA* = *Paulys Realencyclopädie der classischen Altertumswissenschaft*. Ed. G. Wissowa et al. New ed. 24 vols. Stuttgart: J. B. Metzler, 1894–1963.

Pearson *IIsl* = J. D. Pearson. *Index Islamicus*. 1906–1955 (with *Supplements* for 1956–60, 1961–65, 1966–70, and continuing). Cambridge: W. Heffer & Sons, 1958–.

Pellat, Ch. "Hamāsa." *EI*² 3:110–12.

Pellat *MB* = *Le Milieu Baṣrien et la formation de Ǧāḥiẓ*. Paris: Adrien-Maisonneuve, 1953.

Petráček *QAAL* = K. Petráček. "Quellen und Anfänge der arabischen Literatur." *AO* 36 (1968): 381–406.

——— *VAL* = "Die Vorbereitungsperiode der arabischen Literatur." *Orientalia pragensia* III = *Acta Universitatis Carolinae* (1964). *Philologica* 3:35–51.

Pfeiffer *HCS* = R. Pfeiffer. *History of Classical Scholarship from the Beginnings to the End of the Hellenistic Age*. Oxford: Oxford University Press, 1968.

Picard, M. *Man and Language*. Trans. S. Godman. Chicago: H. Regnery-Gateway, 1963.

Poliak *AOS* = A. Poliak. "L'arabisation de l'Orient sémitique." *REI* 12 (1938): 35–63.

Pretzel, O. "Die Wissenschaft der Koranlesung (*ᶜIlm al-Qirāʾa*). Ihre literarischen Quellen und ihre Aussprachegrundlagen (*Uṣūl*)." *Islamica* 6 (1934): 1–47, 230–46, 290–331.

al-Qālī *Am* = Abū ᶜAlī Ismāᶜīl b. al-Qāsim al-Qālī al-Baġdādī. *Kitāb al-Amālī*. 2d ed. 2 vols. Cairo: Dār al-kutub al-miṣrīya, 1344/1926,

al-Qifṭī *IR* = Jamāladdīn Abu l-Ḥasan ᶜAlī b. Yūsuf al-Qifṭī. *Inbāh ar-ruwāh ᶜalā anbāh an-nuḥāh*. Ed. M. Abu l-Faḍl Ibrāhīm. 3 vols. Cairo: Dār al-kutub al-miṣrīya, 1950–55.

Qurʾān karīm. 3d ed. Cairo: Lajnat taṣḥīḥ al-maṣāhif, 1381/1961. (*Sūras* are indicated by Roman numerals, *āyas* by Arabic numerals. *Āya* numbers of the 1906 Flügel edition, where different, are indicated after a slash, following the conversion table given in Bell/Watt *Intro* 202–3.) Translations used are: A. J. Arberry, *The Koran Interpreted*, 2 vols. (New York: Macmillan, 1955); R. Bell, *The Qurʾān Translated, with a Critical Rearrangement of the Sūrahs*, 2 vols. (Edinburgh: T. & T. Clark, 1960 [reprint of 1937 edition]); R. Blachère, *Le Coran* (Paris: Maisonneuve & Larose, 1966); R. Paret, *Der Koran* (Stuttgart: W. Kohlhammer, 1962–63); M. M. Pickthall, *The Meaning of the Glorious Koran* (New York: New American Library, 1953).

Rabin, Ch. "ᶜArabiyya (i & ii.1)." EI^2 1:561b–567a.

Rabin *AWA* = *Ancient West Arabian*. London: Taylor's Foreign Press, 1951.

——— *BCA* = "The Beginnings of Classical Arabic." *SI* 4 (1955):19–37.

Rāḍī *STX* = M. Ḥusayn al-Qazvīnī Kīšvān. *Šarḥ tuḥfat al-Xalīl fi l-ᶜarūḍ wa l-qāfiya*. Ed. ᶜAbdalḥamīd ar-Rāḍī. Baghdad: al-ᶜĀnī, 1388/1968.

Reckendorf *AS* = H. Reckendorf. *Arabische Syntax*. Heidelberg: C. Winter, 1921.

——— *SVA* = *Die syntaktische Verhältnisse des Arabischen*. Leiden: Brill, 1967. (Photo-offset reprint of 1898 edition.)

Renon, A. "Les trois poètes Omeyyades." *IBLA* 7 (1944): 41–59.

Rescher *EU* = *Excerpte und Übersetzungen aus den Schriften des Philologen und Dogmatikers Ǧaḥiẓ aus Baçra*. Part 1. Ed. and trans. O. Rescher. Stuttgart: n.p., 1931.

Reynolds/Wilson *SS* = L. Reynolds and N. Wilson. *Scribes and Scholars*. Oxford: Oxford University Press, 1968.

Rosenthal *HMH* = F. Rosenthal. *A History of Muslim Historiography*. Rev. ed. Leiden: Brill, 1968.

——— *KT* = *Knowledge Triumphant*. Leiden: Brill, 1970.

——— rev *Ar* = Review of Fück *Ar*. *Orientalia* n.s. 22 (1953): 307–11.

——— *TAMS* = *The Technique and Approach of Muslim Scholarship*. = *Analecta orientalia* 24 (1947).

Rutherford, W. G. *A Chapter of the History of Annotation*. = *Scholia aristophanica*, vol. 3. London and New York: Macmillan, 1905.

Sandys *HCS* = J. E. Sandys. *A History of Classical Scholarship*. 3d ed. Vol. 1: *From the Sixth Century B.C. to the End of the Middle Ages*. Cambridge: Cambridge University Press, 1921.

Sauvaget/Cahen *IHME* = J. Sauvaget. *Introduction to the History of the Muslim East: A Bibliographical Guide, based on the second edition as recast by Claude*

Cahen. Ed. Near Eastern Center, U.C.L.A., et al. Berkeley and Los Angeles: University of California Press, 1965.

Sebeok *MS* = *Myth: A Symposium*. Ed. Th. A. Sebeok. Bloomington: Indiana University Press, 1965. (Reprint of 1958 edition.)

——— *SL* = *Style in Language*. Ed. Th. A. Sebeok. Cambridge, Mass.: M.I.T. Press, 1966.

Serjeant *PPH* = R. B. Serjeant. *South Arabian Poetry*. Vol. 1. *Prose and Poetry from Ḥaḍramawt*. London: Taylor's Foreign Press, 1951.

Sezgin *GAS* = F. Sezgin. *Geschichte des arabischen Schriftums*. 5 vols. to date. Leiden: Brill, 1967–.

Shahīd *CKE* =I. Shahīd. "A Contribution to Koranic Exegesis." In G. Makdisi, ed. *Arabic and Islamic Studies in Honor of Hamilton A. R. Gibb*. Cambridge, Mass.: Department of Near Eastern Languages and Literatures, Harvard University, 1965. Pp. 563–80.

——— *MN* = *The Martyrs of Najrân: New Documents*. = *Subsidia hagiographica* 49. Brussels: Société des Bollandistes, 1971.

Sībawayh *Kitāb* = Abū Bišr ᶜAmr b. ᶜUṯmān Sībawayh. *Al-Kitāb*. 2 vols. Būlāq: al-Amīrīya, 1316—17 H.

Smith *EA* = S. Smith. "Events in Arabia in the 6th Century A.D." *BSOAS* 16 (1954): 425–68.

Smith, W. Robertson. *Kinship and Marriage in Early Arabia*. Boston: Beacon Press, n.d. (Reprint of 1903 edition.)

Socin *DC* =A. Socin. *Diwan aus Centralarabien*. = *Abh. phil.-hist. Kl. kgl. sächs. Gesellschaft der Wiss*. 19 (1901). 3 parts.

Sourdel *CIC* = D. and J. Sourdel. *La Civilisation de l'Islam classique*. Paris: Arthaud: 1968.

Spitaler rev *Ar*=A. Spitaler. Review of Fück *Ar*. In *BO* 10 (1953): 144a–150a.

——— rev *VSA* =Review of Bloch *VSA*. In *Oriens* 2 (1949): 317–22.

Spuler *Sem* = *Semitistik*. Ed. B. Spuler. = *Handbuch der Orientalistik* 3. Leiden: Brill, 1954. (Articles by Brockelmann et al.)

Starcky, J. "Pétra et la Nabatène. II, i, 2, g. Ecriture nabatéenne et écriture arabe." In F. Vigouroux, ed. *Dictionnaire de la Bible. Supplement*. Vol. III. Paris: Letouzey & Ané, 1966 (fasc. 1964). Pp. 932–37.

Steinthal *GSW* = H. Steinthal. *Geschichte der Sprachwissenschaft bei die Griechen und Römern*. 2d ed. 2 vols. Hildesheim and New York: Olms, 1971. (Photo-offset reprint of 1890–91 edition.)

Stetkevych, J. "Some Observations on Arabic Poetry." *JNES* 26 (1967): 1–12.

Stevick *OFA* = R. D. Stevick. "The Oral Formulaic Analysis of Old English Verse." *Speculum* 37 (1962): 282–89.

as-Suyūti *BW* = Jalāladdīn ᶜAbdarraḥmān as-Suyūṭi. *Buġyat al-wuᶜāh fī ṭabaqāt al-luġawīyīn wa n-nuḥāh*. Ed. M. Abu l-Faḍl Ibrāhīm. 2 vols. Cairo: ᶜĪsā al-Ḥalabī, 1964–65.

———*Muz* =*Al-Muzhir fī ᶜulūm al-luġa wa anwāᶜ -hā*. Ed. M. A. Jād al-Mawlā et al. 2 vols. Cairo: ᶜĪsa al-Ḥalabi, n.d.

Ṭāhā Ḥusayn *FAJ* =Ṭāhā Ḥusayn. *Fi l-adab al-jāhilī*. Cairo: Dār al-ma^{c}ārif, n.d. (1927 and thereafter).

T̲a^{c}lab *QS* = Abu l-^{c}Abbās Aḥmad b. Yaḥyā T̲a^{c}lab. *Qawā^{c}id aš-ši^{c}r*. Ed. Ramaḍān ^{c}Abdattawwāb. Cairo: Dār al-ma^{c}rifa, 1966.

Thilo *OAP* =U. Thilo. *Die Ortsnamen in der altarabischen Poesie*. = *Schriften der Max Freiherr von Oppenheim-Stiftung* 3. Wiesbaden: Harrassowitz, 1958.

Trabulsi *CPA* =A. Trabulsi. *La Critique poétique des Arabes jusqu'au Ve siècle de l'Hégire (XIe siècle de J. C.)*. Damascus: Institut français de Damas, 1955.

Tyssens, M. "Le Jongleur et l'écrit." In P. Gallais and Y.-J. Riou, eds. *Mélanges offerts a René Crozet . . . à l'occasion de son 70e anniversaire*, Vol. I. Poitiers: Société d'études mediévales, 1955. Pp. 685–95.

Ullmann *UR* = M. Ullmann. *Untersuchungen zur Rağazpoesie*. Wiesbaden: Harrassowitz, 1966.

Van Buren, E. "The Rain-goddess as Represented in Early Mesopotamia." *Studia biblica et orientalia* III = *Analecta biblica* 12 (1959): 343–55.

Vansina *OT* = J. Vansina. *Oral Tradition: A Study in Historical Methodology*. Trans. H. M. Wright. Chicago: Aldine, 1965.

Vollers *VSA* = K. Vollers. *Volkssprache und Schriftsprache im alten Arabien*. Strassburg: Trübner, 1906.

Wace/Stubbings *CH* = *A Companion to Homer*. Ed. A. J. B. Wace and F. H. Stubbings. London: Macmillan; New York: St. Martin's, 1962.

Wagner, E. "War die kontinuierliche Vokalfrequenzabweichung ein Stilmittel der altarabischen Dichter?" *ZDMG* 124 (1974): 15–32.

Watt *IIS* =W. Montgomery Watt. *Islam and the Integration of Society*. London: Routledge & Kegan Paul, 1961.

——— *MMec* = *Muhammad at Mecca*. Oxford: Oxford University Press, 1962.

——— *MMed* = *Muhammad at Medina*. Oxford: Oxford University Press, 1962.

Webber *FDSB* = R. H. Webber. *Formulistic Diction in the Spanish Ballad*. = *University of California Publications in Modern Philology* 34 (1951): 175–278.

Wehr, H. *Der arabische Elativ*. = Akademie der Wissenschaften und der Literatur in Mainz. *Abh. der geistes- und sozialwissenschaftlichen Kl.*, Jahrgang 1952, no. 7. Wiesbaden: F. Steiner, 1953.

Wehr rev *Ar* =Review of Fück *Ar*. In *ZDMG* 102 (1942): 179–86.

Weil, G. "^{c}Arūḍ." EI^2 667b–677a.

——— *GSAM* = *Grundriss und System der altarabischen Metren*. Wiesbaden: Harrassowitz, 1958.

——— *GSBK* = *Die grammatischen Streitfragen der Basrer und Kufer*. = Ibn al-Anbārī *IMX* "Einleitung." Leiden: Brill, 1913.

Wellhausen *RAH* = J. Wellhausen. *Reste arabischen Heidentums*. 3d ed. Berlin: W. de Gruyter, 1967. (Reprint of 2d edition of 1897).

Whitman, C. H. *Homer and the Heroic Tradition*. Cambridge, Mass.: Harvard University Press, 1958.

Wickens *AL* = G. W. Wickens. "Arabic Literature." In E. B. Ceadel, ed. *Literatures of the East: A Survey*. New York: Grove Press, 1959. Pp. 22–49.

Widengren *LPA* = G. Widengren. *Literary and Psychological Aspects of the Hebrew Prophets. Uppsala Universitets Årsskrift* 1948:10.

Wiet *ILA* = G. Wiet. *Introduction à la littérature arabe*. Paris: Maisonneuve & Larose, 1966.

Wild *KA* = S. Wild. *Das Kitāb al-ᶜAin und die arabische Lexicographie*. Wiesbaden: Harrassowitz, 1965.

Windfuhr, G. Review of Bateson *SCP* and Jacobi *SPAQ*. In *JAOS* 94 (1974): 524–33.

Wissmann, H. von. "Badw. (c) Bedouin Nomadism in Arabia." *EI*² 1:880b–887a.

Wolf *SOM* = Wolf, E. "The Social Organization of Mecca and the Origins of Islam." *Southwestern Journal of Anthropology* 7 (1951): 329–56.

Wolf *VSS* = P. Wolf. *Von Schulwesen der Spätantike: Studien zu Libanius*. Baden-Baden: Verlag für Kunst und Wissenschaft, 1952.

Wright *AG* = W. Wright. *A Grammar of the Arabic Language*. 3d ed. Rev. by W. Robertson Smith and M. J. de Goeje. 2 vols. Cambridge: Cambridge University Press, 1962. (Reprint of 1896–98 edition.)

al-Xwārizmī *MU* = Abū ᶜAbdallāh M. b. Aḥmad al-Xwārizmī. *Kitāb Mafātīḥ al-ᶜulūm*. Ed. G. van Vloten. Leiden: Brill, 1960. (Photo-offset reprint of 1895 edition.)

Yāqūt *IA* = Abū ᶜAbdallāh Yāqūt b. ᶜAbdallāh al-Ḥamawī ar-Rūmī. *Kitāb Iršād al-arīb ilā maᶜrifat al-adīb. = Muᶜjam al-udabā'*. Ed. D. S. Margoliouth. 7 vols. London: Luzac, 1923–25.

——— *MG = Kitāb Muᶜjam al-buldān*. Ed. F. Wüstenfeld. 6 vols. Tehran: Maktabat al-Asadī, 1965 (Photo-offset reprint of 1866–70 edition.)

——— *MU* = Yāqūt *IA*.

Zarnūjī *TMTT* = Burhānaddīn az-Zarnūjī. *Taᶜlīm al-mutaᶜallim—ṭarīq at-taᶜallum: Instruction of the Student—The Method of Learning*. Trans. G. E. von Gruenbaum and Th. A. Abel. New York: Iranian Institute and School of Asiatic Studies, 1947.

az-Zubaydī *TNL* = Abū Bakr M. b. al-Ḥasan az-Zubaydī. *Ṭabaqāt an-naḥwīyīn wa l-luġawīyīn*. Ed. M. Abu l-Faḍl Ibrāhīm. Cairo: al-Xānjī, 1954.

Zwettler *BFOT* = M. Zwettler. "Classical Arabic Poetry between Folk and Oral Tradition." *JAOS* 96 (1976): 198–212.

Index

NOTE: Not considered for purposes of alphabetization are the following: the abbreviation "b." (for *ibn*, "son of") and the transliterated definite article in both its unassimilated form (*al-* / *l-*) and its assimilated forms (*ar-* / *r-*, *as-* / *s-*, *aḍ-* / *ḍ-*, etc.).

-*a*/*an*/*ā*, final: *tanwīn* (*-an*) form of, preserved in modern (Bedouin) dialects, 122, 179–80 nn. 64, 80; *tanwīn* or long-vowel forms of, regularly indicated by *scriptio defectiva*, 125–28; tendency of, toward non-inflectional analytic significance, 122, 126–28, 180 n. 78; usage of, differentiated from other short-vowel desinences, 105, 108, 125–28, 180 nn. 76, 80

Abbot, Nabia, 123

ᶜAbdallāh b. Masᶜūd, 178 n. 53

ᶜAbdallāh b. Ṭāhir, 226 n. 12

ᶜAbīd b. al-Abraṣ (poet), 113

Abu l-ᶜAbbās Aḥmad b. Yaḥyā Ṯaᶜlab, 64, 185 n. 129

Abū ᶜAbdallāh ᶜAbdalᶜazī Sahl, 212, 232 n. 104

Abū ᶜAbdallāh al-Ḥusayn b. Aḥmad as-Zawzanī (*Z*), 59, 193, 195–96, 227 n. 22, 274 n. *d*

Abū ᶜAbdallāh Muḥammad b. Sallām al-Jumaḥī, 12, 154, 203–4, 224, 228 n. 50, 230–31 nn. 81–82

Abū ᶜAbdallāh Yāqūt b. ᶜAbdallāh al-Ḥamawī ar-Rūmī, 187 n. 151

Abū ᶜAbdarraḥmān (*or* Abu l-ᶜAbbās) al-Mufaḍḍal b. Muḥammad aḍ-Ḍabbī, 191, 226 n. 5, 231 n. 81

Abū ᶜAbdarraḥmān (*or* Abū ᶜAbdallāh) al-Xalīl b. Aḥmad al-Farāhīdī, 64, 155, 202, 213, 230 n. 76

Abū ᶜAbdarraḥmān Yūnus b. Ḥabīb, 153–55

Abū Aḥmad al-Ḥasan b. ᶜAbdallāh al-ᶜAskarī, 196, 228 n. 49, 268–70 nn. 5, 9, 29, 38

Abu l-ᶜAlā' al-Maᶜarrī, 67–68, 91 n. 58.

Abū ᶜAlī al-Ḥasan Ibn Rašīq al-Qayrawānī, 65–66, 67, 95 n. 107, 212–23, 219

Abū ᶜAmr b. al-ᶜAlā', 12, 212, 229 n. 69

Abū ᶜAmr Isḥāq b. Mirār aš-Šaybānī, 202, 230 n. 78

Abū ᶜAṣīda (*or* Abū Jaᶜfar) Aḥmad b. ᶜUbayd b. Nāṣiḥ, 94 n. 99, 269 n. 18

Abū Bakr ᶜĀṣim b. Ayyūb al-Baṭalyūsī (*B*), 193, 195, 227 n. 27

Abū Bakr Muḥammad b. ᶜAbdaṭṭayyib al-Bāqillānī, 101, 225 n. 3

Abū Bakr Muḥammad b. al-Ḥasan Ibn Durayd, 228 n. 43

Abū Bakr Muḥammad b. al-Ḥasan az-Zubaydī, 226 n. 15

Abū Bakr Muḥammad b. al-Qāsim al-Anbārī (*A*), 43, 59, 92 n. 67, 192–93, 195–96, 226–27 nn. 11, 23; 235, 269 n. 19, 274 nn. *c*, *f*

Abū Bišr cAmr b. cUṯmān Sībawayh, 155, 202, 230 nn. 77, 79; 232 n. 96

Abu-Deeb, Kemal, 43, 225, 227 n. 30

Abū Du'ād al-Iyādī (poet), 93 n. 80

Abu l-Faḍl al-cAbbās b. Faraj ar-Riyāšī, 270 n. 36

Abu l-Faḍl Jalāladdīn cAbdarraḥmān b. Abī Bakr as-Suyūṭī, 185 n. 129

Abu l-Faḍl Muḥammad b. Mukarram Ibn Manẓūr al-Anṣārī, 66–67

Abu l-Faraj Muḥammad b. Isḥāq an-Nadīm, 207

Abu l-Fatḥ cUṯmān b. Jinnī, 66, 174–75 nn. 22, 28

Abu l-Ḥajjāj Yūsuf b. Sulaymān al-Aclam aš-Šantamarī, 91 n. 50, 192–93, 195–96, 209, 226–27 nn. 17–20

Abu l-Ḥasan Aḥmad Ibn Fāris, 116–17, 201, 229–30 nn. 68, 92

Abu l-Ḥasan cAlī b. cAbdallāh b. Sinān aṭ-Ṭūsī (*W*), 192, 196, 226 n. 14

Abu l-Ḥasan cAli b. Muḥammad al-Madā'inī, 231 nn. 90, 92

Abu l-Ḥasan Muḥammad b. Aḥmad Ibn Kaysān (*K*), 65, 75–76, 192, 195–96, 226 n. 15, 269 nn. 19, 32; 274 n. *f*

Abu l-Ḥasan Sacīd b. Mascada al-Axfaš al-Awsaṭ, 64, 66, 90 n. 45, 185 n. 129

Abū Ḥātim Sahl b. Muḥammad as-Sijistānī, 269 n. 23

Abu l-cIrfān Muḥammad b. cAlī aṣ-Ṣabbān, 67

Abū Jacfar Aḥmad b. Muḥammad b. Ismācīl an-Naḥḥās (*N*), 192, 195–96, 226 n. 16, 274 n. *k*

Abū Manṣūr Muḥammad b. Aḥmad al-Azharī, 136, 181 n. 89

Abū Muḥammad cAbdallāh b. Muslim Ibn Qutayba ad-Dīnawarī, 78, 175 n. 28

Abu l-Munḏir Hišām b. Muḥammad al-Kalbī, 163, 231 n. 90

Abu r-Rayḥān Muḥammad b. Aḥmad al-Bīrūnī, 226 n. 4

Abū Sahl Xorābandāḏ (*or* Xarābundāḏ) b. Māxoršīḏ (*Y*), 191–92, 226 n. 7, 274 nn. *f*, *j*, *k*

Abū Sacīd cAdbalmalik b. Qurayb al-Aṣmacī, 90–91 nn. 48, 50; 93 n. 80, 95 n. 116, 191–93, 196, 208–9, 211, 226 nn. 6, 18, 20; 228 n. 33, 231–32 nn. 81, 95; 268–70 nn. 6, 9, 34, 37–38; 274 n. *c*

Abū Sacīd aḍ-Ḍarīr (*X*), 192, 226 n. 12, 269 n. 22

Abū Sacīd al-Ḥasan b. al-Ḥusayn as-Sukkarī (*S*), 192, 195–96, 226–27 nn. 13–14, 21, 29; 274 n. *e*

Abū Tammān (poet), 94 nn. 98, 103

Abū cUbayd al-Qāsim b. Sallām, 113

Abū cUbayda Macmar b. al-Muṯannā, 154–56, 196, 211, 222–23, 228 nn. 48, 50; 231–32 nn. 85, 100; 269 n. 29, 274 n. *c*

Abū cUmar Aḥmad b. Muḥammad Ibn cAbdrabbih al-Andalusī, 64

Abuū cUmar al-Jarmī, 230 n. 79

Abū cUṯmān cAmr b. Baḥr al-Jāḥiẓ, 19, 95 n. 107

Abu l-Xaṭṭāb cAbdalḥamīd b. cAbdalmajīd al-Axfaš al-Akbar, 155–56, 185 n. 129–31, 228 n. 43

Abū Yūsuf Yacqūb b. Isḥāq Ibn as-Sikkīt, 227 n. 20

Abū Zakarīyā' Yaḥyā b. cAlī at-Tibrīzī (*T*), 193, 195–96, 212, 227 n. 23

Abū Zakarīyā' Yazīd b. Ziyād al-Farrā', 112, 118, 129–30, 177 n. 44, 270 n. 41

Abū Zayd cAbdarraḥmān b. Muḥammad Ibn Xaldūn, 75–76

Abū Zayd Muḥammad b. Abi l-Xaṭṭāb al Qurašī (*J*), 193, 195, 227–28 nn. 26, 38, 44

Aḍdād, 111, 177 n. 42

"Adding" style, 70, 74

cAdīy b. Zayd al-cIbādī (poet), 93 n. 80, 168, 186 n. 150

Ahlwardt, A., 12, 197–98, 226–27 nn. 13, 29; 274 n. *e*

acjam/acjamīy/cajam, 163–64, 186–87 nn. 144, 151

al-Aclam aš-Šantamarī. *See* Abu l-Ḥajjāj

cAlī b. Abī Ṭālib, 228 n. 44

Amharic, 121

ᶜAmr b. Kulṯūm: *muᶜallaqa* of, 39 n. 78, 71

Analytic language/linguistic features, 105, 108–10, 127, 134, 136–37, 141–43, 146, 152, 171, 182–83 nn. 102, 109, 115

Anaptyxis, 106, 108, 176 nn. 29–30

Anonymity/"anonymous era", 199–200, 202, 204

Anṣār, 116, 228 n. 44

Apollonius of Rhodes (poet), 73, 89 n. 40

a̲-preformative (of the classical Arabic imperfect), 115–16, 171

Aᶜrāb, 154, 162–63, 186 n. 145. *See also* Bedouins

Arabia (*ᶜAraba*/*ᶜArba*), 162–64

Arabic (language), 48–49, 69–70, 71–72; ancient (epigraphic) forms of, 103, 140; classical (*see ᶜArabīya*); Christian, 102, 179 n. 68, 186–88 nn. 148, 155; Judaeo-, 102; Middle, 132, 136, 140–43, 152–53, 182 nn. 102–3; Nabataean, 144, 146, 149–51; patterned morphology of, 32, 55, 190, *See also ᶜArabīya*; Dialects

ᶜArabīy/*ᶜArab*, 132, 161–64, 186–87 nn. 144, 151

ᶜArabīya, poetico-Qruʾānic: archaic pausal forms of, regularly conserved in rhyme-position, 103–10, 171 (*see also* Pause/pausal forms); as an artistic *Kunstsprache* or *Hochsprache*, 101, 128, 132–35, 171; called the "poetic *koinē*" (*see Koinē*); coexisting with *iᶜrāb*-less dialects (*see Iᶜrāb*); evolution of, parallel to vernaculars, 48–49, 109, 147–49, 183–84 n. 115; frequency in, of parallel or equivalent forms and usages, 103, 110–11, 171; interdialectal and archaic features of, 98–99, 101, 102–3, 110–16, 124, 147–48, 171, 177 nn. 41, 43; as intertribal or super-tribal "language," 101, 111–15, 164, 173–74 nn. 10, 15; intrinsicality of, to classical poetry, 100–101, 132, 133, 145–49, 160, 166–68, 172, 224; as "language" taught, learned, and studied, 166–68, 174 n. 11, 184 n. 115, 188 n. 155; *mubīn*/*(bayān)* as designation of, 186–87 n. 151; non-vernacular nature of, 101, 110, 128–31, 133, 135, 148, 153, 160–61, 167, 171, 174 n. 11, 213; relationship of, to the Qurʾān, 100–102, 117–21, 122–25, 128, 132, 133, 148, 159–61, 165–67, 171–72; spoken sometimes as conventional idiom, 101, 174 n. 11, 184 nn. 115–16; standardization of, as literary *Schriftsprache*, 101, 131, 141, 144, 148, 165–67, 172, 174 n. 11, 184 n. 115, 188 n. 155; standardization of, on the basis of textualized classical poetry, 167–68, 172; structure of, as unsound basis for historical-linguistic speculations, 183 n. 115; and vernacular(s) of Bedouin tribes, 117–20, 128–29, 174 n. 13; and vernacular(s) of al-Ḥijāz, 108, 124, 128–29, 179 n. 61; and vernacular of Najd, 117; and vernacular of Qurayš and Mecca, 98–99, 112, 117, 120, 128–29, 174 n. 13; view of, as upper-class *Hochsprache*, 118–19, 128, 140, 144, 183 n. 108. *See also* Arabic; Dialects; *Kunstsprache*; Oral-traditional diction

Arabs: expansion of, 49, 164

Aramaic script/orthography, 149–51, 164, 180 n. 79, 184 n. 117

Arberry, Arthur J., 227 n. 23

Aristotle, 68, 81

Asad (tribe), 113

al-Asad, Nāṣiraddīn, 84, 187 n. 154, 191–92, 204

al-ᶜAskarī. *See* Abū Aḥmad

al-Aṣmaᶜī. *See* Abū Saᶜīd ᶜAbdalmalik

Attribution (of classical poetical texts), 196–206, 220, 222, 224, 233–34 n. 125; concern for, as later (second/eighth-century) philological development, 199–200, 202–4, 230 n. 75; difficulties of precise, 197–98, 220–21; methodology of, influenced by techniques of Ḥadīṯ-criticism, 203–6. *See also* Anonymity/"anonymous era"; Authenticity; *Intiḥāl*; *Sariqāt*/*sarq*

Audience, 7, 8–9, 16, 18–19, 21–22, 25, 27, 30, 83, 116, 213, 219–20, 221–22, 223; of readers, 16–19, 23, 27, 76, 83, 169

Authenticity (of classical Arabic poetry), 11–13, 32, 42–43, 198–99, 205–6, 220–22, 224, 231 n. 85, 233 n. 25, 262 n. 5. *See also* Attribution

Aws (tribe), 162

Aws b. Ḥajar (poet), 85

Axbār, 84, 95 n. 107. *See also Ayyām al-ᶜArab*

al-Axfaš al-Akbar. *See* Abu l-Xaṭṭāb

al-Axfaš al-Awsaṭ. *See* Abu l-Ḥasan Saᶜīd

Ayyām al-ᶜArab, 201, 204–5

al-Azharī. *See* Abū Manṣūr

Ballad: English and Scottish, 5, 21; Spanish, 5, 21, 30, 39 n. 74

Balogh, J., 37 n. 45

al-Bāqillānī. *See* Abū Bakr Muḥammad b. ᶜAbdaṭṭayyib

Barth's Law, 115–16

Baṣra/Baṣrans, grammatical school of, 176 n. 28, 192–93, 208–9, 212, 227 n. 21, 231 n. 94

al-Baṭalyūsī. *See* Abū Bakr ᶜĀṣim

Bateson, Mary, 43, 59, 87 n. 1, 89 n. 32, 215–20, 225, 232–34 nn. 110, 116–19, 125

Baugh, Albert, 17–18

bayna . . .wa, 52–54

Bede, Venerable, 22, 27

Bedouins (*aᶜrāb, badawīyūn/ahl al-badw*), 74, 114, 122, 129, 154, 162–63, 185–86 nn. 126, 130, 145; 196, 200, 204; "common language" of, 133–35 (*see also Koinē*); dialects of (*see* Dialects); as linguistic and poetic informants, 134, 140, 152–53, 169, 172, 223, 228 n. 43, 274 n. *c*; as maintainers of oral-poetical tradition after first/seventh century, 134, 148–49, 152, 167–68, 172, 221–24; as models of linguistic propriety for early Islamic philologists, 117, 121–22, 132, 136, 151–56, 181 n. 89; poetry of modern, 109, 148, 154, 168, 190, 217, 233 n. 116

Bell, Richard, 118

Benson, Larry D., 15–17, 19, 20, 26–27, 37 n. 43

Bergsträsser, G., 124

Birkeland, Harris, 104, 124–26, 174–75 nn. 15, 26; 180 n. 77

al-Bīrūnī. *See* Abu r-Rayḥān

Bišr b. Abī Xāzim (poet), 67

Blachère, Régis, 30, 34 n. 1, 71, 86, 91 n. 57, 93–95 nn. 94, 108, 110, 113, 115–16; 118, 121, 131, 152, 162, 181 n. 85, 187 n. 151, 190, 197–99, 205, 206, 227 n. 26, 229 nn. 56, 58

Blau, Joshua, 102, 122, 135–39, 141–43, 152–53, 173 n. 10, 179 n. 63, 182 nn. 102–4, 184 n. 121, 187–88 n. 155

Bloch, Alfred, 33, 78, 80, 81, 91–94 nn. 62, 94–95; 103, 111, 114, 225, 230 n. 70

Bloch, Ariel, 115

Books, 18–19, 24, 222

Bowra, Maurice, 29, 55, 97–98, 202, 223

Bräunlich, E., 71, 85–86, 94–95 nn. 101, 110, 113; 189–90

Brockelmann, Carl, 101, 185 n. 129

Browne, Edward, 76

Bundār al-Iṣfahānī, 269 n. 19

Cadora Frederic, 182 n. 102, 186 n. 138

Caedmon, 22, 27

Caesura, 88 n. 19

Campbell, J. J., 31, 37 n. 43

Caskel, Werner, 110

Chadwick, H. and N., 29

Chanson de Roland, 21, 61

Chansons de geste, 16, 21, 30, 61

Chantraine, P., 97

Chaytor, H. J., 16–19, 21, 24, 27, 37 n. 46, 229 n. 70

Chomsky, Noam, 143, 182–83 n. 105

"Classical" (as applied to early Arabic poetry), 34 n. 1

Classicistic/classicization, 34 n. 1, 169, 188 n. 157, 199–200, 203, 224, 230 n. 81

"Corresponsion/corresponsional", 6–7, 9, 35 n. 14, 45, 56

Corriente, F., 139–48, 149, 151, 181–84 nn. 93, 95–96, 100–104, 106–9, 111–13, 115

Croce, Benedetto, 29

Culley, Robert, 30, 50–51

Curschmann, Michael, 19–23, 27, 28, 37 n. 43

Dain, A., 13, 20, 37 n. 35

Ḍarūra/ḍarūrāt aš-šiᶜr. *See* Poetic license

Dialect(s), 93 n. 80, 102, 111–15, 173 n. 7, 178 n. 55, 183 n. 114; of Bedouins, 116, 117–18, 127, 133, 136–38, 146, 152–56, 171, 182 n. 100; of Bedouins = poetical ᶜ*arabīya*, 120–22, 129, 132, 174 n. 13; "cleavage" of, between East and West Arabia, 109, 113, 115, 117–18; of East Arabia, 115–16; of al-Ḥijāz, 108, 113, 116, 117–20, 122, 124, 127, 179 nn. 61, 71; and *iᶜrāb* (*see* ᶜ*Arabīya; Iᶜrāb*); *iᶜrāb*-less, coexisting with ᶜ*arabīya* (*see Iᶜrāb*); of Mecca and Qurayš, 102, 119, 124–25, 181 n. 84; of Mecca and Qurayš = language of the

Qur'ān, 120, 138, 174 n. 13; modern, 120, 122, 125–27, 133, 138, 179 nn. 64–66, 181 n. 84; of Nabataeans, 144, 146, 149–51; traces of, in the Qur'ān, 111–12, upper-class, 119, 128; urban, 116, 122, 136, 152–53, 171, 182 n. 100; of West Arabia, 115

Dictation, 37 n. 35, 180 n. 75; and oral-traditional texts, 4–5, 20, 31

Diction, oral-traditional. *See* Oral-traditional diction

Diem, W., 144, 149–51, 184 nn. 117–19, 203

Dionysius of Helicarnassus, 68

Dow, Sterling, 14

Dual, conventional use of, in *nasībs*, 236, 262 n. 1

D̲u'ayb b. Ka^{c}b at-Tamīmī (poet), 154

Duggan, Joseph, 27, 29, 38 nn. 57, 60; 44, 61–62, 87 n. 6, 89 n. 35

D̲u r-Rumma (poet), 169

Editors and textual critics, 3, 100; Hellenistic and Byzantine, 13, 37 n. 49, 193, 230–31 nn. 81, 85; medieval Arabic, 12, 93 n. 80, 189–90, 193–94, 198–99, 223–24, 230–31 nn. 81, 85; modern, 12–13, 17, 36 n. 24, 37 n. 46, 189, 193. *See also* Literary critics and theorists; Philologists; Tradition, textual

Edwards, G. P., 39 n. 75

Emeneau, M. B., 173 n. 3, 215

Enjambement (*taḍmīn*), 63–76, 82, 90 nn. 41–43, 45; 225 n. 2, 262 n. 4; "necessary," 9–10, 41, 71–73, 90–92 nn. 48, 53, 56, 73, 75; "necessary," more frequent in written poetry, 73–76; "unperiodic," 70–71, 90–92 nn. 50, 52, 68–71; "unperiodic," less frequent in written poetry, 73–76

Epic, 10, 13, 21, 28, 77, 207, 224, 233 n. 117; style, 28–29

fa (coordinating place-names), 51, 114, 209, 232 n. 95, 236, 270 n. 37

al-Farrā'. *See* Abū Zakarīyā' Yazīd

Fischer, Wolfdietrich, 177 n. 39

Fleisch, Henri, 131, 135–38, 175 n. 26, 180–81 nn. 77, 85, 89; 203

Fleischer, H., 172 n. 11

Flügel, Gustav, 94 n. 99

Fluidity (of oral tradition). *See* Variation/variant(s)

Folklore/folk-poetry/folk tradition, 33, 80, 97, 204

Folklorist scholarship, 32–34, 80, 118–19, 128–29, 202, 204

Forgery/fabrication (of classical Arabic poems). *See* Authenticity; *Intiḥāl*

Formulaic analysis, 43–44, 45–47, 49–50, 50–63, 88–89 nn. 12, 27, 33, 35, 37–38; 219, 233 n. 125, 235–62

Formulaic diction. *See* Oral-traditional diction

"Formulaicness"/formularity, 6, 46–47, 51, 56, 57, 59

Formulaic systems, 6, 46, 54, 210; "thrift" of, 54–55

Formulas/formulaic elements, expressions, and usages, 21, 35 n. 17, 41, 219; absorption of, by oral poet-renderant, 7, 100, 102; "economy" (or "thrift") of, 54–56; found in poetry thought to be written, 15–17, 22–23, 37 n. 43; Nagler's generative view of, 6–7, 55–56, 233 n. 120; Parry's definition of, 6; and poetic language (*see* Oral-traditional diction); and the problem of *intiḥāl* and *sariqāt*, 63, 197–99, 205–6, 229 n. 55 (*see also Intiḥāl*; *Sariqāt*); relationship of, to different meters, 44–45, 88 n. 27; relationship of, to theme and thematic elements, 76—77, 79–80, 213–16, 232 nn. 105–6, 109; 236–37, 238, 249, 255; role of, in oral composition and rendition, 9, 22, 79–80, 98, 102, 213–15, 228 n. 46; Russo's broader interpretation of, 6; stabilizing effect of, in oral rendition, 79–80, 100, 213–15, 219–20; syntactic/structural, 6, 46, 51–54, 57–59, 87 n. 9, 214, 240, 241–42, 247–48, 257, 259, 262 n. 4; tendency of, to become adapted to tastes and expectations of different audiences, 221; tendency of, to incorporate and preserve archaisms and dialectisms and reproduce them in oral rendition, 97–100, 102, 106 (*see also* ^{c}*Arabīya*; Oral-traditional diction); usefulness of, 7, 9, 21, 44–45, 54, 102, 112, 214; verbal, 6, 46, 51, 55, 57–59, 89 n. 34, 213–15, 233 n. 125

Frenkel, E., 274 nn. *b*, *k*

Fück, Johann, 101–2, 132–33, 135–36, 151, 174 n. 13

Gandz, Salomon, 42, 193, 209, 227 n. 29, 262 n. 5

Ġaṭafān (tribe), 95 n. 109

Gemination of final consonants, 106, 137–38, 175 n. 26, 181 n. 90. *See also Taḍ*^{c}*īf*

Generative Gestalt *or* mental template, 7–9, 35 n. 20, 45, 171. *See also* Formulas . . . : Nagler's generative view of; Nagler, Michael

Geyer, Rudolf, 113, 118–19, 128–29, 179–80 nn. 61, 80; 183 n. 108

Gibb, H. A. R., 32, 35 n. 9, 94 n. 107, 159

Glottal stop. *See Hamza*

Goldziher, Ignaz, 84, 114–15, 174 n. 15

Grammarians, Arabic. *See* Philologists, medieval Arabic

Greenberg, J. H., 176 n. 33

Grunebaum, G. E. von, 35 n. 9, 81, 85, 90 n. 43, 94 n. 101, 229 n. 64, 231 n. 85

Guillaume, Alfred, 174 n. 15

Guslar, 18. *See also* Tradition, oral: Yugoslav

Hainsworth, J. B., 31

Ḥamāsa anthologies, 81, 94 n. 98

Hamza, 122–24, 179 nn. 70–71

Ḥassan b. Ṯābit (poet), 113

Heroic poetry/style, 29

Heusler, A. 230 n. 70

al-Ḥijāz, 123, 128, 160, 165; dialect of, 108, 113, 115–16, 117–20, 122, 124, 127, 180 n. 78

Ḥīra, 93 n. 80, 165, 188 n. 155

Homer/Homeric poems, 6, 13, 14, 28, 30, 31, 37–38 nn. 37, 53; 44, 54–55, 57, 68–74, 88–90 nn. 18, 40; 95 n. 117, 97–100, 167–68, 170, 177 n. 50, 193, 217, 223, 226 n. 4, 231 n. 85, 236

Houseman, A. E., 36 n. 24

Huḏayl (tribe), 85, 115, 177–78 nn. 43, 53

al-Ḥuṭay'a (poet), 85

Ibn ᶜAbdrabbih. *See* Abū ᶜUmar Aḥmad

Ibn al-Anbārī. *See* Abū Bakr Muḥammad b. al-Qāsim

Ibn Durayd. *See* Abū Bakr b. al-Ḥasan Ibn Durayd

Ibn Fāris. *See* Abu l-Ḥasan Aḥmad

Ibn Jinnī. *See* Abu l-Fatḥ

Ibn al-Kalbī. *See* Abu l-Munḏir

Ibn Kaysān. *See* Abu l-Ḥasan Muḥammad

Ibn Manẓūr. *See* Abu l-Faḍl Muḥammad

Ibn an-Naḥḥās (?), 227 n. 30, 228 n. 43

Ibn Qutayba. *See* Abū Muḥammad

Ibn Rašīq. *See* Abū ᶜAlī

Ibn Sallām al-Jumaḥī. *See* Abū ᶜAbdallāh Muḥammad

Ibn as-Sikkīt. *See* Abū Yūsuf

Ibn Xaldūn. *See* Abū Zayd ᶜAbdarraḥmān

Ibn Xiḏām (poet), 196, 229 n. 58

Ibrāhīm b. Harma (poet), 66

Ibrāhīm, Muḥammad Abū Faḍl, 196, 229 n. 18, 227 n. 30, 269 n. 32, 274 nn. *e, j*

Idġām kabīr, 121

Iġrām (a form of enjambement), 67, 91 n. 58

Iliad. See Homer/Homeric poems

Improvisation, 25–26, 188 n. 158, 214–15 219, 233 n. 115; jazz, 26, 219

Imra'alqays b. Ḥujr (poet), 49, 65, 175 n. 28, 191, 225 n. 3, 229 nn. 55, 58; *muᶜallaqa* of, 42, 43, 46–47, 48, 59–61, 71, 87 n. 4, 89 nn. 32, 33, 37; 191–96, 208–12, 213–15, 219, 221, 225–29 nn. 3, 20–21, 24–25, 33–41, 43, 45–48, 51–52, 54–55; 231–32 nn. 93, 95–103, 105–109; 234 n. 125, 235–74

Instability (of oral-poetical texts). *See* Variation/variant

Interpolation, 196–97, 223, 231 n. 85. *See also Intiḥāl*

Intiḥāl ("misattribution"), 183 n. 112, 197–98, 223, 234 n. 126, 274 nn. *c,e*. *See also* Attribution; Authenticity; Formulas . . . ; *Sariqāt*

i-preformative (of the dialectal imperfects), 115–16, 178 nn. 52, 55

Iqwā' (*sometimes ikfā*), 104–5, 153, 175 n. 24, 184 n. 126, 261; frequency of, as evidence of desuetude of inflectional short vowels, 105, 153–55, 184–85 nn. 125, 130

Iᶜrāb, 100, 104, 109, 116–56, 128, 131; absence of, from vernaculars of Mecca and the Ḥijāz, 117–18, 130, 181 n. 84; alleged absence of, from the Qur'ān as initially recited, 117–18, 129–30, 167; arguments for use of, especially in poetry and more elevated discourse, 117–18, 132–35, 138, 156, 171, 183 n. 110; arguments for use of, in an upper-class *Hochsprache* or for prestige purposes, 118–19, 129, 147, 182–83 nn. 100, 108 (*see also ᶜArabīya*); arguments for use of, in vernaculars of Mecca and the Ḥijāz, 120, 129, 138–39, 179 n. 63;

arguments for use of, in vernaculars of (especially East Arabian) Bedouin tribes, 117–22, 129, 132, 135–37, 140, 144, 151–53, 179–80 nn. 63, 81; arguments that desuetude of is due to non-Arab influence, 132, 136–38, 152; Bedouins' alleged natural propensity for proper use of, 117, 121–22, 151–53 (*see also* Bedouins); dialects without, coexisting with the poetico-Qur'ānic ᶜ*arabīya*, 140–49, 182 n. 100; desuetude of, in Arabic vernaculars, 104–6, 108–10, 117–18, 121, 126, 130–33, 135–36, 139, 146, 167–68, 171, 180 n. 80, 182 n. 102; as element of spoken vernacular of Arabic *at some stage*, 121, 144–45, 148; function of, as synthetic feature (*see* Synthetic language/linguistic features); "functional yield" of, in classical Arabic noun inflections, 140–41, 143, 182–83 nn. 100, 102, 106, 115;—*: i*ᶜ*jām:lahn::hellēnismos: barbarismos: soloikismos*, 178 n. 59; most distinctive feature of poetico-Qur'ānic ᶜ*arabīya*, 116–17, 129, 132, 133, 135, 137–40, 147–48, 149, 156, 167, 171, 181 n. 84, 184 n. 115, 187 n. 151; retention of, as linguistic archaism in poetico-Qur'ānic ᶜ*arabīya*, 135, 145, 147–48, 151, 156, 171, 183 n. 110; suggested meaning of, "to bedouinize," "to speak properly as a Bedouin," 117, 178 n. 59; traces of, in written forms of Nabataean Arab personal names, 149–51 (*see also* Nabataens); use of, in Bedouin (or any) vernaculars of sixth to tenth centuries unlikely, 133–56, 171

-*ī/ū*, final, 114–25, 177 n. 39

Jacob, Georg, 110–11

Jacobi, Renate, 43, 51, 78–80, 81, 89 n. 33, 94 n. 95, 214, 225, 232 n. 108

al-Jāḥiẓ. See Abū ᶜUṯmān

Jamīl (poet), 85

Jinn/šayāṭīn ("demons"), 139, 157–59

Jongleurs, 18, 24, 30

ka/ka-mā/ka-anna/etc., 51, 79, 238, 262 n. 3

ka'ayyin/kā'in, 180 n. 72

Kaᶜb b. Zuhayr b. Abī Sulmā, 65, 85, 86–87, 95 nn. 109, 116; 228 n. 44

Kāhin, pl. *kuhkān* ("seer, soothsayer"), 101, 133, 139, 166, 201, 230 n. 73; association of Muḥammad with, 156–60; Qur'ānic hostility toward, 156–60

Kahle, Paul, 118, 120, 129–30, 167

Kalām (*here*: "prose" [prob. non-casual]), 104–5, 174 n. 22

Kīsvān. *See* Muḥammad Ḥusayn

Koinē: Arabic, 97, 101, 131, 144, 165, 173–74 n. 11, 183 n. 107; Greek, 131, 173 n. 11. *See also* Bedouins: "common language" of

Kosegarten, John, 14, 84

Knox, B. M. W., 37 n. 45

Krenkow, Fritz, 35 n. 9

Kūfa/Kūfans, grammatical "school" of, 177 n. 44, 192–93, 208–9, 212, 227 n. 21, 231 n. 94

Kunstsprache: Homeric, 97–100, 102, 110, 112, 141, 170, 172 n. 2; poetico-Qur'ānic ᶜ*arabīya* as a, 101, 128, 132–35 (*see also* ᶜ*Arabīya*). *See also* Oral-traditional diction

Labīd b. Radīᶜa, 49; *mu*ᶜ*allaqa* of, 43, 48

Laḥn, 130, 136, 153, 178 n. 59, 184 n. 125

Lammens, Henri, 94 n. 106

"Lettered tradition" (Benson's term), 15–19, 26–27. *See also* Benson, Larry D.

Literacy. *See* Writing/literacy

Literary critics and theorists, medieval Arabic, 63–68, 73, 74–76, 81–83, 90 nn. 41, 43–45; 94 n. 102, 169–70, 200

Literary tradition/poetry/poem. *See* Written literature; Writing

Lord, Albert B., 4, 5, 7–15, 21–22, 24, 27, 28–29, 35 n. 15, 41, 44, 48, 51, 55–57, 62, 76–77, 79, 81, 88 n. 18, 95 n. 116, 189, 208, 212, 215, 216–18, 221, 224, 233 nn. 117–19, 23

Lyall, Charles, 114

Lyric, 28–29

al-Maᶜarrī. *See* Abu l-ᶜAlā'

al-Madā'inī. *See* Abu l-Ḥasan ᶜAlī b. Muḥammad

Magoun, Francis P., 9, 20

Majrā, 104–5

Marçais, William, 173 n. 11

Margoliouth, David, 12, 14, 159–60

Maslūt, ᶜAbdalḥamīd, 197

Maṭar, ᶜAbdalᶜazīz, 179 n. 66

Mecca/Meccans, 99, 112, 119–20, 122–23, 128, 130, 138, 156–60, 162, 164, 165, 168, 172

Medina (Yaṯrib), 120, 122–23, 128, 161–62, 165
Memory/memorization, 4, 8, 11, 13–14, 18–19, 14–16, 31–32, 36 n. 26, 207–8, 212–13, 215, 220, 233 nn. 116, 123; emphasized in early education and scholarship, 19
Menéndez Pidal, Ramón, 21, 30, 189, 191, 199, 202, 204, 217, 233 n. 122
Merx, A. 178 n. 59
Meter, 44–45; as conditioning factor in oral-traditional diction, 91 n. 62, 103, 111, 113, 145, 147, 156, 171, 175 n. 28, 177 n. 41, 184 n. 115; as stabilizing factor in oral rendition, 31–32, 220; *basīṭ*, 87 n. 7; *kāmil*, 87–88 nn. 7, 27; *rajaz* (*see Rajaz*); *sarīᶜ*, 75; *ṭawīl*, 44, 86, 87–88 nn. 7, 27; *wāfir*, 87–88 nn. 7, 27
Monroe, James, 43–50, 87–89 nn. 4, 7, 12, 15, 17, 27, 37; 225, 233–34 n. 125
Motifs (*maᶜānī*), 81–83, 94 n. 99. *See also* Themes/thematic elements
Muᶜallaqāt, 70–73, 92 n. 67, 191–92, 215, 226 n. 8. *See also s. n.* of some individual poets
Mubīn/*bayān*, 161, 186–87 nn. 144, 151
al-Mufaḍḍal aḍ-Ḍabbī. *See* Abū ᶜAbdarraḥmān . . . al-Mufaḍḍal
Muḥammad the Prophet, 102, 112, 156–66, 172, 179 n. 71; association of, with poets and *kāhins*, 156, 172, 181 n. 92, 185 n. 132; "false-prophet" rivals of, 185 n. 137; speech of, 111–25, 128–30, 139, 179 n. 71
Muḥammad Ḥusayn al-Qazvīnī Kīšvān, 67, 90 n. 41
Müller, D., 162–63
Muqalladāt (end-stopped verses), 64
Mutammim b. Nuwayra (poet), 66, 222–23, 234 n. 126
al-Mutanabbī (poet), 188 n. 158
Muzayna (tribe), 95 n. 109

Nabataeans, 149, 162; dialect of, 144, 146, 149–51; script of, 122, 180 n. 79, 184 nn. 118–19
an-Nābiġa aḏ-Ḏubyānī (poet), 43, 64–68, 90 n. 48
Nagler, Michael, 6–8, 11, 27, 35–36 nn. 14, 20; 38 n. 71, 47, 55, 56, 57, 225, 233 nn. 120, 124; 262 n. 1
an-Naḥḥās. *See* Abū Jaᶜfar
Najd, 93 n. 80
Najrān, 165, 179 n. 68, 186 n. 148, 188 n. 155
Narrative poetry/elements, 28–29, 77
Nasīb, 79, 80, 103, 214–15, 232 nn. 107, 109; 236–37
Nöldeke, Theodor, 118, 119–22, 128–29, 151, 175 n. 28, 179 nn. 63, 65; 198
Non-Arabs, 132–34, 135–38, 152, 162

Odyssey. *See* Homer/Homeric poems
Oral composition, 4, 21, 24–25, 33, 50, 61–63, 79–80, 171, 194, 206–7, 216–17, 233 n. 124; suggested mode of, in classical *qaṣīdas*, 212–15, 218–20. *See also* Oral rendition/performance
Oral formulas. *See* Formulas . . .
Oral-formulaic technique (of verse composition and rendition), 4, 9, 115, 169–70, 216–17, 222–23. *See also* Formulas . . . ; Oral composition; Oral rendition/performance
Orality, 5, 11, 15, 29, 33–34, 41, 63, 79–80, 95 n. 116, 99, 171, 225
Oral poet (*šāᶜir*, bard, singer, renderant, etc.), 24, 32, 166, 168, 172, 216–17, 233 n. 113; amateur, 30–31, 39 n. 78; professional, 30–31; training of 7–8, 86–87, 95 n. 116
Oral poetry: as different from written poetry, 7, 9, 11, 47–50, 73–76, 87, 169–70, 184 n. 121, 223. *See also* Orality; Oral poet; Oral-traditional texts; Tradition, oral; Written literature
Oral rendition/performance, 4, 8, 10–11, 16–19, 21–22, 24–28, 30–32, 33, 36 n. 25, 50, 61–63, 79–80, 97, 99, 113, 168, 171, 190, 201–6, 209, 213–15, 216–17, 219–20, 223–24
Oral tradition. *See* Tradition, oral
Oral-traditional diction, 9, 16, 41–42, 48–49, 58–59, 73–74, 91 n. 62, 98–100, 112, 121, 145, 147, 160–61, 173 nn. 5, 7; 183 n. 114; anomalous features of, conditioned through oral rendition, 99–100, 106, 147, 170–71, 183 n. 115; conservatism of, 99–100, 102, 147, 170, 173 n. 7, 220, 224; distinct from spoken vernaculars of poets and audiences, 97–98, 101–112, 128–31, 168, 171, 181 n. 85; elements of, 99–100, 102, 170, 173 n. 7
Oral-traditional texts, 5, 95 n. 116; attribution of (*see* Attribution); fluidity of (*see* Variation/variants); fragmentary or "un-

finished'' character of, 11, 35 n. 20; impossibility of conclusively verifying, 22; influence of dictation on form of, 5; as records of oral renditions, 10, 12, 20, 32, 195, 222

Oral transmission, 4, 11, 13–14, 19, 31–32, 33, 37 n. 37, 79, 190, 194, 206

Original version, 11–13, 196–97, 222–24, 226 n. 10; idea of, inappropriate to oral poetry, 10, 189, 221, 225. *See also* Texts: fixed *or* established

Palmer, L. R., 98

Parry, Milman, 4, 7–11, 21, 27, 28–29, 35 n. 12, 44, 45, 54–55, 57, 68–74, 76–77, 89 n. 40, 98–100, 110, 112, 147–48, 170–71, 173 nn. 5–6, 181 n. 86, 183 n. 115, 210

Parry-Lord theory, 4–5, 9, 11, 13, 15, 21, 23, 28–34, 37 n. 37, 41, 50, 89 n. 40, 93 n. 87, 95 n. 117, 98, 194, 216–18, 233 nn. 116–17, 119

Pause (*waqf*)/pausal forms, 125–26, 137, 174–75 nn. 22–23, 180 nn. 73–75; anomalous character of, at verse hemistichs (*waqf* ᶜ*ala l-*ᶜ*arūḍ*), 174 n. 22; occurrences of, in context, 105, 126, 175 n. 28; written forms of words said to be based upon, 122, 124, 125, 180 n. 75

Pause with ''intonation'' (*waqf bi t-tarannum*), 104, 109, 147, 158; as characteristic of ᶜ*arabīya* in classical poetry (in rhyme position), 104, 108, 147, 171; as an archaic usage with respect to prose and sixth-to-tenth-century Arabic vernaculars, 104–5, 108–9

Pause with ''quiescence'' (*waqf bi l-iskān*), 104–5, 109, 126, 137, 154, 158, 175 n. 26; as characteristic of ᶜ*arabīya* in the Qur'ān and non-casual prose, 104–5; vocalic (or semi-vocalic) non-inflectional modifications of (*išamām, rawm, taḍ*ᶜ*īf*), 105, 175 n. 26, 177 n. 39, 180 n. 77

Performance. See Oral rendition/performance

Petráček, Karl, 33, 80, 95 n. 111, 172 n. 1, 202, 204

Pfeiffer, Rudolf, 13, 37 n. 37, 89 n. 40, 177 n. 50

Philologists/philology, medieval Arabic, 81, 93–94 nn. 80, 99; 98, 101, 106 111–12, 129, 134, 140, 167–68, 175 n. 26, 188 nn. 155, 157; 190, 193–94, 198–99, 202–6, 220, 222–24, 228 n. 43; anecdotes of, about Bedouin linguistic superioity, 117, 121–22, 134, 136, 151–56, 181 n. 89, 183 n. 113. *See also* Editors and textual critics: medieval Arabic; Literary critics and theoritsts, medieval Arabic

Place-names. *See* Toponyms

Plagiarism. *See Sariqāt/sarq*. *See also* Attribution; Authenticity; *Intiḥāl*

Poetic license (*ḍarūra, ḍarūrat aš-ši*ᶜ*r*), 106, 110–11, 171, 177 n. 41. *See also* Oral-traditional diction

Poetry/poems: ''individual'' and ''traditional'' (Menéndez Pidal), 199, 202, 233 n. 122; ''individual'' and ''traditional'' aspects of, 25, 30, 214, 219–20, 233 n. 124

Poets: ''ancient'' (= *jāhilī, muxaḍram, islāmī*; pre- and early Islamic), 63, 64, 74–76, 81–83, 94 n. 102, 169, 188 n. 157, 223; association of Muḥammad with, 156–61, 172; bio-bibliographical literature about, 199–201; ''dynasties'' of, 85, 95 n. 110; ''modern'' (= *muḥdaṯ*), 63, 64, 74–76, 81–83, 94 n. 102, 169, 223; Qur'ānic hostility toward, 156–61; role of, in sociocultural life of early Arabs, 200–202, 208, 229–13 nn. 69–70; ''schools'' of, 85, 94 n. 101, 229 n. 64, 262 n. 5

Pretzl, Otto, 124

Psalms, 21, 30

Qāfiya. *See* Rhyme.

Qāfiya muqayyada (''fettered rhyme''), 104

Qāfiya mutawātira mujarrada, 107, 176 nn. 32, 37

Qāfiya muṭlaqa (''loose rhyme''), 104

Qāri', pl. *qurrā'/qirā'a*, 84, 111, 127, 178 n. 53–55

Qaṣīda (''ode''), 17, 21, 28–29, 42–43, 55, 61–62, 74, 94 n. 105, 100, 177 n. 49, 200, 207, 212–15, 217, 220, 224, 232 n. 110, 234 n. 125, 238; relative brevity of, as stabilizing factor in oral rendition, 31–32, 100, 220; thematic elements in, 78–82, 94 n. 98, 103, 238, 249, 258 (*see also* Themes/thematic elements); toponyms in, 114–15, 236–37 (*see also* Toponyms)

*Qiṭ*ᶜ*a* (pl. *qiṭa*ᶜ), 80–81

Qur'ān, 116, 156–67, 158, 187–89 nn. 145, 151–52; 222; hostility of, toward poets and *kāhins*, 156–61; *i*ᶜ*jāz* (''inimitability'') of, 157, 160, 177 n. 44, 185 n. 137; language of,

Qur'ān (*continued*)
as different from spoken vernaculars, 123, 128–30, 138, 167, 181 n. 84 (*see also* ᶜ*Arabīya*); pausal forms in, 105–9; relationship of classical inflective ᶜ*arabīya* to, 101–2, 111–12, 117–21, 129–30, 156–67, 171–72, 186 n. 138 (*see also* ᶜ*Arabīya*); textualization of, 48–49, 121, 138, 165, 172, 179 n. 70, 222; tribal dialectisms in, 111–13; ᶜUṯmānic text of, 120, 122–29, 178 n. 53; variant readings (*qirā'āt*) of, 112, 115–16, 120, 140, 178 nn. 53–55

Qur'ānic scholars/scholarship, 111, 124, 177 n. 44

al-Qurašī. *See* Abū Zayd Muḥammad

Qurayš (tribe), 99, 101, 112, 116, 119, 128–29, 158, 162, 169; dialect of, 124–25, 130, 179 n. 71, 181 n. 84. *See also* Dialect(s); Mecca/Meccans

-*r̲* and -*l̲* as final consonants in *CVCC*- word-forms, 107–8, 176 nn. 32, 36–37

Rabin, Chaim, 102, 110–11, 113, 115–16, 118, 130–31, 151–52, 174 n. 15, 177–81 nn. 41, 55, 71, 77, 84; 187 n. 155, 231 n. 85

Rajaz/*urjūza*, 29, 74–75, 92–93 nn. 62, 80; 95 n. 114, 101

Rāwī, pl. *ruwāt*, 14, 18, 24, 31, 84–87, 93–94 nn. 80, 106; 166, 168, 172, 175 n. 28, 184 n. 121, 195, 197–98, 205, 216–17, 219, 228 n. 43, 231 n. 84; early poets (*rāwī*-poets) combining function of, 85, 94 n. 107, 221–22, 224, 233 n. 112; meaning and evolution of term, 84, 94 n. 105, 109, 224; as oral informants to early philologists, 152–53, 155–56, 223 (*see also* Bedouins); as poetical "apprentices," 85–87, 94 n. 107, 109, 216, 233 n. 113

Rawīy (rhyme-word/-constant), 94 n. 105, 104, 109–110, 176 n. 32

Reading: aloud (of literary works), 16–19, 37–38 nn. 45, 50, 58; audience (*see* Audience of readers); difficulty of, in Antiquity and Middle Ages, 16–18, 37 n. 49

Recitation, 11, 18–19, 31, 100, 175 n. 26, 219. *See also* Oral rendition/performance; Rhapsodes

Reckendorf, Hermann, 232 n. 101

Rendition, oral. *See* Oral rendition/performance

Rhapsodes, 13, 18, 24, 38 n. 53, 217

Rhyme (*qāfiya*), 39 n. 81, 64, 126, 156, 158; as conditioning factor of oral-traditional diction, 69, 91 n. 62, 103–110, 111, 113, 145, 156, 171, 184 n. 115; "fettered" (*qāfiya muqayyada*), 104–6, 109; "loose" (*qāfiya muṭlaqa*). 104–7, 109, 175 n. 26; "loose," as evidence of much more archaic stage of language, 104–6; as stabilizing factor in oral rendition, 31–32, 220. *See also Iqwā'*; Pause with intonation; *Qāfiya mutawātira mujarrada; Rawīy*

Riwāya. *See Rāwī*

Rosenthal, Franz, 133, 137, 187 n. 152, 230 n. 81

Ru'ba b. al-ᶜAjjāj (poet), 95 n. 107

Russo, Joseph A., 6–11, 35 n. 12, 45, 87 n. 9

aṣ-Ṣabbān. *See* Abu l-ᶜIrfān

Šāᶜir/*šiᶜr*, 104, 109

Sajᶜ (rhymed prose), 101, 157–58

Sariqāt/*sarq* ("plagiarism"), 11, 63, 82–83, 94 n. 103. *See also* Attribution; Authenticity; Formulas . . . ; *Intiḥāl*

Šayāṭīn. *See Jinn*/*šayāṭīn*

šay' Vn/*ša'n*, dialectal, 179 n. 65

as-Sayyid b. Muḥammad al-Ḥimyarī (poet), 153

Scholia, 185 n. 129, 192–93, 226–27 nn. 13, 20, 23; 231 n. 85, 263

"Schools" of poets. *See* Poets: "schools" of

Schriftsprache, 119, 128, 131, 165, 174 n. 15, 178 n. 60, 181 nn. 85–86

Schwartz, Paul, 92 n. 62

Scribes/scribal techniques, 16, 20, 223

Script, 13, 14; early Arabic, 122–29, 165; inadequacies of early Arabic, in transcribing poetico-Qur'ānic ᶜ*arabīya*, 122–25, 138

Scriptio defectiva. *See* Qur'ān, ᶜUṯmānic text of; Script, early Arabic

Sebeok, Thomas A., 215

Semitic languages, 120, 139, 177 n. 41; general desuetude of desinential inflections in, 133–34, 141, 182–83 nn. 102, 109

Sezgin, Fuat, 78, 95 n. 117, 226 n. 7

Shahīd, Irfan, 185 n. 134

Sībawayh. *See* Abū Bišr

Singing (as mode of oral rendition), 18–19

Skalds/skaldic poetry, 17, 18, 27, 215–16, 222, 230 n. 70

Spitaler, Anton, 100, 103, 133–35, 136–37, 153

Stability (of poetical text). *See* Variation/variants; Written literature

Staiger, E., 28

Stevick, Robert, 26

Structural formula. *See* Formula . . . : syntactic/structural

as-Sukkarī. *See* Abū Sa^{c}īd al-Ḥasan

as-Suyūṭī. *See* Abu l-Faḍl Jalāladdīn

Syntactic formula. *See* Formula . . . : syntactic/structural

Ta'abbaṭa Šarrā T̲ābit b. Jābir (poet), 59, 196

Taḍ^{c}īf (gemination of pausal rhyme-consonants), 175 n. 26

Taḍmīn: (enjambement), (*see* Enjambement); (quotation, literary allusion), 90 n. 41

Taġlib (tribe), 114

Ṭāhā Ḥusayn, 12, 14, 85, 95 n. 108

Ṭāhir b. ^{c}Abdallāh b. Ṭāhir, 226 n. 12

T̲a^{c}lab. *See* Abu l-^{c}Abbās

Ta^{c}līq ma^{c}nawī ("semantic dependence"—a form of enjambement), 67

Tamīm (tribe), dialects of, 117, 180 n. 77

Tanwīn (nunation), 104, 122–27, 148, 179–80 nn. 65–66, 72; 183 n. 106; —— *at-tarannum*, 180 n. 77

T̲aqīf (tribe), 116

Ṭarafa b. al-^{c}Abd (poet), *mu^{c}allaqa* of, 70–71, 90 n. 45

Taṣrī^{c} (internal rhyme at hemistich), 42–43, 87 n. 3

Taxalluṣ, 79, 103

Ṭawīl (meter). *See* Meter: *ṭawīl*

Texts: of classical poems as song lyrics, 202, 230 n. 75; fixed *or* established, 5, 11, 12, 16, 15 (*see also* Original version); oral autograph, 20; oral dictated, 20; of oral poems (*see* Oral-traditional texts); of poems essential to education and scholarship, 19, 25; possibility of transitional, discussed, 15–16, 19–23; as sources for classical Arabic poetry, 37 n. 40, 204–5; traditional, 23–28, 32, 34. *See also* Writing/literacy

Textual critics. *See* Editors and textual critics

Textualization (of oral poems), 3, 5, 13, 20–21, 36 n. 20, 190; effects of, on oral tradition, 10–11, 24

Textual tradition. *See* Tradition, textual

Themes/thematic elements, 41, 76–83, 93–94 nn. 87, 101; 234 n. 125, 236–37

Thilo, U , 114

at-Tibrīzī. *See* Abū Zakarīyā' Yaḥyā

Toponyms, 114–15, 171

Tradition, literary *or* written. *See* Written literature

Tradition, oral: African, 207–8, 233 n. 111; Anglo-Saxon/Old English, 15–17, 20, 30, 31, 221; characteristic features of, 8, 9, 11, 22, 41, 80, 87, 225; conventional views of, 4, 10–11, 13–14, 32, 83–84, 190, 218; Yugoslav/South Slavic, 7, 11, 20, 24, 28, 30, 79, 95 n. 116

Tradition, textual, 3–4, 12–13, 19, 21, 35–37 nn. 8, 24, 46; 192–94, 206, 221, 222–24, 225, 226–27 nn. 20, 24–25; 230 n. 75

Transmission, oral. *See* Oral transmission

aṭ-Ṭūsī. *See* Abu l-Ḥasan ^{c}Alī b. ^{c}Abdallāh

Tyssens, M., 38 n. 58

^{c}Ukāẓ, 160

Ullmann, Manfred, 92–93 nn. 62, 80

^{c}Umar b. Abī Rabī^{c}a (poet), 92 n. 62

Umayyads, 75, 188 n. 157

^{c}Utba b. Rabī^{c}a, 159

Utley, Francis, 33

Vansina, Jan, 39 n. 81, 207–8

Variation/variant(s), 11–12, 24–25, 39 n. 78, 194, 206, 263–74; as characteristic of oral poetry and traditional texts, 10–11, 21, 36 n. 25, 189–91, 212, 220, 224, 233 n. 116; editorially induced, 208–9, 227–28 nn. 20, 42, 44; 232 n. 95; extent and scope of, neither constant nor predictable, 207–8, 224; increases toward the ends of oral poems, 212; kinds of, 10, 190–91; in number and sequence of verses, 194–96, 210, 228 nn. 34–42, 45–47; 271–74; scribally induced, 25, 206, 208, 229 n. 54, 231 n. 88; significant non-scribal (i.e., orally induced), 209–212, 231 n. 93

Vernacular/*Vulgärsprache*. *See* Dialect(s)

Virgil (poet), 73

Vollers, K., 112–13, 117–20, 128–29, 131, 156, 174 n. 15, 178 nn. 55, 58; 180 nn. 80–81

Wagner, Ewald, 232 n. 110
al-Walīd b. Muġīra, 158–59
Waqf. *See* Pause/pausal forms
Watt, W. Montgomery, 118
Weber, Ruth House, 30, 39 n. 75
Wehr, Hans, 123–24, 133–35, 136–38, 185 n. 127
Wetzstein, J., 117
Wiet, Gaston, 113
Whitman, C. H., 95 n. 117
Word-order, 69–70, 91–92 nn. 62, 66; 132, 133, 140–43, 155, 182 nn. 103–5
Wright, William, 110
Writing/literacy, 14, 17, 18–19, 21, 24, 49, 63, 74, 90 n. 40, 123, 138, 165–68, 187 n. 152, 222–24; conventional association of, with verbal creativity, 102, 119, 174 n. 15, 178–79 nn. 60–61, 184 n. 121, 222–23; relation of, to oral tradition, 11, 26–27, 74–76, 83, 89 n. 34, 95 n. 117, 119, 165, 167–69, 182 n. 101
Written literature, 16, 119, 167–80, 188 n. 158; coexistant with oral poetry, 14, 95 n. 117; distinguishable from oral poetry, 7, 8, 9–10, 20, 27, 34, 47–50, 73–76, 83, 87, 169–70, 176 n. 37, 186 n. 150, 188 n. 156, 223; relative "stability" of, 10, 25, 222

al-Xalīl b. Aḥmad. *See* Abū ᶜAbdarraḥmān al-Xalīl
al-Xansā' (poet), 177 n. 38
al-Xaṣafī al-Muḥārbī (poet), 186 n. 144
Xaṭīb ("orator"), 133
Xazm (adding extra syllable at head of verse), 269 n. 32
Xazraj (tribe), 162

Yāqūt. *See* AbūᶜAbdallāh Yāqūt
Yaṯrib. *See* Medina/Yeṯrib
Yūnus b. Ḥabīb. *See* Abū ᶜAbdarraḥmān Yūnus
Yūnus al-Kātib, 230 n. 75

zaᶜamū ("they allege"), 229 n. 53
ẓalla (*taẓallu*, *ẓa/ilta/u*, etc., 52, 88 n. 20, 112–13, 241, 257
az-Zawzanī. *See* Abū ᶜAbdallāh al-Ḥusayn
az-Zubaydī. *See* Abū Bakr Muḥammad b. al-Ḥasan az-Zubaydī
Zuhayr b. Abī Sulmā (poet), 43, 85, 86–87, 95 n. 109, 217, 220; *muᶜallaqa* of, 70